The Idolatry of the Actual

SUNY series in the Philosophy of the Social Sciences

Lenore Langsdorf, editor

The Idolatry of the Actual

Habermas, Socialization, and the Possibility of Autonomy

David A. Borman

SUNY PRESS

Published by State University of New York Press, Albany

Printed in the United States of America

For information, contact State University of New York Press, Albany, NY
www.sunypress.edu

Production by Eileen Meehan
Marketing by Michael Campochiaro

Library of Congress Cataloging-in-Publication Data

Borman, David A.
The idolatry of the actual : Habermas, socialization, and the possibility of autonomy / David A. Borman.
p. cm. — (Suny series in the philosophy of the social sciences)
Includes bibliographical references and index.
ISBN 978-1-4384-3737-8 (hardcover : alk. paper)
ISBN 978-1-4384-3736-1 (pbk. : alk. paper)
1. Social sciences—Philosophy. 2. Socialization. 3. Social structure. 4. Habermas, Jürgen. I. Title. II. Title: Habermas, socialization, and the possibility of autonomy.

H61.15.B667 2011
300.1—dc22 2011003123

10 9 8 7 6 5 4 3 2 1

To James L. Marsh,
for cultivating in me both the philosophical desire to make sense of the world,
and the practical desire that it should make sense.

Contents

Acknowledgments

The bulk of the research that went into this work was originally completed as my doctoral dissertation at Fordham University under the supervision of James Marsh, to whom I have dedicated the book. I also would like to express my gratitude to the Graduate School of Arts and Sciences at Fordham for a research grant that enabled me to work full time on the dissertation for the academic year 2007–08, without which I might still have been writing it today. Additionally, I owe my thanks to the other members of my committee—especially Merold Westphal and John Davenport—both for their comments on specific portions of the text as well as for their invaluable advice regarding how to go about turning what was a much longer dissertation into what I hope is a readable book. My wife, whose patience greatly exceeds my own, also provided much assistance with the editing and formatting of the text. And, finally, I owe a great deal of thanks to the staff at SUNY Press, particularly Jane Bunker and Andrew Kenyon, as well as to Lenore Langsdorf, and the anonymous readers of the manuscript, all for their support and assistance.

Introduction

There are perhaps few aspects of what I do as satisfying as introducing first- and second-year university students to philosophy. I mean those cases where a genuinely interested student discovers through my class a radically new way of thinking about the world, knowledge, social reality, and so on, a kind of world of problems, forces, and concepts hidden within what is, in other respects, already familiar to them. And yet, despite this kind of general, formal insight, the vast majority of even such genuinely interested students seem, in the end, to regard this philosophical perspective in purely academic terms. That is, even where the course material succeeds in engaging and challenging their existing convictions—and this, it must be admitted, is rare enough—the impact of this challenge is subtly undermined: It succeeds in inducing only a fractured sort of *aporia*. Beliefs and social institutions that are revealed as being without warrant or legitimacy are nevertheless declared, sometimes openly and sometimes not, to be inevitable. Often the result is, in philosophical-logical terms, incoherent; yet there seems to be some nearly irresistible pull felt by so many first- and second-year students toward the view that, for instance, what Kant argues in the *Groundwork* sounds good on paper, but that people "just aren't like that." No amount of explicit thematization of the problems involved in such a response—for example, that if people were already "like that," why would Kant bother to write the book?—seems to diminish the unarticulated conviction that the sheer reality of the status quo, of how people or things "are," somehow lends it normative force. In a word, the conviction seems to be that, as Margaret Thatcher callously declared, "there is no alternative."

Although when I began teaching, I found the pervasiveness of this attitude surprising, as a critical theorist, I should have been expecting it. And although, in my initial surprise, I took it as a pedagogical problem, both critical-theoretical and empirical research quickly pointed me in a more or less sociological direction. From Marx, through Adorno and Horkheimer, to the early Habermas, this attitude of passivity or helplessness in the face of the status quo—which Horkheimer, quoting Nietzsche, once aptly described as the "idolatry of the actual"[1]—has been identified as the ideology of last resort for an advanced capitalism for which many of the traditional legitimating narratives, such as religion or unrestricted entrepreneurial freedom, have lost plausibility. All of these authors agree in seeing the "idolatry of the actual" as an obstacle to both effective critical insight and meaningful social transformation; but they disagree in deep ways about the causes of this syndrome or attitude, the means by which it is produced and sustained, and the prospects and possibilities for its overcoming. In what follows, I hope to accomplish two things: first, to offer a more or less novel, empirically informed analysis of these questions, in methodological concordance with the original program of critical theory; second, while drawing for my theoretical framework on the thought of Jürgen Habermas, to demonstrate that his earlier work contained the resources—although largely undeveloped—for a far more adequate, more genuinely critical answer than is actually to be found in his later work. The two tasks are intertwined because it is the empirically informed analysis that offers at least some preliminary and independent justification for my critical modifications of Habermas' social theory and theory of the subject; as a result, there is in fact one single argument that stretches the length of the book. Given that it would thus otherwise be some time before the whole would come into view, it seems worthwhile to summarize my main contentions by way of introduction. Before I do so, however, I also need to clarify—by way of a rather simplified sketch—just what it means to say that this argument attempts to advance the original program of critical theory.

The Structure of Critical-Theoretical Argument

As Seyla Benhabib noted, the argumentative structure of critical theory owes a great deal to Hegel and, specifically, to Hegel's (sometimes misplaced) critique of Kant.[2] To put the point succinctly, Hegel formulated the doctrine of immanent critique as a rather conservative reaction against the normativism of Kant's practical philosophy, a rejection of the pure "ought" that would justify the attempt of individuals to jump ahead of the historical process, of the level of development of their society, an attempt that Hegel feared could only end in the sort of terror manifested, for him, in the outcome of the French Revolution. The new order is not to be brought about through a process in which individuals iconoclastically sever their ties with the social world that has shaped them; to the contrary, the source of stable and just transformation is to be found not outside the world as it is, but within it. The seeds of the new are nourished in the heart of the old, in the internal contradictions that, over time, lead to its self-overcoming. In the place of a "utopian" critique that would harshly juxtapose to existing reality an external and "abstract" ideal, immanent critique entails an illumination of the ways in which societies are unable to fully realize their own purported nature, or fail for intrinsic reasons to achieve their own purported ends.

Despite their differences, Marx absorbed this structural element of Hegelianism, transposing it into a radical context. For Marx, the utopianism against which was posed the necessity of immanent critique was not Kantian rationalism but a vapid and anesthetizing sort of theoretical socialism, which contented itself with vivid descriptions of the Crystal Palace while remaining more or less uninterested both in a detailed critique of the operations of the present order and in any serious consideration of the conditions under which socialist ideals could become realizable. But if socialism is to have a genuine claim to practical realizability, it must be shown to be a potential outcome of developments within the present capitalist order itself. As the Habermasian educationalist R. E. Young has written, "historically-immanent critique is the form in which we hope,"[3] that is, the form in which we are able to hope without succumbing to an impotent idealism. Immanent critique can fully support this hope, however, only by fulfilling two conditions: First, it must unmask capitalism as a system of injustice, not only as a violation of the abstract norm of distributive justice (e.g., insofar as it entails the private appropriation by the capitalist class of socially produced wealth), but as hypocrisy, as ideological—in other words, as violating its own legitimating principle of equality in the market or the exchange of equivalents. Marx's analysis of capitalism demonstrated that, in the exchange of labor power for wages, the former was systematically undervalued and, indeed, that this undervaluing was the source of profit.

But this element of immanent critique is not, on its own, enough. There was a point, early in his career when, under the influence of Ludwig Feuerbach, this was not as clear to Marx. Feuerbach had sought to expose religion as an illusion, a projection of humanity's own essence. Because religion is a system of belief, this unmasking of its true nature is itself sufficient to bring about its dissolution. It was not long before Marx realized that this method wasn't going to cut it when it came to social theory: Capitalism, while relying for its stability in part on legitimating beliefs, is not itself merely a system of beliefs. Were I to succeed in convincing myself that money was no more than colorful paper, I would not thereby end its power over me: The police will go on being paid to keep me in line. Ideas gain power when they meet up with the motives of social agents and, for Marx, this meant that immanent critique must not only demonstrate the perfidiousness of capitalism; in uncovering the truth about the social order, it also must reveal a connection to the motives of a group of social agents with the ability, under the right conditions, to bring about practical transformation. This latter demand—the second condition mentioned earlier—has come to be known, in critical theory, as the problem of the addressee.

For Marx, as is well known, the answer was the proletariat. His critique of capitalism argues not only that it violates its own purported normative basis; it also reveals that the true interests of the working class are inherently antagonistic to capitalism, that they cannot be advanced (as a class) *through* the market, but only by overcoming it. Although capitalism is identified as unjust on the basis of specifically normative arguments, the motivations with which this critique links up are the interests of the proletariat, particularly (but not exclusively) their material interests. Thus, the proletariat, because they have an interest in overcoming the capitalist system, are the addressee of critical theory; put otherwise, critical theory has a socially immanent practical foothold through its articulation of the genuine interests of the proletariat, through its service, in this sense, to the struggle of the working class. As capitalism, according to Marx's analysis, drove more and more people into poverty through the increasingly frequent crises it visited on itself, the truth of his critique would become increasingly patent. The concentration of workers in large-scale factories would confirm the impression among them that their suffering was more than just the result of individual bad luck. Capitalism, in its "vampire-like thirst" for profit, is without restraint; its undoing was, in long run, inevitable. Marx was so hopeful that it appeared, at times, he no longer needed hope.

Neoliberal triumphalism notwithstanding, history is not yet over. Still, it could hardly have been denied for long that things weren't quite that simple. In the very historical moment in which the conflict seemed to be coming to a head—as capitalist imperialism plunged unsatisfied through eruptions of unprecedented growth and headlong into world wars and economic catastrophe—capital appeared (temporarily, it turns out) to have gained an uncharacteristically sober appreciation of longer-term interests. The emergence of the welfare state, with its ability to stabilize comparatively high levels of economic growth, and the consequent emergence of a consumer society and "culture industry" throughout the developed world—these transformations radically altered the context for critical theoretical analysis. The first generation of Frankfurt School critical theorists—Adorno, Horkheimer, and Marcuse principal among them—witnessed the absorption of the working class into the welfare state compromise, which seemed to offer it ceaselessly increasing standards of living, social rights, and protections. At least so far as its material interests were concerned, its structural antagonism to a capitalism unchanged in its fundamentals appeared to be blunted. As a practical matter, the investment of the working class in the new consumerist society and, worse still, its complicity in the rise of fascism in Germany in the 1930s, robbed critical theory of its addressee. Hope began to appear extraordinary.

But critical theorists like Adorno and Horkheimer did not simply let the matter stand there. To the contrary, they initiated an ambitious research program that aimed to investigate how a capitalism unchanged, as I have said, in its fundamentals, could succeed in producing such allegiance: What makes human persons so willing to sacrifice to their material interests the specifically human interest in autonomy and creativity, an interest to which welfare state capitalism no less than its predecessor denies expression? Adorno and Horkheimer observed this same phenomenon both in the absorption of workers into a consumer capitalism that is rigidly hierarchical and pervasively bureaucratic, and in the surrender to authoritarian fascism: What happened to the ideals of enlightenment, the dream of an emancipated society, the cornerstone of which was individual autonomy? In its initial phase, the Frankfurt School produced a series of fascinating, empirically informed, interdisciplinary studies on the transformation of the processes of socialization, which aimed to explain the patterns of psychological development underlying the acceptability of these broader social changes, and so also to explain the disappearance of meaningful protest and opposition. Central to the former explanation was the intellectual dominance of positivism in the sciences, both natural and social, and its correlative cultural and popular manifestation in the syndrome summarized as the "idolatry of the actual": a slavish deference to "the facts," disconnected from any sense of the role of human agency in their creation, especially regarding the social world; a dismissal of values, encouraged by positivism in the intellectual world and by the media and school curriculum in the practical world, as "merely subjective," as "opinion," as impervious to "objective" verification and so not "rationally" grounded; and, finally, a reduction of rationality to a pragmatic accommodation to "objective" reality, as when we say to someone whose expectations appear to us to be naïve or extravagant, "be reasonable." In the face of this cognitive complex, the real takes on a kind of spurious normative authority and "the way things are," an aura of inevitability and inalterability. In Adorno and Horkheimer's terminology, this collection of attitudes reveals and stems from the dominance of "instrumental reason." Needless to say, it is extremely valuable for those who profit under the terms of the status quo.

The focus on the individual that characterizes many of the increasingly hopeless studies of the Frankfurt School reflects more than merely a reaction against the homogeneity and anonymity of the society they saw emerging. As critical theory continued to separate itself from the remnants of the philosophy of history—on which Hegel's and at least some of Marx's comparative confidence had rested—it could only become more apparent that advances in the level of learning of society must wait upon the ability of individuals to enter history as agents, to make history, individually and cooperatively. At the same time, it was (and is) not at all clear how this change could come about under the present constellation of the forces of socialization. Nevertheless, as Habermas himself once noted, such a positive conception of the autonomous ego remained—if only implicitly—normative for critical theory, even in its darkest hours when, as in the work of Adorno and Horkheimer, "it makes the gloomy prognosis that this ego is losing its basis."[4] The norm of the autonomous ego, of the individual who actively participates in the creation of his or her society, is present in these works by its absence, as precisely that personality formation that the totalizing society will not allow.

I believe Horkheimer's assessment of the problem to be still accurate today. The "idolatry of the actual" describes reciprocally supportive deformations of society, culture, and subjectivity that appear to preclude the possibility of radical social change. To the extent that this syndrome remains dominant, critical theory is without an addressee. This is both the ultimate practical conclusion of Horkheimer and Adorno as well as the background for my argument in this work. But although I share this much with them, from here we part ways. For these authors, the terrible default of Enlightenment ideals called for a deeper explanation: The devolution of Enlightenment into a domination exalted as freedom was not a merely contingent failure. Influenced by the sociology of Max Weber, in their classic co-authored text, *Dialectic of Enlightenment*, they purport to uncover an impetus toward such domination—of ideas, of nature and, ultimately, of humanity—at the very heart of reason as it was conceived of by the European Enlightenment. Reason has always suffered from, indeed, *will* always suffer from, an intrinsic instrumentalism such that the "rationalization" of society could never have ended other than in its total administration. Critical theory thus found itself at a kind of dead end: Not only was it without an addressee, but its immanent critique of "Western" reason was forced to take on a new perversity, having no option but to employ the very intellectual resources and concepts it had identified as the problem. Especially for Adorno, this entailed the self-limitation of critical theory to a kind of negativity alone.

Habermas is widely credited with a reinvigoration of critical theory. Through a renewed investigation into the nature of reason that is tremendously ambitious in scope, Habermas recontextualizes the critique of instrumental reason and rationalization as defended by Weber, Horkheimer, and Adorno, arguing that these authors more or less accurately describe an historical one-sidedness in the rationalization of society. The institutionalization of instrumental rationality has occurred not only at a faster pace, but also often explicitly at the expense of reason's other half, the communicative. What this means is something to be dealt with in the text itself. But the general significance of this insight is that it made possible a reinstatement of the positive in critical theory: Reason is not instrumental reason, not domination, alone. Particularly in his early work, Habermas returned to the question of socialization as a communicative process, with the aim of demonstrating the continued possibility of rationally justified resistance, of making explicit and defensible the invocation of autonomy as a normative reference point and a practical goal. On the basis of this expanded conception of reason, the identification of new potentials for crisis was possible; advanced, welfare state capitalism was not seamless after all, and immanent critique as Marx had conceived of it was thus once again possible. Hope may be considerably less sure-footed than Marx had thought, but there is yet ground beneath its feet.

The Argument

My aim here is to advance a critical theoretical argument in the above-described sense: that is, to formulate an immanent critique of the contradictions of contemporary society—described as advanced capitalist and multicultural—and to establish a practical connection between this critique and potential motives for effective insight and action among a socially and politically significant portion of the population. Having accepted Horkheimer's account of the primary obstacle to be faced, I too am compelled to turn to the question of socialization. Within this broad area of study, however, I have focused my attention on the school, which has received less attention than the media and the family in the mainstream of critical theory. In addition to this relative historical neglect, the existence of a wealth of empirical research on the sociology of the school would be enough, it seems to me, to justify this focus as a means of elaborating and testing a critical theory of the interrelation of society and the subject. But there are additional grounds internal to Habermas' social theory that recommend such an approach: The school finds itself at the reproductive crossroads of what Habermas has called system and lifeworld. On the one side (the side of "system," in Habermas' terms) the school is both in practice and in popular perception crucially involved in the reproduction of the economy, particularly of the occupational sphere: It is routinely invoked in hand-wringing discussions of economic competitiveness; as entrepreneurial capitalism withers under the weight of the now dominant monopoly sector, appeals to equal educational opportunity have assumed the burden of legitimating social inequality (as "everyone" knows, doing well in school is the key to "getting ahead"); and members of underprivileged groups who take this legitimation at face value have made the school the focus of struggles for the attainment of greater economic equality. On the other side (the side of the "lifeworld"), the school is also the focus of controversy surrounding the reproduction of privileged perspectives regarding culture and history (which is not unconnected to the educational success of members of the underprivileged): It is routinely invoked in hand-wringing discussions of the absence of civic-democratic habits and the purportedly associated virtues of character. On the one hand, in a multicultural society, which permits (and even encourages) the reproduction of minority cultures in the family (and through support for community centers, and so on), the public schooling system takes on essential burdens in the maintenance of broader social integration. On the other hand, in an advanced capitalist society, characterized by labyrinthine occupational hierarchies and—so it is argued—increasingly dependent on technical skills and knowledge, the school takes on essential burdens in reproducing the economy and in legitimating individual economic and occupational success or failure.

My argument, in short, is that optimally fulfilling these two reproductive imperatives is impossible: They require that the school foster, through practices of socialization, two incompatible forms of subjectivity. In light of evidence drawn from the sociology of schooling, I will argue in the Intermediate Reflections that the hardwiring of the school to the occupational system that is necessary for the reproduction of advanced capitalism and, more importantly still, for its legitimation, results in a reduction of education to a form of strategic, exchange relation—from the perspective of both students and teachers—and that this, in turn, constitutes a context of socialization that reinforces the attitudes captured by Horkheimer with the phrase "the idolatry of the actual." This includes competitive individualism, an instrumental attitude toward work and social interactions, an orientation toward leisure and consumer choice and, in general, a self-limitation of individual expectations to the "reasonable" boundaries set by a reified social system. In the Concluding Reflections, on the other hand, I argue that stable integration in a multicultural society requires individuals capable of discursively resolving conflicts and maintaining integration through a shared commitment to the nonviolent pursuit of collective self-determination. Or, rather, I argue that deliberative democratic social institutions provide the only stable and just basis for the resolution of the conflicts that are inevitable in diverse societies, which cannot be processed administratively; thus, citizens are required who possess the willingness and ability to participate in such discourses, to critically evaluate taken-for-granted presuppositions and, in general, to adopt a hypothetical attitude toward the status quo (and thereby to shatter its pseudo-naturalness) without which all consciously and democratically directed social change is an impossibility. If the school is to serve the end of social integration in a multicultural society, it must contribute to the socialization of these critical competencies.

The incompatibility of these reproductive processes represents an immanent contradiction, but it does not serve as the basis for a prediction of any kind: We cannot do better than hope. The contradiction could be resolved in either direction and, as a matter of fact, the wind has for a very long time now seemed always to blow at capitalism's back. Nevertheless, if correct, my argument would still point to a cost that would accompany the victory of capitalism, one that has been little remarked on: namely, that in light of the irreducibility of cultural difference and its increased subjective and public connection with the idea of basic rights, the absence of the conditions under which cultural conflict could be satisfactorily negotiated entails an ongoing deficit of social integration and the persistence of apparently irresolvable social conflict. Of course, there are a variety of more or less Orwellian alternatives for managing such conflicts and the politicization they threaten; indeed, the informed reader will not require that I should list examples already in evidence in nations throughout the so-called "West."

As summarized thus far, this immanent critique still does not fulfill the dual tasks of a critical theory, insofar as it lacks any substantive connection with the motives of socially and politically significant agents. This element of the argument relies on a further contrast drawn between the operations of advanced capitalism and the nature of stable and just multicultural integration. With respect to the former, I attempt to show—drawing partially on an argument made by Nancy Fraser—that capitalism instrumentalizes, is parasitic upon, the patterns of social prejudice within any given society. This includes, first, in pursuit of the maximization of profit, the super-exploitation or total economic exclusion of socially marginalized groups, racial minorities and racialized immigrant groups, ethnic minorities, and women, as well as the populations of the developing world generally; second, negatively, in pursuit of legitimation, the asymmetrical distribution upon "underprivileged" groups of the burdens incurred by the welfare state in fostering capitalist growth, such as strategic cuts to social spending (which aims to avoid the legitimation deficit that would result should such deprivation be demanded of the socially or politically powerful); and, third, positively, the mirroring of status asymmetries in occupational hierarchies, such that the latter can maintain legitimacy or even appear "natural" by, as it were, feeding off of the former. Capitalism not only necessarily generates unequal outcomes with respect to wealth, but also is organized as intrinsically hierarchical and authoritarian. The ideology of a purportedly meritocratic schooling system can go some way toward legitimating both; but the evidence suggests that education alone cannot bear the weight and that, to the contrary, the requisite attitudes toward education (especially among the working class) are themselves dependent on the same patterns of sexism and racism. In short, capitalism is inseparable from a system of prejudice.

If correct, this would already be rather problematic for a multicultural yet capitalist society. But, in the Concluding Reflections, I attempt to go some distance further and, through a perhaps somewhat creative reading of Habermas' notion of constitutional patriotism, defend the claim that a more or less successful pursuit of the shared project of democratic self-determination could present the real possibility of a transformation, a decentering, of individual identity. Multiculturalism, if successful, has the potential to result in an identity that is, as Hegel might have said, "at home in otherness," an identity for which diversity has become constitutive. Moreover, in question is not "otherness" or "diversity" in general, but a kind of solidarity with or loyalty to the particular forms of diversity around which one's social and political experience revolves. The presence of such an identity, developed on the basis of fledgling successes in genuine multiculturalism, could provide a form of long-term reinforcement to social integration when cases of conflict arise that, in the near-term, appear to allow of neither consensus nor settled compromise. In the absence of any predictive implication it can be argued that, to the extent that multiculturalism succeeds and is prepared for in the school, individuals so socialized would be in a position to see threats to the value of diversity, the exploitative buttressing of prejudice by the operations of the capitalist economy—and of the welfare state in its name—as threats to their own identity, as assaults on their own values. The significance of such an argument is not only to indicate a potential solidarity of interest between leftist struggles for economic justice and struggles for cultural, racial, ethnic, and sexual equality, a solidarity based on a common set of obstacles to the realization of their respective aims. It is also to point, hopefully, toward a form of solidarity that transcends considerations of interest. A good deal of work pointing back far beyond the age of "identity politics" has demonstrated that questions of identity, of constitutive values and culture, have played a much greater role in motivating sustained social struggle than the imperatives of self- or even of group interest. Thus, one aspect of the contribution offered by this work toward the general project of reinvigorating critical theory is to reinforce existing voices calling for a broader conception of the sorts of motives through which potential addressees may be identified.[5] Indeed, in the absence of such a conception, the emergence of antiglobalization movements, immigrant solidarity groups, and the halting appearance of genuinely cosmopolitan orientations among young people, must remain mysterious at best.

The Critique of Late Habermas

That is my main argument here. In fact, however, the text is structured such that more than half of it is given over to a detailed exposition and critique of Habermas' work. After the pattern of Habermas himself, I have conceived of this as a form of secondary scholarship with "practical intent." And, in fact, I have organized this material in a way that roughly corresponds to Habermas' approach in each of the two volumes of *The Theory of Communicative Action*: namely, critical-interpretative sections of the text are interspersed with attempts to make use of their conclusions in original, critical-theoretical reflections. Accordingly, in Chapters 1 and 2, I examine Habermas' social theory; the critically modified version of this theory for which I argue is then tested through an attempt, in the Intermediate Reflections, to use it as a framework for integrating diverse research trends in the sociology of schooling. However, this is not merely one-directional application: On the one hand, by drawing on the theory of communicative action, I am able to go beyond sociological confirmation to provide a normative basis for a critique of the subordination of the school to the reproductive imperatives of the economy and welfare state; on the other hand, this review of sociological literature highlights the need to adequately root claims about sociological forces in an explanatory account of their mediation by individual agency and consciousness. Thus, we are led in turn to the need for a more detailed account of the subject in relation to society. Chapters 3 and 4 take up this task through an examination of Habermas' work on socialization and the development of the subject. This is the most novel of the interpretive sections of the text and the climax of my critical engagement with Habermas (specifically, Chapter 4); although his developmental conception of the subject is crucial to his defense of deliberative democracy, his account of social evolution, and his normative theory of communicative reason, it has not been the focus of any of the most well-known, detailed treatments of Habermas' work. Beyond providing such a detailed account and assessing the adequacy of Habermas' position on the subject and socialization, my argumentative aim in these chapters is to construct a schema for the identification of the consequences of the stalled forms of development that result from the instrumentalization of socialization processes by capitalism, and also to indicate the consequences of and conditions for individual competencies that are prerequisite to the form of multicultural integration I then defend in the Concluding Reflections.

The presentation is complicated, however, by the need to deal with profound changes that occur in Habermas' thinking over the course of his career. Not to put too fine a point on it: My sense is that Habermas' thinking has become progressively less critical over time, in two distinct but interrelated senses, one substantive and the other, methodological. With respect to the substantive point, I am far from alone in this having this sense. As William McBride wrote of Habermas, for instance,

> [d]espite his laudable disapproving allusions to the "colonization of the lifeworld" by money and power, the tone of all his more

> recent work with which I am familiar strikes me as being that of, at best, a liberal critic who finds some worrying trends in contemporary society but is on the whole not deeply unhappy with its evolution—or, if one prefers, "progress."[6]

Yet McBride goes on to concede that this claim is "a rather difficult one to prove with rigor when such lengthy texts, filled with analyses of still other thinkers, are involved."[7] It is one of the principal contributions of this book, I hope, to offer detailed support for this at least somewhat widely shared intuition concerning Habermas' development. This effort also is of some independent value, since the majority of the major works on Habermas do not deal substantively with the changes in his thought. Accordingly, in what follows, I attempt to document this transition not in general (which would indeed be difficult to do rigorously), but by focusing on a single although absolutely central issue, already mentioned: Habermas' changing assessment of the significance and contemporary reality of individual autonomy, of that culmination of human development that he customarily calls "postconventionality."[8] The centrality of this issue for critical theory has already been noted, when I observed that in the absence of a philosophy of history, and in the face of the "idolatry of the actual," all just social transformation must wait upon the widespread realization of such autonomy.

Indeed, in his early work, Habermas concurred: He argued there that advanced capitalism depends on depoliticization, on the maintenance of merely formal democracy admitting of no alternatives; this depended, in turn, on the fragmentation of individual consciousness for its spurious legitimacy. The central thesis of *Legitimation Crisis* was precisely that postconventionality at the level of the individual, when realized on a broad enough scale, threatens that legitimacy by undermining citizen passivity in the face of a purportedly "natural" and inalterable social order. By accepting Marx's conception of crisis as limited to the economic sphere, the earlier Frankfurt School had failed to see that the success of the welfare state in absorbing the economic contradictions of capitalism did not so much dissolve as displace the potential conflict. Social and cultural changes, at least some of which are a response to the actions of the welfare state on behalf of capital accumulation, threaten to undo the fragile positivist legitimation by creating conditions under which autonomy or postconventionality could become more widespread. In other words, although he considered it rare at the time of writing *Legitimation Crisis*, Habermas thought there was some reason to foresee the possibility of a pervasive cultivation of postconventional subjectivity and, as a result, the possibility of genuinely transformative social change.

By the time of *The Theory of Communicative Action*, he appears less optimistic, and the trends opposing individual autonomy appear much more starkly. The interference by capitalism in domains of socialization such as the family and the school undermines the basis for postconventionality—indeed, for communicative action generally—leaving in its wake a positivist, "postmodern" form of individuality that may be described, on Habermasian grounds, as a stalled form of development. But in this same work, there also begins to emerge another, exculpatory explanation of the apparent failure of autonomy, of communicative action: We begin to see signs of Habermas' progressive retreat from his earlier, radical critique of capitalism and merely formal democracy, in the name of concessions to social complexity. Individuals now appear more or less correct in their estimation that basic features of their society—such as the capitalist market, and the bureaucratic organization of states and workplaces—are essentially inalterable because the tasks with which these institutions are charged are simply too complex to be subjected to democratic direction or even to structural transformation by nonexperts.

By the time of *Between Facts and Norms*, this transition is basically complete: The complexity of society is such that the communicative resources of individuals are described as being "hopelessly overtaxed"; mechanisms like the market and bureaucracies, which integrate individuals and coordinate action without the need for communication or consensus, are indispensable. What marks this position off from a straightforward endorsement of liberal ("merely formal") democracy as it is practiced today are the claims that, first, communicative discourses are to help determine the proper sphere of strategic, self-interested action through legal regulation; and, second, that political representatives and processes ought to be open to influence by enlightened public opinion. Habermas concedes that the robust, repoliticized public sphere that is prerequisite to this realization of democratic principles under current conditions—which can restrain administrative and economic power, subordinate the political and economic subsystems to the lifeworld—is contingent on the self-understanding and actions of its citizens. And that is to say, that it is contingent on forms of life and practices of socialization that foster the sorts of postconventional competencies and identities necessary for citizens to assume this burden.[9] The burden itself is, of course, noticeably reduced: The sorts of social transformations anticipated in *Legitimation Crisis* appear to have been taken off the table. That is the substantive point: Habermas no longer deems necessary the kind of deep, structural changes he did in his earlier work and is, accordingly, increasingly sanguine about the status quo. But, even here, we can ask: Are even these comparatively modest empirical preconditions realized? At the very least, there is a strong suggestion throughout *Between Facts and Norms* that proceduralist legal forms are *in the process* of assuming the burden of integration in pluralistic, complex societies; to that extent, there is an implicit, unargued assumption that there indeed exist the sort of postconventional individuals who alone could make this possible, although this fact apparently no longer presents any serious, transformative threat to the maintenance of the status quo. But his ambiguity on this empirical question points to the absence of a critical theoretical argument in the second, methodological, sense: Habermas appears to have given up on the insistence, central to the program of critical theory, that the theorist account for the conditions on the realization of his ideals, and so has simply offered a traditional (i.e., normative) liberal theory of law (albeit with interesting, proceduralist modifications).

These two senses of "critique," substantive and methodological, are pragmatically related: It is precisely a sense of the depth of the current problems and distortions, and precisely with respect to the question of the socialization of the individual, which suggests the need to account for the possibility of critique and transformation and to specify in what sense it is not a hollow or apologetic indulgence. In this book, I argue that Habermas' most recent work is no longer adequately critical, neither in the substantive nor in the methodological sense. But the distinction is worth maintaining because, although the senses are related, one can be substantively but not methodologically critical—although doing so raises important practical questions—and one can be methodologically critical without being deeply critical in the substantive sense. And, in fact, Habermas' retreat from critical theory has not been uniform: *The Theory of Communicative Action*, like *Legitimation Crisis* and unlike *Between Facts and Norms*, remains critical in the methodological sense, yet is already marked by a reduction in the scope of the proposed social transformation as contrasted with *Legitimation Crisis*. As Johannes Berger has noted, the concept of social crisis in *Legitimation Crisis* is replaced, in *The Theory of Communicative Action*, by the concept of social pathology: but a social crisis is the result of an immanent, fundamental contradiction and is either resolved or results in destruction, whereas a social pathology, by contrast, can be externally corrected or treated.[10]

The details of this story, and what exactly is lost or surrendered in this transition, will have to await the body of the text. But it is worth anticipating here one final element of my argument. From *The Theory of Communicative Action* onward, Habermas' increasing appreciation for the practical significance of social complexity has motivated his flight from his earlier, radically democratic position. But, simply put, we can only talk straightforwardly of an "overburdening" of communicative resources, of the limits on the exercise of autonomy that would make unavoidable the degree of systemic structuring of life that Habermas himself has come to accept, if we *presuppose* that available communicative resources themselves are already developed to the limits of their capacity—which is precisely why it is so valuable to insist on the connection between social theory and the theory of the subject. Yet

Habermas never gives us any reason to accept this presupposition of full development, which I think would strike most educators, for example, as an unlikely one. The closest he comes is what appears to be an inference from existing levels of law and social organization, especially the market that, he suggests in *Between Facts and Norms*, draws on capacities for autonomous action and judgment that only become available at the postconventional level. But such a direct, undialectical inference from the developmental level of society to that of the individual is discounted by Habermas' own argument in *The Theory of Communicative Action*, in which he claimed that, while the institutionalization of the market—among other modern social institutions—required postconventional moral insights, the uncontrolled growth of the economy and the state have resulted in such a high degree of interference in the process of socialization that the communicative bases for autonomy have subsequently been widely undermined.

There is, then, no reason to suspect against all evidence that postconventionality or autonomous subjectivity has been realized on a broad scale, or that the "idolatry of the actual" that is cultivated and reinforced in homes, in schools, and in the media, has been overcome. None of this is to say that forms of systemic integration might not be required for complex societies; only that we cannot stipulate in advance the degree to which that would be the case, nor how such institutions would be structured, under the changed circumstances of a postconventional society. It strikes me as particularly perverse that one consequence of a social formation that is deeply antithetical to rational self-determination, and that therefore works pervasively to enforce the immaturity of its members, should be that intellectuals—both on the left and the right—come to argue that, in the face of this immaturity, meaningful social transformation is not just difficult, but impossible.[11] This is to forget that all legitimate, democratic social transcendence requires first individual transcendence, requires that we ask more of ourselves than is demanded or encouraged by the social order which has, in the first instance, shaped our expectations. As R. E. Young observes, today this sort of demand immediately runs up against a very widely shared "neoconservative" pessimism regarding the limits of "human nature," a view characterized by

> an individualistic, and relatively narrow understanding of our capacity to solve problems by a reason which goes beyond the absolute givenness of traditional values or expansion of technology. This pessimism concerning the scope of our capacity for rational problem-solving is so pervasive in the English-speaking world that it has become the unacknowledged background for much of the debate. In our characteristic fear of Utopian Grand Theory

> we have turned our backs on the very kind and level of reasoning with which our forefathers constructed the democratic institutions we presently enjoy.[12]

Neoconservatives, neoliberals, and technocrats from whom Habermas has become harder and harder to distinguish, believe that "[w]e can no longer afford egalitarianism. . . . The mass of people are not all equally competent to govern," and therefore so-called "ordinary" people will be forced to submit ever more to the direction of credentialed experts.[13] I suspect that thinkers of all such stripes will accuse me of idealism or naivety; I let the structure of my argument in the body of the text answer that charge. But I would like to respond, in conclusion, to another possible accusation: that in my critique of the predominance of the "idolatry of the actual," of the present state of human subjectivity, I evidence the sort of false humanism described by Dostoevsky's Ivan Karamazov, which can indulge in the love of a neighbor in the abstract alone and only so long as he doesn't get too close. In other words, to a neoconservative, for instance, the demand for human development beyond the constraints of capitalism may smack of nothing so much as a disdain for human nature "as it really is." This, of course, entirely begs the question, since the point of my whole argument is to counter the claim that there is anything natural about the current level of development. But even still, I want to stress that the philosophically elaborated form of autonomy is not an imposition foreign to human nature, to the essence of a species characterized most profoundly by its ability to learn. Self-determination is indeed an intellectual endeavor; but the work of intellectuals, which today seems so "unreal" to so many, is simply an extension and specialization of competencies that are, as Habermas shows, made available in the development of all individuals. As the Italian Marxist Antonio Gramsci wrote, "All men are intellectuals, one could therefore say: but not all men in society have the function of intellectuals."[14] This takes us full circle: The function of the intellectual is not only, as Albert Camus advises, to be on the side of the victims and not the executioners, but as critical theory has insisted since Marx, to attempt to clarify the nature of the injustice inflicted upon the oppressed and the nature of the obstacles that frustrate their self-fulfillment.

Chapter 1

Capitalism and Contradiction in *Legitimation Crisis*

My ultimate aim in the first sections of this book is to present Habermas' mature social theory, his two-tiered theory of society as system and lifeworld, and to show how this theory, after the pattern of classical critical theory, serves to point out and articulate the interests of groups who embody a potential for protest or resistance within the societal formation of advanced capitalism. On the basis of this discussion, in the Intermediate Reflections, I then turn to the sociology of schooling as a means of critically evaluating the empirical adequacy of the theory. But, although it is in the two volumes of *The Theory of Communicative Action* that Habermas develops his mature social theory, I'd like to make a running start at that account by way of an earlier and much less discussed work, *Legitimation Crisis*. There are a few reasons for this:

1. It is in *Legitimation Crisis* that Habermas first attempts to articulate the concepts of system and lifeworld.
2. Objections made against the argument of *Legitimation Crisis* set the stage for the theory of system and lifeworld as it is elaborated in *The Theory of Communicative Action*.
3. The analysis of the welfare state offered here is presupposed by the later thesis of the "colonization of the lifeworld by system."
4. The argument I advance in this work actually bears a closer resemblance to the structure of *Legitimation Crisis* and, as I argue, represents an alternative response to some of the critical issues raised against it—an alternative, that is, to the path Habermas himself takes in *The Theory of Communicative Action* and thereafter.

On the Concept of Crisis

In its earliest employment, in the vocabulary of medicine, "crisis" referred to a critical situation in which the "self-healing" powers of the organism were put to the test: The crisis is that point at which the possibility of a recovery of the normal state of health hangs uncertainly in the balance. Such a crisis is induced by something external: the illness. Its effects are likewise objective deviations from the healthy, well-functioning state of the organism. But although the consciousness of the patient is, in that sense, immaterial, the critical connotations of the idea of a crisis imply a necessary connection to the "patient," the one who is made passive precisely by the objectivity of the illness from which he or she helplessly suffers. There is an inevitable association between the idea of a crisis and the idea of domination, the deprivation of the powers of the individual by some objective force. Thus, the concept of crisis is inherently normative: "The resolution of the crisis effects a liberation of the subject caught up in it."[1]

It was Marx who first developed a socioscientific conception of crisis that remains the basis of this idea in the economic domain, for instance, as expressed by systems theory in sociology. Put simply, systems theory is a sociological methodology that views societies as a whole, and/or the various subsystems of society (economy, political administration, culture, family, etc.), as adaptive systems that self-regulate their interactions with their environment, something after the fashion of Adam Smith's view of the capitalist market or a biologist's view of an organism. So a crisis, according to such a view, occurs when the structure of the system or subsystem prevents it from adequately adapting to new problems in a way that permanently or deeply threatens its integration or coherence. One consequence of this approach is that, as Habermas argues, it makes the possibility of crisis contingent on changes in the "environment," that is, on changes in those things external yet relevant to the system: When the environment changes in some way to which the system cannot accommodate itself, the system is destroyed, just as a biological organism is destroyed if, for instance, a new parasite or contaminant is introduced into its environment that overwhelms its defenses and compromises the organic processes on which its life depends. Habermas does not deny that this can and does occur; but he insists that there are also internal causes of social crisis to which such a theory is necessarily blind. An internal crisis results from the inherent structure of a social system if that system issues contradictory imperatives that cannot be hierarchically ordered, so that one or the other obviously has priority and thus cancels or relativizes its competitor. In short, as a model of society, systems theory suggests—as a sort of methodological presumption—a greater degree of seamlessness, homogeneity, and harmony than is to be found in actual, existing social systems.

In order to be able to identify such an internally generated crisis, we need to be able to differentiate between the essential structures of a society, those directly related to what Habermas refers to as its "organizational principle" and that cannot be altered without undermining the identity of the system (i.e., without destroying it, turning it into a different kind of system), and those structures that can be altered to meet new challenges. Systems theory fails on this score as well, according to Habermas, because it is impossible to distinguish on the basis of its vocabulary between a reorganization that should count as a learning process contributing to the evolution of a given system, and one that should be interpreted as system dissolution. The reason is that the unity of a social system, defined relative to its goals and identity, can only be assessed from the perspective of its members—as we will see, from the perspective of the "lifeworld."

> Thus, only when members of a society experience structural alterations as critical for continued existence and feel their social identity threatened can we speak of crises. Disturbances of system integration endanger continued existence only to the extent *social integration* is at stake, that is, when the consensual foundations of normative structures are so much impaired that the society becomes anomic. Crisis states assume the form of a disintegration of social institutions.[2]

System integration refers to the functional interweaving of the actions and action consequences of individuals, irrespective of both their personal motive and intent; for example, individuals are integrated with one another in the economic system by being integrated into the market, which their individual actions serve to reproduce and sustain. The unity or integration of the system is ensured so long as individuals continue through their behavior, howsoever motivated, to carry out the operations necessary for the maintenance of the system as a whole, to perform, for example, those acts from which Adam Smith's "Invisible Hand" would purportedly emerge. So, disturbances in system integration, which open a gap between individual performances and the functional needs of the system itself, only present the possibility of crisis, Habermas has said, if they threaten social integration.

Social integration is more difficult to explain; it will be necessary in the course of this chapter and the next to critically examine Habermas' account of social integration as it develops and varies over his career. For now, let us say that social integration, for Habermas, seems to refer to the ability and willingness of individuals within a society both to (a) recognize one another as belonging to the same society, and (b) see themselves, as a group, in continuity with the traditions of previous generations that have been constitutive for their society and its institutions. It should be clear that these are in fact two distinct—although often interrelated—questions: We can easily imagine a case in which a society remained integrated in the first sense but not in the second.[3] In *Legitimation Crisis*, however, Habermas appears to equivocate with respect to these two senses although, in its main argument regarding the diagnosis of the crisis tendencies of advanced capitalism, he focuses on the latter question (b) at the expense of a consideration of the conditions for (a), mutual recognition between contemporary citizens. But with respect to this historical conception of integration, he notes that it contains rather too much idealism: Experiences of rupture of tradition are not only inexact as a criterion for identifying crises, it is often the case that a contemporary sense of crisis turns out to have been a false alarm, even one that was intentionally—that is, ideologically—sounded.

Thus, objective disturbances of system integration only count as a crisis if they threaten social integration; but we can't rely on the subjective sense of a crisis alone to tell us when social integration is truly threatened. Habermas' solution is to attempt to combine the merits of both perspectives: Objectively describable problems that overwhelm steering capacity (not limited to problems introduced by contingent changes in the environment, but including those that arise from internal contradictions) will count as crises only insofar as their consequences affect the consciousness of individuals "precisely in such a way as to endanger social integration."[4] The crisis theory Habermas articulates in *Legitimation Crisis* is intended to catalogue the vulnerability of advanced capitalist societies to crises that meet this criterion. The first step in constructing such a theory is to elaborate the distinction between system and lifeworld.

System and Lifeworld

> The two expressions "social integration" and "system integration" derive from different theoretical traditions. We speak of social integration in relation to the systems of institutions in which speaking and acting subjects are socially related. Social systems are seen here as *lifeworlds* that are symbolically structured. We speak of system integration with a view to the specific steering performances of a self-regulated *system*. Social systems are considered here from the point of view of their capacity to maintain their boundaries and their continued existence by mastering the complexity of an inconstant environment. Both paradigms, lifeworld and system, are important. The problem is to demonstrate their interconnection. From the lifeworld perspective, we thematize

> the normative structures (values and institutions) of a society. We analyze events and states from the point of view of their dependency on functions of social integration . . . while non-normative components of the system serve as limiting conditions. From the system perspective, we thematize a society's steering mechanisms and the extension of the scope of contingency. We analyze events and states from the point of view of their dependency on functions of system integration . . . while the goal values serve as data. If we comprehend a social system as a lifeworld, then the steering aspect is screened out. If we understand a society as a system, then the fact that social reality consists in the facticity of recognized, often counterfactual, validity claims is not taken into consideration.[5]

The difference between system and lifeworld is, thus, in the first instance, defined perspectivally: They refer to aspects of social systems considered as a whole that are illuminated by competing theoretical perspectives. But at the same time, they are more than that: The *aspects* of the social system so thematized are distinct structures, namely, the structures relevant to the reproduction of modern, differentiated societies. These theoretical perspectives recommend themselves, in other words, in the light of considerations regarding the object domain of social theory.[6] Although it is possible to view all of society from either perspective, it is not possible to do so with equal felicity, since each perspective suffers from its aforementioned weakness. To put it crudely, because system and lifeworld therefore are also *things*—they refer to distinct phenomena—there is a real question about their relation and potential interaction. Systems theory, however, cannot respond to this question, because it either screens out normative structures entirely or reinterprets actions in the service of social integration as mere "behavior," the consequences of which are to be analyzed from the perspective of their functional effects. And because systems theory cannot even identify bounded systems and their goal states (or crises) except through appeal to the vocabulary of action theory, lifeworld analysis retains a kind of priority. Action theory, on the other hand (as in a theory of communicative action), successfully avoids one-sidedness, but only at the cost of a brute "dichotomy between normative structures and limiting material conditions"[7] (the dichotomy is brute in that one half, the systemic half, remains opaque to such a theory). This is a limitation of action theory that holds not only at the macro-level of society as a whole (composed of system and lifeworld) but also with respect to the individual subsystems themselves (the components of system and lifeworld, such as subcultural forms of life, the political system, and the economic system), all of which combine social and system elements.

The point is that action theory alone cannot ground a social theory adequate to contemporary reality. What is required is a theory that is able to explicate both the operations of system, the material substratum of society and its resources for solving steering problems, and the normative structures of society, including the ways that they are affected by disturbances in the substratum. Habermas claims that these conditions are met by an "historically oriented analysis of social systems" that allows us to determine the range "within which the goal values of the system might vary without its continued existence being critically endangered. The boundaries of this range of variation are manifested as boundaries of historical continuity"[8] (i.e., (b), the historical sense of social integration). The "goal values" for a society as a whole include both imperatives issued by the normative cultural system—which must be more or less satisfied if the social system is to be perceived as legitimate by its members—and the requirements of system integration—which must be more or less satisfied if the society is to function, to reproduce itself stably. By proposing an "historically oriented analysis," Habermas intends a theory of social evolution. These aspects of the theory—the determination of goal values and social evolution—come together in the following thesis: "Change in the goal values of social systems is a function of the state of the forces of production and of the degree of system autonomy; but the variation of goal values is limited by the logic of development of world views on which the imperatives of system integration have no influence."[9] Thus, the logics of the development of productive forces and of normative structures are independent of one another, although both are important factors in the evolution of society as a whole. This is the basic argument of Habermas' theory of social evolution.

In both cases, the sequence of development is irreversible so long as the continuity of tradition is not broken: Cognitive advances with respect to technical knowledge, as well as those that underwrite the stages of (in this case, collective) moral consciousness, cannot simply be forgotten (although they can be repressed, on pain of pathological side effects). But there is nevertheless an asymmetry between them: Although the development of productive forces always results in increasing contingency in the sociocultural sphere—that is, as production expands and intensifies, social relations become more complex, necessitating new learning—evolutionary advances in the development of the normative structures governing the sociocultural sphere do not necessarily result in an advance of (new learning in regard to) productive forces. Habermas points to the experience of developing nations as evidence for the claim that modernization of economic and political structures often does overwhelm traditional, stratifying, and limiting social institutions; the development of productive forces can also stimulate sociocultural change when knowledge produced in the service of technical goals has the effect of discrediting traditional worldviews. But the fact that these technical developments act as catalysts for the sociocultural development of normative structures does not tell us anything about what the latter developments will look like. This is the point of insisting that the respective logics of development are independent and asymmetric: It may be the case that, rather than resulting in new normative structures that satisfy the imperatives of expanding production, which spurred the development in the first place, the changed normative structures may instead end up restricting the autonomy of economic systems by resulting in new demands for legitimation that alter the goal values of the society as a whole. It is Habermas' argument in *Legitimation Crisis* that this may well be what happened in advanced capitalist societies in the 1960s.

Liberal Capitalism and Contradiction

In *Legitimation Crisis*, Habermas offers some limited substantiation for this theory of social evolution, particularly for the way in which the organizational principle of a society relates to its characteristic vulnerabilities to crisis, through a sketch of primitive (kinship), traditional (feudal), liberal capitalist, and advanced capitalist societies. The first two are not crucial for understanding the details of advanced capitalism, but its specific difference from liberal capitalism is. In his analysis of the latter, Habermas relies quite heavily on Marx, who saw in the relationship between wage labor and capital—enshrined in bourgeois legal codes—the fundamental, in Habermas' terms, "organizational principle," of liberal capitalism. The key structural change in the development of this social formation (from the crumbling feudal system) is the emergence of an autonomous civil society in which individual commodity owners pursue their private interests. The autonomy of the political and economic systems seems to depoliticize class relations and to turn the patently still prevalent class domination into something impersonal and anonymous.[10] Under feudalism, by contrast, one's position with respect to the "honor system" defined in a single stroke one's economic, social, and political position, one's options with respect to occupation, marriage, education, and so on. The asymmetrical distribution of wealth was directly political, justified by appeal to the authority, ultimately divine in origin, of the Absolutist monarch.

Within the economic subsystem as differentiated from the lifeworld, a new realm of strategic, self-interested action is opened to participants, a legally enshrined space for the pursuit of self-interest without regard for normative structures. This development allows considerable leeway for the expansion of the forces of production and, concomitantly, for the development of normative structures, such as bourgeois law and morality. In the first instance, as Marx carefully documented, the openly strategic relations of the market economy, their unchecked liberation from normative regulation, led to egregious levels of exploitation of workers (men, women, and children) in the pursuit of "absolute surplus value"—that is, the essentially unpaid labor that results from the nearly indefinite extension of the working day.[11] This is one of the most obvious self-destructive tendencies of the market: to undermine the ability of workers to reproduce themselves and their labor power through rest, meeting of basic needs, and so on. The introduction of the legally regulated working day served to counter this tendency, with a tremendously important side effect: Once increased profit can no longer be pursued by extending the working day temporally, capitalists turn to increasing the intensity of labor within the legal time frame, in pursuit of what Marx called "relative surplus value." Labor-/time-saving technical innovations mean that fewer workers can produce more commodities in the same or even less time; or, if market opportunities exist for selling greater product, the same number of workers can produce even more product in the same or even less time. In either case, the result is a driving down of the amount of capital that must be spent on labor relative to the amount that will be realized through exchange; in other words, increased profits. The fateful evolutionary consequence is that the accumulation of capital becomes tied to the development of technical innovations that increase the efficiency of labor in this way.

At the same time, there is an important transformation in the structure of legitimation in liberal capitalist societies, an inversion of a sort. In traditional, feudal societies, the sociocultural sphere provided the legitimation required for the operations of the economy, specifically for the private appropriation of social wealth in accord with the status hierarchy. As mentioned previously, the religious worldview of feudalism justified the patent economic inequality. In liberal-capitalist societies, this worldview is undermined and the autonomy of civil society is justified on the basis of an independent, universal moral principle: the exchange of equivalents (or equality, generally). The market, in a sense, needs no justification; to the contrary, it now both provides the legitimation for the actions of the state, so long as the latter limits itself to actions that are complementary to the apparently inherent justice of civil society, and directly contributes to the integration of society as a whole according to the newly autonomous pattern of system integration. The market is open to the talent and effort of all, equally, to make from it what they will. With this new contribution, however, comes a new danger: steering problems, that is, disturbances in the operations of the system, present for the first time direct dangers to the integration of society. The potential for class conflict has been transferred, by the organizational principle of liberal-capitalist society, to the steering dimension, "where it expresses itself in the form of economic crisis"[12]—that is, in the cycle of growth, crisis, and recession/depression. These crises are problematic precisely because the ideology of equality in the market plays a legitimating function for the entire social system; when the market shows itself to be dysfunctional, and if these disturbances cannot be passed off as natural catastrophes, then the opposition of classes that sits at the basis of liberal capitalism may come explicitly to the fore.[13] This is precisely what Marx's theory of value intends to accomplish: both to analyze the steering mechanism of the capitalist market and, in so doing, to unmask its ideological pretension to equality, to show that what is institutionalized in the market through the system of bourgeois civil law is not the principle of equal exchange, but a particular constellation of power. This contradiction in liberal capitalism is fundamental to its very existence:

> We can speak of the "fundamental contradiction" of a social formation when, and only when, its organizational principle necessitates that individuals and groups repeatedly confront one another with claims and intentions that are, in the long run, incompatible. In class societies this is the case. [But] As long as the incompatibility of claims and intentions is not recognized by the participants, the conflict remains latent.[14]

The key to Marx's argument for the inescapability of this confrontation, precipitated in turn by the inescapability of economic crisis, is his theory of the falling rate of profit. Through this, he intends to reveal to the proletariat in particular that the source of their suffering is not the result of natural, inexplicable catastrophe, but of domination, a basic antagonism of interests that is irresolvable within the present social system. The argument, very briefly, runs as follows: profit is derived from the private appropriation of socially produced surplus value (a violation of distributive justice) which, as we have already seen, is increasingly reliant on relative sources, that is, on technical innovations. But this means that continued accumulation is dependent on increasingly capital-heavy, near-term investment in innovation, machinery, and the like, aimed at reducing expenses in the long run. As a result, at ascending levels of accumulation, and correlatively of technical progress, the total composition of capital, made up of both constant capital (raw materials, machinery, tools, etc.) and variable capital (wages and, in the end, profit), alters to the detriment of the latter: Constant capital absorbs more and more of the total amount. Yet it is precisely from variable capital that relative surplus value is derived.[15] The result is a falling rate of profit relative to investment, which undermines the incentive for reinvestment, and the collapse of economic growth, which leads to recession or depression. It also is worth recalling that accumulation is dependent on more than just increased productivity, since production must be kept in a careful balance with the opportunities for capital realization, with opportunities for realizing investment by selling your product. Because overproduction drives down market prices, increased production is only worthwhile in connection with increased consumption; but the masses can only increase consumption through higher wages, which would again require surrender of some amount of the variable capital from which relative surplus value is derived.[16] The collapse of incentives for reinvestment results in mass unemployment and economic crisis, but this economic crisis immediately becomes a social crisis because it lays bare the opposed interests of social classes and threatens social integration. Note, however, that social integration here appears to be predominantly concerned with the mutual recognition of contemporary members of society; the revelation in question is the one long ago observed by Plato, that a city governed by the pursuit of wealth is not one, but two—a city of the wealthy and a city of the poor. The continuity of socioculturally constitutive traditions appears to have very little to do with it; if anything, the ideals of that tradition are reinforced, that is, the ideals of equality and justice are reasserted *against* their contradiction by social practice.

"A Descriptive Model of Advanced Capitalism"

There are two phenomena that are particularly important for the delimitation of liberal from advanced capitalism, both of which have to do with the "advanced stage of the accumulation process." The first is the complementary and intertwined processes of economic concentration and the globalization of markets.[17] The result of this phenomenon is the emergence of "oligopolistic" or monopoly capitalism in the place of competitive capitalism. Although the former often continues to rely on the market as a steering mechanism in the implementation of strategic decisions aimed at company profit, monopoly capital is able to exert extensive control over market operations. The second is the rise of the interventionist state, which attempts to manage economic growth and, especially, to prevent economic crisis. Although these interventions restrict the autonomy of private commodity owners in some ways, the state refrains from any direct political management of the system of resource distribution, which could not take place without completely dismantling the market system. Accordingly, "the priorities of society as a whole [continue to] develop in an unplanned, nature-like manner—that is, as secondary effects of the strategies of private enterprise."[18] Habermas traces out the significance of these developments for the organization and operations of (a) the economy, (b) the political-administrative system, (c) the sociocultural legitimation system, and (d) the class structure of advanced capitalism, all with an eye to the diagnosis of possible crisis tendencies.

The Economic System

Habermas' analysis of the economic system of advanced capitalist nations is based on the three-part model developed by economists whose studies focused on the United States. The three parts are: The private sector, comprised usually of (1) smaller, competition-driven enterprises and (2) oligopolies that tolerate a "competitive fringe," but whose own investment decisions are based on "market strategies" (monopoly) rather than competition; and (3) the public sector, including especially the arms and space travel industries (and today we should certainly add so-called "defense contractors," the nuclear industry, etc.), which are either government controlled or reliant on enormous government contracts and which, as a result, make investment decisions without regard for the market. Both oligopolies and the massive public-sector corporations are capital-investment heavy and are today responsible for the majority of economic growth (and are, Habermas claimed in *Legitimation Crisis*, now outdatedly, faced with strong unions).

The Political-Administrative System

The administrative system in advanced capitalism, as in liberal capitalism, executes the imperatives of the economic system. Its activities on this account can be divided into two classes: (a) regulating the economic cycle through global planning, and (b) the creation of opportunities for capital realization and the improvement of conditions for the use of "excess accumulated capital."[19] Global planning strategies (a) are limited by the freedom of investment of private enterprise, which cannot be infringed upon, and so are reduced to the "avoidance of instabilities." Actions taken to this end—ultimately, of maintaining economic growth—include monetary and labor market policy, income redistribution, loans and subsidies of various sorts, and so on.[20] The most these strategies can accomplish, however, is to alter the circumstances and considerations that enter into the decision-making process of private enterprises, in order in this indirect way to "correct the market mechanism." This is to be contrasted with the activities of the second class (b), in the service of capital realization, in which the market mechanism is directly supplanted. The most patent, time-honored, and ongoing example of this second strategy is imperialism, the direct conquest of foreign markets; the "structural adjustment" policies of the World Trade Organization, International Monetary Fund, and World Bank, which demand (among other things) the opening of markets to foreign investment and trade, are merely the subtler, younger siblings of the same parentage. The extensive list of means described by Habermas as employed to this end include:

> "strengthening the competitive capability of the nation" by organizing supranational economic blocks [e.g., NAFTA, the proposed Central American Free Trade Agreement, the European Union free trade zone], securing international stratification by imperialist means [e.g., U.S. interventions in the Middle East and Latin America] . . . unproductive government consumption (for example, armaments and space exploration) . . . guiding, in accord with structural policy, the flow of capital into sectors neglected by an autonomous market . . . improvement of material infrastructure (transportation, education, health, recreation, urban and regional planning, housing, construction, etc.) . . . improvement of immaterial infrastructure (general promotion of science, investments in research and development, provision of patents, etc.) . . . heightening the productivity of human labor (general system of education, vocational schools, programs for training and re-education, etc.) . . . relieving the social and material costs resulting from private production (unemployment compensation, welfare, repair of ecological damage).[21]

These changes in the role of the state are, according to Habermas, of great significance for Marx's law of value and its role in his analysis of the capitalist economy. That is, the form of the production of surplus value is transformed where the state assumes responsibility for the production of collective commodities, infrastructure, education, and so on, which reduces the balance of constant capital and the cost of the reproduction of labor power, and so frees up additional surplus value. In particular, Habermas points to the significance of government organization of science/innovation and of education/qualification in this connection. Teachers, engineers, scientists, etc., are all engaged in forms of labor that are, in Marxian categories, directly unproductive; and yet their labor has become of crucial indirect significance in the attempt to increase the productivity of labor and so, too, surplus value.[22]

The Sociocultural Legitimation System

The functional problems in the market undermine the core ideology of liberal capitalism, the exchange of equivalents, the basic fairness or justice of the market. What is worse, government intervention intended to stabilize the economic system—for instance, corporate bailouts—"re-politicizes the relations of production," which increases the need for legitimation. It is no longer possible, as the traditional state did, to appeal to cultural traditions that have, in the meantime, been "undermined and worn out during the development of capitalism."[23] Universal moral and legal norms have since made their appearance in the normative structures of liberal-capitalist society, where they served to ideologically conceal the domination of the proletariat by the bourgeoisie through a selective interpretation of the "rights of man." But these developments are irreversible and so new sources of legitimacy may only be sought in accordance with universal legal and moral principles, such as human rights and, especially, popular sovereignty. Habermas claims that this obstacle is overcome through a system of merely "formal democracy," a kind of periodic plebiscite on administrative personnel that shields the basic operations of government administration—typically presented as "technical questions"—from genuinely democratic determination.[24] This relative independence of the administrative system from the process of political will formation signals the depoliticization of the public sphere, which is itself made to appear acceptable to citizens through the cultivation of attitudes summarized by Habermas under the heading of "civil privatism." The latter refers to "political abstinence combined with an orientation to career, leisure, and consumption . . . [which] promotes the expectation of suitable rewards within the system (money, leisure time, and security)."[25] In some places, Habermas differentiates this syndrome into civil privatism, referring to a high interest in system output (goods and security) coupled with a low interest in system input (participation), and a complementary familial-vocational privatism, referring to a family orientation paired with a high interest in leisure time and consumption, as well as a "career orientation suitable to status competition."[26] Diffuse mass loyalty is thus ensured through economic output alone and, in that sense, despite democracy, the merely formal character of which is perceived to be acceptable by individuals socialized into the syndromes of privatism just so long as there is sufficient pay-off.

But things aren't entirely this simple. First, these pay-offs are increasingly in the form of use values (social services, transportation, health care, etc.), which places the administration in an awkward position because the imperatives of capital realization and system maintenance generally prohibit the consideration of use value in preference to exchange value. Second, the process of depoliticization itself requires justification (and not only compensation), which must be provided by democratic elite theories and technocratic systems theories that translate practical problems of politics into technical, administrative problems accessible only to the reflection of experts. Thus, just as bourgeois political economy had suggested that the capitalist system was a spontaneous outgrowth of human nature, so too these theories argue that the transfer of decision making to experts is a natural and unavoidable consequence of increased social complexity.

The Class Structure

Although relations of production have been repoliticized under advanced capitalism, this does not necessarily undermine the anonymity of domination that prevailed under its liberal predecessor. The sort of crisis of integration that would entail is avoided through a management of class relations that intends to keep class divisions latent: for instance, through such measures as political compromises on wages between unions and companies, particularly in the public and monopolistic sectors that are crucial to economic growth. This compromise, Habermas argues, absorbs the conflict potential of increasingly reformist labor politics; the increased labor costs that result are passed on to the consumer in the form of higher commodity prices. Because there is an overlap of the moderate demands made on the state by workers and companies regarding, for example, productivity, social services, the qualifications of labor, and so on, "[t]he monopolistic sector can, as it were, externalize class conflict." This externalization has a number of important consequences:

> *(a)* disparate wage developments and/or a sharpening of wage disputes in the public service sector; *(b)* permanent inflation, with corresponding temporary redistribution of income to the disadvantage of unorganized workers and other marginal groups; *(c)* permanent crisis in government finances, together with public poverty (that is, impoverishment of public transportation, education, housing, and health care); and *(d)* an inadequate adjustment of disproportional economic developments, sectoral (agricultural) as well as regional (marginal areas).[27]

But perhaps the most important cumulative result is the fragmentation of class conflict, the dispersion of the effects of crisis avoidance over a wide range of unorganized "quasi-groups" that, in Habermas' estimation, are lacking in serious protest potential: consumers generally; those reliant on (permanently bankrupted) government services of some form, such as the sick or elderly, transportation users, school children, and their parents; and finally, "natural" groups lacking in political power whose marginalization is acceptable for reasons of prejudice, such as immigrant communities and racial and ethnic minorities. This last consequence is particularly important for my argument.

Having offered this sketch of the structure of advanced capitalism, Habermas turns to the question of whether it indeed represents a new social formation, that is, whether a change has come about in the organizational principle of liberal capitalist society. This question centers on the identification of characteristic susceptibilities to crisis, but also more generally on whether exchange remains "the dominant medium of control over social relations."[28] The fact that the exchange principle has continued to migrate into areas from which it had once been excluded does not conclusively answer this question for us. Habermas addresses the issue of crisis susceptibility first.

Crisis Tendencies in Advanced Capitalism

Habermas' first comment on this issue is that he will not rule out the possibility that advanced-capitalist strategies for the avoidance of economic crisis could be indefinitely successful. However, the absorption of the basic contradiction of capitalist society, its administrative processing and transference into the sociocultural system, necessarily reintroduces the permanent possibility of political conflict, although no longer in the direct form of political class conflict predicted by Marx. Thus, the pessimism of the earlier Frankfurt School was premature: The dissolution of the threat of inevitable economic crisis does not itself entail the establishment of a seamlessly administered society. Before elaborating this position in any detail, however, Habermas discusses three kinds of problems faced by advanced capitalism that, although not taking the form of crisis, potentially present limits to its indefinite development: the limits of the natural environment to sustain economic exploitation, which are today clearer than ever; the threat of globally destructive warfare presented by economically functional arms proliferation; and the shaping of individuals' motives in favor of compliance and complacency. Only the third is relevant for my argument here, which concerns the possibility of a "violation of the consistency requirement of the personality system."[29]

The development of the steering capacity of society, which is a condition for growth, expands in two directions: through the development of the forces of production, by which systems gain control of outer nature (and encounter environmental limits); and through increasingly complete forms of socialization, by which it attempts to gain control over the inner nature (motivations, etc.) of its members. The former relies on the accumulation of technically useful knowledge, knowledge that implies a truth claim relative to the objective world; socialization, on the other hand, shapes inner nature through "normative structures in which needs are interpreted and actions licensed or made obligatory," which structures imply claims for the validity of underlying norms.[30] According to Habermas, although there is nothing in human nature or psychology itself to prevent the complete socialization and instrumentalization of individual psychology decried by earlier generations of the Frankfurt School, there are restrictions related to the nature of the socialization process as it has hitherto operated, on the basis of the internalization of interpretive, identity-securing normative structures with a criticizable claim to normative validity (which I discuss in detail in Chapters 3 and 4). Thus, Habermas claims, in the absence of a radical change in the nature of socialization and so of individuation, "it is inconceivable that there should be legitimation of any action norm that, even approximately, guarantees an acceptance of decisions without reasons."[31] In other words, at the limit where individuals would be shaped so as to "automatically" produce the sorts of performances required for system maintenance, without any (even implicit) appeal to normative legitimacy, we would at the same time be faced with a social system radically different than what has existed up until the present. As Habermas has already observed in his critique of the self-sufficiency of systems theory: Up to the present, at least, the identity of social systems has been dependent on the identity of its members.

In addition to the three problems representing challenges in the "environments" of system, Habermas describes four possible, internally generated crisis tendencies to which advanced capitalist societies are vulnerable. However, his argument on this score is very strongly qualified: The division, first of all, is analytic and in actual practice compensating substitute relations are possible, where one system alleviates pressure on another. More importantly, although he believes advanced capitalism will—unless the above transformation of the nature of socialization is carried through—remain *vulnerable* to one of these crisis tendencies at any given time, it is not possible to predict that any form of crisis will actually occur.

Economic Crisis Tendencies

The economic system, according to Habermas, is characterized by an input of work and capital, and an output of consumable values distributed according to system mechanisms as well as status hierarchies. Economic crises in liberal capitalism, resulting from the undermining effect of the falling rate of profit on incentives for reinvestment, describe disturbances in output. In bourgeois society, these disturbances repeatedly brought to the consciousness of members the pattern of distribution of (in times of crisis) increasingly scarce values and, in so doing, threatened to unmask the legitimating pretence of equality. So the question of economic crises refers to whether the administrative system of advanced capitalism can, through the two classes of action on behalf of capital described previously, successfully manage and promote continual growth and so forestall the falling rate of profit. Habermas has declared it at least possible, but not without a cost. The other three forms of crisis illuminate this cost.

Political Crisis Tendencies

The input required by the political-administrative system is the generalized mass loyalty already described, as independent as possible of the specific motivations of citizens; its output is in the form of administrative decision making. An output crisis is indeed possible, which Habermas refers to as a "rationality crisis," if these decisions do not satisfy the imperatives issued by the economic system. This would result in a disturbance of system integration. An input crisis, on the other hand, would mean a loss of loyalty, that is, a "legitimation crisis" in which mass loyalty, and so social integration, cannot be secured at the same time as the imperatives of the economy are carried out; in particular, Habermas has in mind cases where the satisfaction of economic imperatives threatens the depoliticization of the public sphere and the acceptability of merely formal democracy.

The fundamental problem underlying a rationality crisis is the inability of the state to adequately steer the economy, either (a) because of the basic anarchy of the market, which could only be tamed through recourse to the kind of economic planning that would infringe upon the autonomy of private enterprise; or (b) because the absorption of economic imperatives into the medium of administrative power is not possible without introducing "foreign orientations" into the system. These foreign orientations refer to the socialization of increasing numbers of workers engaged (in Marx's terms) in concrete (oriented to use value) rather than abstract (oriented to exchange value) labor—for example, in public service (health, education, etc.)—as well as to those not engaged in productive activity at all—such as students, welfare recipients, the sick, criminals, and unemployed. The problem here, in the first instance, is that the system steers actions by altering the external facts in the light of which strategic decisions oriented to exchange value are made (after a pattern describable in terms of rational choice theory); but to the extent that individuals are no longer primarily orientated by exchange value, the alteration of such external facts becomes ineffective.[32] Put plainly, individuals not adequately socialized by school and work to orient their actions by the individualistic pursuit of monetary rewards are exceedingly difficult to control through manipulating the conditions for the distribution of these rewards. Habermas concedes, however, that this negatively described steering difficulty does not possess the force of a logical contradiction in the system because limited forms of participation, as well as other potential means, may prove equally or more effective in steering action than external behavioral stimuli. The larger issue, potentially productive of crisis, is the positive possibility of dysfunctional motivational developments that would more or less directly oppose cooperation with the status quo administration of society.

Thus, in the attempt to adequately steer the continuous growth of the capitalist economy, the administrative system gradually extends its boundaries both into the economic system—where it supplements or replaces the market mechanism—and into the sociocultural system, where it attempts to secure for itself legitimation and functional motivations. The latter effort is what Habermas will later call "colonization," in which system imperatives and systemic forms of integration spread into and undermine domains of cultural tradition, social integration, and communicative socialization. "The residue of tradition must, however, escape the administrative grasp, for traditions important for legitimation cannot be regenerated administratively"—as Habermas will say elsewhere, more generally, "*[t]here is no administrative production of meaning.*"[33] Cultural tradition is reproduced in an unplanned, nature-like way; even when it is consciously and critically appropriated by reflective, autonomous individuals, it remains a delicate medium for the crucial tasks of social integration and self-understanding, the potential for which it surrenders wherever tradition is patently manipulated or strategically employed. This presents a structural or systematic limit to the ability of the administration to "compensate for legitimation deficits through conscious manipulation."[34] This limit only indicates an immanent potential for crisis, however, when seen in conjunction with the insight that the expanding scope of state action necessarily calls for increasingly more legitimation.

Habermas offers a number of familiar examples of the way in which the state attempts to secure the legitimating depoliticization of the public sphere, which include,

> the personalization of substantive issues, the symbolic use of hearings, expert judgments, juridical incantations, and also the advertising techniques (copied from oligopolistic competition) that *at once confirm and exploit existing structures of prejudice* and that garnish certain contents positively, others negatively, through appeals to feeling, stimulation of unconscious motives, etc. The public realm, set up for effective legislation, has above all the function of directing attention to topical areas—that is, of pushing other themes, problems, and arguments below the threshold of attention and, thereby, of withholding them from opinion-formation.[35]

Although interventions of this kind attempt to avoid the direct manipulation of cultural tradition or meaning, they are nevertheless equally problematic from a different angle: Every intervention of the administrative system within the realm of tradition has the perverse side effect of thematizing elements that hitherto had been accepted uncritically as natural; the awareness that things could be otherwise actually expands the potential scope for democratic will formation among the population, and so undermines the depoliticization of the public sphere that is so crucial for system legtimation.[36] An example of the administrative processing of cultural tradition that has resulted in just such thematization is educational, especially curricular, planning. In the past, school administrations based general curricula around a codified canon that represented the essential developments of a culture that unfolded in an unplanned, nature-like manner. Curriculum planning today, on the other hand, in the service of administratively determined goals including both long-term economic planning and the cultivation of functional patterns of socialization, "is based on the premise that traditional patterns could well be otherwise. Administrative planning produced a universal pressure for legitimation in a sphere that was once distinguished precisely for its power of self-legitimation."[37] Disputes over the role of "core curriculum" at the university level, and value issues in public education, reflect the high degree of politicization that has been unwittingly introduced by administrative interference in education. And the problem extends beyond disputes regarding the content of education and tradition to include the form or method of socialization itself, competition between the family and the school, and the "problematization of childrearing routines" that is reflected both in the growing socializing significance of the school and in the "pedagogical-psychological, scientific journalism on the subject."[38]

So there are two possibilities lurking beneath the idea of a rationality crisis: The administration may fail the economy by providing adequate legitimation, but at the cost of inadequate efforts to forestall the falling rate of profit and so too economic crisis (which, in the long run, threatens legitimation again); or it may fail the economy by not providing adequate legitimations, or worse, by perversely undermining the crucially important depoliticization of the public sphere on which rests the entire legitimating enterprise of formal democracy. Once the latter has occurred, and the unquestionable character of tradition has been undermined, legitimating validity claims can only be restabilized through discourse, that is, through the genuinely democratic, communicative achievements of citizens.[39]

Sociocultural Crisis Tendencies—Legitimation Crisis, Motivational Crisis

Input for the sociocultural system refers to the products of the economic system (consumable goods) and the political system (legal acts, provisions for public safety, etc.). As a result, an output crisis in either of those systems will result in an input crisis here, leading to a withdrawal of legitimation. Because the sociocultural system does not produce its own input, there are no internally generated input crises. However, all forms of crisis are "filtered," as it were, by the sociocultural system, because it is on its output that social integration depends; that is, social integration depends "directly on the motivations it [the sociocultural system] supplies to the political system in the form of legitimation and indirectly on the motivations to perform it supplies to the educational and occupational systems."[40] There is an output crisis in the sociocultural system whenever normative structures are transformed—in conformity with their own independent logic—such that the needs, expectations, or identities of individuals rooted in these structures become dysfunctional with respect to the political or occupational system. Additionally, if the political structure changes (even if normative structures do not) such that a need for legitimation arises that cannot be met by existing resources, a legitimation crisis results. A motivational crisis, on the other hand, is directly the product of changes in the sociocultural system itself. On this basis, Habermas offers the thesis at the heart of *Legitimation Crisis*:

> In advanced capitalism such tendencies are becoming apparent at the level of cultural tradition (moral systems, worldviews) as well as at the level of structural change in the system of childrearing (school and family, mass media). In this way, the residue of tradition off which the state system of social labour lived in liberal capitalism is eaten away (stripping away traditionalistic padding), and core components of the bourgeois ideology have become questionable (endangering civil and familial-professional privatism) [the negative possible threat mentioned earlier]. On the other hand, the remains of bourgeois ideologies (belief in science, post-auratic art, and universalistic value systems) form a normative framework that is dysfunctional [the positive potential threat].[41]

In the first place, at issue is the rise of expectations in society that either cannot be satisfied because of insufficient value (the bankrupting of public finances will have, in this case, reached a crisis point where it can no longer adequately mitigate the painful side effects of capitalist growth through compensation), or because the expectations in question are not amenable to the form of value with which the system must operate, namely, a rise in use-value expectations that will not be satisfied through conversion into exchange value (monetarized compensation). Because expectations play the key role in this argument, Habermas claims, "[a] legitimation crisis . . . must be based on a motivation crisis—that is, a discrepancy between the need for motives declared by the state, the educational system and the occupational system on the one hand, and the motivation supplied by the socio-cultural tradition on the other."[42] This second part is crucial: A crisis only results if, in addition to the erosion of the traditions that support civil privatism, there are other motivations still fostered by the remnants of bourgeois tradition (scientism, postauratic art, and universal morality) that ground expectations that are not amenable to system compensation. This argument also serves to deny that the decay of bourgeois cultural traditions have left in their place a socialization altogether without reference to norms, the radical transformation of the socialization process discussed earlier.

It is helpful to divide Habermas' argument into two theses: (a) that the ideologies of bourgeois society have been undermined—specifically, the relevant forms of privatism, the achievement ideology, and "possessive individualism"—and that functional equivalents for these undermined ideologies cannot be produced; and (b) that the remnants of bourgeois traditions—scientism, postauratic art, and especially universal morality—continue to secure a normative socialization for significant sectors of the population and, in so doing, foster needs, expectations and identities that are dysfunctional with respect to the imperatives of system.

The End of Bourgeois Ideologies.

Civil privatism, according to Habermas, is the result of a peculiar mixture of both bourgeois and precapitalist elements of tradition. Bourgeois society, in other words, relies on the remnants of earlier cultural traditions in order to secure the motivational resources that it cannot itself produce. Habermas cites the work of Almond and Verba in support of his contention that, although bourgeois formal law grounds the expectations that individuals have of the administrative system generally, the passive attitude toward will formation typical of civil privatism is in fact rooted in the older "traditionalistic civic ethic or, even . . . [in] familial orientations."[43] Although the political theorists of the bourgeois era called on citizens to actively and rationally engage in processes of collective will formation, the practice of bourgeois societies required that this call be screened out and replaced with authoritarian demands for respect for political elites, which had formed the core of pre-bourgeois political traditions. According to Almond and Verba, this "mixed political culture" results in contradictory demands being made of citizens to be passive yet active, influential yet deferential.

Both the bourgeois attitude of possessive individualism—so well analyzed in its theoretical dimensions by C. B. MacPherson—and utilitarianism reflect at the cultural level the syndrome described by Habermas as "familial-vocational privatism." At the level of the individual, it, too, required additional motivational resources:

> the achievement-oriented vocational ethos of the middle class, as well as the fatalism of the lower class, need to be secured by

> religious traditions. These traditions are transposed into educational processes through corresponding family structures and techniques of childrearing. The educational processes lead to motivational structures that are class specific, that is, to the repressive authority of conscience and an individualistic achievement orientation among the bourgeoisie, and to external superego structures and a conventional work mentality in the lower class. The "Protestant ethic," with its emphasis on self-discipline, secularized vocational ethics, and renunciation of immediate gratification, is no less based on tradition than its traditionalistic counterpart of uncoerced obedience, fatalism, and orientation to immediate gratification. These traditions cannot be renewed on the basis of bourgeois society alone.[44]

Bourgeois ideologies have in fact always been limited in scope; they have always required supplementation if one's experience and needs are to be adequately interpreted and one's identity stabilized, for example, in the face of sickness, guilt, death, and contingency. Bourgeois ideologies offer no means of establishing a nonobjectifying relation to nature, including one's own body; they "permit no intuitive access to relations of solidarity with groups or between individuals"; and they support no real "political ethics" insofar as they are only able to ground objectivistic interpretations of actors in social and political life.[45]

The problem is that the process of capitalist development has weakened and in many cases entirely dissolved the precapitalist traditions and worldviews through which bourgeois ideologies were provided with these necessary supplementations. The aspect of this process that Habermas has principally in mind is what Max Weber called "rationalization," in which, on the one hand, the cultural tradition is differentiated into specialized knowledge spheres of science, art, and law/morality while, on the other hand, areas of life that had been regulated by tradition are subjected to the expansion of strategic-utilitarian reason. Examples of these developments include the "scientization of professional practice" (which results in the formation of expert cultures severed from the lifeworld of ordinary citizens); "the expansion of the service sector through which more and more interactions were subsumed under commodity form"; "administrative regulation and legalization of areas of political and social intercourse previously regulated informally" (examples offered elsewhere include the provision of geriatric and child care); the "commercialization of culture and politics" (in which the advertising industry plays a leading role); "and finally, scientizing and psychologizing processes of childrearing."[46] As this rationalization proceeds, traditional worldviews increasingly are contradicted by the results of science, to which individuals are exposed in general formal schooling and that tends to foster a positivistic, decisionistic consciousness in place of the old interpretative schemes. The ability to construct a holistic interpretation of the world, history, and nature, is accordingly undermined and replaced by "changing popular syntheses of isolated items of scientific information." The attitudes underlying belief, that had already been subjectivized, detached from the cult practice of the community under the rigor of the Protestant ethic, are yet again displaced: "The liberal disposition of taking-for-true, which is relativized from the start by the taking-for-true of another persuasion, corresponds to the recognition of a pluralism of competing beliefs that is undecided as to truth. Practical questions no longer admit of truth; values are irrational."[47] Finally, the connection between theoretical systems of interpretation and moral conceptions is also severed, such that the "utilitarian secular ethic" is cut loose from its original moorings in natural law theory and set adrift, posing as "common sense," the utterly unproblematic. The result is that the utopian kernels of philosophy and religion, which had formed a critical backdrop to the wretchedness of existing social orders, are lost in what Horkheimer referred to as "the idolatry of the actual," the reduction of reason to "reasonableness," the surrender of critique in deference to "the facts"—in short, an accommodation to the status quo social order that has been reified, turned into a kind of "second nature."

It is not only the traditional cultural bases that are eroding; the material basis of the achievement principle has also undergone a transformation:

> According to bourgeois conceptions that have remained constant from the beginnings of modern natural law to contemporary election speeches, social rewards should be distributed on the basis of individual achievement. The distribution of gratifications should be an isomorphic image of the achievement differentials of all individuals. The condition for this is equal opportunity to participate in a competition that is regulated so as to neutralize external influences. The market was such an allocation mechanism. Since it has been recognized, even among the population at large, that social force is exercised in the forms of economic exchange, the market has lost its credibility as a fair (from the perspective of achievement) mechanism for the distribution of life opportunities conforming to the system. Thus, in more recent versions of the achievement ideology, occupational success mediated through formal schooling takes the place of success in the market.[48]

The market can no longer credibly support the basic bourgeois ideology of equality, the burden of which has therefore been shifted to an interpretation of the significance of equal opportunity in schooling. This obviously makes the school a crucially important institution for the legitimation of capitalist society. But it can only support this burden, according to Habermas, if it meets the following conditions:

1. There is equal access to the relevant levels of education.
2. Success within the school is determined in accord with nonprejudicial methods of evaluation.
3. Developments in the educational and occupational systems remain synchronous.
4. The material structure of labor processes allow for evaluation according to the criteria of individual achievement.

Habermas claims that since World War II, advances have been made with respect to both conditions 1 and 2 although, as we will see in the Intermediate Reflections, there is in fact a wealth of literature suggesting that the advances have in both cases been at best inadequate, and often quite illusory. Nevertheless, Habermas himself argues that condition 3 is largely unmet: The development of systems of education has become independent of the development of the occupational system and, as a result, success in the former may fail to adequately translate into success in the latter.[49] With respect to condition 4, he contends that increasingly numerous sectors of the occupational system involve forms of labor that are not amenable to individualized evaluation processes. Moreover, occupational status has become more and more a question of "the extrafunctional elements of professional roles"[50]; in other words, individuals are increasingly motivated not by individually distributable, external rewards for performance, but by an internalized sense of the use value-oriented prestige of certain occupations, such as medicine. At the same time, the increasingly fragmented, monotonous, *alienated* character of labor processes even in sectors where occupational role used to be able to support positive identities, is serving to undermine the intrinsic motivation to achieve that had once flowed from such comparatively fulfilling labor. Finally, even the extrinsic, instrumentalist motivation to achieve provided by wages among lower income brackets is being diminished by a tendency toward equalization between the standard of living of the lowest wage earners (the working poor) and that of the "inactive labor population," the unemployed, the sick, welfare recipients, and so on.

The remaining element of the bourgeois ideologies described here is "possessive individualism," which relies on two conditions for its stabilization: (a) strategically acting subjects can reliably calculate the motivating needs of others when acting competitively, and (b) the needs in question permit individual distribution, in particular, that they be translatable into money.

Neither of these conditions attains under circumstances of increased social wealth, where a well-known catalogue of basic goods is no longer the motive force for predictable action. In the liberal era, upper-class culture had set the agenda for new consumption opportunities, but this too is no longer true.

> The constant interpretation and reinterpretation of needs has become a matter of collective will-formation. In this process, free communication can be replaced only by massive manipulation, that is, by strong, indirect control. The more freedom the preference system has, the more pressing become the problems of market policy for suppliers. This is true, at least, if the appearance that consumers can decide privately and autonomously—that is, according to monologically certain preferences—is to be preserved. Opportunistic adaptation of consumers to market strategies of monopolistic competition is the ironic form of the consumer autonomy that is supposed to be maintained as the façade of possessive individualism.[51]

As the latter part of this quote seems to indicate, collective will formation has, in fact, been replaced by the massive manipulation of the advertising and market research industries, that claim to track and discover the elusive preferences of their "demanding, independent consumers," but whose efforts are almost exclusively directed at finding convincing ways to pitch whatever they have been contracted to sell such that it will match up with reported/manipulated consumer desires. In either case, the accountability premise of possessive individualism is forfeited in favor of the leaderless, Ouija-board push and pull of unpredictable, if nevertheless unfree, consumer fads. As for the second premise, the individually distributable character of the goods in question: This, too, is undermined by the nature of the needs that emerge beyond the level of basic requirements. Especially in urban centers, in which increasing numbers of the world's population live, these needs more and more take the shape of demands for collective commodities such as transportation and health care services. And, as we already observed, the socializing effects of the market are unable to effectively reach the expanding segments of the population that do not reproduce their life through labor, or that are engaged in concrete as opposed to abstract forms of labor in the public-service sector.

The Remnants of Bourgeois Traditions.

Habermas sees three elements as relevant in this respect: scientism, postauratic art, and universal morality. The state and character of each of these elements is a product of an irreversible sequence of developments in accord with the internal logic of normative structures. As a result, they represent cultural barriers to a number of system strategies that could only be overcome at the cost of psychological regression and its attendant pathologies.[52] Universal morality is undeniably the most important for Habermas, and so I will be rather brief regarding the others.[53]

Scientism: The immense prestige enjoyed by science, which Habermas believes characteristic of contemporary society, has made possible a critique of the prejudices ingrained in traditional worldviews that cannot meet justificatory burdens, a critique that has been widely disseminated in popular consciousness. At the same time, the positive authority that is granted to science is of the most abstract variety, such that the results of this increasingly expert culture only make their way into ordinary consciousness in the form of "short-lived popular syntheses of isolated pieces of information" that, as mentioned previously, take the place of the holistic interpretations of traditional worldviews. Habermas rather unconvincingly maintains that, although scientism in this way results in "a positivistic common consciousness that sustains the [depoliticization of the] public realm . . . scientism also sets standards by which it can itself be criticized and convicted of residual dogmatism."[54] It isn't that this is false: Science can and should (and has been by Habermas) so criticized; but it can only be so by someone for whom its authority is precisely *not* abstract, someone who, to the contrary, recognizes its basis in rational methodology. On his own terms, "common consciousness" is not in a position to engage in such critique.

Postauratic Art: Habermas sees in postauratic art a counterculture directly antagonistic to the practice and ideology of bourgeois society, yet emerging from the core of bourgeois society itself. Modern art had initially played a confirming role in relation to bourgeois consciousness, offering an image of the beautiful as the anticipated fruit of bourgeois rationalization, the promise of reward for the self-denials of the present. But the emergence of an avant-garde shatters this illusion, adopting a critical posture toward rationalization and the bourgeois social order based on it. In surrealism, even the "shell" of the beautiful maintained by the autonomy of art is broken in an attempt to level the divide between art and life. Yet this move contains within it a significant danger: On the one hand, a popularly accessible mass art could provide the basis for a broad counterculture; but, on the other hand, a premature integration into life could just as easily result in its degeneration into propaganda, commercialism, and so on. Alternatively, the attempt to avoid this danger by retaining autonomy risks the loss of critical power by remaining inaccessible or esoteric. Habermas offers no resolution of this dilemma, and thus his appeal to art in *Legitimation Crisis* seems intended to provide no more than a kind of countercultural model, rather than its reality.[55]

Universal Morality: Along with bourgeois formal law, universal morality grows out of the collapse of traditional societies that could not adapt their nature-like substance sufficiently quickly to the processes of modernization. Into the place of this monolithic "ethical substance" steps consciously constructed positive law, justified in light of principles, and set off as public in contradistinction to the newly privatized domain of moral norms enforced by conscience. For liberal capitalism, the internal tension thus established (and diagnosed by Marx) between *citoyen* and *homme*—member of a particular legal community versus member of the universal moral community of reason—served a crucial legitimating purpose. Universalistic orientations are necessary to the operations of the market and to the endorsement of the legitimacy of the law that institutionalizes it, out of respect for the universal principle of equality. As we have seen, however, the equality of the market has been unmasked even in popular consciousness; yet the introduction of universalistic principles into moral consciousness cannot be undone. A morality based on principle is inescapable but, Habermas claims, its only credible form after the collapse of the nature-like reproduction of cultural traditions and the worldviews rooted in them, is that of a communicative ethics. In other words, this is the form morality must take once need- and identity-securing traditions are no longer simply given. The problem, and this is the crucial part of Habermas' argument, is that such a morality "cannot function without conflict in the political-economic system" that demands individualistic, privatistic orientations.[56]

Habermas believes that there is evidence suggesting that these three elements of the otherwise desiccated bourgeois tradition have taken on socializing force in "*experimental complexes of countercultures*." In particular, he is interested in evidence suggesting the motive-forming power of these remnants for an un-(or post-)conventional outcome to the adolescent crisis, one in which the young person, by adopting a "reflective attitude toward socially tendered patterns of interpretation . . . [comes] to terms with these cultural interpretations, [allowing him] to work out his definition of identity for himself"[57]—that is, autonomously. He cites the research of Keniston to support this claim, which the latter had described in terms of James' distinction between the once- and twice-born, referring to individuals who, while they may hold identical beliefs in terms of content, do so in different ways: unreflectively in the first case and reflectively in the second. Habermas appeals to a number of social changes that support the claim that such unconventional outcomes are increasingly probable. They include (a) that the extension of the number of years of required schooling is delaying the need for a definitive resolution of the adolescent crisis until, in some cases, the late 20s, with the result that resolution is made in circumstances of greater cognitive and emotional maturity; (b) higher-quality education in more numerous segments of the population increases the likelihood that young people will perceive disparities between traditional interpretive patterns and present social reality (this challenge to interpretive patterns also entails an intensification of the problem faced by the adolescent with regard to securing identity); (c) as Horkheimer argued in his study of authority and the family, increasingly egalitarian family structures result in patterns of socialization that make adolescent identity problems more likely (because highly structured and gender-assigned parental roles, for example, don't establish rigid models for adult identity); (d) innovations in birth control, which also temporarily liberate sex from economic pressures, expand the scope for relatively anxiety-free sexual experimentation. There are two possible practical forms taken by an unconventional outcome to the adolescent crisis, both documented by Keniston:

1. Withdrawal as a reaction to an overloading of personality resources (a behavioral syndrome that Keniston has observed and examined in the "alienated"); and
2. Protest as a result of an autonomous ego organization that cannot be stabilized under the given conditions (a behavioral syndrome that Keniston has described in his "young radicals").[58]

Examples of the latter include participants in the student movement of the late 1960s, the women's liberation movement, and pacifists. However, the student movement has a kind of priority here, for Habermas, because it draws from a demographic, youths, who are by definition those affected by changes to the nature of adolescent crises.

In summary, then, Habermas sees hopeful empirical indicators that postconventional identity, which he implicitly recognizes has hitherto been rare, may become progressively more widespread in the future. Most importantly, if this is the case, it may have transformative consequences for the existing social order in the form of a motivation crisis that would precipitate a legitimation crisis. As Thomas McCarthy cautions, however, Habermas' appeal to the significance of youth protest should not be read as the claim that youths will somehow constitute themselves as a social class that might overthrow the existing order.[59] Instead, the transformation in question is, at least in the first instance, pictured as a kind of crumbling of the reproductive processes of the social system, as young people cannot be convinced to maintain it and assume the positions of previous generations (in particular, they refuse to accept merely formal democracy). But the political questions, which McCarthy insists "remain open," concern whether (a) withdrawal and protest could conceivably occur on a wide enough scale to endanger the system as a whole (as we know now, this did not occur in the 1960–70s); and (b) if it did, whether the groups in question—feminists, pacifists, environmentalists, and the like—could respond with effective political action.

I will return shortly to some other questions raised by McCarthy with respect to the argument of *Legitimation Crisis*; first, however, I want to discuss in more detail the other, pessimistic possibility entertained by Habermas and already mentioned, namely, the possibility of a new form of socialization not reliant on the internalization of norms. If this were to occur, and the connection were severed between individual motivation and internalized norms and values with criticizable claims to validity, the very possibility of a motivational crisis would evaporate, and "the social system would no longer establish its unity [i.e., would no longer be socially integrated] through formation of the identities of socially related individuals."[60] This would entail a complete conversion to systemic integration, and the communicatively oriented remnants of bourgeois traditions would be displaced by the total absorption into system of the inner "environment" of individual personality. Habermas maintains that, at least up until the recent past, motivational development has been tied to validity, to truth of a kind, and therefore has been dependent on cognitive elements of the process of moral development that can be hierarchically reconstructed, and that culminates in a form of universal morality rooted in the structure of discourse (i.e., *this* is postconventionality, or the developmental meaning of autonomy—see Chapter 3). The question is: Have the sociocultural and political-administrative systems now been "uncoupled" in the manner described by Niklas Luhmann, for instance, as a *fait accompli*? Habermas poses this question by noting, following Durkheim and classical sociology generally, that human beings have secured for themselves a stable identity only through establishing a connection to the socially integrating worldviews that are the basis of *meaning*. So, if these worldviews have begun to disintegrate, or have perhaps collapsed entirely under the pressure of societal rationalization, what fulfills the tasks today of constituting group and ego identities? Has a universal communicative ethics begun to do so, and could it credibly accomplish this task? Or, on the other hand, have the normative elements of these identities simply withered and been replaced by an objectivistic self-understanding on the part of human beings? Have we seen the "end of the individual"?

Habermas, in the end, doesn't offer a definitive answer. He mentions a number of alternative possibilities, developments that either present possible sources of meaning, or that adequately overcome the contingencies that shake the foundations of identity in the first place. This serves only to demonstrate the admittedly "comforting" fact that "the developmental logic of worldviews does not exclude the continuance of a mode of socialization related to truth"—that is, that rationalization does not inherently lead to this dystopian result. It still does not conclusively disprove the claims of systems theorists like Luhmann that social complexity has, as a matter of fact, necessitated the uncoupling of motive formation from norms requiring justification. The problem is that, according to Habermas, in none of its versions—including those offered by Adorno and Horkheimer, and conservatives like Arnold Gehlen—has this thesis been sufficiently removed from "the malaise and self-experience of intellectuals" and made amenable to empirical corroboration.[61] It isn't that there is no evidence. To the contrary, Habermas agrees that advanced capitalist societies are increasingly alienated, severed in their structural operations from the actual motives and values of individuals. Moreover, such societies have proven themselves remarkably adept at translating social conflicts into private psychological problems of individuals; even in those cases in which psychic conflicts are successfully "repoliticized as protest," they are administratively absorbed, neutralized, and offered "as proof of the extended scope of tolerance."[62] But, despite regarding the question of the balance between system and social integration as an empirical one, Habermas argues that it does not appear possible at present to actually determine empirically whether these verifiable phenomena are attributable to the violation of normative structures by the imperatives of the economic-political system, including interferences in processes of socialization as well as the basic inability of this system to seriously countenance use value-oriented demands as such, or whether we are witnessing emergence of a radically new pattern of socialization.

The Critical Reception of *Legitimation Crisis*

I confine my comments here to a set of criticisms from two writers, both of whom are largely sympathetic to Habermas' overall project, and whose criticisms (or others like them) seem to have been influential for the way in which his social theory continues to develop into *The Theory of Communicative Action*. The writers in question are David Held and Thomas McCarthy.

Held's first concern with the argument of *Legitimation Crisis* regards the obscurity of the distinction between a legitimation crisis and a motivation crisis. According to Held, this lack of clear differentiation results from an ambiguity in the distinction between the two kinds of "scarce resources to which the two types of crisis are, respectively, linked—'generalized motivations' and 'action-motivating meaning.' "[63] Legitimation crises result from a shortfall of "generalized motives" or "diffuse loyalty," but this only occurs if traditional "action-motivating meaning" is undermined (which Habermas believes is occurring as a result of capitalist development and rationalization). In a reply to Held, Habermas concedes this point and attributes it to a more general failure to have clearly worked out the relationship between the basic concepts of system and lifeworld. And, in fact, he indicates there that he is in the process of completing a more adequate, systematic account of this very issue—that is, he is writing what would become *The Theory of*

Communicative Action. I discuss the relevant sections in some detail later; for now, suffice it to say that Habermas admits that an adequate typology of potential disturbances in the interactions between system and lifeworld requires distinctions that were absent from *Legitimation Crisis*. Specifically, we must distinguish between (a) disturbances that result from the inflexibility of the normative structures of the lifeworld, which threaten system maintenance, and of which the persistence of universalist morality in the form of a communicative ethics was an example in *Legitimation Crisis*; and (b) "manifestations of deficiencies in the reproduction of the lifeworld itself"[64] such as loss of meaning, anomie, and personality disorders, which all are discussed in the account of the lifeworld in *The Theory of Communicative Action*, and which are connected to the key diagnoses there of both the intrusion or "colonization" of system imperatives into core domains of the lifeworld (especially socialization processes) and the phenomenon of "cultural impoverishment."[65]

So Habermas concedes Held's criticism in full but, it turns out, not really the point behind the criticism. According to Held, the deeper problem underlying Habermas' confusion in *Legitimation Crisis* is to be found in "an inadequate conception of the way societies cohere—that is, in a problematic emphasis on the centrality of shared norms and values in social integration and on the importance of 'internalization' in the genesis of individual identity and social order."[66] In particular, Held contends that we need to distinguish—as Habermas does not—between the, as it were, official normative structures that provide legitimation, and the interpretive frameworks that underlie the motives of people in their ordinary lives.[67] With the exception of wartime, the moral approval of the majority of the members of a society is neither forthcoming nor necessary; in other words, social integration, the basis of social stability, does not in practice lie in a shared sense of legitimacy understood as "the worthiness of a political order to be recognized."[68] What is important, according to Held, is the approval of dominant groups, the politically powerful, state personnel.

> The notion of legitimation crisis presupposes that the motivation of the mass of the population was at one time constituted to a significant extent by the normative structure established by powerful groups. But Habermas, in my view, overestimates the degree to which one may consider the individual as having been integrated into society, as well as the degree to which bourgeois identity has been eroded and the extent to which contemporary society is threatened by a "legitimation/motivation" crisis.[69]

I am not so sure that the retrospective assumption of genuine mass loyalty is particularly important to Habermas' argument, even if it is true: If the socialization of dominant groups in bourgeois society is altering such as to increase legitimation demands beyond the resources of the state to meet them or, more likely, that they are changing qualitatively such that system rewards cannot satisfy them, then the crisis argument holds. Held's competing diagnosis of social trends, on the other hand, appeals repeatedly to the state of class consciousness among workers; but this seems rather tangential to Habermas' point, which has to do most prominently with the socialization of middle-class and even upper middle-class youths (from which student protest and countercultural movements, and even the women's liberation movement, draw most heavily). If Held's additional point holds good, that Habermas has exaggerated the erosion of bourgeois identity, this would indeed present a significant problem. But again, in his defense of this position Held appeals instead to workers' consciousness: He argues that any generalizations regarding the conditions for social integration,

> must recognize that a "dual consciousness" is often expressed in communities and workplaces. This implies a quite radical interpretation of many everyday events—often linking dissatisfactions with divisions between the "rich and poor," the "rulers and the ruled"—and a relatively "conservative" . . . privatistic interest in dominant political parties and processes. Many institutions and processes are perceived and hypostatized as "natural," "the way things have been and always will be"; but the language used to express and account for immediate needs and their frustration often reveals a marked penetration of ideology or dominant interpretative systems.[70]

The groups predominantly implied by Habermas' crisis argument are not located in the economic and political systems such that the divisions between rich and poor, rulers and ruled would be particularly apt lenses through which to interpret their experience: They do not fit neatly into either class. However—and this is the reason Held's critique is relevant for my argument—his appeal to the hypostatization of social reality is worthy of further consideration. He maintains that the stability of advanced capitalism relies on the fragmentation of culture, the "atomization of people's experience of the social world," which undermines their ability to form a "coherent conception of social totality." Habermas himself had said as much with reference to the effects of scientism on common consciousness. As a direct effect of this cognitive and imaginative limitation, the present order is not so much accepted as legitimate or worthy, rather the individual simply shifts their attitude toward this apparently incomprehensible Leviathan to one of practical accommodation. In Held's words, "compliance most often comprises pragmatic acquiescence to the status quo."[71] Acquiescence is precisely pragmatic because individuals who wish to survive have to act "rationally"—must "be reasonable," as Horkheimer would say—where acting rationally means, as a matter of fact, "acting according to the standards which ensure the functioning of the apparatus."[72] In Habermas' terms, this means maintaining the orientations needed for systemic integration. But there also is an element of false consciousness here inasmuch as workers, in Held's example, do not fully appreciate the systemic significance of their actions because, again, they are lacking the conception of social totality relative to which such functions find their place.

By overestimating the role of shared values in social integration, Held argues, Habermas becomes blind to the significance of this phenomenon of pragmatic adaptation. Held offers a variety of speculations, most of them reinforcing his emphasis on worker consciousness, to explain how the cognitive incapacity that underlies the adoption of this accommodating strategy comes about: He appeals to the work of Braverman, Mann, Aronowitz, and Willis to illustrate the ways in which the increasing fragmentation of social labor into meaningless snippets forms an obstacle to understanding the social relations that underlie production; he points to the way in which the fragmentation of class solidarity through sexual, racial, and ethnic divisions, as well as through the seniority system and credentialism, frustrates cooperative efforts to discuss and come to understand the functioning of society; finally, he notes the socially reinforcing effect of the culture industry, as analyzed by Adorno.[73]

Given that Held and Habermas appear to part ways at a much more general level, it isn't clear that this evidence is directly relevant to the critique of *Legitimation Crisis*, although much of it will be interesting to reconsider in the context of the sociology of schooling. Additionally, the social significance of the specifically cognitive incapacity implied by fragmented consciousness will be treated in detail toward the end of Chapter 4. But it is worth noting here that Held appears not to appreciate the similarity between his argument and critical versions of the "end of the individual" thesis; in other words, that "pragmatic acquiescence" simply describes the acceptance of the expanded scope of systemic over social forms of integration and is not, therefore, a competing account of *social* integration. The adoption of a strategic perspective toward social reality as a whole means that normative structures that are, as a matter of fact, based on criticizable validity claims, are instead treated as social facts to be considered as boundary conditions in the making of decisions in which the individual is oriented by personal preference—in Held's example, the usually very strong preference not allow oneself or one's family to starve to death. Held has added, however, that the individuals themselves don't entirely surrender the normative attitude, even while practically speaking they renounce any action on its behalf. I argue in Chapter 4, following the lead provided by Habermas in his reconstruction of the cognitive stages of moral development, that we can identify the crucial psychological-structural element that appears to be lacking in a "conservative" consciousness unable to conceive of alternatives to the hypostatized status quo: It is the ability to adopt a hypothetical attitude on the social world from within a norm-conformative perspective. The incapacity, in other words, refers to the ability to seriously conceive of the possibility that things could be otherwise: "the idolatry of the actual." Following Held, on the other hand, I argue that this incapacity has a stabilizing function in advanced capitalist societies that is altogether independent of a normative conception of social integration and is, I argue, reproduced at least partially through socialization in the school. Habermas, in any case, appears to realize the basic direction of Held's criticism and responds by simply repeating that it is an empirical question to what extent system integration (to which Held is essentially referring) can absorb the surplus need for integration that overruns the socially integrative capacity of highly rationalized lifeworlds.

In addition to sharing Held's skepticism regarding the evidence for a motivational crisis, McCarthy, too, counterposes what he sees as a third option to "the alternative posed in *Legitimation Crisis* between acceptance of decisions as the expression of a rational consensus" and acceptance of decisions without reasons, which dilemma, he believes, "may well be too broad to capture effective motivations." But again, just like Held, McCarthy doesn't appear to realize how similar his argument is to the basic intuition underlying systems theory. He argues:

> [o]ne face of the growing "cynicism of bourgeois consciousness" to which Habermas frequently refers might be described as the willingness to accede to a political order *because* it provides an acceptable flow of system-conforming rewards. This too is a reason that can and does serve to legitimate political systems. The point here is not to side with the "brave new world" theorists against Habermas but to introduce a middle ground: acceptance of decisions *for the reason* that nothing better seems practically possible in the given circumstances.[74]

This only appears to be a "middle ground" because McCarthy is overly literal in his interpretation of the dilemma as Habermas poses it. Habermas' conception of a reason is normative: not just any sort of reason will do. This is clear when he describes the dilemma as one between socialization on the basis of internalized norms and socialization without such norms. Norms have the form of criticizable claims to *normative validity*, that is, to moral or ethical rightness. The ability to address oneself to such claims—which is necessary if their presence is not to be merely ideological—entails that one can at least temporarily suspend one's endorsement of that validity and to see the norm in question as one among competing hypothetical alternatives. The idea that the present normative order is but one alternative among other "live" options is just what the systems-theoretic individual cannot seriously conceive—and not merely in light of contingent considerations regarding present circumstances that could themselves be thematized and critically evaluated. In this sense, McCarthy's final comment in the above quote strikes me as misleading. But the real point is still that the promise of financial reward in exchange for the performance of some act does not intend to justify that act as a morally legitimate; it asks me to put that question aside in favor of a different kind of non-normative consideration. Of course, it is still the case that individuals act for *a* reason: In question are the *kinds* of reasons they take to be salient. Extended to the level of society as a whole, the "brave new world" is precisely that society in which individuals are socialized without the sense that social demands make precisely *normative* claims on them, criticizable claims to rightness, a society in which they fail to develop the competencies that would allow them to carry through such criticism and in which, instead, the "reason" of system rewards, the carrot and the stick of social facts, are sufficient to induce general compliance. Habermas claims that, in such a situation, legitimation crises would no longer be a threat.

A much more interesting objection raised by McCarthy—and one that appears to have influenced Habermas going forward—regards the "predictive" form of the argument of *Legitimation Crisis*. That is, despite the fact that the argument is thoroughly qualified, and despite Habermas' concession that in light of these necessary qualifications it is not possible to predict the occurrence of crises, nevertheless the argument is advanced in a predictive form. What is surprising about this, as McCarthy notes, is that *Legitimation Crisis* is unique among Habermas' work in this respect: In his other writings, he has always confined himself to the attempt to enlighten the practical addressees of his theory about the nature of their situation, interests, and possibilities, and has maintained that beyond this, only practical action can go. Here, however,

> the structure of the argument is such that no appeal to the practical self-consciousness of any identifiable social group is made, or its seems, need be made. The discrepancies in question [although they involve the expectations of social subjects] appear to issue from the very structure and functioning of the "sociocultural system" in the context of advanced capitalist society as a whole.

> Although they are in a sense "subjective," they arise, it seems, with something like "objective" necessity.[75]

Habermas, as McCarthy notes, surely does not intend his argument to be read in this way, which contradicts the prescriptions of his own methodological writings. The problem is a result of what McCarthy sees as the alternating and unintegrated use of systems- and action-theoretic concepts in *Legitimation Crisis*, where the former carry the burden in the crisis argument, in particular. As a result "the practical-political activity of social agents tends to recede into the background."[76] A similar sort of puzzling "objectivity" is observable in Habermas' presentation of the model of ideology critique, described in *Legitimation Crisis* as the identification of "the suppression of generalizable interests." I haven't discussed this model thus far, as it isn't relevant to my main theme; but McCarthy's criticism is comprehensible even still.

The interests suppressed by an unjust society are particular, historical interests belonging to a given community; they are those interests that all affected could agree on through a process of unconstrained discourse (thus, they are "generalizable"). Their suppression is effected by preventing such discourse from occurring, in order to protect a status quo favorable to the particular ("nongeneralizable") interests of some other class. This suppression can be identified and critiqued by a social theorist who hypothetically projects how members of the community would have interpreted their needs if the conditions for discourse were met. This projection is intended to make its addressees, the members of the community in question, "aware of the 'domination' or 'injustice' built into prevailing normative structures and their interpretations," and in so doing, "to motivate them to replace 'value-oriented action with interest-guided action . . . in politically relevant domains.' "[77] To give a classic example, a Marxist projects the way in which a collective discourse among workers regarding their needs and interests would, if the divisions sown in the proletariat could be overcome, issue in the realization that the "exchange of equivalents" in the market and its legal protection actually represent the institutionalization of their domination. The system is inherently unjust on normative grounds, and it is in the interest of the proletariat to struggle against it practically.

McCarthy's point is that the interest in unconstrained discourse, which is a "quasi-transcendental interest" rooted in the structure of speech,

> is not the *immediate* basis of sociopolitical critique; it is rather its *mediate*, normative-theoretical basis, the procedural criterion for assessing the rationality or legitimacy of concrete interests. But *Legitimation Crisis* itself—and this is true, by and large, of Habermas' other critical writings as well—clearly does not move

> at the level of identifying the "interest positions" of specific social groups. In part this is because he has been primarily concerned with reworking the foundations of critical theory.[78]

McCarthy concedes, however, that in his critique of the depoliticization of the public sphere—which is not only central to the argument of *Legitimation Crisis*, but is in many ways central to the argument spanning his career—Habermas has identified a suppressed interest that is universal, generalizable at the level of humanity as a whole: namely, the emancipatory interest in communication free of domination embedded in language itself. Thus, the quasi-transcendental converges with the historically rooted interest and, at the same time, the addressee of critical theory is universalized. On the other hand, the interest to be articulated is now so abstract that it is difficult see, according to McCarthy, how it "could serve to orient effective political practice."[79] Which concrete actors will engage in political struggle for the sake of communication free from domination? The bourgeois appeal to the universal values of liberty, equality, and justice was politically effective precisely because they were ideologically interpreted to be of service to the particular interests of an emerging class. Marx's critique of these same values, which rested on a moral critique of capitalism, similarly retained a connection to the interests of a particular social class (although Marx did not see those interests as particular, precisely because their realization was to be a liberation for all humanity). Given that these "two levels of critique do not seem to be mutually exclusive," McCarthy asks why Habermas, after having unmasked a particular class interest posing as universal, and having contrasted it with the identification of a truly "fundamental interest of mankind," does not return to the level of the particular where it links up with the universal. The answer, McCarthy believes, is to be found in Habermas' contention that social struggle today no longer takes the form of direct class conflict. That is not to say that there do not remain conflicts related to disparities in the distribution of social wealth; but, Habermas writes,

> unless they are connected with protest potential from other sectors of society no conflicts arising from such underprivilege can really overturn the system—they can only provoke it to sharp reactions incompatible with formal democracy. For underprivileged groups are not social classes, nor do they potentially represent the mass of the population. Their disenfranchisement and pauperization no longer coincide with the exploitation [*sic*], because the system does not live off their labour . . . as long as no coalitions are made with privileged groups, such a civil war lacks the chance of revolutionary success that class struggle possesses.[80]

This argument is in fact a constant in Habermas' work from *Toward a Rational Society* to *The Theory of Communicative Action*. In *Legitimation Crisis*, according to McCarthy, this consideration leads Habermas to conclude that there is no appropriate or adequate practical addressee for critical theory, much as Adorno and Horkheimer concluded, although for their own reasons. But, as we will see, in *The Theory of Communicative Action*, Habermas will make the return trip from the identification of a universal interest in undistorted communication, via the theory of colonization, to the articulation of the interests of potential protest groups confronted with the encroachment of system imperatives. As we will also see, the argument there represents a dramatic scaling down of the transformative significance of protest from the crisis argument of *Legitimation Crisis*. McCarthy's criticism, however, is not only interesting in light of these further developments; my own argument, to be elaborated in the Concluding Reflections, intends to offer the possibility of the sought after practical complement (and so to answer McCarthy's objection) without sacrificing the hope of radical and just social transformation that sends the critical theorist looking for potential leverage points in the first place.

Chapter 2

Rationalization and Social Pathology in *The Theory of Communicative Action*

The Theory of Communicative Action is Habermas' magnum opus. At the same time, it is, in light of the later development of his philosophy, a profoundly transitional work. Because it does preserve many of the insights of *Legitimation Crisis*, I will focus here on the differences that emerge in this later work, particularly where they reflect Habermas' response to the criticisms just described. These responses are based on a more comprehensive account of the system/lifeworld distinction and the processes by which each is reproduced, as well as what Habermas now refers to as their "interchange" relations. However, this account emerges from a detailed theory of social evolution that depicts both the transformation of the structure of social integration over the course of modernization, as well as the emergence of the modern lifeworld and its differentiated subsystems. Consideration of this theory of social evolution will allow us to clarify Habermas' altered account of the way in which the colonization of the lifeworld by system imperatives interferes with the symbolic reproduction of the former and results in various kinds of social pathologies (mentioned in his reply to Held). This, in turn, forms the basis for Habermas' revised assessment of protest potential, which represents a response to the objections raised by McCarthy. Finally, the account offered in *The Theory of Communicative Action* of the effects of "colonization" on socialization processes arguably helps explain why the possible crises anticipated by *Legitimation Crisis* failed to materialize.

Habermas introduces his discussion of social evolution as "linguistification" in order to explain how the integration of society and the individuation of subjects are transferred from a basis in pregrammatical religious rituals and the complete identification of the individual with the group, to the forward-looking solidarity of individuated citizens achieved through communication and mutual understanding. As a whole, this story is intended to link Durkheim's aporetic account of social evolution to Habermas' own theory of communicative action and, on that basis, to reformulate a version of the rationalization thesis that escapes the paradoxes of Weber's "Iron Cage" or the "dialectic of enlightenment" as described by Adorno and Horkheimer. The theory of communicative action thus serves both to redeem the emancipatory potential of reason and to specify—as Durkheim could not—the meaning of a new, posttraditional form of social integration ("organic solidarity," in Durkheim's terms). Habermas' thesis is that the rationality inherent in the structure of speech is released in a rationalization of the lifeworld to the extent that processes of cultural reproduction, social integration, and socialization, come to be increasingly mediated by language—or, in other words, to the extent that these reproductive processes are "linguistified."[1] In order to explain this thesis, then, it is necessary to make clear the basic outlines of Habermas' theory of communicative action, his account of the rationality of speech.

The Theory of Communicative Action in a Nutshell

At its heart, the theory of communicative action is intended to explain how social integration is possible in a complex society:

> The question in social theory of what makes social order possible has a counterpart in action theory: How can (at least two) participants in interaction coordinate their plans in such a way that alter is in a position to link his actions to ego's without a conflict arising, or at least without the risk that the interaction will be broken off? If the actors are interested solely in the success, i.e., the consequences or outcomes of their actions, they will try to reach their objectives by influencing their opponent's definition of the situation, and thus his decision or motives, through external means by using weapons or goods, threats or enticements. Such actors treat each other strategically. In such cases, coordination of the subjects' action depends upon the extent to which their egocentric utility calculations mesh. The degree of cooperation and the stability is determined by the interest positions of the participants. By contrast, I speak of communicative action when actors are prepared to harmonize their plans of action through internal means, committing themselves to pursuing their goals only on the condition of an agreement—one that already exists or one to be negotiated—about definitions of the situation and prospective outcomes.[2]

It isn't that individuals pursuing communicative action don't continue to be motivated by their ends; the difference is that, unlike strategic action, we cannot describe communicative action purely teleologically but must also include a description of the conditions for reaching understanding. Reaching understanding means coming to a rationally motivated agreement regarding the content of some utterance. Thus, the smallest unit of communicative action includes a claim raised by one participant in interaction and a "yes" of acceptance or a "no" of refusal by at least one other participant. The "yes" must be rational, which is to say, for Habermas, that it cannot be the result of manipulation or external force, but must instead reflect the acceptance of a claim to validity that is "in principle criticizeable."[3] To say that the validity claim is "in principle criticizable" means that, if necessary, ego could give reasons why alter should accept it, reasons that depend on the kind of claim it is. In his mature work, Habermas claims that there are three mutually irreducible kinds of validity claims that are implicitly raised by every utterance: claims to truth (that something is the case); claims to rightness (that something ought to be the case); and claims to sincerity (that what I say is said in earnest).[4] So if I, the author, say to you, the reader, "Habermas' theory of communicative action, though difficult, is worth learning about," then along with the propositional content of that statement there are three other things I have additionally claimed: (a) *that it is true* that the theory is worth learning about; (b) that as the author of a work dedicated to explaining this theory, *it is appropriate* (morally acceptable, in keeping with social roles, etc.) for me to make such a claim to you, the reader; and (c) that I really do believe that the theory is worth learning about and in so saying, I am not engaging in an elaborate practical joke at your expense. For the first two types of validity claims, it is understood that I could offer reasons should you raise doubts about them: Sincerity, on the other hand, usually is demonstrated convincingly only through consistent future action and not through repeated protestations (I demonstrate my sincerity, I hope, by the seriousness of my discussion throughout this section). If you accept my claim that the theory of communicative action is worth learning about, you have implicitly accepted as well both my sincerity and the nature of the interpersonal relation that I seek to establish between you and I, as author and reader. The process of giving justifying reasons for validity claims is what Habermas refers to as their "discursive redemption"; that is, they are redeemed from the doubt into which they were cast by engaging in discourse. In ordinary communicative action, however, it is not the process of discourse, which is both rare and costly in terms of time and energy, that provides the coordination of action; rather, it is the implicit promise of discourse contained in the structure of communicative action that provides the bonding force of social integration.

The aim of action, in general, is to master a situation, either through the successful implementation of a plan (strategic action), or (as in communicative action) by arriving at a common interpretation of the situation itself (which we believe, for that reason, to be at least provisionally true or justified). A "situation" in this sense refers to a "segment of a lifeworld that has been delimited in terms of a specific theme. A *theme* arises in connection with the interests and objectives of actors. It defines the *range* of matters that are *relevant* and can be thematically focused on."[5] Individual actions, then, serve to make a theme relevant, in light of which the need for consensual understanding of the situation is assessed: Is there a complementarity of self-interest such that those affected do not need to come to an independent agreement? Or is there a conflict of interests, such that the only choices are either violence, or an agreement in light of which one (or possibly both) party (or parties) agree(s) to subordinate their interest? Action situations that raise themes for consideration in this way call simultaneously for action and for speech, "in which the actors take turns playing their *communicative roles* of speaker, addressee, and bystander. To these roles correspond first- and second-person *participant perspectives* as well as the third-person *observer* perspective from which the I–thou [first- to second-person] relation is observed as an intersubjective complex and can thus be objectified."[6]

The system of speaker perspectives, of first, second, and third persons links up with three different ways of relating to the world in light of which one might encounter three different kinds of problems. When an actor encounters a problem, a thematized situation, he or she is both faced with some segment (formerly) of his or her lifeworld and yet is simultaneously supported by the lifeworld as a whole. The lifeworld is, in part, the store of culturally rooted assumptions, interpretive patterns, and shared knowledge that individuals of a common language and/or culture, society, and so on, can take for granted in trying to come to an understanding with one another. When faced with a problem, a disagreement, some one aspect of the lifeworld has been separated from the background and is now thematized by the actor; but the lifeworld as such remains at the actor's back, a resource to draw on. In fact, the lifeworld as such "cannot become problematic . . . it is prior to any possible disagreement and cannot become controversial in the way that intersubjectively shared knowledge can; at most it can fall apart."[7] But the lifeworld is comprised of more than just these cultural givens (generally, "culture") that prestructure our interpretations and provide a semantic resource for mutual understanding; it also includes the solidarity of the various groups making up a culture, based on membership-constraining shared norms (generally, "society"); and it includes the "competencies of socialized individuals" who are also members of that culture or potential participants in processes of communicative interaction through which they may assert their identities (generally, the "personality system"). Both of these additional structures—social solidarity and individual competencies—contribute to the resources that can be employed in mastering a situation, communicatively or strategically.

Although the problem faced by participants may have emerged from the lifeworld, the point of communicative action is to come to an understanding not about the presupposed lifeworld but about something *in the world.* Agreement can be sought regarding something in the "objective world," understood as the sum total of existing facts or states of affairs; it can be sought regarding something in the "social world," which is comprised of the system of "legitimately ordered interactions" or normative expectations; or it can be sought regarding the sincerity of an expression of something in the "subjective world" of the speaker. (This way of putting it can be misleading, however, since there is only one world and every utterance, as I indicated with my previous example, raises all three kinds of validity claims at once—the question is one of emphasis). When ordinary communicative action proceeds without interruption, it is resting on antecedently shared propositional knowledge, normative agreement, and reciprocal trust, and the difference between these kinds of agreements will remain unnoticed. However, competent speakers are able to differentiate between these three relations to the world and, when ordinary communication is interrupted by misunderstanding or disagreement, they do so differentiate in conscious pursuit of concord regarding the problematic aspect or aspects.

Flexibly correlated with these three "world perspectives" are the three speaker perspectives or attitudes. This means, for instance, that every speaker has a choice between three modes of language use: cognitive (focused on the expression of facts, leaving the appropriateness of the expression and its sincerity implicit), regulative (focusing on the rightness of the claim and leaving its factual presuppositions and sincerity implicit), and expressive (focusing on the sincerity of the claim and leaving its factual presuppositions and the appropriateness of the expression implicit). These perspectives reflect the attitude of the speaker toward the world. The fact that the correlation is flexible rather than strict is important:

> the decentered understanding of the world enables [the actor] to confront external nature [the "objective world"] not only in an *objectivating* attitude but also in a *norm-conformative* or an *expressive* one, to confront society not only in a norm-conformative attitude but also in an objectivating [e.g., social-scientific, but also a strategic attitude] or an expressive one, and to confront inner nature not only in an expressive attitude but also in an objectivating [e.g., from a psychological-scientific perspective] or a norm-conformative one.[8]

The decentered understanding of the world that is the culmination of the development of perspectives, as well as the basis of communicative action, presupposes (to begin with) that the three relations to the world, the three kinds of validity, and the three basic attitudes have been differentiated. This is accomplished, in turn, on the basis of the differentiation of the lifeworld and the world, which is an effect of participation in communicative action in which the three types of validity claims are raised with their varying world referents. The significance of the distinction between lifeworld and world is that it creates a domain of things about which we can *pursue* agreement through the discursive redemption of criticizable validity claims, distinct from the domain of things about which we unquestioningly *assume* agreement. But decentered understanding requires more than just distinction: The actor must be able to integrate the speaker and world perspectives, to adopt the appropriate attitude in each case.

In Chapter 3, I take up this presentation again in the discussion of ontogenetic development; but for the time being, this is sufficient for the illumination of the lineaments of Habermas' theory of social evolution as a simultaneous rationalization/linguistification of the lifeworld that, following Durkheim, he understands as an increasing separation of the structural components of the lifeworld from one another—that is, of culture, society, and personality.

Linguistification as Rationalization: An Evolutionary Account of the Lifeworld

Habermas' offers his description of linguistification in the form of a thought experiment, beginning with a fictional, limit state archaic society that is totally integrated and dominated by a religious cult. Cultic practice assures the unity of the group and represses conflict in such a way that the significance of language for cultural tradition is minimal. The structural components of the lifeworld—culture, society, and personality—remain fused in the collective consciousness that constitutes both group and individual identity at once. Linguistification of this sacred, bonding, total institution results in the differentiation of these lifeworld components, beginning with cultural tradition.

Habermas' explanation of the linguistification of culture starts out from the role of background knowledge—the lifeworld as background—in the formation of situation definitions. Background knowledge is drawn upon by communicating individuals for the negotiation of such situation definitions which, when achieved, feed back into the lifeworld and so become a part of shared knowledge. This means, however, that an initially sacred background consensus is faced with the task of assimilating a more or less constant stream of knowledge coming from instrumental and cooperative profane action (e.g., cooperative labor processes, hunting, etc.). This results in a "fusion of meanings; moral-practical and expressive contents [sacred in origin] with cognitive-instrumental contents [from the profane realm] in the form of cultural knowledge."[9] With this, the transition is made from a religious worldview—that is, religion in its background, situation-structuring function—to religion as a cultural tradition—that is, as a store of cultural knowledge that must be communicatively renewed.

The emergence of propositionally articulated cultural knowledge underlies the linguistification of social integration: It establishes the significance of the structure of speech for consciousness and action. The acceptance of the validity claims inherent in speech, their intersubjective recognition, has a bonding effect that is distinct from integration achieved through institutionalized ritual and religious practice. Since the binding force of communicative action rests on the promise of discursive vindication (however limited in practice), to the extent that such communicative interaction becomes a part of everyday consciousness, the unquestionability of the sacred is sacrificed in principle. That doesn't mean that its authority evaporates: But it does mean that its authority increasingly rests on the justificatory articulation of its contents by religious and cultural experts. This again entails that it take the form of cultural knowledge to be drawn upon by communicative actors. Conflicting experiences among actors present one kind of challenge to this knowledge; but the more significant one, according to Habermas, is that increasingly complex action situations require more and more abstract norms with greater room for flexibility in their interpretation. This explains part of the force behind the universalization of law and morality: Law emerges as the specialized domain of norms governing action contexts in which the increasingly large burden of justification and application is institutionally removed from the shoulders of actors; universal morality, on the other hand, governs those contexts of action in which this burden must increasingly be borne by individuals. The application of these general norms involves negotiating situation definitions—coordinating actors' views regarding the objective, normative, and subjective elements of the situation—and so sets loose still further the differentiation of validity spheres in accordance with the rational structure of language.

Finally, Habermas appeals to the dual, expressive, and normative senses of the performatively employed "I" in explaining the linguistification of the personality system. On the one hand, use of the "I" signals the expression of the experiences of the ego; at the same time, however, it signals that the ego as a member of a social group thereby takes up, in the first person, an interpersonal relationship with other members. This grammatically rooted structure has sociological implications, because the socialization of individuals as "first-persons" gives impetus to the process of their individuation—according to the degree to which social life is communicatively regulated—and prevents the direct instantiation of the group identity in the individual. As a first-person agent in communicative action, the individual must demarcate him or herself, and the "inner world" to which he or she has privileged access, from other participations, their normative expectations, and from the objective world of facts.[10]

In point of fact, Habermas is actually not clear in his presentation that these three changes are cumulative; but as far as I can see, that must be the case. In other words, we can summarize the above as follows: The rationalization of worldviews into cultural traditions occurs as a result of the need to assimilate profane knowledge emerging from the domain of material reproduction and cooperative, instrumental action; this loosens the bond of traditionalistic integration, which is no longer up to the task of action coordination; instead, cultural knowledge must be interpreted and applied by actors themselves and this means that integration is shifted to an increasingly communicative basis; to the extent that individuals are socialized under such circumstances, that socialization takes the form of the cultivation of the (increasingly formal) competencies required for communicative interaction. Habermas himself describes these trends as the rationalization of the lifeworld, the differentiation of its structural components—culture, society, and person—which had been fused in the collective consciousness. But, in addition, rationalization involves changes within each of these components: the processing and articulation of the cultural tradition by authorities/experts leads to the differentiation of its rational basis (i.e., the separation of science, morality, and art, according to the different kinds of validity claimed in each); in the social sphere, law and morality come to be increasingly separated and increasingly formal or universal; and the personality system (as a result) takes on greater autonomy regarding both judgment and self-expression.

Once again, these developments count as rationalization because through them the reproduction of the elements of the lifeworld comes more and more to depend "on outlooks that refer, when problematized, to yes/no positions on criticizable validity claims," which is to say, on the promise or process of reason-giving.[11] Habermas turns to Mead in order to elaborate upon the details of this communicative rationalization of the reproductive processes of the lifeworld, treated analytically under the headings: (a) cultural reproduction, (b) social integration, and (c) socialization. It is the interrelations between these three processes that allows Habermas to formulate his revised account of social pathologies that, in turn, reflects his response to Held's critique of *Legitimation Crisis*; that is, the account of possible deformations in the reproduction of the lifeworld is intended to alleviate the overextension of the concepts of motivation and legitimation crises.

Cultural Reproduction

Successful processes of cultural reproduction ensure the "*continuity* of tradition and *coherence* of knowledge sufficient for daily practice." Inversely, when cultural reproduction is unsuccessful, there results a loss of meaning for members of the lifeworld ("the resource 'meaning' becomes scare"): cultural knowledge stored in shared lifeworlds no longer ensures mutual understanding in new situations and, ultimately, crises of legitimation and orientation appear.[12]

Social Integration

Social integration involves a process of reproduction in the form of the maintenance of social unity: That is to say, it coordinates the actions of individuals "by way of legitimately regulated interpersonal relations"—as opposed to appeal to complementary interests, function, or coercion—and it "stabilizes the identity of groups to an extent sufficient for everyday practice." Solidarity is the criterion for success and so, when social integration is disturbed such that accepted patterns of social membership and normative expectation no longer adequately coordinate action, anomie results ("the resource 'social solidarity' becomes scare").[13]

Socialization

Socialization secures for upcoming generations the competencies required for action, as well as ensuring that "*individual life histories are in harmony with collective forms of life*." The responsibility of individuals is the criterion in light of which interactive competence and lifestyle are judged. Deformations of the process of socialization result in psychopathologies and "alienation" and, in general, in the lack of adequate competencies on the part of the individual for maintenance of successful intersubjective relations: "The personality system can preserve its identity only by means of defensive strategies that are detrimental to participating in social interaction on a realistic basis, so that the resource 'ego strength' becomes scarce."[14]

These reproductive processes are not hermetically sealed off from one other; to the contrary, they exist in a complex balance and complementarity. By renewing vital cultural traditions, successful processes of cultural reproduction also provide legitimations for existing institutions as well as general patterns for socialization (typically, culturally defined social roles) and goals for systems of education.[15] The maintenance of social integration contributes to the regulation of identity-structuring social and cultural memberships, as well as actualizing moral duties and obligations rooted in cultural knowledge by incorporating them into social institutions (and, in so doing, shielding these norms from the constant testing of informal processes of reaching understanding). Finally, if processes of socialization succeed in cultivating ego structures and personal identities able to consciously manage problem situations in the lifeworld, that will also signal the presence of the interpretative competencies necessary for the renewal of cultural tradition, as well as providing the motives and competencies required for norm-conforming social interactions. Because of these complex interrelations, disturbances to any of the three reproductive processes results in corresponding deficits in the other two: A loss of meaning resulting from disturbed processes of cultural reproduction also will result in a withdrawal of legitimations for social institutions and in a crisis of orientation in self-formation and education; failures of social integration result in phenomena of alienation and the unsettling of collective identities; and disturbed processes of socialization produce not just psychopathologies in individual personality structures, but also cause a withdrawal of the motivations needed for norm-conforming integration and action coordination, as well as resulting in a rupture in the continuity of tradition.[16]

The rationalization of the lifeworld entails not just the separation of its structural components, culture, society, and personality, but also the specialization of these reproductive processes. I have already mentioned the differentiation of the cultural system into the professionalized, validity-based spheres of science, morality, and art, an example analyzed in detail by Weber. Mead and Durkheim, on the other hand, focused on the evolutionary significance of the emergence of democratic processes of will formation, which they regarded as a rationalization of both social integration generally, as well as of the specific process whereby political domination is legitimized.[17] With regard to the rationalization of socialization, Habermas cites the "increasingly pedagogical approach to child-rearing" which begins to appear in the eighteenth century (with the so-called "discovery of childhood"), and which Durkheim also discussed. Connected to this is the emergence in the twentieth century of a system of public education freed, at least to a considerable extent, from the demands of churches and families. Habermas notes that over the course of the century, formal education has been extended further and further into the early years of childhood and has explicitly taken over socializing functions that had once been the exclusive purview of the family.[18]

This structural picture of reproductive processes, including the susceptibility to various pathologies, does not answer the question of social dynamics: that is, although it is constructed with an eye to explaining deformities of the lifeworld, it does not illuminate what causes such deformations or disturbances in the first place. Counter-enlightenment social critics accuse the process of rationalization itself as, in a more dialectical fashion, did Weber. Habermas rejects this explanation and appeals to Marx instead. By developing a two-tiered theory of society, Marx was able to accept and endorse the rationalization of the lifeworld while attributing the distortion of its structures to the operations of the material base of society. Similarly, the thesis Habermas defends is that it is the internal dynamics of functionally differentiated subsystems that causally accounts for interferences in the symbolic reproduction of the lifeworld, which in turn result in social pathologies. This is the "colonization of the lifeworld by system imperatives," which is yet another part of Habermas' revised account of the pathologies of advanced capitalist societies. Before we can discuss that thesis, however (and having now clarified the concept of the lifeworld), we need to clarify his conception of "system." This is not only a requirement of theory; it is Habermas' position that the rationalization of the lifeworld itself, as described previously, calls forth systemically integrated subsystems as a solution to the problem of social complexity, as a mechanism for the alleviation of the increasing communicative burden foisted upon individuals. So we need to return to the story of social evolution, this time from the observers' perspective of the systems theorist, in order to trace out the path by which subsystems are "uncoupled" from an increasingly rationalized, communicatively burdensome lifeworld.

Mediatization as Rationalization: An Evolutionary Account of System

Although I have just anticipated a certain kind of link between the rationalization of the lifeworld and the emergence of subsystems, in *The Theory of Communicative Action* Habermas offers an independent account of social evolution in general from the systems-theoretical perspective in order to avoid prejudging, to leave open as an empirical question, the specific relationship between system differentiation and forms of societal integration. His thesis is the following:

> It is possible to analyze these connections by distinguishing mechanisms for coordinating action that harmonize the action orientations of participants from mechanisms that stabilize the nonintended interconnections of actions by way of functionally intermeshing action consequences. In one case, the integration of an action system is established by a normatively secured or communicatively achieved consensus, in the other case, by a nonnormative regulation of individual decisions that extends beyond the actors' consciousness. This distinction between a societal integration of society, which takes effect in action orientations, and a systemic integration, which reaches through and beyond

> action orientations, calls for a corresponding differentiation in the concept of society itself.[19]

That is, it calls for a distinction between the communicatively reproduced "lifeworld of a social group," and the "system of action" as seen from the observer's perspective. As was the case in *Legitimation Crisis*, the distinction between system and lifeworld is in the first instance a methodological one. The problem with the concept of the lifeworld is that it is rooted in a communication-theoretic perspective that "has only limited analytical and empirical range." There is more to society than communicative interactions: Social functions and subsystems of action in society itself are what recommend the complementary methodological perspective of systems theory. But, in light of persistent misunderstandings of Habermas, we need to be particularly careful here: Habermas does not intend—as he once did[20]—to categorize lifeworld and system simply by corresponding types of action, as consisting exclusively of communicative or strategic actions, respectively. Empirically speaking, strategic actions occur routinely in the lifeworld, and communicative actions within "systems." We are free, in other words, to conceive of processes of material and symbolic reproduction from either the vantage point of action theory or of systems theory; but, according to Habermas, they are not equally illuminating since, as he has claimed above, forms of systemic integration often remain opaque to the consciousness of actors. We arrive at the concept of system by taking an objective view of social interactions with an eye to thematizing stable forms of the interconnection of action consequences, irrespective of motive or orientation; that is to say, analyses of systemic integration lead to the concept of system. On the other hand, analyses of social integration, coordination on the basis of language, lead to the idea of the lifeworld as the resource that, as we have seen, makes such coordination possible.[21] However, the connection between the lifeworld, social integration, and communicative action orientations is still less direct than this might make it seem: Social integration relies on a more or less *counterfactual* assumption of communicative action orientations, without which agreement is impossible. But this means that the two types of integration also do not empirically map directly on to action types anymore than do the concepts of system and lifeworld derived from them. Moreover, the approaches also are not mutually exclusive: The consequences of actions oriented to communication, for instance, may very well have systemically integrating effects that escape the consciousness of the actor. Finally, it is important to note that Habermas retains his insistence on the methodological priority of lifeworld analyses that was evidenced in his account of the concept of crisis: Systems theory cannot define for itself what counts as the boundaries of a given system, what would count as learning and what would count as destruction.

It must be conceded that Habermas is very largely to blame for misunderstandings regarding the nature of the system/lifeworld distinction: His account of system differentiation, to which we now turn, is offered under the heading of the "uncoupling of system and lifeworld." But this is a terribly misleading use of his own terminology, and critics have understandably assumed that, despite having explicitly repudiated his initial linking of action types to given domains, the idea of an empirical-historical uncoupling of system (network of action consequences) from lifeworld (network of communication) necessarily suggests that—as increasingly independent of communication—"system" must be a more or less monolithic block of strategic action. Habermas clarifies, in light of the reception of *The Theory of Communicative Action*, that what are "uncoupled" is the lifeworld, on the one hand, from *media-steered subsystems* on the other—and *not "system"* per se. As we will see, it is the institutionalization of these steering media—money and power—that is definitive for the process of uncoupling. These media do indeed demand a strategic-action orientation for their effectiveness (whereas stable patterns of interwoven action consequences may well not), and not just counterfactually, because they steer actions precisely by altering in quantifiable ways the facts taken into consideration in processes of self-interested decision making. As a result, such subsystems, *in terms of their inner workings*, become almost entirely opaque to communicative-theoretic analysis. As this claim, too, is controversial, let me therefore stress once more: It entails no symmetrical assertion regarding action orientations in the lifeworld. Although a strategic orientation is functionally necessary for the operation of media-steered subsystems, communicative orientations only are *counterfactually* presupposed by the reproductive processes of rationalized lifeworld domains in which, as a matter of fact, strategic action persists to greater and lesser degrees.[22] In what follows, then, wherever Habermas discusses the uncoupling of system from lifeworld, we are to understand the specific, legally organized and institutionalized subsystems that are steered by media rather than by language, and not a process by which society moves more and more into a kind of bicameral purity consisting of communicative lifeworld and strategic system.

From the "observer's" perspective, Habermas defines social evolution as a "second-order process of differentiation": "system and lifeworld are differentiated in the sense that the complexity of one [system] and the rationality of the other [the lifeworld] grow. But it is not only qua system and qua lifeworld that they are differentiated; they get differentiated from one another at the same time."[23] This second-order process is what Habermas refers to as the "uncoupling" of system and lifeworld, which occurs in the transition from tribal to traditional to modern societies and that, in fact, continues to occur today.[24] Because it is the phenomenon of the "uncoupling" of subsystems that is most relevant here, I am going to pass over Habermas' long discussion of the evolution of power within tribal and traditional societies, and focus instead on the process of system evolution through which the economic subsystem is uncoupled from the lifeworld, only then returning to the more complicated question of the status of power as a steering medium in contemporary societies.

Although money emerges in traditional, state-organized society, it does not result in a structural transformation of society until there exists an economic system at least largely independent of political governance and steered by money alone. This occurred in Europe during the early modern period with the appearance of a distinctly capitalist economy. Money, as the medium by which the autonomous economy is steered, must retain an institutional anchoring through bourgeois private law; but the economy itself that is "differentiated out via this medium is, as a whole, a block of more or less norm-free sociality"[25] (i.e., it is "uncoupled" from the lifeworld). It is the steering medium that is responsible for this: As I noted earlier, although the operation of a system as such (i.e., a stable nexus of action consequences) is logically indifferent toward the action orientations of its constituent members, steering media *do* require a strategic orientation, because they steer action by altering the conditions under which self-interested decisions are made. This means that only at the point at which systemically integrated, media-steered subsystems are differentiated out of the society component of the lifeworld does the use of systems theory become more than an analytical difference; it becomes a necessary part of an account of the *real transformations* of the lifeworld.[26] The emergence of the money-steered capitalist market, in turn, required a reorganization of the state and, out of the bourgeois revolutions, there emerged a modern administrative state complementary to the new economy. Specifically, a state based on taxation emerged as the complement to the institutionalization of wage labor, and it ensured the autonomy of the media-steered market by allowing the latter to regulate its interchanges with its "environment" in its own terms, as it were—namely, in money. This is necessary since the market could not be "norm free" if it had to constantly answer to the political system in terms of normative legitimacy. At the same time, this reflects a new dependence of the state on the economic subsystem. In traditional, politically stratified societies, programs for defining membership, regulating interactions, and so on, had to link up in some way with existing cultural traditions and lifeworlds. The uncoupling of subsystems from the lifeworld, on the other hand, frees the capitalist economy from these lifeworld constraints, allowing it to function as an independent and norm-free subsystem. As Luhmann has argued, this independence from lifeworld expectations is achieved empirically by the fact that the functionally specified public and private institutions that make up the capitalist economy actually realize, at least to some extent, the fiction of voluntary membership that arose at the traditional stage with its theories of the social contract. In other words, it is through the voluntary acceptance of membership conditions that individuals are made to check such expectations at the door to systemically organized domains; communicative value orientations are, in this way, pushed into the environment of subsystems.[27] From the perspective of systems theory, this makes it seem as though the lifeworld is the junior partner, a kind of historical relic that, in the wake of increasing complexity, is reduced to an ever smaller portion of social organization. But, as Habermas makes clear in his model of social evolution in *Legitimation Crisis*, this impression is false: It is not changes in social complexity which result in transformations of the structure of the lifeworld; rather "increases in complexity are dependent on the structural differentiation of the lifeworld," where the latter follows its own immanent logic (described as a process of rationalization).[28] In other words, mediatization, or the uncoupling of subsystems from the lifeworld, is dependent upon rationalization.

Habermas argues this by demonstrating the way in which the rationalization of morality and law in the lifeworld makes possible the institutionalization of new system mechanisms like money and power, in response to problems that originate in the "base" of society. He appeals to the ontogenetic account of moral development defended by Lawrence Kohlberg (discussed in Chapter 3) for his general model. According to Kohlberg, moral development may be divided into three levels of moral consciousness: the preconventional, at which the consequences of action alone are judged; the conventional, at which norm conformity and intent are judged, but relative to uncritically accepted social norms; and the postconventional, at which norms themselves are critically evaluated with reference to principles. According to Habermas, Klaus Eder has established that there are "homologous structures of consciousness in moral and legal developments of archaic, traditional, and modern societies."[29] Eder argues that at the preconventional social level, at which archaic societies operate, magical ethics and revealed law remain fused. Punishment for the violation of taboos is not a matter of establishing and enforcing individual accountability but of reestablishing the disturbed cosmic order through expiation. When it comes to dispute resolution (i.e., civil law), the legal structures of tribal societies were without means of coercion: The feuding parties themselves must reach an agreement. It is the institutionalization of political power as a steering medium that signals the transformation to the next stage of development in the institution of "royal judgeship," but this is itself dependent on a change in the cognitive structure of moral consciousness; that is, an offence must be seen as "a violation of intersubjectively recognized norms for which an individual is held accountable"[30] before the idea of the office of judge—specifically, the power over the means of sanction attached to that office—can gain legitimacy in the eyes of the public. This means that the transition must be made to the conventional level, at which the separation is at least begun between the ethics of law (an internalized morality) and the traditionalistic law itself. The legitimacy of the latter, of the legal order as a whole, grounds the office of the judge and the willingness to obey on the part of citizens; and this office, in turns, provides the nucleus around which political domination crystallizes. But, although the legal order now offers a kind of insurance against breakdowns in the ordinary, traditionalistic coordination of action and resolution of conflict, it remains "laid like a shell around a society whose core domains are by no means legally organized throughout. Social intercourse is institutionalized much more in forms of traditional mores than through law. This changes in modern societies."[31]

Whereas law had functioned as a backup for a society coordinated in the first instance through shared expectations rooted in a traditional lifeworld, in modern societies it serves to directly organize important spheres of daily life, as in the economy. This innovation requires postconventional moral and legal developments, in particular, the completion of the separation between morality and law: Morality is deinstitutionalized and anchored in internalized behavioral controls, whereas positivized law is regarded as an external code governing state force and detached from the question of the motivations of the legal person (it doesn't matter whether an individual person obeys the law out of fear or respect). This last point reflects the increasing separation of the components of the lifeworld: The system of social institutions anchored in law is increasingly independent of the system of personality; but it also is increasingly separated from culture, dependent upon formal procedures for its justification rather than on traditional norms.[32] Private civil law anchors the capitalist, money-steered market, differentiated out the lifeworld, and functions as a higher-level insurance for a delinguistified coordination of action consequences (systemic integration) based on the success-oriented, competitive action of private legal subjects. Opposite this, a domain of public law, including penal law, takes shape in which consensus can be pursued in cases of conflict. The positivization of law, which is entailed by its complete separation from morality and traditional ethics, saves it from the immediate justification problems that had plagued particularistic traditional law in its entirety. At the same time, a new sort of justification problem arises: Appeals to the legality of procedures of enactment only temporarily eases the burden of legitimation, which must now rest on the legitimacy of the legal order as a whole in the light of basic principles, the two most important of which are human rights and popular sovereignty. These principles mediate between deinstitutionalized morality and positivized law.

The point of this sketch of the development of law is to show how legal-moral developments form necessary prerequisites to the institutions of political and economic class societies, the institutionalization of their steering media, power and money. In summary, Habermas' position is that new levels of system differentiation wait upon required levels of rationalization of the lifeworld: "My thesis is that higher levels of integration cannot be established in social evolution until legal institutions develop in which moral consciousness on the conventional, and then the postconventional, levels is embodied."[33] There seem to be two significant claims implied by this thesis. The first, which is critically important for my ultimate argument, is that the institutionalization of the level of social complexity *currently present in society* required the emergence of postconventional levels of moral and legal consciousness at the level of society. I cannot yet indicate why this claim is so important, although a reader of *Legitimation Crisis* may already see why it is surprising; nevertheless, note it well, as I return to it later. The second is that the hypothesized link between system complexity and social rationalization seems at first to suggest that Habermas has, despite his proposal to leave the question open as an empirical one, already solved at the level of theory the problem of the relationship between system and social integration. Specifically, the impression would be that the reliance of system complexity on social rationalization indicates that the relationship is one of complementary dependence: namely, the freeing of communication from concrete, traditionalistic normative constraints results in an ever expanding burden on the communicative resources of individuals; at the same time, the differentiation of moral and legal norms makes possible the parallel differentiation of communicative and strategic action orientations; this enables, in turn, the establishment of mediatized subsystems of action governed by strategic or instrumental action[34] (i.e., the uncoupling of subsystems from the lifeworld) that alleviates the communicative burden by uncoupling action orientations "from consensus formation in language," and neutralizing it "with respect to the alternatives of agreement or failed agreement."[35] So, for example, the money medium, severed from lifeworld contexts, makes functional a uniform instrumental attitude toward quantifiable amounts of value and, in so doing, makes it possible for strategically acting individuals to calculate and attempt to influence the interest-oriented actions of others in a way that does without communication oriented to mutual understanding.

The matter is rather more complicated in the case of power, which differs from money with respect to means of circulation, institutionalization, calculability, and in requiring a more demanding form of legitimation. Money functions as a medium so long as individuals have confidence in the structural stability of the economic system: Legal provisions mandating that currency be accepted as legal payment is an example of a basic mechanism for the inspiration of such confidence, as is the regulation of inflation. Power requires greater legitimation because, although we can at least imagine cases of exchange in the equal interests of all parties, the structural disadvantages in relationships of power seem inherent: The asymmetry between those who command and those who obey can only be mitigated if the orders issued are seen to be directed toward the realization of "legitimizable collective goals." This suggests that power is dependent upon an ultimate consensus in language that money is not. And indeed, sympathetic critics like Nancy Fraser, Thomas McCarthy, and David Ingram have objected to Habermas' characterization of workplaces, for example, especially those that are bureaucratically structured, as subsystems regulated by language-replacing power.[36] But the empirical fact that in such organizations action is often coordinated consensually misses Habermas' point which is, first of all, that even though subsystems steered by power may make use of both communicative action and lifeworld presuppositions, "*in the final instance*," they do not depend for their stability on either.[37] We can add to this that, as Habermas noted following Luhmann, what empirical independence there is of subsystems from the lifeworld is attained largely through the voluntary acceptance of membership conditions, including willingness to follow orders, carry out requisite performances, and so on.[38] In the case of bureaucratically structured workplaces, this entails acceptance of a hierarchy of power. Power functions as a medium in such a structure because superiors *need not* coordinate the action of subordinates communicatively; they need not explain why or justify with reasons their demand that a task be done or that it be done in a certain way. Habermas concedes that,

> [e]ven within formally organized domains of action, interactions are still connected via the mechanism of mutual understanding. If all processes of genuinely reaching understanding were banished from the interior of organizations, formally regulated social relations could not be sustained, nor could organizational goals be realized. Nevertheless, the classical model of bureaucracy is right in one respect: action within organizations falls *under the premises* of formally regulated domains of action. Because the latter are ethically neutralized by their legal form of organization [which demands only obedience to positive, external laws], *communicative action forfeits its validity basis* [the promise of discursive redemption] *in the interior of organizations*.[39]

This is essentially to say that, within such subsystems, power is trump: Communicative orientations and the spaces in which they operate persist at the pleasure of power alone; they can be revoked, redefined, and stripped of the lifeworld at will (especially by appeal to the conditions of membership: if you don't like it, then quit!).[40] The lifeworld and its orientations are thus exiled from the domains of power and money; from the perspective of the former, the mediatization of domains of action appears as an expansion of the scope for interest-oriented individual freedom, as a reduction in the risks and costs of dissensus, but also as a "technicizing of the lifeworld," a provincializing of its concerns. In the delinguistified spheres of money and power, responsibility, in the Habermasian sense of an orientation to criticizable validity claims, is not called for: No one is responsible for the "deworlded" coordination of action consequences and, indeed, for the most part, it escapes the consciousness of actors.

Thus, as I have said, although Habermas offers independent analyses of both the evolution of the lifeworld and of system/media-steered subsystems, as well as of their internal dynamics, there seems to be an implied complementarity between the accounts: The uncoupling of media-steered subsystems from the lifeworld is a language-replacing means of alleviating the burden on communication that results from rationalization as linguistification; the differentiation of subsystems is thus both genetically and normatively dependent on rationalization, because only a rationalized lifeworld permits of domains of distinctly strategic interaction that can be formally organized, and because that formal organization requires institutional anchoring in the lifeworld via legitimizing postconventional legal representations. This allows for a higher level of complexity and integration by supplementing social integration with system integration. But this initial impression of complementarity is shattered by what Habermas has to say about the contemporary relationship between the dynamics of lifeworld and subsystems. His account of this begins with the following warning: "[w]e cannot directly infer from the mere fact that system and social integration have been largely uncoupled to linear dependency in one direction or the other." This warning may seem rather surprising since, at the level of genesis, Habermas has clearly indicated a linear dependence of subsystems on the lifeworld. But his real point is about contemporary dynamics, which becomes evident as he continues:

> Both are conceivable: the institutions that anchor steering mechanisms such as power and money in the lifeworld could serve as a channel either for the influence of the lifeworld on formally organized domains of action or, conversely, for the influence of the system on communicatively structured contexts of action. In one case, they function as an institutional framework that subjects system maintenance to the normative restrictions of the

> lifeworld, in the other, as a base that subordinates the lifeworld to the systemic constraints of material reproduction and thereby "mediatizes" it.[41]

In other words, Habermas does not believe the question of the directionality of contemporary influence answerable at the level of theory (despite having suggested functional complementary at that level): Instead, he offers an hypothesis on the basis of an account of the internal dynamics of subsystems—that is, the account of the advanced capitalist welfare state familiar to us from *Legitimation Crisis*—while insisting that the question of the balance between system and social integration can only be answered empirically. His hypothesis is the colonization of the lifeworld by the imperatives of subsystems: that, as a matter of fact, the directionality of the interchange relations between lifeworld and these subsystems is one-dimensional, noncomplementary, and points to the subordination of the former to the latter. This is still not to say that the transformation to systemic forms of integration is complete, that we have realized the "socialization without norms" discussed in *Legitimation Crisis*. To the contrary, Habermas maintains that the need for systems media to be anchored in the lifeworld is at least one indication that the process he now calls colonization, although progressing, is not complete.[42] Thus, while avoiding the Weberian thesis of an inherent paradox in the idea of rationalization, Habermas poses the question whether there is not an empirically verifiable "irony" to this development, in that "[t]he rationalization of the lifeworld makes possible the emergence and growth of subsystems whose independent imperatives [ultimately] turn back destructively upon the lifeworld itself."[43]

System and Lifeworld Interchange Roles and the Thesis of Colonization

The problem we had put on hold, which has waited in the wings while we completed Habermas' account of the nature of media-steered subsystems, regards the dynamics that explain disturbances in the reproductive processes of the lifeworld. Habermas' hypothesis, we have just seen, is that it is the extension of subsystem imperatives into the lifeworld that is (primarily) to blame. In explaining how this occurs, however, we must first specify more clearly the interchange relations between the lifeworld and these subsystems, their points of contact and exchange, through which processes of colonization can proceed. Habermas maintains here, too, that these interchange relations are not themselves tantamount to colonization, since they could serve as conduits for influence in either direction and, moreover, in light of his account of system evolution, he argues that the mediatization of certain segments of the lifeworld actually counts as an evolutionary advance and not, per se, as a deformity. In other words, we must distinguish as neither Marx nor Weber did, according to Habermas, between the "unavoidable pains of modernization"—for example, the undermining of traditional forms of life that must accompany structural differentiation both within the lifeworld itself (between culture, society, and personality) and in the form of the uncoupling of subsystems from the lifeworld—and the colonization of the lifeworld that results when system imperatives subordinate core processes of symbolic reproduction (cultural reproduction, social integration, and socialization).[44]

In the face of the splitting off of the subsystems of economy and state, the socially integrated lifeworld is formed into complementary private and public spheres. The nuclear family is the central institution of the former and, in modern societies, is "relieved of productive functions and specialized in tasks of socialization; from the systemic perspective of the economy, it is viewed as the environment of *private households*." This environment is important to the economy with respect to the generation of motives. The public sphere, on the other hand, is comprised of communicative networks linking cultural institutions, the press, and the mass media; through participation in these networks, an art-enjoying public of private citizens aid in the reproduction of culture, and the "public of citizens of the state . . . participate in the social integration mediated by public opinion. From the systemic perspective of the state, the cultural and political spheres are viewed as the environment relevant to *generating legitimations*."[45]

The economic system exchanges with its environment as follows: The labor of private individuals is exchanged for wages, and goods and services are exchanged for the satisfaction of consumer demands. In the case of the administrative welfare state, it is "organizational performances" that are exchanged for taxes, and political decisions for mass loyalty. These "exchanges" indicate the points of contact between the media-steered subsystems and the communicatively structured lifeworld, namely, the social roles of "employee and consumer, on the one hand, and those of client and citizens of the state, on the other."[46] Both employee and client roles are legally constituted in dependence on an organization; that is, they are roles within already legally structured, formally organized domains—they are system roles. Habermas' account of the significance of this, however, strikes me as problematic: "Actors who assume the roles of employees or of clients of the public administration," he writes, "detach themselves from lifeworld contexts and adapt themselves to formally organized domains of action."[47] The fact that these domains are already legally structured—for example, the fact that the economic-occupational system has, as long as it has been differentiated, always been subject to forms of private law—appears to lead Habermas to view the forced adaptation of individuals to systemic-functional imperatives, which is to say, the imperative to adopt a strategic orientation toward monetarized compensations, as a *fait accompli*. This structuring of occupational roles appears to be integrated into his theoretically motivated acceptance of system differentiation as functionally complementary to societal rationalization, even though he concedes that "[v]iewed historically, the monetarization and bureaucratization of labour power and government performance is by no means a painless process"; it is accompanied by the "unavoidable" pains of the loss of traditional forms of life, by resistance manifested in revolts over the uprooting of rural populations and the creation of the urban proletariat, the imposition of taxes and the regulation of trade, and so on. Nevertheless,

> [i]n spite of the destructive side effects of the violent processes of capital accumulation and state formation, the new organizational forms gained wide acceptance and considerable permanency on the strength of their greater effectiveness and superior level of integration. The capitalist mode of production and bureaucratic-legal domination can better fulfill the tasks of materially reproducing the lifeworld.[48]

It is difficult to know what exactly we are to make of this claim. First of all, we might remind ourselves of Held's critique of *Legitimation Crisis*, and ask whether social integration today (or ever) proceeds on the basis of recognition of normative legitimacy; there seems to be ample room for dispute over what the grounds are, as a matter of fact, for the apparent acceptance of the status quo and the historical pacification of resistance. But, second, on Habermas' own account, since the uncoupling of subsystems from the lifeworld entails that the former slip further and further from the consciousness of individuals, increasingly exceeding our ability to comprehend them even if we wanted to, it doesn't seem possible that their acceptability could proceed directly from an apprehension of their greater effectiveness, or from an appreciation of the merits of systemic integration. To the contrary, Habermas argues that

> [t]he constitution of action contexts that are no longer socially integrated means that social relations are separated off from the identities of the actors involved. The objective meaning of a functionally stabilized nexus of action can no longer be brought into the intersubjective context of meaningful action. At the same time . . . it makes itself felt as a causality of fate in the experiences and sufferings of actors.[49]

Subsystems appear as a block of more or less norm-free sociality "jutting out" from the lifeworld and confronting their members as a kind of "second nature." That certainly suggests that Held may be right: Subsystems become historically acceptable because, once established, "ordinary" people, who recognize a connection between the existing system and their experiences of injustice and suffering, are unable to conceive of alternatives to the status quo. Indeed, at least so far as the economic system is concerned—he will turn out to be more flexible regarding the decolonization of client roles—the victims of the imposition of system will receive no help from Habermas' critical theory on this score.

The situation is different with respect to the roles of consumer and citizen that, although they are "defined *with reference* to formally organized domains of action"—the economy and the state—are not constituted *in dependence upon* those domains but instead reflect at least to some extent the independent logic of culturally rooted conceptions of demand and legitimation (although I would be inclined to add that the advertising strategies employed by both producers of commodities and political parties and interest groups—e.g., "branding" of young people, focus-grouping vocabulary, and so on—aim as far as possible to put an end to this independence). Rather than being legally constructed from the ground up, as it were, they are based on "contractual relations and civil rights."[50] As a result, they cannot be so neatly severed from the lifeworld inasmuch as they rely on action orientations, values, and preferences that are shaped through socialization in a form of life. These orientations, according to Habermas, cannot be "bought" or "collected" by private or public organizations, after the pattern of labor power and taxes, respectively. Their independence in this respect may explain why bourgeois ideals are connected predominantly to these roles of the "individual consumer and the sovereign citizen," although both remain largely fictions of bourgeois economic and political theory.[51] For that matter, however, Habermas admits that labor too is by nature neither sellable nor buyable; he recalls Marx's theory of the "real abstraction" that labor undergoes in the process of commodification, its violent separation from its own qualitative nature, its use-value orientation. Something like this process of "real abstraction" is the condition for the transformation of lifeworld orientations in conformity to the structure of steering media, through which interchanges with subsystems take place at all four points of contact:

> Just as concrete work has to be transformed into abstract labor so that it can be exchanged for wages, use-value orientations have to be transformed, in a certain sense, into demand preferences, and publicly articulated opinions and collective expressions of will have to be transformed into mass loyalty, so that they can be exchanged for consumer goods and political leadership.[52]

In the private sphere, the adaptation of action orientations to the imperatives of the economic system results in phenomena of "consumerism and possessive individualism [through which] motives of performance, and competition gain the force to shape behavior."[53] It is interesting to recall that, in *Legitimation Crisis*, Habermas had described this very phenomenon, possessive individualism, as a core, functional ideology of bourgeois capitalism. He asserted there that it rests on two presuppositions: (a) that strategically acting economic competitors engage in behavior that can be predicted on the basis of the relative uniformity of human need; and (b) that the needs in question be translatable into individually dispensable value, namely, money. With the growing prosperity of developed nations—which results in an explosion of extra-basic, unpredictable, and rapidly changing consumer "needs"—and with the increasingly collective nature of new basic needs—for example, health care, environmental protection, social services, and infrastructure—both these presuppositions are undermined. In other words, possessive individualism was, according to Habermas, eroding along with the majority of bourgeois ideology and it was on this basis that he offered the crisis argument of *Legitimation Crisis*. In *The Theory of Communicative Action*, on the other hand, possessive individualism is made the result of a distinctly modern phenomenon of the colonization of the lifeworld. We can expect already, then, a correlated change in his ultimate practical argument, his assessment of the potential for transformation.

Just as the economic system intrudes on the private sphere, the administrative system intrudes upon the public sphere: "[t]he bureaucratic disempowering and desiccation of spontaneous processes of opinion- and will-formation expands the scope for engineering mass loyalty and makes it easier to uncouple political decision making from concrete, identity-forming contexts of life."[54] Habermas cites two mechanisms through which this uncoupling occurs: The first has long been in his critical sights, namely, the redefinition of practical questions as technical ones that can only be responsibly handled by experts; the second, the focus of more recent writings on law, is the attempt to evade questions of substantive justification through appeal to "legitimation through procedure" or, in other words, legal positivism.

More generally, however, processes of colonization take place through a "specific kind of juridification"; that is, having defined subsystems most basically by their formal legal organization (which secures the operation of steering media), rather than by the empirical predominance of instrumental action orientations within them, their formation and expansion—the transfer from social to system integration—must take the form of "the juridification of communicatively structured areas of life."[55] Correlated to the distinction between interchange roles that are dependent upon formal organizations (employee and client) and those that are independent of them (consumer and citizen), juridification processes may represent either an intensification of the density of law in domains that already are legally regulated, or the expansion of legal regulation, through the creation of new legal institutions, into domains that had been regulated informally. There are, according to Habermas, four historical "waves" of juridification underlying contemporary society, through which the bourgeois state of the European state system emerged, followed by the constitutional state, the democratic constitutional state and, finally, the democratic welfare state. The first wave institutionalized the media by which the economy and state are steered: This legal constitution of civil society was considered a liberation of the individual into system, freeing him from the rigidity and paternalism of the feudal social order. The lifeworld appeared to persist in the private domain alone, as a reservoir on which absolutist political domination and the market both drew for functionally necessary motives and legitimations. The second wave subjected political power to constitutional limitation, established actionable civil rights for citizens over against the monarch and, in general, represented a moralization of personal freedom and a reassertion of the lifeworld against the political subsystem. The third wave subjected political power to regulation yet again, this time in accordance with democratic processes of will-formation and a new principle of legitimacy: popular sovereignty. Citizens gained rights of political participation, institutionalized in representative parliaments intended to be responsive to public opinion. This amounts to a juridification of the process of legitimation; the universalization of franchise, at the same time, completed the institutional anchoring of the power medium in the lifeworld as a whole.[56]

The first wave is marked by the ironic freedom satirized by Marx in *Capital*, in that the worker is simultaneously freed both from the servitude of feudalism as well as from any means of independently reproducing his or her own existence. But the second two waves, at least, are unambiguously freedom-giving assertions of the lifeworld against political domination. The emergence of the welfare state in the fourth wave, however, is ambiguous in a new way. On the one hand, it extends the tradition of bourgeois emancipation by subjecting the economic subsystem, this time, to normative restrictions. Since the domain of social labor is already legally structured, this juridification takes the form of an increasing density of law manifested in additional protections for labor, rights to collective bargaining, and social security benefits. These measures have, for their beneficiaries, a freedom-guaranteeing character. But this cannot be said for all welfare-state measures, many of which, because of the intrinsic form of juridification itself, seem to seek the protection of their "clientele" while simultaneously bringing about a relationship of domination.[57] Although legally granted entitlements to monetary compensation in case of unemployment, disability, old age, or illness, are certainly preferable to traditional treatment of the poor, they nevertheless "exact a noteworthy price in the form of *restructuring interventions in the lifeworlds* of those who are so entitled."[58] It is the individualistic form of bourgeois legal entitlements, as well as the processing requirements of large, government bureaucracies, that are responsible for this "restructuring" or distortion. The individualism of the client role demands an instrumental, strategic orientation to the pursuit of private interests that is inappropriate to many of the circumstances requiring regulation, as in the cases of family and school law, two examples on which Habermas focuses. Additionally, the role structuring exacted through bureaucratic compensation has deleterious effects on "the self-image of the person concerned, and for his relations with spouse, friends, neighbors, and others."[59] In this connection, both Habermas and Nancy Fraser have discussed the stereotype-reinforcing, paternalistic structuring of welfare provisions of which women are the primary recipients. With reference to single mothers, Fraser writes,

> many welfare systems are internally dualized and gendered . . . they include two basic kinds of programs—"masculine" social insurance programs tied to primary labor force participation and designed to benefit principal breadwinners, and "feminine" relief programs oriented to what are understood as domestic "failures," in short, to families without a male breadwinner. Not surprisingly, these two systems are separate and unequal. Clients of feminine programs, virtually exclusively women and their children, are positioned in a distinctive, feminizing fashion as the "negatives of possessive individuals": they are stigmatized, denied rights, subjected to surveillance and administrative harassment and generally made into abject dependents of state bureaucracies.[60]

The legal structuring of candidate situations in all welfare state programs effects a "violent abstraction" from the life contexts of the individuals in question that is a parallel to the "real abstraction" of labor described by Marx: Administrative processing operates on the basis of selection from preformulated conditions and means, suited "to the needs of a centralized and computerized handling of social exigencies by large, distant organizations," which undermines the ability of individuals to interpret their needs for themselves. According to bureaucracy, for the most part, there is only one need, one form of the "indemnification of life risks," and that is money. But when faced with the reality of retirement, or sudden unemployment, the sorts of life changes that occur, Habermas claims, "cannot as a rule be subjected to consumerist redefinition."[61]

On final example, significant for my argument in the Concluding Reflections, is the attempt by the welfare state to respond to cultural and ethnic mobilizations; here, too, the desire to interpret one's own needs, to intersubjectively pursue self-understanding, is replaced by monetarization and ascription of identity. As Seyla Benhabib notes of the United States:

> The number of children from mixed-race families grew from 500,000 in 1970 to 2 million in 1990 and to 6.8 million, or 2.4 percent of the population, according to the results of the 2000 census. Individuals from a mixed-race background want a census category that registers these mixtures—be it among African-Americans, Asian-Americans, Hispanic-Americans, or whites. Opponents of this classification and, primarily among them, major civil rights organizations like the NAACP (National Association for the Advancement of Coloured People) argue that the introduction of this new category into the census will have the effect of only reducing the numbers of African-Americans, and will effectively result in the diminution of entitlements specific to this group, ranging from affirmative action advantages to the reduction in the number of black congressional districts.[62]

Negotiating cultural politics while protecting the depoliticization of the public sphere takes the form of colonization, reflected here in interferences in the self-understanding of groups and individuals. The result is that political actors, even where they do not accept reduction of their demands to the pursuit of individually distributable rewards, must assume a fundamentally strategic posture, as is the case with the NAACP here.[63]

Habermas summarizes the paradox reflected in these examples of juridification-as-colonization as follows:

> The more the welfare state goes beyond pacifying the class conflict lodged in the sphere of production and spreads a net of client relationships over private spheres of life, the stronger are the anticipated pathological side effects of a juridification that entails both a bureaucratization and a monetarization of core areas of the lifeworld. The *dilemmatic structure of this type of juridification* consists in the fact that, while the welfare-state guarantees are intended to serve the goal of social integration, they nevertheless promote the disintegration of life relations when these are separated, through legalized social intervention, from the consensual mechanisms that coordinate action and are transferred over to media such as power and money.[64]

It is worthwhile to pause here and note briefly another transformation of Habermas' argument from *Legitimation Crisis*, although it is perhaps only a change of emphasis. In the earlier work, he had argued that the interventions of the welfare state were in the service of capital, securing the conditions for its stability and growth, but that the state was constrained in this activity by expectations emanating from the lifeworld in that it must secure for itself both legitimacy (through formal democracy and welfare provision buy-offs) and functionally necessary motivations (through instrumentalizing bourgeois and pre-bourgeois cultural traditions). These latter tasks are indeed a means of ensuring integration; but they appear to be largely secondary measures, conditions on the true aim of facilitating capital accumulation. In *The Theory of Communicative Action*, on the other hand, the interventions of the welfare state are regarded as being in the service of social integration; however, as we will see, they are constrained by the requirements of capital—specifically, that the redistribution of wealth will be permitted only so long as the growth continues from which alone it is to be funded.

This change becomes clearer still in the two examples employed by Habermas in some detail to clarify the idea of juridification, the use of law as a channel for money and power to enter the lifeworld: family and school law. Juridification in these areas protects "the welfare of the child" and the norm of "equal opportunity" against sexism and racism, protects children from parents, teachers, and school administrators, wives from husbands, and so on. In other words, these restructuring interventions are ostensibly well intentioned, even just. In the case of family law, juridification is driven by adjudication and resultant court decisions (and is evidenced in child-custody laws, for example); although initiated through litigation, the legal formalization of schooling was very rapidly absorbed into "government educational bureaucracy" and this entailed, once again, a process of violent abstraction: "[t]he bureaucracy had to ensure that instructional procedures and school measures, as far as they were relevant to the pupil's later life and the parent's wishes, were given a form in which they were accessible to judicial review."[65] Standardized testing, litigation-proof grading procedures, and procedures for handling plagiarism, all are familiar versions of this which subject teaching methods and curricular development to organizing imperatives reflecting the needs of a bureaucratic system. Both the school and the family, however, are informally organized domains of action in which coordination is based on the (at least) counterfactual assumption of an orientation toward mutual understanding; juridification here signals not an increase in the intensity of legal regulation, but its expansion into a new domain. "The formalization of relationships in family and school means, for those concerned, an objectivization and removal from the lifeworld of (now) formally regulated social interaction in family and school. As legal subjects they encounter one another in an objectivizing, success-oriented attitude."[66] Socialization processes in the family, no less than teaching processes in the school, must be able to function according to their own communicative, socially integrative logic. Legal norms may supplement these contexts with certain types of protections; but they result in "functional disturbances" where they interfere with the processes themselves, attempt to convert these contexts over to the medium of law—that is, disturbances in the reproductive functions of these institutions, in particular, in the process of socialization. As we already know, such disturbances have consequences that reverberate throughout the lifeworld.

So, although his emphasis changes regarding at least some of the motives behind the interventions of the welfare state, the real dynamics behind colonization are essentially the same as those identified in *Legitimation Crisis*: The welfare state absorbs the class conflict institutionalized in the sphere of production and, in so doing, displaces conflict into the political sphere at the same time as it disperses the burdens created through this absorption in less and less class-specific ways. As Habermas remarked in reply to critiques of *The Theory of Communicative Action*,

> I still explain these pathologies [manifested in contemporary society] by referring to the mechanism driving capitalism forward, namely economic growth, but I *assess* them in terms of the systematically induced predominance of economic and bureaucratic, indeed of all cognitive-instrumental forms of rationality within a one-sided or "alienated" everyday communicative practice.[67]

The basic dynamic factor remains the need to maintain the ceaseless growth of capital through targeted interventions, while simultaneously attempting to mitigate its destructive side effects; the difference is that Habermas' critical project has been narrowed down to the phenomenon of colonization, and this leads him to focus on the compensating interventions of the welfare state, which results in the change of emphasis noted above.[68] But it remains the case that the welfare state must never, in any of these actions, infringe on "the sovereign right of private enterprise in matters of investment"[69] because to do so would undermine the basis of capitalism itself. From imperialist military and legal actions to regulation of the business cycle, the provision of infrastructure at public expense, and the compensation paid to the victims of growth—the actions in the service of facilitating capital realization operate by altering the "boundary conditions" with reference to which private enterprise governs itself.[70] Once again, Habermas notes that the absorption of economically generated problems in this way leads to crises of public debt, planning capacity, and so forth, and occasionally results in attempts to foist problems back onto the economy. We need not rehash this material, having already dealt with it in some detail. Instead, let me call attention to some additional differences that have emerged in Habermas' account.

First, going along with his change of emphasis regarding the intentions of the welfare state is a new reason for the prohibition against interference with the basic mechanism of capitalist growth: In *Legitimation Crisis*, it had seemed that the reason the welfare state could not interfere with freedom of enterprise is that its entire *raison d'être* had been the service and protection of capitalism; the basic motivation for state interventions now, however, appears to be the maintenance of social stability. Problems that overloaded the steering capacity of liberal capitalism (economic crises) inspire a new level of societal learning that, by drawing on existing normative resources within worldviews (expanding the interpretation of the principle of equality to include substantive conditions on the realization of formal rights) enables the society to renew integration at a higher level of complexity and to solve the initial crisis through expanded means of regulating the economic cycle and compensating for its side effects. In short, then, this evolutionary solution takes the accumulation problems of capital for granted; the issue then becomes one of finding a way to neutralize class conflict so as to ensure integration and stability. The means by which this is done is the provision of social welfare benefits, including collectively used infrastructure such as housing and health care, rights to collective bargaining, and so on: The pathological side effects of capitalist growth, which at first manifest themselves as private burdens, thereby are politicized and are "transformed into mortgages on legitimation."[71] But (and this is the new reason), "adjustments to the pattern of distribution of social compensations trigger reactions on the part of privileged groups unless they can be covered by increases in the social product and thus do not affect the propertied classes; when this is not the case, such measures cannot fulfill the function of containing and mitigating class conflict."[72] Elsewhere Habermas adds that only on the condition that welfare state interventions do not interfere with capitalist growth (indeed, it must do much more than adopt this passive respect), "is there a mass of compensation available that can be distributed according to implicitly agreed upon criteria, in ritualized confrontations, and channeled into the roles of consumer and client in such a way that the structures of alienated labor and alienated political participation develop no explosive power."[73] In other words, the goal of the welfare state system is to neutralize class conflict and so ensure stability, but it cannot appease the toiling, expropriated masses at the expense of the privileged without reigniting class conflict at the top of the social hierarchy; and so the only solution is to say yes to everyone, and to fund social welfare compensations only on the basis of the ceaseless growth demanded by the propertied. Thus, far from a compromise that resolves class conflict, the welfare state represents its institutionalization. Yet because the conflict is deflected through strategic compensations and by an asymmetrical distribution of burdens over the population, the problems that continue to manifest themselves are no longer ascribable to class positions in any direct way: Crises of public debt, the bankrupting of public services, and the like, certainly do affect the poor disproportionately, including especially marginal segments of the poor, immigrants, racial minorities, the elderly, single mothers, and so on. But the haves and have-nots no longer confront one another across a clear line drawn in the structure of the process of production. Parallel to this downgrading of the citizen role in favor of client compensation, Habermas notes that the normalization of alienated, heterogeneously determined occupational roles is compensated for by means of an upgraded consumer role, and by the conversion of private households "over to mass consumption."[74] This, of course, is also functionally necessary, since economic growth is always contingent on increased consumption.

All the information just presented has focused on the question of the stability of the capitalist economy; but the use of political power to this end obviously entails that the latter, too, be legitimized in some way. Habermas claims that only democratic processes of will formation can provide this legitimacy in a rationalized lifeworld, "with highly individuated members, with norms that have become abstract, positive, and in need of justification, and with traditions that have, as regards their authority, been reflectively refracted and set communicatively aflow."[75] This claim manifests another difference of emphasis from *Legitimation Crisis*: Habermas no longer discusses democracy as "merely formal" in the first instance; instead of being directly explicable in terms of meeting system legitimation needs, democracy, on the contrary, is a product of a rationalization of the lifeworld that constrains subsystems—as we saw earlier, it is a form of juridification in which lifeworld asserts itself against the power of the political subsystem. Habermas writes:

> [b]etween capitalism and democracy there is an *indissoluble* tension; in them two opposed principles of societal integration compete for primacy. If we look at the self-understanding expressed in the basic principles of democratic constitutions, modern societies assert the primacy of a lifeworld relative to the subsystems separated out of its institutional orders. The normative meaning of democracy can be rendered in social-theoretical terms by the formula that the fulfillment of the functional necessities of *systemically* integrated domains of action shall find its limits in the integrity of the lifeworld, that is to say, in the requirements of domains of action dependent on *social* integration. On the other hand, the internal dynamics of the capitalist economic system can be preserved only insofar as the accumulation process is uncoupled from orientations to use value. The propelling mechanism of the economic system has to be kept as free as possible from

> lifeworld restrictions as well as from the demands for legitimation directed to the administrative system. The internal systemic logic of capitalism can be rendered in social-theoretical terms by the formula that the functional necessities of systemically integrated domains of action shall be met, if need be, even at the cost of *technicizing* the lifeworld.[76]

Although this represents a real change of emphasis from *Legitimation Crisis*, we could easily be misled into overstating the practical difference by an overhasty interpretation of this "indissoluble tension": It prevails not between capitalism and the self-understanding of citizens in "real existing" democracies, but between the principles of democracy itself and capitalist dynamics. In other words, the tension is indissoluble only at the level of theory; at the level of practice, it is a different story.

It is not that there is no tension at all at the empirical level: To the contrary, capitalist welfare mass democracies are empirically confronted with the use-value demands of citizens, which they must satisfy at least to some minimal extent in order to keep the economic system pure of such orientations. This practical paradox is particularly evident in theoretical reflections on the public sphere, in what at first appears to be merely a difference between two methodological perspectives: According to the first, polls of public opinion in a democratic society make manifest a general interest formed across a plurality of groups, voters, political parties, and so on, and represent the basis and origin of legitimate political decision making. According to the second, that same "general interest" is viewed as the product of efforts by the administration to manufacture legitimation for political decisions.[77] Although, at first glance, this contrast might seem to map on to the difference between normative and sociological conceptions of democracy, Habermas argues that, as a matter of fact, they both capture one element of democracy as it is actually practiced, in all its ambiguity. On the one hand, he argues that competition between political parties really is a part of a communicative process through which public will formation occurs; at the same time, this competition reflects the organizational goals of the established political bureaucracy.[78] This picture still seems rosier than that of *Legitimation Crisis*, but a closer look at the process of the colonization of the public sphere by the imperatives of subsystems shows that Habermas sees the communicative elements of democracy as being in decline. Mass loyalty is today secured through two avenues, neither of which includes substantive, rational deliberations: Positively, the provision of social welfare benefits reflects a downgrading of the citizen role, compensated for through the expansion of the role of the client; and negatively, the political system filters access to the public sphere through the "bureaucratic deformation of the structures of public communication, or through manipulative control of the flow of communication [especially by the colonization of the mass media]. . . . This arrangement amounts to a neutralization of the possibilities of political participation opened up by the role of the citizen."[79] Electoral politics are, in accordance with Habermas' earlier position, reduced to periodic plebiscites on administrative personnel, whose self-presentation in the public sphere is purely symbolic and whose motives remain outside the process of discursive will formation.

The dynamics behind colonization, then, are to be explained by the need to maintain continuous growth of the capitalist economy, which results in parallel increases in system complexity, including both the extension of juridification into areas of life hitherto regulated informally, as well as the intensification of law in domains already formally organized. This colonization,

> triggers conflict within the lifeworld . . . first of all, where socially integrated contexts of life are redefined around the roles of consumer and client and assimilated to systemically integrated domains of action. Such processes have always been part of capitalist modernization; historically, they have been successful in overriding the defensive reaction of those affected so long as it was primarily a question of transferring the material reproduction of the lifeworld over to formally organized domains of action. Along the front between system and lifeworld, the lifeworld evidently offers stubborn and possibly successful resistance only when functions of symbolic reproduction are in question.[80]

I have already raised the question of what exactly we are licensed to infer from this empirical victory of systemic integration: Certainly in claiming that resistance is possibly successful only in areas of symbolic reproduction, Habermas seems to turn the historical failure of struggles against capitalist modernization into a matter of fate. Nevertheless, at this point, I am more interested in his account of this new potential for protest, which he believes to be gathering primarily in the roles of consumer and client, which shoulder the positive weight, as it were, of welfare state interventions. Before I can address this issue, however, I need to take one step back in order to explain a distinction that is relevant to Habermas' account of social struggle under advanced capitalism.

Habermas insists on a distinction between the thesis of colonization and what he describes as a distinct but "complementary" phenomenon: the "cultural impoverishment that threatens a lifeworld whose traditional substance has been devalued."[81] Although this phenomenon is related to rationalization in a less mediated way than is colonization, unlike Weber, Habermas is still unwilling to reduce one to the other. The rationalization of the cultural component of the lifeworld, as we have seen, takes the form of a differentiation of cultural tradition into spheres of science, morality and law, and art, each specializing in one validity domain and developing according to their own inner logics. This development is, as a result, increasingly carried out by professional experts. But, according to Habermas, the separation of such expert cultures need not itself have impoverished the lifeworld of everyday consciousness; as a matter of fact, however, in the process of capitalist modernization these expert cultures have been severed from the everyday lifeworld such that individuals in daily life are thrown back on traditions that have already been discredited but that have not been replaced by new, accessible cultural learning. This is particularly problematic because communicative action relies on there being a vital cultural tradition "across the whole spectrum," that is, inclusive of "cognitive interpretations, moral expectations, expressions, and valuations," which interpenetrate in ordinary processes of reaching understanding. The adequacy and depth of this tradition are under assault from both colonization and cultural impoverishment.[82]

The culturally differentiating character of rationalization also entails an overcoming of the rationality differential between the sacred and profane domains such that classical ideology, which hid system imperatives behind this differential, is no longer possible. It is in this connection that Habermas endorses Daniel Bell's proclamation of the "end of ideology." Thus, it might seem that the demerits of cultural rationalization with respect to the impoverishment of the lifeworld are more than compensated for, in the form of a new, sober apprehension of the deformations of the lifeworld by system imperatives that, in this case, must penetrate the lifeworld as transparently foreign. It turns out, however, that system imperatives discover a functional equivalent for ideology in the phenomenon of cultural impoverishment itself, which obscures the evidence of system violence:

> In place of the positive task of meeting a certain need for interpretation by ideological means, we have the negative requirement of preventing holistic interpretations from coming into existence. The lifeworld is always constituted in the form of a global knowledge intersubjectively shared by its members; thus, the desired equivalent for no longer available ideologies might simply consist in the fact that the everyday knowledge appearing in totalized form remains diffuse, or at least never attains that level of articulation at which alone knowledge can be accepted as valid according to the standards of cultural modernity. *Everyday consciousness* is robbed of its power to synthesize; it becomes *fragmented*.[83]

The separation of expert cultures from everyday consciousness thus means not only that the latter is left dependent on cultural traditions the validity of which has already been undermined, but that even when it is able to avoid recourse to "traditionalism," it remains "hopelessly splintered."[84] Lacking the resources to construct the sort of global interpretation of the lifeworld against which processes of colonization would become manifest, and forced to assimilate to media-oriented interchange roles, it surrenders the communicative orientation altogether in favor of a system-conforming orientation to reward. The unity of a differentiated reason can, according to Habermas, only be re-established at the level of reflective discourse; but discourse is accessible only from within the communicative framework (more on this in Chapter 4).

In *Legitimation Crisis*, too, Habermas had argued that the destruction of traditional worldviews by scientism increasingly left in its wake a positivism with respect to values and an inability to construct a holistic picture of the world. Despite the similarity, it is not too hard to read this as another concession to Held's criticism of *Legitimation Crisis*, although Habermas, in that case, will have generalized Held's account of the consciousness-fragmenting effects of alienated labor to a much broader account of the dynamics behind capitalist modernization. In any case, forms of fundamentalism and neoconservativism, which are a part of the contemporary landscape of social protest, represent anachronistic attempts to restore the stability and unity of the lifeworld by reinvigorating devalued traditions. Like Weber and the early Frankfurt School, as well as conservative social theorists like Gehlen, fundamentalists and neoconservatives indict the process of rationalization itself, rather than the elitist autonomy of expert cultures and the colonization of the lifeworld by system imperatives; in blurring this necessary distinction, they seek to legitimize regressive social programs that are inadequate to the realities of the modern world. Before concluding my account of *The Theory of Communicative Action* with a more detailed discussion of Habermas' assessment of the nature and significance of the full range of contemporary protest potential, I want to summarize the picture of social evolution that is now essentially complete. This summary stresses something that is quite important for my critique of Habermas' later position in Chapter 4.

Summary

Habermas' theory of social evolution asserts that individuals or marginal groups in a society are the first to acquire new learning capacities; these new insights make their way into the interpretive system of mainstream society by way of what Habermas unhelpfully calls "exemplary learning processes." Without ever elucidating this opaque concept, he is at least clear that social movements are a key aspect of this societal learning. The transformed interpretive system in this way gains additional cognitive potential, which is stored in the dominant worldview. Problems that arise in the domain of material reproduction, and that overwhelm existing steering capacities, are what actually provoke the transformation of social structures; the latter occurs when a society draws on the hitherto unexploited cognitive potential stored in worldviews, particularly legal and moral insights, in order to institutionalize new systems of action or forms of social integration. Finally, this new form of integration can make possible an expansion of productive forces and so too of systemic complexity, by freeing up or producing "technical-organizational knowledge" that is able to meet the new steering needs. Thus, as we saw earlier, "learning processes in the area of moral-practical consciousness function as a pacemaker in social evolution."[85]

Although reducible to neither in detail, this amounts in a general way to an endorsement of Weber over Marx, the latter of whom thought that technical innovations relevant to the mode of production held the evolutionarily leading role. Weber's account of the Protestant ethic and the spirit of capitalism, on the other hand, serves as an illustration of Habermas' theory: "In studying ethical attitudes, Weber discovered that evolutionary learning processes began with a rationalization of the lifeworld that first affected culture and personality structures and only then took hold of institutional orders." He recognized that "a conception of *law based on principles of enactment and justification* was needed for the value-rational anchoring of purposive-rational action."[86] In other words, Weber saw that the differentiation of the capitalist economy and administrative bureaucracy—through the institutionalization of language-replacing steering media—required that individuals be satisfied with a positivistic justification of legal regulations within these domains, which demanded only external conformity as opposed to the sort of substantive justification encompassing character and intent that is typical of morality. Thus, the separation of morality and legality must be completed, while "the legal system as a whole had to rely upon an autonomous justification possible only in terms of posttraditional morality."[87] Neither Habermas nor Weber puts the cart before the horse: These transformed cultural and personality structures did not emerge because the economic and political structures of the future required them. Their explanation appeals instead to steering problems in feudal society, which could draw for their solution on already available levels of learning contained in worldviews, in this case, according to Weber, in the unique path of rationalization taken by monotheistic cultural traditions.[88]

The details of this story are not crucial for the point I want to make. At the moment, I just want to stress that the prerequisites to the emergence of postconventional legal institutions, which include, for Habermas, the formal organization of autonomous subsystems, are to be located in individual learning; in other words, that the ontogenetic level has priority in the historical emergence of postconventionality, followed by resultant changes in cultural tradition. The rationalization of the lifeworld that makes this possible, or rather, of which this is a part, results in an overburdening of the communicative resources of these emerging postconventional individuals; steering problems, problems of action coordination, begin to emerge. The institution of formally regulated subsystems, which ease the burden of communication through systemic integration, draws on the postconventional separation of legality and morality, which has subsequently made its way into the cultural tradition. As we have already seen, the wave of juridification through which this occurs counts as a process of liberation: It is heralded as the institutionalization of bourgeois ideals of freedom and equality. But, ironically, these subsystems, which continue to develop autonomously, soon react upon and threaten the very rationalized lifeworld to which they owe their existence. The inherent dynamics of capitalist growth initiate this process, but the absorption of its side effects by welfare state mass democracies results in an increasing impulse toward the colonization of the lifeworld. This colonization, as well as the complementary, ideology-functional phenomenon of cultural impoverishment, interfere with core processes of the symbolic reproduction of the lifeworld and undermine the resources on which communicative action relies; this results in the phenomena of alienation, loss of meaning, and fragmentation of consciousness. In short, these complementary processes undermine the postconventionality of individuals who are either thrust back into traditionalism (a sort of super-rigid conventionalism), or are unable to form a coherent, unified, normative picture of society and are instead trapped, as it were, in a strategic attitude toward a social order that seems to permit of no alternatives. This is the crucial argument for Chapter 4: The result of this "irony" is that, despite the presence of ostensibly postconventional legal institutions, under advanced capitalism there are no longer (or are ever less frequently) the personality structures that could make these institutions real with respect to their essential meaning. As Habermas says, "the explosive contents of cultural modernity have been defused."[89]

Protest Potential in *The Theory of Communicative Action*

Habermas claims that, in advanced capitalist societies, the point of entry for the imperatives of subsystems that threaten the lifeworld is predominantly the private household; that is, it is principally to this sphere that crises of system maintenance are shifted. System crises directly threaten social integration, in the first instance, by harboring the potential to unmask class conflict. But before social integration and the maintenance of the social system can be challenged seriously, crises are shifted into the environment.

> We can represent the replacement of steering crises with lifeworld pathologies as follows: anomic conditions are avoided,

> and legitimations and motivations important for maintaining institutional orders are secured, at the expense of, and through the ruthless exploitation of, other resources. Culture and personality come under attack for the sake of warding off crises and stabilizing society . . . instead of manifestations of anomie (and instead of the withdrawal of legitimation and motivation in place of anomie), phenomena of alienation and the unsettling of collective identity result.[90]

Given the intertwining of reproductive contributions, it isn't entirely clear that the pathologies that result from the displacement of crises can be confined even this successfully: A crisis of orientation and in educational goals is almost certain to result from the unsettling of collective identities (although system imperatives will happily take over the setting of educational goals); the psychopathologies that result from alienation will also cause ruptures in the cultural tradition and a withdrawal of motivation; and, finally, the rupture of cultural tradition may lead to a loss of meaning, thus undermining the resources needed for legitimation.[91] These, however, may well indicate comparatively long-term effects of the interference of subsystems in symbolic reproduction; Habermas' point about the primary targets for displacement seems plausible, although not precisely as he has made it. The reason is that he is constrained by his presentation of systems and their dual environments, such that the options for displacement appear to be either the family or the public sphere. But it quickly becomes clear that what he really means to say is that the reproductive process most directly threatened is socialization, which he has rather narrowly identified as the specialization of the family. That this limitation is misleading is evident in Habermas' own examples, to which he returns here: It is not only the family (family law) that is implicated in this, but the school (school law), as well. And insofar as it is the socialization of the strategically oriented, competitive attitudes necessary for system maintenance (and for the suppression of alternatives) that is at issue, it is arguably the case that the school rivals the family in importance.[92]

In this connection, Habermas argues that his reformulation of the pathologies of modernity in terms of the uncoupling of subsystems from the lifeworld necessitates a reassessment of the changes in "family, education, and personality structures" that interested the first generation of critical theorists. In particular, the rationalization that has taken hold of the family, its freedom from economically reproductive functions and its specialization in processes of socialization, entails that system imperatives that intrude there result in disturbances in personality formation, especially in the adolescent phase during which the continuity of identity-securing traditions is tested.[93] As a result,

> there is a tendency toward disparities between competencies, attitudes, and motives, on the one hand, and the functional requirements of adult roles on the other. The problem of detaching oneself from the family and forming one's own identity have in any case turned adolescent development (which is scarcely safeguarded by institutions anymore) into a critical test for the ability of the coming generation to connect up with the preceding one. When the conditions of socialization in the family are no longer functionally in tune with the organizational membership conditions that the growing child will one day have to meet, the problems that young people have to solve in their adolescence become insoluble for more and more of them. One indication of this is the social and even political significance that youth protest and withdrawal cultures have gained since the end of the 1960s.[94]

It seems to me that there are actually a number of possible tendencies confused in this ambiguous passage. Colonization, Habermas claims, is reflected in the conversion of the private household over to a unit of mass consumption; the disparity with adult roles might therefore suggest that young people lack the postconventional ego capacities needed for interactions in contemporary society. But this would have no obvious connection to youth protest. And, in fact, we have just seen that the mechanisms by which advanced capitalist societies achieve stability under conditions of mass democracy require the hollowing out and undermining of postconventional identity. Thus, there would appear to be a complementary relationship between a colonized family structure and a colonized, instrumentalized and desiccated public (and occupational) sphere in relation to which adult identities are largely constructed. The connection to the protest potential of youth only makes sense if we revert to a position closer to that of *Legitimation Crisis*: namely, that the socialization patterns typical of the bourgeoisie, despite the threat of colonization, may foster postconventional competencies that are dysfunctional from the perspective of the alienated occupational sphere, trivialized citizens' role, paternalistic state–client relationship, and consumerist self-image of the capitalist welfare state. This disjunction presents the possibility of a crisis of motivation and inspires resistance movements. Even in this case, however, it remains somewhat difficult to see the connection to ruptures of historical integration that occur between generations, which Habermas also mentions here. If we assume that the prior generation manifests an essentially conventional, traditionalist self-image, the problem is dissolved: The divide occurs because of the autonomy young people increasingly demand for themselves, in their identities and in their judgments. But the actual situation certainly is much more ambiguous: If we also take into account the complementary phenomenon of cultural impoverishment, it is far more plausible to say that, although certain patterns of socialization may point in the direction of a system-dysfunctional postconventionality; at the same time, the undermining of cultural traditions and fragmentation of consciousness results in an impoverishment of the resources available to young people for the construction of an autonomous identity, and the colonization of the family suggests that consumerist and status-oriented self-definition may be the only option.

In any case, perhaps with McCarthy's criticism of *Legitimation Crisis* in mind, Habermas does not conclude his assessment of protest potential here with this comparatively gloomy prognosis, but makes the return trip from the identification of the universal interest in unconstrained communication, the sanctity of the lifeworld, to the identification of empirical groups whose interests are violated by logic of self-expanding systems. Perhaps also recalling Held's criticism, he identifies a series of potential sites of social struggle that are discernable on the basis of the thesis of colonization, and that are distinct from the issue of motivational and legitimation crises—which are, in turn, given only cursory treatment in *The Theory of Communicative Action* and in which, it would appear, Habermas has lost hope. He writes,

> the fact that in welfare-state mass democracies class-conflict has been institutionalized and thereby pacified does not mean that protest potential has been altogether laid to rest. But the potentials for protest emerge now along different lines of conflict—just where we would expect them to emerge if the thesis of the colonization of the lifeworld were correct. . . . They no longer flare up in domains of material reproduction; they are no longer channeled through parties and associations; and they can no longer be allayed by compensations. Rather, these new conflicts arise in domains of cultural reproduction, social integration, and socialization; they are carried out in subinstitutional—or at least extraparlimentary—forms of protest; and the underlying deficits reflect a reification of communicatively structured domains of action that will not respond to the media of money and power. The issue is not primarily one of compensations that the welfare state can provide, but of defending and restoring endangered ways of life.[95]

Compared with the "old politics" of class, this "new politics" draws heavily from the middle classes, especially from young people and those with a high degree of formal education. According to Habermas, the line of conflict separates, on the one hand, the central strata of capitalist society, those invested in the maintenance of growth as the basis of the welfare state compromise and, on the other, "a periphery composed of variegated groups that are lumped together," united through a common critique of growth, through being "more strongly sensitized to the self-destructive consequences of the growth in complexity" and, finally, through their being distanced from " 'the productivist core of performance' in late capitalist societies."[96] Habermas gives a number of examples taken from the situation in Germany, although most are familiar throughout the "West": environmental groups; antiwar groups; various groups dedicated to alternative lifestyles; minorities; lesbian, gay, bisexual, and transgender rights groups; disability rights groups; the feminist movement; various movements for regional, cultural, linguistic, or religious autonomy; various forms of religious fundamentalism; anti-tax libertarian groups; parents' associations engaged in school-related protests; community associations opposed to development projects, and so on.[97] He divides such struggles into those that aim at resistance, and those that aim at withdrawal. Feminism stands outside this dichotomy as a liberation movement in the bourgeois-socialist tradition, an offensive (as opposed to defensive) movement for the realization of the universalistic promise of modern morality and law. By comparison, both sides of the divide described here are defensive: They seek to protect communicatively structured domains of life from the encroachment of system imperatives. Beyond this, resistance movements can be internally subdivided into those that are essentially conservative—those, for instance, that aim to protect traditional, property-based forms of social rank—and those that are comparatively progressive, and that aim to protect an already rationalized lifeworld, including those that experiment with "new ways of cooperating and living together." In the first category are included the protests of traditional middle classes against technical projects that threaten neighborhoods (related to infrastructure or security), against certain kinds of school reforms, against taxes; also included here are most of the aforementioned autonomy struggles, which define themselves in conventionalist terms. In the second category fall the new conflict potentials, examples of which include youth movements, alternative movements, in particular those oriented by a critique of growth in the dimensions of peace and ecology. According to Habermas, "[i]t is possible to conceive of these conflicts in terms of resistance to tendencies toward a colonization of the lifeworld."[98] In other words, *The Theory of Communicative Action* singles out these empirical groups as the addressees of its theory, whose social position and interests it serves to clarify.

Habermas' insistence on the distinction between the rationalization of the lifeworld and its colonization—a distinction not always clear to these movements themselves, nor consistently made by their critics—provides a criterion for distinguishing between those movements that regressively and implausibly seek to reconstitute the destabilized traditional order (often based on ascriptive identities—race, gender, etc.), and those that accept the rationalization of the lifeworld and seek to protect it from system imperatives, or even to regain some ground lost to colonization. Alternative practices directed toward this latter end crystallize, once again, around the interchange roles between lifeworld and subsystems. The groups in question intend to resist the "profit-dependent instrumentalization of work in one's vocation . . . the extension of pressures of competition and performance all the way down into elementary school" and, in general, the ongoing commodification of human life and activity. In opposition to this colonization of the lifeworld, they raise the demand for the democratization of public service agencies.[99]

Compared with the crisis argument of *Legitimation Crisis*, this account of protest potential represents a dramatic scaling down of the scope of potential transformation. Importantly, Habermas appears to remain committed to a position he first articulated in *Toward a Rational Society*, at a time when serious structural transformation of capitalist society was still on his agenda, and that I cited in connection with McCarthy's discussion of *Legitimation Crisis*. Referring to the fragmentation of the lines of class conflict as a result of welfare state interventions, and the dispersion of the worst of the burdens over "underprivileged," marginal groups, Habermas wrote that in the absence of solidaric relations with dominant sectors of society, such underprivileged groups pose no serious, potentially transformative threat to the system: "For underprivileged groups are not social classes, nor do they even potentially represent the mass of the population. Their disenfranchisement and pauperization no longer coincide with exploitation, because the system does not live off their labour."[100] Such marginal groups, including—for my purposes, especially—immigrant groups, ethnic minorities, and so on, form part of the periphery once again in the protest argument of *The Theory of Communicative Action*. Habermas' minimization of the significance of their protest coheres well with his new acceptance of the inescapability of language-replacing subsystems as they exist today. His critique has been scaled down to the phenomenon of colonization: As long as the system remains in its proper place, it not only is acceptable, but it is unavoidable for any modern, complex society. Over the course of this work, I aim to refute the entirety of this claim: I argue that (a) "system" today *does* live off the labor of "underprivileged groups," both within developed nations and at the global level; and (b) Habermas portrays the prospects for solidarity with groups in the center of society as being dim, precisely because he confines the chances for solidarity to a narrow reading of interest: My presentation of the structure of multicultural identities in the Concluding Reflections is constructed to challenge this premise. Accordingly, I restrict my comments here to a critique of Habermas' position on the systematic lack of importance of "underprivileged groups," which receives further substantiation in the Intermediate Reflections.

Culture and Economy: On the Instrumentalization of Status Distinctions

The work of Nancy Fraser and, in particular, her debate with Axel Honneth, provides a helpful resource for considering the relationship between social status—or marginalization and underprivilege—and the operations of the money-steered economy or, as Fraser puts it, the relationship between recognition and redistribution. Additionally, she presents her theory as an alternative, richer account of social injustice than she sees available in Habermas' "colonization" thesis, which she regards as being too one-sided. Fraser defends a political conception of justice as "participatory parity," understood substantively to include both recognition-oriented (or cultural) and redistributive-oriented (or economic) conditions on the effective realization of one's autonomy. By encompassing recognition and redistribution, this conception of justice allows her to identify the differing sources of injustice in the spectrum of cases of social struggle, from those that, like class struggle, unionization, and so on, are primarily economic, to those that, like the gay rights movement, are primarily cultural.[101] Her real interest, however, is in the middle ground of cases, in "two-dimensionally subordinated groups" who "suffer both maldistribution [economic injustice] and misrecognition [cultural marginalization or oppression] *in forms where neither of these injustices is an indirect effect of the other, but where both are primary and co-original.*"[102] Gender and race are Fraser's two main examples: She claims that both function as "basic organizing principle[s] of the economic structure of capitalist society." In the case of gender, she has in mind the distinction between paid and unpaid, or productive and "unproductive" labor, according to which domestic labor performed overwhelmingly by women is unpaid and deemed socially unproductive. Additionally, she observes within the paid workforce the gender-coded division between better-paid blue- and white-collar "man's" work and poorly paid, feminine "pink-collar" work. The result of this "structuring" of the economic by sexist value patterns is "an economic structure that generates gender-specific forms of distributive injustice, including gender-based exploitation, economic marginalization, and deprivation."[103] This makes gender a "class-like" structure that should be overcome through broadly redistributive measures, in this case, an ultimately transformative reorganization of the occupational system. Fraser considers that Habermas' colonization thesis is unable to account for such phenomena, in which deformities in the lifeworld (i.e., prejudice) exert an influence on the structure of the economy.

But gender is also a status category distinct from class, as is demonstrated by the fact that all low-status groups risk "feminization and thus depreciation."[104] Sexist patterns of cultural value are encoded in family and criminal law, in ideas of privacy, self-defense, equality, and autonomy; they are reflected in government policies with respect to immigration and asylum, and in the professional practice of medicine and psychotherapy. Correlated to these social realities are forms of gender-specific status subordination suffered by women, including domestic abuse, demeaning representations in the media, high levels of harassment in everyday life, exclusion from public spheres, underrepresentation in deliberative bodies, and the like. These harms cannot be reduced to economic injustices or to their effects.

Race similarly structures economic divisions between menial and nonmenial jobs, and between superfluous labor and labor worth exploiting. As a result, "the economic structure generates racially specific forms of maldistribution. Racialized immigrant and/or ethnic minorities suffer disproportionately high rates of unemployment and poverty and over-representation in low-paying menial work."[105] To this extent, race, too, is a class-like category; but just as with gender, it is more than that, as can be seen in the way non-white racial categories and ascribed characteristics are stigmatized in the public sphere, resulting in pervasive discrimination, harassment, and marginalization. Again, neither element is reducible to the other.

In any given case, the balance between the economic and cultural forces at work in status and class assignment is an empirical question (and, at the level of the individual, it is complicated by the fact that all individuals belong to diverse collectivities, and so may, e.g., be privileged along one axis or in one set of institutions, and disadvantaged in others). In short, then, Fraser takes a broadly Habermasian view of contemporary societies, describing them as encompassing "two analytically distinct modes of social ordering; an economic mode, in which interaction is regulated by the functional interlacing of strategic imperatives, and a cultural mode, in which interaction is regulated by the institutionalized patterns of culture value. . . . In all societies, economic ordering and cultural ordering are mutually imbricated."[106] The difference, as she sees it, lies in the "analytical" nature of the distinction. Of course, Habermas claims that the system/lifeworld distinction is analytical—or rather, methodological—but Fraser argues that he substantializes both. I have already discussed the basis of this misunderstanding. What concerns me here is that Fraser primarily distinguishes her account from Habermas' with the assertion that her theory, unlike his, is two-directional; that is, she can account for the mutual interpenetration of lifeworld and subsystems, while he reduces their interaction to the unidirectional question of "colonization." Although the market is indeed a legally institutionalized domain of strategic action, it is not norm-free; although the differentiation of the market represents, in one sense, a fissure in the cultural ordering of society,

> [e]ven on their own turf . . . markets do not simply dissolve status distinctions; rather, they instrumentalize them, bending pre-existing patterns of cultural value to capitalist purposes. For

> example, racial hierarchies that long predate capitalism were not abolished with the dismantling of New World slavery or even of Jim Crow, but reconfigured to suit a market society. No longer explicitly codified in law, and no longer socially legitimate, racist norms have been wired into the infrastructure of capitalist labor markets.[107]

It seems to me that there is a kind of ambiguity to this account. Fraser is rightly critical of the kind of "culturalism" she sees in Axel Honneth's work, in his insistence that cultural values so deeply influence the pattern of distribution in capitalist societies that there is no need to consider systemic economic structures. But although the instrumentalization of existing status distinctions by capitalism provides strong support for that critique, the claim we have seen repeated several times here, which reappears in her last sentence above, sounds rather like Honneth's own position. The only example either he or Fraser describe in any detail to explain the structuring of the economic system by cultural values is the distinction between socially productive and unproductive labor, which is the basis of the exclusion of predominantly women's domestic labor.[108] But there is nothing mysterious about why domestic labor isn't remunerated within the capitalist system of distribution: It isn't commodified. There was no founding of the labor market at which it was determined what would count as labor and at which, motivated by sexism, it was resolved to exclude domestic work. Rather, the labor market is based on the "ironic" freedom described by Marx, "enjoyed" by those liberated from the bonds of the feudal status order and simultaneously from any means of independently reproducing their own existence. And so they sold their labor, alienated from its use-value orientation and from their own enjoyment of it, to the owners of capital and of the means of production. Domestic labor is not like this: It is use-value oriented and so unalienated, at least in that respect (although perhaps not in others).

To be clear: I fully endorse the justice of the claim that, under a democratically determined distribution of social wealth, domestic labor would deserve direct remuneration; I also endorse the claim that, under market conditions, domestic labor merits redistributive remuneration that will have to be based on taxation. My point is that I can see no way in which this example, the only one offered, can support the claim that the economic system is deeply, actively structured by cultural values. Honneth has no more to say on the matter; Fraser, however, gives numerous other examples of the way capitalism instrumentalizes, parasitically feeds on distinctions in the cultural status order and, in fact, tends to recur to this argument whenever she tries to offer a more detailed account of the interactions between cultural status and economic class.[109] The exclusion and underemployment of young black men in the Bronx, of young Arab men in the urban suburbs of France, of women in sub-Saharan Africa, the rise of pink-collar labor in developed nations—all are good examples of the way in which, in the pursuit of profit, capitalist enterprise exploits existing distinctions of status (with respect to exclusion, recall that an "industrial reserve army of the unemployed," in Marx's terms, has a salutary effect on the overall price of labor, and is required to make employer control effective through credible threats of dismissal). Equally strong examples can be found in the fear-mongering surrounding "illegals" and Hispanic immigration generally in the United States; in the economic and occupational status of new immigrants and so-called "guest workers" or "sans-papiers" throughout the so-called "West"; and in the morally repugnant exploitation of labor in the developing world vis-à-vis the developed. These examples are particularly good not simply because the exploitation of the populations in question is, without being justified in an explicit way, not widely perceived as unacceptable or intolerable. This is also true of the earlier examples: It is acceptable to pay workers in Africa and China mere cents a day, whereas it would be an outrage if done "here," or to people "like us"; 50 percent unemployment rates are acceptable for young black men, but would be a hot-button issue were it to be true of young white men across the country. What sets the second set of examples apart is that they highlight forms of exploitation on which the current economic system can *easily* be shown to be dependent: For instance, the U.S. economy not only depends on immigration for economic growth, as do nearly all Western nations, but whole sectors of the economy depend on "illegal," exploitable, Hispanic laborers who, as it is sometimes said in justification, "do the jobs Americans won't do."[110]

In summary, the convincing part of Fraser's position is, at the level of cultural–economic interaction, essentially the same as Habermas': that is, this opportunistic instrumentalization moves in the same direction as colonization. And yet she enables us to see something terribly important regarding Habermas' practical argument: The system *does* depend on the labor (and exclusion) of marginalized groups, which fails to present a threat to system legitimacy precisely because the system feeds parasitically on existing forms of status inequality. The practical significance of this observation is great: At least some of the obstacles faced by economic struggles and struggles for gender, racial, ethnic, or cultural equality, are one and the same—namely, core operations of capitalist reproduction. This offers potential grounds for something approaching the kind of solidarity described by Habermas as requisite to genuine transformation. But, in fact, on the basis of this argument and its extension in the following chapters, I argue in the Concluding Reflections for a much more substantive form of solidarity that transcends such merely negative characterization.

The "Inevitability" of System

Finally, let me note following another, later critique offered by Thomas McCarthy, that Habermas' acceptance of the need for media-steered subsystems in modern societies, which he repeatedly insists upon in *The Theory of Communicative Action*, is mysterious at best. If we are to accept his characterization of such systems, which McCarthy does not, this would appear to entail that even an emancipated society would require the creation of institutions in which the functional interconnection of interactions was kept latent and in which "members just take orders without regard to the legitimacy of goals."[111] Yet Habermas has elsewhere criticized this insistence on latency as a neoconservative position, which seeks to shield decisions from "insight and variation." To be sure, in a complex society, we will need some mechanisms for the implementation of general, collective goals that do not depend on achieved consensus for each and every decision; but this is a long way from accepting subsystems that are defined in principle as inaccessible to everyday consciousness. It is hard to see, as McCarthy notes, how such a view could be compatible with Habermas' endorsement of participatory, deliberative democracy: The establishment of the latter would require institutional change that, McCarthy claims, Habermas "runs the risk of not being able to formulate" as a result of his accommodation of systems theory.[112] Of course, Habermas himself noted that the systems-theoretic and action-theoretic models highlight an irresolvable tension that is more than a methodological difference, but which is a function of a society compromised of both media-steered subsystems and lifeworld. The problem is that he still wants to see the process of colonization halted, and to see these subsystems subjected to the influence of the lifeworld via the interchange relations; this is a problem because, on his account of such subsystems, or—because I am more sympathetic than McCarthy is to Habermas' account as a description of practice—*given his acceptance of such subsystems in their current form*, this influence does not appear to be possible.

What is most puzzling about all of this, however, and most relevant for my own argument, is also McCarthy's basic question: Why exactly does Habermas think he *needs* system? The answer, McCarthy agrees, is social complexity and the overburdening of communicative resources. Surely in a pluralistic society, in which there is no longer a culturally rooted, antecedent consensus that serves to coordinate action, there must be *some* form of repre sentative (as opposed to direct) democracy, some form of party system, "*some* way of selecting leaders with some measure of latitude for decision-making, *some* administrative apparatus for carrying out decisions. This is the point, I take it, of characterizing schemes in which all of this is simply thought away as 'utopian' in a negative sense."[113] But, McCarthy adds, there is no way to determine the character of the *"some"* in each of these cases purely at the theoretical level, which is to say, *a priori*. By Habermas' own lights, these questions can only be answered "through learning processes that test the limits of the realizability of the utopian elements of our tradition."[114] In short—and I return to this at the conclusion of Chapter 4—the question of the overburdening of the communicative resources of individuals is an empirical one that Habermas has made no attempt to answer.[115] Nevertheless, this reverence for the problem of complexity as *the* problem of modern societies continues to determine his work beyond *The Theory of Communicative Action*. Before revisiting Habermas' social theory with an eye to research in the sociology of schooling, and before returning to discuss in more detail the nature and structure of postconventional identities, it is worth sketching very briefly Habermas' own path from here.

Postscript

Between Facts and Norms, in Which Law Saves Us from Ourselves

It might seem rather odd to treat *Between Facts and Norms* in a mere postscript, after having devoted whole chapters to both *Legitimation Crisis* and *The Theory of Communicative Action*. After all, it surely ranks as one of Habermas' major works and, within North America, has been among the most widely discussed of Habermas' writings. But there are two rather specific reasons for this brief treatment. First, my basic question in this book concerns the relationship between Habermas' social theory and his theory of the subject. As I discussed in the Introduction, the idea that there is a dialectical relationship between the subject and society has been at the core of critical theory, as a methodological program of immanent critique, from the very beginning. Habermas' work up to and including *The Theory of Communicative Action* is squarely within the tradition of critical theory in this methodological sense. This is no longer true of *Between Facts and Norms*: Despite its great sophistication and interest in other respects, what is remarkable about this text is that it is basically silent on this key question. This is the primary reason, then, for the brevity of my treatment: My aim here is to show that, in *Between Facts and Norms*, Habermas gives up on the attempt to deal in a serious and central way with the empirical preconditions upon the attainment of the normative ideals he defends. All I can really do to show this is to point to an absence.

The second reason is that, despite a number of other differences, *Between Facts and Norms* represents a continuation of Habermas' retreat from the demand for systematic social transformation, a further step toward his increasing accommodation to the status quo social order. This change has already been discussed in this chapter in some detail, and the motives for it in *Between Facts and Norms* remain the same: It is the problem of social complexity that is invoked by Habermas in justification for his increasing critical modesty. Accordingly, my only additional aim in this postscript is to point to at least one reason for Habermas' turn to a normative philosophy of law in light of the unfolding of his social theory. The changes that explain this outcome occur, as I have argued, in *The Theory of Communicative Action*.

Briefly, then, the "between" of *Between Facts and Norms* refers to the tension between facticity and validity—literally, its German title—which is characteristic of modern, positive, coercive law: Such law, in other words, is a social fact backed by force at the same time as it makes a context-transcendent claim to legitimacy. As Kant argued, legitimate law must be such that, although it demands only external conformity (e.g., we cannot legislate religious convictions or other motivations), individuals subjected to it *can* obey out of "respect for law." This dual character of law turns out to be crucial for Habermas' solution to the problem of social complexity and for his revised account of social integration. He begins by reminding us once again that, as the rationalization of the lifeworld sets in, the burden of social integration is more and more placed on the communicative resources of individuals, eventually overwhelming them. In support of this latter contention, he stresses more strongly than he has elsewhere that, ordinarily, communicative action relies on "the backing of a massive background consensus" embodied in shared lifeworlds comprised (in part) of utterly unproblematic "knowledge"—that is, premises or assumptions in which validity and facticity remain fused as a result of the lack of critical distance.[116] The problem, as he sees it, is that

> [t]he more societal complexity increases and originally ethnocentric perspectives widen, the more there develops a pluralization of forms of life accompanied by an individualization of life histories, while the zones of overlapping lifeworlds and shared background assumptions shrink. In proportion to their disenchantment, secularized belief complexes fall apart, under differentiated validity aspects, into the more or less freely thematizable contents of a tradition set communicatively aflow. Above all, however, processes of social differentiation necessitate a multiplication of functionally specified tasks, social roles, and interest positions. On the one hand, this allows communicative action to escape its narrowly circumscribed constitutional boundaries for a wider range of opportunities. On the other hand, in a growing number of spheres social differentiation not only unshackles but requires the self-interested pursuit of one's own success. . . . According to this scenario, the increasing need for integration *must hopelessly overtax the integrating capacity of communicative action*, especially if the functionally necessary spheres of strategic action are growing, as is the case in modern societies.[117]

In this long quote are contained a number of themes with which we are already familiar: The foundations of communicative action are under assault from two directions—from the pluralization of worldviews, which undermines the prerequisites of communicative action, and from the expansion of complexity, which calls forth the differentiation of language-replacing subsystems of strategic action. In a revision of his earlier critical position regarding at least some kinds of juridification, Habermas here suggests that the structure of modern law simultaneously provides solutions to both problems, that is, if individuals themselves come to a democratically produced understanding regarding the *"normative regulation of strategic actions."*[118] In other words, actors are to make use of the citizen's role to reverse the flow of influence, from the subsystem *to* lifeworld directionality of colonization, to the regulation and boundary-demarcation of subsystems *by* the lifeworld. Because of its dual character, modern positive law is uniquely suited to this task: It can act as a "hinge between system and lifeworld" because, while communicatively acting individuals can address themselves to it normatively (and, if it is legitimate, obey it out of respect), strategically acting individuals can address themselves to law as a social fact, a premise to be considered in self-interested deliberations.[119] Law can speak to power and to money in a way that morality, Habermas now claims, cannot.

His proceduralist account of the legitimacy of law, which ties together public autonomy (citizenship and participatory rights, etc.) and private autonomy (so-called negative rights or freedoms), can be read as a response to McCarthy's critique of Habermas' account of system; that is, he advances a normative conception of law that allows him to formulate answers to questions regarding alternative, more just, democratic, administrative models. Although his conception of law is indeed normative, it is offered as an explication of the essentially normative contents built into empirically existing constitutional democracies. But is that sufficient to shield Habermas from the potential charge of utopian thinking? He does concede, and spends some time discussing, the external tensions that result from the social facts of complexity, the need for expert knowledge in fulfilling administrative functions, as well as the attempt by special interests and constellations of money and power to instrumentalize the political process. This discussion is parallel to, but weaker than, the assertion in *The Theory of Communicative Action* of an "indissoluble tension" between capitalism and democracy. But as we saw there, this tension is resolved (in favor of capitalism) in the practical dimension through the reduction of democracy to merely formal status, carried out ultimately through the undermining of trends toward postconventionality at the ontogenetic level. In *Between Facts and Norms*, on the other hand, although he does not reject sociological evidence pointing toward such instrumentalization, he "insists on the empirical relevance of deliberative democratic ideals accepted by the citizens themselves as engaged participants."[120] In other words, what now forms the opposing pole of this tension is not merely the theoretical significance of constitutional democracy itself, its meaning *in principle*, but the self-understanding of citizens. The critique of formal democracy and of the functionally necessary interference in processes of socialization, without being rebutted, evaporates into thin air. From whence did these citizens come? Or better, casting a glance over the quality of democratic politics and rates of political knowledge and engagement in developed nations in the last thirty years, one would be inclined to ask: *Which engaged participants*?

In the end, the status of the argument of *Between Facts and Norms* is much more difficult to puzzle out than is the case with any of Habermas' earlier works. As William Scheuerman documents in some detail, it is in many ways a work divided against itself, riven by an ultimately unsuccessful attempt to accommodate both normative and descriptive accounts of democracy and the public sphere.[121] Habermas concedes that the robust, repoliticized public sphere that is prerequisite to the realization of democratic principles under current conditions—which can restrain administrative and economic power, subordinate subsystems to the lifeworld—is contingent on the self-understanding and actions of citizens. And that is to say, that it is contingent on a rationalized lifeworld and on forms of life and practices of socialization that foster the sorts of postconventional competencies and identities necessary for citizens to assume this burden.[122] The burden itself is, of course, noticeably reduced: Citizens require these competencies in order to participate in discourses regarding the regulation of the boundaries of spheres of strategic action, and in discourses in the political public sphere to which political parties and the administrative system should be receptive. The sorts of social transformations anticipated in *Legitimation Crisis* have been taken off the table. Nevertheless, are even these comparatively modest empirical preconditions realized? While on the one hand, Habermas offers concessions to sociological theories that suggest that this normative picture is without empirical foundation, on the other, he brushes the critique of these practical shortcomings under the rug in favor of an illumination of essential principles. At the very least, there is a strong suggestion throughout *Between Facts and Norms* that proceduralist legal forms are *in the process* of assuming the burden of integration in pluralistic, complex societies; to that extent, there is an implicit, unargued assumption that there indeed exists the sort of postconventional individuals on the basis of which alone this would be possible. I return to what this means for the status of postconventionality today in Chapter 4.

Intermediate Reflections

Habermas and the Sociology of the School

Chapters 1 and 2 laid out the main aspects of Habermas' theory of society as it has developed over the course of his career; to that extent, the main purpose there was expository. Although I also offered a number of critical considerations, many of which were related to changes in his theory, I have not yet really discussed its adequacy to reality. Habermas, however, has always suggested that his work be understood as the outlines of a research project to be taken up in empirical research and so confirmed or disconfirmed. That, more or less, is what I propose to do in this chapter by focusing on the issue of the school. I am not a social scientist by training, however, and so what I will offer here is not my own empirical vindication or refutation; rather, I propose that, by offering a survey of research trends in the sociology of schooling—that is, of empirically oriented research into the place and function of the school in society—we can assess the degree to which Habermas succeeds in providing a framework for the illumination and critique of social reality. One could justify the choice of the school more or less contingently: It is simply a more manageable task to focus on one set of institutions rather than on society as a whole and so, without claiming to be an exhaustive concern, the school might serve as well as any other complex theme relative to which there exists a rich body of empirical research. But the school is more than just a contingent example: In light of the key role played by socialization in Habermas' theory, the institutions involved in this reproductive function recommend themselves for special attention on immanent grounds. Of course, that includes the family and the media, alongside the school. I have already adduced some considerations for the particular relevance of the latter, although I certainly do not deny that all three are crucial; accordingly, I make no pretense here to an exhaustive testing Habermas' theory on this point. Habermas himself, in any case, has not had much to say at the empirical, sociological level, about any of these institutions that nevertheless seem so central to his theory. Much of what he has said concerning educational socialization has already been discussed in the previous chapter.[1] Let me briefly summarize the relevant claims.

Habermas on the Function of the School

In *Legitimation Crisis*, Habermas offered four theses relevant to the significance of the school in society, through which he portrayed:

1. Public schooling as a tool for increasing relative surplus value;
2. Schooling as a tool for maintaining the depoliticization of the public sphere;
3. Interference of the state in schooling as an example of the pathologies of the welfare state; and
4. Economically or politically "dysfunctional" schooling as contributing to the likelihood of a motivational crisis.

Public Schooling as a Tool for Increasing Relative Surplus Value

Habermas saw the expansion of the system of education, especially after World War II and the solidification of the welfare state, as an innovative part of the attempt by the state to increase available surplus value and so to maintain economic growth. Provision of a general system of education, as well as specialized vocational training, is intended to increase the productivity of labor at no cost to capital, funded instead through public taxes. In short, in the language of the sociology of schooling, the school serves capitalist reproduction.

Schooling as a Tool for Maintaining the Depoliticization of the Public Sphere

Increasing qualifications, however, is not enough to ensure the stability of capitalist growth. As discussed in Chapter 1, in order to dedicate itself to the needs of capital, the state has to be shielded from substantively democratic demands, from the use-value orientations of its citizens that would presume to put human needs before profit. The depoliticization of the public sphere, through the cultivation of attitudes of civic- and familial-vocational privatism among citizens, is what enables the state to succeed in this. Recall that these attitudes entail "political abstinence combined with an orientation to career, leisure, and consumption . . . [which] promote the expectation of suitable rewards within the system (money, leisure time, and security)."[2] In short, an instrumental, "possessive individualist" attitude toward the state and the social world underwrite the acceptability of the trade-off of meaningful autonomy for system rewards. Particularly important for this chapter is Habermas' additional observation that this depoliticization requires transference of the achievement principle—that is, the meritocratic principle according to which inequality of outcomes is legitimate as long as it reflects unequal use of equal opportunity—from the market to the school. In light of the dominance of monopoly capital in advanced capitalism, especially in the main growth sectors of the economy, this principle can no longer be credibly applied to the market itself. Shifting it to the school is intended to justify inequality of outcomes in personal fortune by arguing that, because qualifications are increasingly important for hiring in bureaucratic firms, equality of opportunity in a competitive schooling system is sufficient to legitimate the occupational structure.

Habermas does not place too much weight on this principle, however, arguing instead that, although this may help to secure the loyalty of "the achievement-oriented" middle classes, both the "Protestant ethic" of the bourgeoisie and the "fatalism of the lower classes" continue, in part, to rely on eroding "religious traditions." Recall, as well, that Habermas argued that the school could only support the ideological burden of the meritocratic principle on the condition that (a) there is equal access to the relevant levels of education; (b) success within the school is determined in accord with nonprejudicial methods of evaluation; (c) the development of the educational and occupational systems remain coordinated; and (d) the material structure of labor processes allow for evaluation according to the standpoint of individual achievement. Although he claims—quite controversially—that significant advances have been made with respect to the first two conditions, he notes that schooling and occupational success have become uncoupled as a result of the hyper-expansion of education, in a way that ultimately threatens the meritocratic premise. And, finally, he believes that changes in the occupational sphere are rendering problematic individualistic assessments of achievement as the basis for occupational status. Moreover, even in the traditional professions—for example, medicine, law, and teaching—the labor process is increasingly rationalized and fragmented, undermining the meaningfulness of work and the ability of occupation to support the sort of strong identifications formerly typical of the middle class. As a result, instrumentalist attitudes toward labor are spreading throughout the occupational hierarchy, which is relevant to the possibility of a motivation crisis.

Interference of the State in Schooling as an Example of the Pathologies of the Welfare State

Foreshadowing the central critical thesis of *The Theory of Communicative Action*, Habermas argued in *Legitimation Crisis* that the interventions of the welfare state on behalf of capital have the perverse effect of eroding, by bringing to consciousness, elements of tradition on which capitalism parasitically draws. He cites the "administrative processing of cultural tradition in educational planning, especially curriculum planning," as an example of this.[3] Perhaps the clearest instance of such thematization occurred subsequent to the writing of *Legitimation Crisis*: the struggle over multicultural education. The formal regulation and standardization of curriculum poses the question of the legitimacy of the use of schooling for the inculcation of the dominant culture or the dominant cultural perspective on history, and so on. The thematization of educational techniques and dominant cultural traditions occurs in part because schools are increasingly "competing with family upbringing" in the early and formative socialization of children. Although the family obviously continues to be an important influence on the relation the child takes up toward schooling itself, the temporal extension of formal education increases the importance of the school in the cultivation of those attitudes toward work and achievement that are necessary for social reproduction, in many ways supplanting the family in this respect.

Economically or Politically "Dysfunctional" Schooling as Contributing to the Likelihood of a Motivational Crisis

The temporal extension of schooling is also considered by Habermas to be a factor increasing the chances of a motivation crisis. Specifically, its extension over the duration of the adolescent years postpones the need for a definitive resolution of the adolescent crisis. As a result, this resolution eventually occurs in circumstances of improved intellectual competence, such that the probability is increased that young people will themselves see through conventional patterns of interpretation to the disjunctive reality beneath—thus, it increases the probability of a dysfunctional, postconventional outcome. Surely time itself is not enough, however, and so one would suspect that this outcome depends rather heavily on the nature of socialization in the school.

As a matter of historical fact, the sort of resistance anticipated in *Legitimation Crisis* failed to materialize. But as Raymond Morrow and Carlos Alberto Torres note, in the colonization thesis, *The Theory of Communicative Action* offers a mechanism for explaining this failure: "the suppression of potential resistance is traced to the processes related to the colonization of the lifeworld by bureaucratic power and commodification. . . . 'Everyday consciousness is robbed of its power to synthesize; it becomes fragmented.' "[4] Habermas in this way identifies the sphere of socialization as the primary point of entry into the lifeworld of the imperatives of subsystems and, thus, suggests that such interference is the primary means by which the attainment of postconventionality—the basis for social transformation—is forestalled.

In *The Theory of Communicative Action*, in other words, Habermas argues that the legal regulation of the school, and its role in the legitimation of capitalism—manifested in the way that "the school palpably takes over the functions of assigning job and life prospects"[5]—is an example of the illegitimate encroachment of money and power on a domain of life that relies on informal, communicative regulation. This argument is a curious one in that it reaffirms Habermas' argument in *Legitimation Crisis* that the school assumes the burden of a meritocratic justification of the capitalist occupational structure and yet, as discussed in Chapter 2, this servicing of capital is now somchow carried out through the ostensibly good intentions of bureaucratic actors, who seek to protect "the welfare of the child" and "equal opportunity" regardless of gender and race; to protect children from teachers and administrators; to guarantee that the selection and measurement processes that are increasingly relevant to the occupational fate of children are made "accessible to judicial review."[6] This apparent ambiguity may reflect (I suspect quite unintentionally) a real tension in the forces exerted on the school by parents and administrators. But, good intentions notwithstanding, where the legal regulation of the school goes beyond the provision of external protections and so interferes with the inherently communicative process of teaching, "functional disturbances arise and, notably, teachers and students, as "legal subjects," more and more confront one "in an objectivizing, success-oriented attitude."[7]

The crucial advance of this formulation is to better specify with *what* the extension of economic imperatives interferes; that is, if, as appears to be the case in *Legitimation Crisis*, the function of the school is exhausted in its relationship to the occupational structure, then it is hard to see what would make the use of the school for the aims of capital realization morally or politically suspect per se (we might well think those aims suspect, as I do, but the involvement of the school would be of no separate concern). Here, however, by identifying the school as an institution rooted in the lifeworld, dependent on the presupposition of a communicative orientation for its functioning, Habermas has developed the resources for a specifically educational critique of the *colonization* of the school. Litigation-proof grades and promotion procedures, the proliferation of high-stakes standardized testing as a measure for both teacher and student performance, the administrative regulation of curricula—all undermine the communicative freedom on which the pedagogical relationship depends. Depersonalization, abstraction, rote learning, become the central features of an increasingly strategic context in which students and teachers pursue the maintenance or enhancement of their respective positions. The U.S. "No Child Left Behind" Act is quintessential in this regard: a high-stakes testing regime linked to the threat of privatization of schools, loss of job security for teachers who are not fully performing, and their effective deskilling through the proliferation of scripted lesson plans produced by textbook companies guaranteeing better performance on standardized tests.[8]

On the whole, although the significance of the school with respect to a meritocratic legitimation of the occupational system is less fore-grounded in *The Theory of Communicative Action*, Habermas does suggestively argue in one place that, while the decolonization—that is, the dejuridification—of child-custody regulations, for example, may be relatively unproblematic,

> [f]or a public domain such as the schools, the analogous demand for deregulation and debureaucratization meets with resistance. The call for a more strictly pedagogical approach to instruction and for a democratization of decision-making structures is not immediately compatible with the neutralization of the citizen's role: it is even less compatible with the economic system-imperative to uncouple the school from the fundamental right to education and to close-circuit it with the employment system.[9]

This is precisely why the school is such an interesting institution relative to the attempt to test Habermas' social theory: It finds itself squarely at the reproductive crossroads of media-steered subsystems and the lifeworld. Indeed, this is the crucial element of Habermas' social theory for my proposed integration of research trends in the sociology of schooling: The identification of socialization, social integration, and cultural reproduction as analytically distinct but practically intertwined reproductive processes of the lifeworld, each also intertwined with and affected by its material reproduction—ensured by the differentiated subsystems of economy and state—provide four dimensions in which the social function of the school may be specified. These dimensions, as I argue here, seem to correlate to existing research findings in the sociology of schooling that themselves are often overgeneralized and so remain unintegrated with insights derived from other analytical perspectives. The merit of approaching the question from a Habermasian perspective is that, not only does his social theory gain support, supplementation, as well as critical modification from this research, but it allows us to demonstrate the complex interrelations between the competing functions of the school and, crucially, to see the practical consequence of this competition for the socialization of individuals and future citizens, as well as for the integration of society. The rootedness of the reproductive processes of the lifeworld in communicative action, and the role of the school in these processes, makes it possible (as it is often not in the sociology of schooling, even where critically oriented) to defend the claim that pedagogical or educational action is inherently, if counterfactually, communicative (i.e., nonstrategic, cooperative). Put simply, learning is contingent on an orientation to understanding. Finally, such an approach makes room for the necessary accommodation of the agency of teachers and students that, as we will see, is often implausibly trivialized by structuralist and functionalist educational sociology. Before I explain this proposal in more detail, let me simply note one final observation Habermas makes of the school.

It will not surprise the reader, given the argument of Chapter 2, that Habermas has had least to say about the school in his most recent work. Although he recurs again and again to the need for practices and institutions of socialization to meet postconventional social and legal structures halfway, he no longer makes any attempt to deal seriously with the reality or absence of these prerequisites. In *Between Facts and Norms*, he merely registers his support for Parsons' assessment of the significance of the "educational revolution," the pursuit of universal education which, although declared in the Enlightenment to be a condition on inclusive processes of democratic will formation, was not institutionalized until the first half of the twentieth century.[10] In what is now only the faintest trace of the claim that the school plays a crucial legitimating function through its purportedly meritocratic structure—a claim made by Parsons without irony—Habermas notes that the educational revolution combines the demand of the industrial revolution for equal opportunity (by the transference of the achievement principle from the market to the school) and the demand of the democratic revolution for equality of citizenship (through universal enrollment).[11]

To summarize the foregoing, then: The school is more than merely a potential example for the testing and illumination of Habermas' theory. The implication of the school in the reproductive processes of the lifeworld—socialization, social integration, and cultural reproduction—and in the reproduction and legitimation of the subsystems of economy and state, pick it out as one of the central institutions through which his claims regarding the relationship between lifeworld and subsystems, culture, society, and individuals, should be vindicated. Moreover, not only must his descriptive claims prove true in the school, but his normative proposals should help explain, on the one hand, what is unjust about colonization and, on the other, how social transformation is encouraged or forestalled by changes to the process of socialization. The first step toward making this argument, however, is undoubtedly the least pleasant: As one might suspect, not only do sociologists disagree among themselves regarding the dominant function of the school, but they do not even agree on a standard set of terms for discussing these functions. Additionally, despite the widespread acceptance of "schools of thought" regarding the school (e.g., functionalism, conflict theory, etc.), almost no writer of any sophistication fits without qualification into a single category. In what follows, then, I first present a rather stereotypical summary of the main research trends, before moving on to discuss the work of specific authors who fall somewhere between these clean, categorical lines. These caveats duly registered, it would not be implausible to say that there are three principal approaches to the sociology of schooling: (a) functionalist or technocratic accounts, (b) structuralist or conflict theoretical accounts, and (c) interpretivist or hermeneutical accounts.

Dominant Perspectives in the Sociology of the School

Functionalist and Technocratic Sociologies of the School

This approach includes thinkers like Parsons, Luhmann, and Jeffrey Alexander; Durkheim typically is regarded as its founder. Three elements of Durkheim's sociology have become crucial premises for functionalism in education:

> First, he advanced the historical thesis that changes in educational systems were the causal consequence of external social and economic changes in society as a whole . . . Second, he asserted that the specific characteristics of educational structures and their cultural contents had a strong functional relationship with the needs of society—as defined by the groups concerned—for cultural integration and a specialized division of labour. . . . Third, he asserted that, as a consequence of the transition from mechanical to organic solidarity . . . greater individuation was necessary and that this was expressed in shifts in pedagogy and school organization.[12]

Although he was acutely aware of the contradictory aspects of the division of labor, functionalism from Parsons on gave near exclusive emphasis to the conservative elements of Durkheim's thought, ignoring these conflicts and contradictions as well as the "very truncated conception of individuation implied by his theory of socialization."[13] The focus, instead, was on the "needs" of society and on social stability.

Parsons, for instance, analyzed the school in terms of four functions:

1. An academic function, through which the school cultivated the cognitive skills required for a variety of social and economic tasks;
2. A distributive function, through which the school competitively selects and prepares individuals for certain social and economic roles;

3. An economic function, through which the school, especially through the expansion of higher education, promotes economic growth by increasing the productive skills of future laborers; and
4. A political socialization function, through which the school socializes individuals with an eye to social integration and social control.

In this last connection, functionalists often have linked social integration to the cultivation by the school of a "single, national identity," conceived of (in accordance with historical fact, to be sure) as the assimilation of minorities to the dominant culture. Even within the majority culture, however, a broadening of loyalties and a kind of standardization has been necessary. Depending on the functionalist in question, this process is seen as meeting the legitimation needs either for democratic decision making or for redistributive measures aimed at social stability. By and large, however, on closer examination, the sort of integration envisioned is more accurately characterized as system integration; indeed, there is very little of anyone's culture in the final product. Socialization for integration refers to conformity with the "meritocratic, bureaucratic, and individualistic form of life that is associated with modern society and is viewed as a prerequisite for technological and economic development."[14] Cultural assimilation, in other words, at bottom refers to a conception of "modernization": "Assimilation involves, among other things, a change in the wants of the members of newer groups. Modernization presupposes just such a change in wants. After all, a meritocracy depends on people wanting what it offers as rewards."[15] So political socialization and integration appear to be reduced to the function of cultivating an acceptance of media according to which the capitalist pattern of systemic integration operates.

The distinctive claim on which criticisms of functionalist accounts of the school center is its endorsement of meritocracy. Parsons' argument in this respect goes as follows: Individuals have, at birth, an ascribed status based on the socioeconomic standing of their family, as well as their personal gender and the order of birth among siblings. Education understood as a system incrementally transforms this ascribed status into a competitively and justly acquired one. Crucial to this is the (patently outlandish) claim that children enter primary schooling "relatively homogenous in terms of socioeconomic status and age," and so the competitive trial of the school is initiated under circumstances of "equal opportunity."[16] A number of structural, systemic features of the school encourage this transition: Because of the number of students in the class, particularistic treatment of pupils is precluded, and the teacher necessarily has relatively generic expectations regarding the academic potential of students.[17] As a result, the students are accustomed to universal expectations taking precedence over emotional bonds (a notable break with socialization in the family); the changing of teachers each year teaches the child to distinguish between the role of the teacher and the person of any particular teacher, which similarly promotes the adoption of generalized models of behavior. The cumulative result is a displacement of the orientation to ascriptive status by an orientation to achieved status based on grades, qualifications, and academic success. Parsons portrays this, moreover, as a *shared* orientation to certain meritocratic values that safeguards integration even when status stratification emerges on the basis of achievement, because this status is taken by all to be rational and just. The secondary school then solidifies educational differentiation on the basis of achievement, and streams students accordingly toward terminal, vocationally oriented studies, or to university education. The university is described as a "cognitive complex" that not only reinforces the meritocratic pattern of society, but furthers its increasingly cognitive culture. The most important role of the university in this respect is the reproduction of the academic professions themselves. In addition, however, the university educates and continues to socialize young people, supports the development and inculcation of applied knowledge relevant for the professions and, in times of crisis, may provide "intellectual definitions of critical problems for the culture and society."[18]

Parsons, and functionalists following him, give little evidence of concern that the stratification of higher levels of education may simply offer a stamp of legitimacy to inherited inequalities of status by filtering them through the educational process: Their crucial thesis is that schooling provides a just selection procedure for meeting economic needs, and that higher qualifications indeed reflect greater potential productivity (which is the specifically technocratic premise). To the extent that evidence is undeniable of persistent correlations between academic achievement and family socioeconomic status, as well as gender and race, functionalists dogmatically invoke a kind of implicit philosophy of ineluctable progress: Such evidence is explained away as the persistence of *pre*modern obstacles (which is tautologous with respect to racism and sexism, given the functionalists' equation of modernity with achieved status) or as institutional inertia which unfortunately impedes the progress of societal rationalization. As critics have frequently observed, however, this *a priori* link drawn between the function of the school and the needs of society as a whole precludes the possibility of asking whom these "impediments" and apparent "failures" of meritocracy might serve: If there is no society-as-a-whole with determinate needs, but instead a plurality of groups whose interests and needs are mutually antagonistic, then the question becomes, which part of society has its needs served by the school? This is the premise of structuralist and conflict-theoretical sociologies of the school.

Before I turn to them, let me note one additional problematic feature of functionalist theories: At the methodological level, they are in danger of a fallacy of teleological explanation. The argument is that the school operates in the way it does *in order* to meet the needs of the economy; but careful documentation is required of any reproduction theory to explain causally how these outcomes are achieved, how these functions are served, through the mediation of daily life in the school, school policy, and so on. All too often, this careful analysis has been lacking in both functionalist and structuralist theories; it is a main theme in my own discussion here.

Structuralist and Conflict Theoretical Sociologies of the School

This broad category of approaches conceals considerable diversity. Perhaps the dominant version of conflict theory has been Marxist, but included here as well are some feminists, critical race theorists, cultural reproduction theorists (like Pierre Bourdieu), and Foucaultean sociologists.[19] The connection to structuralism is more or less loose, depending on the thinker in question. In general, the common suspicion is that the surface phenomena of the school are limited and shaped by a deeper organization or system of relations.[20] For instance, the neo-Marxist sociologists Samuel Bowles and Herbert Gintis, in what is arguably the classic of structuralist-conflict theory, argue that there is a relationship of "correspondence" between the social relations of the school and the social relations of production, such that socialization in the former serves to reproduce the latter. In this light, it becomes clear that the "needs" served by socialization in the school are not those of "society," but of the dominant social class, the capitalist-bourgeoisie, and that, therefore, the migration of the meritocratic principle to the school is of ideological rather than real significance. Bourdieu, though a conflict theorist and, in some sense, a structuralist, does not begin from Marxist premises. His theory of social reproduction through cultural reproduction holds that the stratifying structures of the school serve to confirm, reinforce, and legitimize the superiority of those who possess "cultural capital." By the latter, Bourdieu and his early co-author, Jean-Claude Passeron, mean culturally rooted status markers, such as language and speech patterns, modes of dress, and so on. These elements cumulatively constitute a kind of code, or "habitus" through which individuals interpret their experience and communicate. The argument is that these codes are class-differentiated, but that the pedagogical practices of the schools—in particular of those streams of the schooling system that actually promise the possibility of mobility—employ the code of the socially dominant class. This has several consequences: academic success is far easier for those of high socioeconomic background whose family socialization also employed this high-status code; as a result of this academic success, these privileged individuals go on to inherit the socioeconomic privileges of their parents; most students from lower-class backgrounds will find education alienating and difficult, and will either drop out or fail; and those who remain will be overselected for conformity to the cultural norms of the dominant class. Yet because the school presents itself as a culturally neutral, meritocratic selection mechanism, based on standardized testing and fair grading procedures, it has the effect of convincing those excluded of the legitimacy of their exclusion and of the real superiority of the values represented by the school.[21] Thus, here, too, the meritocratic claims of the school are ideological. However, unlike Marxist conflict theory, Bourdieu does not address the relationship between the structure of schooling and production, but focuses instead on the effects of the cultural embeddedness of educational socialization. A similar approach is employed by critical race theorists and feminists, as well as by proponents of multicultural reform of curriculum, who have attempted to extend reproduction theory to subordinated groups other than class, and to investigate the way in which the school is implicated in reproducing gender, racial, and ethnic inequality.

Interpretivist Sociology of the School

In general, interpretivist (or hermeneutic) sociology of the school is less interested in offering global accounts of the role or function of the school in society than in "the culture-bound framework of particular schools and the ways individuals understand and act in specific social contexts."[22] The idea is to uncover the "language-games" operative in particular schooling situations, both as understood by participants and as manifested in the practices themselves, which reflect "shared systems of meanings" that may not be consciously accessible to any given participant. These investigations take on socioscientific significance through the observation that the process of active interpretation, as described by hermeneuticists from Dilthey to Gadamer, is itself a process of socialization: As Gadamer indicates with his notion of the "fusion of horizons," interpretation does not leave the interpreter unchanged. A number of researchers who adopt this perspective in fact eschew the term *socialization* in light of its connotations of passivity. In contrast to some orthodox Marxist accounts in particular, in which subjects appears as little more than empty vessels to be filled with ideology "as a container is filled with water,"[23] interpretivists argue that by accounting for the participation of subjects in their own socialization, we are better able to appreciate the evident variety of beliefs and attitudes among individuals socialized in the same culture and institutions. What these individuals share, according to the interpretivist, is not a set of necessary beliefs or attitudes, but "a structure of intelligibility that enables communication and intersubjective understanding to take place and provides a foundation for shared commitments to be expressed."[24] The competence for interpretation that facilitates this communication does not entail the unqualified acceptance of proposed contents; rather, individuals have the capacity to reject certain proposals, for example, of the school culture.

For the interpretivist, then, the "function" of the school is to cultivate the shared social structure of intelligibility. In a sense, neither the functionalist nor the Marxist or structuralist would necessarily reject this view. But they would want to put certain qualifications on it that the interpretivist doesn't and, in some cases, won't allow. For example, functionalists, structuralists, and Marxists maintain that the social rules and interpretations in question can themselves be explained by more fundamental, objective social mechanisms related to the given social formation: Functionalists see socialization as encouraging children to acquire knowledge of, and to shape their desires in accordance with, the rules that actually govern modern, bureaucratic, individualistic societies; Marxists, on the other hand, see socialization in the school as fostering desires and interpretations among at least certain classes of young people that conceal the actual workings of modern, capitalist societies. In order to decide between these hypotheses, we would need to know what the real practices of society are, apart from the interpretations; but that is precisely what the interpretivist will not allow.[25] Nevertheless, interpretivism in educational sociology has done a great service to social theory by demonstrating the importance of hermeneutical methods for an adequate explanation of how the macro-sociological processes identified by functionalism and conflict theory operate through the agency of individuals.

In what follows, I first relate Habermas' account of the four reproductive processes of society to the research strategies just outlined, both in order to settle on the terms to be employed here and to suggest that they capture the sense of the terms employed by others. To put it simply, there appears to be a consensus in sociology that everyone else's perspective is one-sided or overgeneralized; and indeed, this critique appears roundly well deserved, if we consider only the stereotypical representations so far discussed. The problem with functionalism is that it overgeneralizes the needs served by education, linking them to "society as a whole"; the problem with Marxist conflict theory (as well as Bourdieu's non-Marxist version) is that it is overgeneralized, allowing of only one dimension of conflict (class, or social class); and the problem with interpretivism is that it is overgeneralized in that it screens out all systemic imperatives constraining possible interpretations in favor of an unqualified hermeneuticism. Integrating these perspectives into the reproductive processes identified by Habermas allows us to recast these differences as a matter of emphasis.

First, all forms of education, and all accounts of the school, include a dominant place for socialization so that there is no theory of socialization in the school that is independent of a theory regarding its purpose or aim.

Functionalist and class-oriented conflict theorists agree that the overriding purpose of this socialization is systemic integration, the reproduction of the occupational/economic system—although their descriptive agreement on this general point occurs across an inverted estimation of the legitimacy of this reproduction. Similarly, cultural reproduction theorists, including feminists, critical race theorists, and proponents of multicultural schooling, as well as interpretivist sociologists, share an estimation of the importance of the school for cultural reproduction. Socialization is, as Habermas says, crucial for ensuring that upcoming generations receive the interpretive competencies needed to draw on and renew their cultural traditions, whereas cultural tradition in turn guides the establishment of goals for education that ensure that "individual life histories are in harmony with collective forms of life."[26] Feminists, critical race theorists, and multiculturalists, as well as cultural reproduction theorists like Bourdieu, argue that what is reproduced here are patterns of subordination and exclusion and, since they too recognize a connection between the school and the economy, this exclusion has material consequences for those affected. Interpretative sociologists, on the other hand, see this function of cultural reproduction as overlapping with the maintenance of social integration. In this, many follow a certain conservative, communitarian-nationalist view of schooling that has its roots in Hegel, according to which socialization in the school immerses the young person in their national culture, in the *Sittlichkeit* that mediates the mutual recognition between citizens. Social integration among the adult population is, in this sense, manufactured by shared socialization in a nationalist educational system.

John Dewey, who was sharply critical of what he considered to be the nationalist instrumentalization of education in Hegel, insists on the separation of cultural reproduction and social integration, and argues that socialization should serve the latter.[27] That is, education in the school should socialize individuals for forward-looking social integration in democratic society, should give them the resources needed to perceive the legitimacy of democratic processes of decision making, and so on. Of course, social integration plays a role in all the other theories as well, for example, in the transformed guise of system integration in functionalism and Marxism. According to various conflict theories, the school cultivates the attitudes and orientations in light of which the responsibility for social exclusion and inequality can be convincingly laid on the doorstep of the excluded and, in so doing, maintains levels of legitimation required for the integration of society.

Thus, although the terminology differs, it is possible to reformulate the main insights of diverse trends in the sociology of schooling in terms of the concepts of socialization, social/system integration, cultural reproduction, and material reproduction. Moreover, it is patent that schools play a role in all four functions; indeed, it is patent that a role for the school in each of these dimensions is inescapable. Multicultural disputes over the role of the school in cultural reproduction do not argue for its abolishment, but for its transformation in favor of greater inclusiveness and justice of representation. However, what the effective politicization of the issue of multiculturalism has entailed is that, in any society committed to multiculturalism—any society that explicitly rejects a policy of assimilation—the goal of social integration can no longer be unproblematically pursued directly through cultural reproduction. The school in a multicultural society cannot manufacture integration in the manner called for by Hegelians and conservative communitarians (who are, in any case, typically opposed to multiculturalism). I want to postpone now, until the Concluding Reflections, discussion of the form this integration must instead take, since it will first require an investigation of the significance of multiculturalism itself. Let me just note that it will entail distinguishing, as Habermas failed to do in *Legitimation Crisis*, between social integration in the sense of mutual recognition between contemporary consociates, and social integration in the sense of individuals and societies as a whole seeing their identity as historically continuous. The latter, we can now say, rests on a conflation of social integration and cultural reproduction. In this chapter, I nevertheless examine the relationship between the operations of the economy and issues of race, gender, and ethnicity, as they are mediated by the school; in this way, we can begin to test the hypotheses of Habermas and Fraser discussed in Chapter 2.

In light of the conclusions of this chapter, then, I go on in the Concluding Reflections to answer the question of the relationship between socialization and both social integration and cultural reproduction in multicultural societies. That discussion relies, as well, on the more detailed account of the subject provided in Chapters 3 and 4; but, inversely, it is in part the need for a better account of the way in which social forces are mediated by and expressed in individual agency—a need that is revealed over the course of this chapter—which demands, first, the more detailed discussion of subjectivity. So that leaves us here with the question of material reproduction. Accordingly, I want to consider primarily the work of Bowles and Gintis as well that of Jean Anyon and Paul Willis; both of the latter authors take important lessons from the ethnographic orientation of interpretivist sociology, while insisting that this does not preclude links to macro-level sociological theory (which is to say that, like Habermas, they want to maintain the independence and interrelation of system and lifeworld). In this way, Anyon and Willis save reproduction theory from the pitfalls of teleological explanation, by offering detailed analyses of interaction within the school that demonstrate how the reproductive "needs" of the capitalist economy are met through the mediation of the actions of teachers and students.

Schooling in Capitalist America: The Correspondence Principle

At first glance, Bowles and Gintis offer an analysis of the schooling system in the United States that very closely parallels both Habermas' specific comments on the school in *Legitimation Crisis*, as well as more generally complementing his social theory there. For instance, they argue that the education system serves two central functions in the material reproduction of society: First, it aids in the increase of the productivity of labor, both by providing technical skills and by cultivating appropriate social skills and motivations; second, it helps to legitimize the general form of material reproduction as capitalist, and the specific acceptability of the private appropriation of surplus value, by depoliticizing class relations (largely through its own claim to serve as an individualistic, meritocratic selection mechanism).[28] But, in the end, the authors turn out to be far less convinced of the straightforwardness of that first, technocratic claim, which is also endorsed by Habermas: namely, that education increases technical qualifications in ways that result in increased productivity. In fact, the main critical target of their book is liberal educational theory, including Progressivism as defended by Dewey as well as the technocratic theories common today, both of which argue that, in light of this connection to productivity, it is therefore possible to employ school reform directly as a means of bringing about socioeconomic equality under capitalism. Before discussing in greater detail how the school performs the reproductive functions described by Bowles and Gintis, it is instructive to consider first the error of these alternatives.

Dewey identifies three functions for the school, putting his own spin on the same broad functions I have identified via Habermas: (a) to integrate young people into a variety of adult roles in the economy, family, and political society; (b) to ensure that all individuals have equal opportunity to succeed in society (the meritocratic-egalitarian function); and (c) to promote the psychic and moral development of young people (the socialization function, here normatively aligned with self-fulfillment). Dewey is representative of the specifically liberal tradition in that he not only endorses all three functions but, in *Democracy and Education*, argues for their mutual implication. The plausibility of this argument rests on three assumptions, each of which is demonstrated by Bowles and Gintis to be false:

> [1] he assumed that occupational roles in capitalist society are best filled by individuals who have achieved the highest possible levels of personal development. For Dewey, personal development is economically productive . . . [2] Dewey assumed that a free and universal school system can render the opportunities for self-development independent of race, ethnic origins, class

> background and sex. Hence, the integrative, egalitarian, and development functions of schooling are not only compatible, they are mutually supportive.[29]

And, finally, [3] Dewey assumed that the social institutions of U.S. society were democratic in character. Since self-development, for Dewey, meant autonomy in the sense of gaining insight into and control over one's relationships, it is expressed in democratic self-determination and in the private use made of equal opportunity.

The immediately obvious problem is Dewey's radically distorted appraisal of the nature of the institutions of contemporary capitalist society. In fact, however, Dewey recognized that the occupational structure, into which young people were to be integrated by the school, was deeply alienating and unfulfilling, sharply incompatible with the ideals of self-fulfillment. But his solution to this problem was also quintessentially liberal: he attributes the stunted nature of modern labor to a "one-sided stimulation of thought" on the part of the captains of industry, which has led them to reduce their focus to efficiency and scientific management alone. For this problem, education is again the answer: By cultivating "well-balanced interests" on the part of social and economic elites, education can bring them to see the importance of human relationships in production while, on the other hand, the education of workers will inspire in them a new interest in sharing in control over their circumstances.[30] Bowles and Gintis conclude "[h]ere Dewey exhibits in raw form the liberal proclivity to locate the source of systemic failures [e.g., the inherent drive for the maximization of profit and control] in the shortcomings of individuals and to propose 'expert' solutions which respect—even reinforce—the top-down control of social life under corporate capitalism."[31] This strategy becomes a "fundamental tenet" of Progressive educators; namely, that education could be a means for promoting an internally motivated humanization of industrial work, thus bringing its integrative and socializing functions into line.[32] Although the ideal is indeed worthy, it could hardly be in starker contrast to the reality of a capitalist occupational structure that is hierarchical and autocratic, rather than democratic; which relies on extrinsic motivation on the basis of sanctions (the threat of unemployment) and rewards (wages, promotion), rather than on the intrinsic motivation characteristic of the pursuit of self-fulfillment. There is some truth to the defense often made of Dewey's program: that Progressivism, as he defended it, was never actually tried in practice, that progressive reforms were historically co-opted by the school of scientific management *ala* Frederick Taylor, which remade education in the image of bureaucracy; which recruited administrators from the business world rather than from academia; which made efficiency and cost-saving paramount; which made teachers into workers and students into consumers. But notwithstanding this truth, Bowles and Gintis argue that there is a more fundamental problem: The goals identified for education by Progressives like Dewey himself are contradictory under the conditions of an unreformed capitalism.

According to the technocratic view, although the functions identified by Dewey may not be mutually implicating, they are at least compatible. Such thinkers see the economy as a technical system in which successful work performance is based on technical competence. Levels of income reflect levels of productivity, and so inequalities with respect to income and status in turn reflect the empirical distribution of the skills relevant to given occupations.[33] The socialization function of the school, then, is related to the acquisition of knowledge and skills; beneath the correlation of years of schooling with levels of income, the technocrat postulates the competence-based increase in potential productivity. So long as the opportunity for such development is extended equally to all, the resultant inequalities in society are legitimate on meritocratic grounds: Because evaluation in the school is—as in the labor market—meritocratic, credentials serve as reliable indicators of talent and thus their correlation with income and status is similarly just. Inversely, the persistence of forms of unjust inequality can only be the result of unequal opportunity for entrance into the technical system. And while, in line with Durkheim's functionalist premise regarding the extrinsic source of school reform, the technocrat interprets the rise of mass schooling as a response to the increasingly complex and cognitively demanding occupational sphere in industrialized societies, this transformation simultaneously entails that higher levels of the occupational hierarchy are opened up to those with the ability and willingness to attain the requisite qualifications: "Hence, the increasing economic importance of mental skills [more or less accidentally] enhances the power of a fundamentally egalitarian school system to equalize economic opportunity."[34] In light of the continuing prominence of this argument, which is, in a sense, *the* form of the legitimating idea of meritocracy today, I follow Bowles and Gintis in dealing with it in detail, while updating their data in places. This enables us to begin to accumulate evidence for considering the factual relationship between the school and the task of the material reproduction of society, especially of the capitalist occupational structure.

The first, at least intuitively problematic, issue encountered by the technocrat is the strong correlation between the length of education attained by an individual and parental socioeconomic status: "If we define socioeconomic background by a weighted sum of income, occupation, and educational levels of the parents, a child from the ninetieth percentile may expect, on the average, five more years of schooling than a child in the tenth percentile."[35] Individuals in the lowest income brackets at the time of Bowles and Gintis' study were more than six times as likely not to attend college than those in the upper brackets; and those from lower-class families were not only more likely to drop out of high school, but they were also more likely to attend an inexpensive two-year community college rather than a four-year bachelor's program, if they made it to college at all.[36] At the same time, data collected by the U.S. Office of Education indicated that among white high school students, those whose parents were highly educated—which is a dominant factor in socioeconomic background—also tended to outperform their peers in terms of academic achievement. The technocrat might thus argue that the greater likelihood that those from higher social classes will attend college simply reflects the factual distribution of cognitive ability. But, as Bowles and Gintis demonstrate,

> [t]his view is unsupported by the data. . . . [E]ven among children with identical IQ test scores at ages six and eight, those with rich, well-educated, high-status parents could expect a much higher level of schooling than those with less-favoured origins . . . [O]nly a small portion of the observed social class difference in educational attainment is related to IQ differences across social classes.[37]

Thus, as I have mentioned, individuals from the top socioeconomic decile are, on average, likely to receive five additional years of schooling as compared with those in the lowest decile; but the former are still likely to receive 4.25 more years of schooling than the latter, even when the individuals compared attained identical test scores. The same pattern is evidenced with respect to both rates of college enrollment and rates of college graduation. As the sociologist Steven Brint confirms (in 2006), "the correlations between fathers' social status and children's educational attainments has remained roughly constant over time—and the reproduction of family social status with the help of schooling has become, over the last quarter of a century [i.e., since Bowles and Gintis' writing], if anything somewhat more common."[38]

The meritocratic view of school promotion appears to be falsified by the evidence. But that is not the whole issue because schooling is nevertheless correlated with economic success. Brint notes that the disparity between those with higher and those with lower educational attainments is most pronounced today in the United States, in which a college graduate earns on average 86 percent more than a worker with only a high school diploma. In other nations, the figure is around 50 percent.[39] The technocrat attempts to explain this fact by reference to the acquisition of productivity-enhancing technical competence. In the case of white males, however, at least one-third of this correlation actually is attributable to the common correlation of both years of schooling and economic success with socioeconomic background. In other words, "people whose parents have higher-status economic positions tend to achieve more income themselves, independent of their education, but they also tend to get more education."[40] And, once again—with the exception of the far extremes of the IQ distribution and test score curve—the dollar pay-off for each year of education in terms of future income is, at best, "tenuously" related to IQ.[41] If this is the case with white males, what about everyone else?

> In 1940, most black male workers (but a minority of whites) earned their livelihoods in the South, by far the poorest region; the education gap between nonwhites and whites was 3.3. years (38 percent of median white education). By 1972, blacks had moved to more affluent parts of the country, and the education gap was reduced to 18 percent (4 percent for young men aged 25-34 years). Richard Freeman has shown that this narrowing of the education gap would have virtually achieved black/white income equality had blacks received the same benefits from education as whites. Yet the income gap has not closed substantially: The income gap for young men is 30 percent, despite an education gap of only 4 percent. Clearly, as blacks have moved toward educational (and regional) parity with whites, other mechanisms—such as entrapment in city-centre ghettos, the suburbanization of jobs, and perhaps increasing segmentation of labor markets—have intensified to maintain a more or less constant degree of racial income inequality.[42]

Bowles and Gintis do not at all deny that African Americans suffer educational inequality: As expensive college-level education has become the norm, the trend has in fact been toward increasing inequality. Brint confirms that "the age of increasing educational opportunity ended around 1980." Although college enrollments have continued to expand, racial and class inequalities in graduation rates have been on the rise as well: "For African Americans who enrolled in college [already a highly selected group], graduation rates in the later 1980s fell to about half the rate of whites."[43] Importantly, however, Bowles and Gintis maintain that the source of broader social and economic exploitation lies outside education, "in a system of economic power and privilege in which racial distinctions play an important role."[44] The same pattern is evidenced more dramatically still in the case of gender, where female enrollment, academic performance, and graduation levels have surpassed that of males (although still unequally distributed across faculties), without leading to the equalization of income and occupational status levels that the technocratic argument necessarily predicts.[45] Here, too, the operations of the school seem to serve other aims, and economic and social inequality to result from mechanisms other than differential use of equal educational opportunity. Across the board, the number of years of schooling depends as heavily as ever on socioeconomic background; and although the length of schooling has been generally extended, driven by extensions in the length of compulsory education, the pattern of relative disparity has remained constant.[46] In those cases where there has been an improvement in educational opportunity—as with African Americans and women—this has not resulted in meaningful narrowing of disparities in income.[47] General income inequalities are at their highest levels since the so-called roaring twenties, while the degree of wealth concentration is without parallel in the modern era. Although college enrollment has continued to expand, since 1980 "virtually all growth in the number of graduates came from the top quarter of the income structure. Graduation rates for students from the top quartile of family income approached 70 percent, but graduation rates from the second quartile of family income remained in the high 20 percent range."[48] This should hardly be surprising, given that tuition even at public colleges has risen at nearly three times the rate of inflation, far faster than the wages of all but the richest few.[49]

So, the technocratic argument cannot be sustained in the face of available evidence: Cognitive ability explains neither years of schooling, nor economic success; whatever it is about years of schooling that explains its correlation with socioeconomic status, it isn't that it results in greater technical competence. At the same time, this isn't to deny that modern economies in fact require skills acquired through education. The argument entails only that

> the mental skills demanded of workers are sufficiently limited, the skills produced by our educational system sufficiently varied, and the possibilities of acquiring additional skills on the job sufficiently great so that skill differences among individuals who are acceptable for a given job on the basis of other criteria including race, sex, personality, and credentials are of little economic import. At most levels in the occupational hierarchy mental skills are productive, but are not scarce, and hence do not bear a direct monetary return.[50]

At the same time, additional studies have suggested both that there is no evidence to indicate that more educated workers are more productive and that, in the face of massive deskilling extending even into the professions, many jobs today require less skill than they once did. These facts fly in the face of the most common invocation of the technocratic argument today: that disciplined school reform is indispensable for economic competitiveness in the new global economy, where the price of any shortfall in highly technical skills is "steep economic decline."[51] We will turn directly to consider the other relevant criteria, that is, to what is the *real* function of the school, according to Bowles and Gintis. But the first thing to note in this regard is that the schools themselves foster the notion that the economic success of the individual—and indeed, of society—is contingent on the acquisition of technical and cognitive skills that it is structured to provide in an efficient and meritocratic manner. And yet, as we have just seen, in reality the schooling system reliably reproduces a set of hierarchical economic and occupational relations—which are, at most, only partially linked to technical requirements—while simultaneously giving them the appearance of legitimacy and necessity. Thus, the authors conclude, "[t]he linking of technical skills to economic success via the educational system," that is, the transference of the meritocratic justification of capitalism from the market to the school, described by Habermas, "strengthens rather than weakens the legitimation process."[52]

Correspondence and Legitimation

It has been argued already that the evidence belies the explanatory connection posited by technocratic theorists between cognitive ability and economic success; the former explains neither the latter, nor its apparent heritability. What statistical correlation there remains between cognitive achievement and occupational success must therefore be seen as a "by-product of selection on the basis of other traits." Many readers already will be familiar with studies that reveal the astonishing degree to which personal appearance in either sex, or the height of a man, or his weight, will influence his likelihood of economic success.[53] Most people also will have some familiarity from their own experience with an apparently obvious point against the technocratic position: namely, that the majority of students—everyone save for the top 15 or 20 percent in academic performance—are focused almost exclusively on nonacademic interests, do not retain course content subsequent to testing, do not recall course material from their educational pasts, and recall their schooling in terms of teachers they did or did not like or, generally, as an opportunity to socialize with friends. Put bluntly, "schools do not actually succeed very well in transmitting the lessons of the curriculum."[54] Yet this is not to say that the schools effectively transmit nothing: Rather, it suggests we direct our attention to elements of school socialization beyond considerations of content for the real significance of education. In short, this fact points toward one of the crucial concepts of the sociology of schooling: The "hidden curriculum," the implicit messages built into the form of pedagogy, the nature of assignments, the organization of the classroom, etc., through which the attitudes and habits of students are shaped with respect to work, authority, and motivation. Bowles and Gintis write,

> [t]o capture the economic import of education, we must relate its social structure to the forms of consciousness, interpersonal behavior, and personality it fosters and reinforces in students. . . . The free-school movement and other related efforts to make education more conducive to full human development have assumed that the present school system is the product of irrationality, mindlessness, and social backwardness on the part of teachers, administrators, school boards, and parents. On the contrary, we believe the available evidence indicates that the pattern of social relationships fostered in schools is hardly irrational or accidental. Rather, the structure of the educational experience is admirably suited to nurturing attitudes and behavior consonant with participation in the labor force. Particularly dramatic is the statistically verifiable congruence between the personality traits conducive to proper work performance on the job and those which are rewarded with high grades in the classroom. . . . As long as one does not question the structure of the economy itself, the current structure of the schools seems eminently rational.[55]

This is the basis of the "correspondence" principle: Irrespective of the conscious intent of more or less progressive educators and administrators, the hierarchical form of social relations in the school—from administrators, to teachers, to students—accustoms students to subordination and so prefigures the workplace, the utter lack of control possessed by workers over the direction of their own energies, a motivational system that operates on the basis of external inducements and threats (with grades and failure corresponding to wages and the threat of dismissal) rather than on the intrinsic value of the activity (learning, understanding, self-development). Through the "correspondence" between the social relationships of the school and the capitalist occupational sphere, schools facilitate a smooth transition on the part of young people into the "workforce," in particular, by the way in which the ostensibly meritocratic basis of success and failure in the school feeds into the selection process whereby individuals are assigned to distinct positions in the occupational hierarchy. Thus, the school plays a key legitimating function for social inequality. But schools also accustom young people to their "proper" place in the hierarchy by reinforcing patterns of class, race, and sexual identification; schools socialize subjects in contexts of the same sorts of dominance and subordination that characterize the capitalist economy; and finally, they "create surpluses of skilled labor sufficiently extensive to render effective the prime weapon of the employer in disciplining labor—the power to hire and fire."[56] Let us look more closely at each of these economic functions, as described by Bowles and Gintis, which we can classify generally as follows: (a) motivational functions, including the socialization of students in conformity with a system of external motivation, and so on; and (b) legitimation functions, including the cultivation of an acceptance of domination and hierarchy that is differentiated according to class position, but also according to race, ethnicity, and gender.

Motivational Functions

Grades and the prospect of failure are the cornerstones of the motivational system of the school and research demonstrates that, independent of cognitive ability, students tend to be rewarded for performances that conform to and reinforce the social order of the school and are punished for violations of that order.[57] The school is not a meritocracy; or, if it is, the merit it rewards is behavioral rather than cognitive. In this connection, Bowles and Gintis cite (among others) John L. Holland's study of data gathered on 639 finalists for National Merit Scholarships, which included four measures of cognitive development employed in the College Entrance Examination Board tests and "sixty-five measures of personality, attitude, self-concept, creativity, and home-life," attained through testing and ratings from students, teachers, and parents. On the basis of Holland's data, they conclude:

> while the group's high academic rank is doubtless related to their above-average IQs . . . many of the personality variables were significantly and positively correlated to grades [and variations of grades within the group]. Most important were teachers' ratings of students' *Citizenship* [conformity to the social order of the school] and the students' self-evaluation of *Drive to Achieve* [personal motivation to succeed within this order]. Neither of these variables had any significant impact on actual achievement measures! . . . Students who are ranked by their teachers as high on *Citizenship* and *Drive to Achieve* are indeed more likely to be diligent (e.g., they are high on such measures as *Deferred Gratification*, *Perseverance*, and *Control*) and socially popular (e.g., they are high on *Social Leadership* and *Popularity*). But they are, in fact, significantly below average on measures of creativity and mental flexibility (e.g., they are low on such measures as *Cognitive Flexibility*, *Complexity of Thought*, *Originality*, *Creativity*, and *Independence of Judgment*). Moreover, further statistical analysis shows that these same traits of creativity and mental flexibility

> are directly penalized in terms of school grades, holding constant test scores, *Citizenship*, and *Drive to Achieve*. . . . The conclusions from this body of data seem inescapable. Conformity to the social order of the school involves submission to a set of authoritarian relationships which are inimical to personal growth.[58]

Although they characterize these conclusions as inescapable, they do not apply uniformly to the different groups of the school; rather, the form and extent of conformity demanded is refracted through the differential treatment of boys and girls, young women and young men, whites and blacks, rich and poor, high school and college students, and elite university and community college students. Of course, this is to be expected if the role of the school is to prepare individuals destined for all stations in a hierarchical occupational system. This brings us to the legitimation functions of the school.

Legitimation Functions

Bowles and Gintis use the expression "legitimation" with reference to forms of consciousness that both prevent the formation of solidarity on a scale that would be threatening to the status quo and, to this end, frustrate the kind of critical understanding that would be prerequisite to such solidarity or potential social transformation. Legitimation may be expressed either as an active belief in the justice of the social order or as a passive acceptance or resignation in the face of the apparent naturalness or inevitability of this order. They also discuss a kind of middle ground, in which individuals judge the system to be acceptable if, in the long-term, they believe it will satisfy their needs and wants—which requires that their needs and wants take the form of system rewards. This definition diverges from Habermas', who reserves the idea of legitimation for active endorsement or valuing and who sees (in *Legitimation Crisis*, at least) resignation toward to the status quo in the absence of such moral reasons as undermining the very idea of legitimation. We saw in Chapter 1 that both McCarthy and Held believe Habermas puts too much emphasis on active valuing, in light of the empirical dominance of pragmatic accommodation. Like Habermas' critics, then, Bowles and Gintis lump together active acceptance and passive forms of consciousness that are necessary on a broad scale for the stability of the capitalist system. All forms of inequality, they argue, require both a pervasive legitimating ideology, as well as an organization of social relationships and everyday life that reinforces this ideology while fragmenting the ruled "into mutually indifferent or antagonistic subgroups."[59] In the case of advanced capitalism, the ideology is the technocratic version of the meritocracy thesis, in which the school plays the leading part; the relevant structure of social relationship is the division of labor, the bureaucratic or hierarchical organization of power, and a "system of stratification . . . by race, sex, education, and social class," which fragments workers and which, recall, is mirrored in the school.[60]

Because the organization of the economy has precedence in this relation, it is helpful to offer some additional observations regarding its form. First, like Habermas, Bowles and Gintis remark on the rapid expansion of the bureaucratically organized corporate-monopolistic and state sectors of the economy at the expense of the entrepreneurial. This process initiated an increasingly pronounced "segmentation" of the labor force into "primary" and "secondary" sectors. The primary sector corresponds to comparatively stable, well-paying labor in high-growth areas of the corporate and state economy, where unionism is [was] widespread, labor hierarchically organized with clear, if short, lines of promotion, and in which credentials play a major role. The secondary sector, on the other hand, is characterized by high levels of job insecurity and worker turnover, low wages, little to no unionization, little to no opportunities for promotion or development of additional job skills, and in which credentials are more or less irrelevant for entry-level positions and are not meaningfully correlated with wages. This segmentation in part maps onto racial, ethnic, and gender distinctions, and reflects the ways in which oppressed groups are drawn into the economy in successive waves, at its lowest rungs and in situations of intense exploitation. Historically, the arrival of a new wave has served to displace some groups into the primary economy, as was the case with Irish and Italian immigrants to the United States, for example, but that has never occurred for African Americans, even in the face of massive Hispanic economic immigration. Today, employment in the secondary sector "is the expected lot of the most oppressed social groups: blacks, Puerto Ricans, Chicanos, Native Americans, women, the elderly, youth, and other minority groups."[61]

The main reason this more detailed account of economic stratification is called for is that Bowles and Gintis argue that a principal condition on maintaining the legitimacy of the hierarchical division of labor is that the "relationships among superiors, subordinates, and peers must not violate the norms of the larger society. The right of the superior to direct as well as the duty of the subordinate to submit must draw on general cultural values."[62] The meritocratic principle rooted in the school underwrites a number of instances of this: For example, superiors must always be paid more than inferiors, regardless of the inherent nature of the work involved or the relative supply of the two kinds of labor because greater wages should correspond to greater contributions and not to the irrational laws of supply and demand. Educational credentials are directly serviceable in justifying this hierarchy, irrespective of their relevance in terms of technical needs: The myth of meritocracy, that educational achievement results in economic success, makes the superiority of those with higher educational credential seem an expression of well-earned desert. Additionally, those with higher levels of education often appear fit to lead, as manifested in patterns of speech especially, but also in action, dress, and demeanor. It is thus hardly surprising that hiring firms—contrary to what the technocratic argument would lead us to suspect—almost never make any effort to verify the cognitive substance purportedly represented by credentials.

The very same consideration of consonance with cultural value patterns that underwrites credentialism also entails that African Americans and women cannot, for the most part, be placed in positions of superiority over whites and men, and that young people, in general, should not be the bosses of the old (although today, cultural values seem somewhat in flux on this point). For example, nearly all women who had attained the level of supervisor at the time of Bowles and Gintis' writing were employed in that capacity over other women; in general, women workers were seventeen times more likely to have a female supervisor than was a male worker.[63] For Bowles and Gintis, this is part of the underlying explanation for why educational credentials fail to result in the same economic rewards for women and African Americans as they do for white men: Because the former are not considered suitable for higher levels of employment irrespective of their educational qualifications, since they would threaten the ability of the occupational hierarchy to draw parasitically on social prejudice. As a result, "[t]he economic return to schooling is twice as high for white males as for blacks or females."[64] The exception to this—which demonstrates the "mutual imbrication" of class and status, as Fraser puts it—is that among those classified as "workers," as being of low socioeconomic status, some studies have suggested that the economic return is equally poor irrespective of race and gender. However, for those classified as "managers," a group that is (as Bowles and Gintis' argument leads us to suspect) disproportionately white and male, the rate of return is substantially higher; according to one study, "whites of high social class background enjoy economic returns to education that are 66 percent higher than those for either whites of low social class background or blacks."[65] Nevertheless, Bowles and Gintis are careful to avoid the errors of an orthodox Marxist reductionism:

> We make no claim that these distinctions originated as a capitalist contrivance, although a strong case could probably be made that the form and strength of both sexism and racism here are closely related to the particular historical development of class relations in the United States and Europe. Save credentialist distinctions, all predate the modern capitalist era. "Rational business practice" has reinforced and extended them, while consigning less useful prejudices to gradual extinction. . . . The individual employer, acting singly, normally accepts social values and beliefs and will

> violate them only in the interests of long-term financial benefits. The broader prejudices of society are thus used as a resource by employers in their effort to control labor. In this way, the pursuit of profits and security of class position reinforces racist, sexist, and credentialist forms of status consciousness.[66]

In other words, the capitalist occupational system instrumentalizes existing status distinctions, as Fraser has argued and, to that extent, the former presents itself as an obstacle to anyone seeking to overcome the latter. But how is the school implicated in this? First, it offers the ideological justification for the general structure of occupational stratification through the idea of meritocratic selection. This is important because the operation of discriminatory value patterns must be largely implicit, given that it is no longer possible to advance inherent racial or sexual superiority as an explicit principle of legitimation. But more than this, we have seen that ethnic minorities and those of low class origins are disproportionately likely to be tracked into lower-level vocational schooling, to attend less expensive and prestigious two-year colleges, to advance no further than high school, or to drop out of school altogether. According to the dominant ideology, the responsibility for their subsequent poor economic situation is their own because, as we all know, a good education is the ticket to success in today's world.

Bowles and Gintis have some additional arguments to make about the operation of the correspondence principle, specifically regarding the manner in which the relationships of authority and the nature of work and motivation differ by level such that, in general, high school education is structured by relatively rigid rules which correspond to the "close supervision of low-level workers" while, at the other extreme, "the internalization of norms and freedom from continual supervision in elite colleges reflect the social relationships of upper-level white-collar work."[67] In between are the state universities and colleges that cater to the attitudinal needs of technical occupations, service and low-level supervisory personnel. Even within the same level of schooling, however, there are differences of organization between different schools that "reflect both the social backgrounds of the student body and their likely future economic positions. Thus blacks and other minorities are concentrated in schools whose repressive, arbitrary, generally chaotic internal order, coercive authority structures, and minimal possibilities for advancement mirror the characteristics of inferior job situations."[68] Predominantly working-class schools are characterized by rigid rules and an emphasis on behavioral conformity, whereas comparatively affluent suburban schools are governed by flexible rules, with less supervision, and more student participation and course choice. These differences in patterns of socialization reflect the expectations and objectives of teachers, parents, and administrators, rooted in perceptions of social class appropriateness. I will return to the significance of expectations shortly, in conjunction with the discussion of Anyon, who not only provides more detailed evidence than do Bowles and Gintis, but also challenges their estimation of the straightforwardness of socialization processes with respect to the "correspondence" thesis. The need for supplementation in this regard stems from the structuralist tendency in Bowles and Gintis to overstate the success of socialization, the passivity of the subject whose attitudes appear to be determined without remainder.[69] But first, I turn to another potential problem mentioned already, with respect to which Bowles and Gintis fare much better: the danger of teleological explanation in functionalist and structuralist arguments.

We have just seen that Bowles and Gintis link the correspondence between the social relations of a given school and a given station in the economy to the expectations of parents, teachers, and administrators. At the same time, they also stressed that reproduction of the economic system cannot be reduced to the intentions of these groups, but results primarily from structural features of the school. It is important that they be able to provide some explanation, then, for how these structures came to have the shape they do; otherwise, it would appear that they intend to explain the structure of the school directly by the function it is to play relative to the economy, and so to invoke the result of the process of education in explaining its cause. As I have said, it seems to me that Bowles and Gintis successfully avoid this error.

In the United States, it is possible to pinpoint with some accuracy the moment at which the school began to assume the burden of a meritocratic legitimation of social inequality: at the closing of the Western frontier. "Go West, young man," had been the directive given to those who demanded the opportunity to alter their life circumstances for the better, and who were willing to do so through hard work and on the basis of sufficient ability. With the closing of the frontier, a new avenue was sought; with the advent of the common school movement in the mid-nineteenth century, a new avenue was, let's say, postulated. As a matter of fact, the aims of the reformers who led this movement equivocated between establishing equality of opportunity and establishing social control: In the record of their writings, "the merger of these two threads is sometimes so complete that it becomes impossible to distinguish between the two. Schooling has at once been something done for the poor and to the poor."[70] In practice, however, the competition is easier to call: That the desire for social control, the desire to reconcile the poor to their fate, was decisively victorious over the qualms of social justice is amply borne out by the realities of the education system today, which "provides eloquent testimony to the ability of the well-to-do to perpetuate in the name of equality of opportunity an arrangement which consistently yields to themselves disproportional advantages."[71] Bowles and Gintis describe in great detail the successive transformations of the school that, from the closing of the Western frontier, correlated with sweeping changes to the U.S. economy and with the need to integrate previously excluded workers who were, in many cases, understandably reluctant. This history includes the origins of the common school movement, in which public education as we know it was established, the role of the schools in the "Americanization" of immigrants, the emergence of corporate capitalism and the explosion of white-collar labor after World War II. Both because it concerns the transformations that resulted in the present structure of education under advanced capitalism, and because it lends confirmation to the thesis of the colonization of the school, I want to focus on the most recent stage described by the authors, roughly encompassing the period from World War I to the present. Bowles and Ginits demonstrate the overriding role played by capital in educational reform over this period. The influence of J. P. Morgan and John D. Rockefeller's "philanthropy" on the development of vocational tracking around the turn of the twentieth century is particularly striking—calculated, out of the goodness of their hearts, to thwart worker control over job training, and pursued in tandem with union breaking and deskilling through techniques of scientific management.[72] Closer to home, however, is the role of corporate funding in the researching, development, and institutionalization of testing regimes, including intelligence testing, following World War I. These tests became the justificatory basis for tracking, which had earlier relied on patently classist, racist, and sexist "realism." Henceforth, inequality would be scientifically administered and justified according to the principle of achievement.

The charitable foundation of Andrew Carnegie initiated this effort through generous funding for the attempt to impartially establish the inherent feeble-mindedness of black prison inmates, single mothers, and essentially anyone from the dominant countries of immigration at the time (which "evidence" was used to justify an end to open immigration).[73] The Rockefeller Foundation soon stepped in to find specifically educational uses for these tests, and Carnegie provided $3 million for the Rockefeller initiative over the next two decades. The 1931 report that resulted from this research lauds educational tracking according to both ability and sex as the just form of universal education, tailored to the potential of each. But although the captains of industry may have been convinced, the real aim was institutionalization of the testing system as the basis for tracking. Carl Brigham, another Carnegie-supported researcher who confirmed the unfortunate and apparently universal cognitive inadequacies of immigrants, was the man for the job: In his capacity as secretary of the newly formed College Entrance

Examination Board, Brigham developed the Scholastic Aptitude Test, better known as the SAT.

In 1930, Rockefeller's General Education Board gave half a million dollars for the founding of the Cooperative Test Service to the American Council of Education (itself established in 1918 by Rockefeller and Carnegie money). In addition to the Cooperative Test Service, Carnegie and Rockefeller supported the Educational Records Bureau, the Graduate Records Office, and the National Committee on Teachers Examinations, and the College Entrance Examination Board. Prodding and a substantial grant from the Carnegie Foundation achieved the consolidation of these testing units under the aegis of the Educational Testing Service in 1948. In the first half of the twentieth century, these organizations alone received over $7 million from the Rockefeller and Carnegie foundations.[74]

The "educational efficiency binge of the 1920s," underwritten by Rockefeller and Carnegie, resulted in the widespread application of "business methods" to secondary schools. The result for teachers was just what it had been for workers in countless other industries: a loss of control over their labor—in this case, over curriculum, to be planned by educational bureaucrats and "experts," and over methods of evaluation and teaching, to be determined in accordance with uniform, scientific standards. In the interests of the efficiency of the educational system as a whole, individual schools and class sizes became larger and more impersonal, more and more resembling a sort of educational factory. This influence was neither confined to the formative period of the early twentieth century, nor was it exclusively focused on secondary schooling and college selection standards. With regard to the first, Brint agrees that large business interests were responsible for the introduction of the "one best system" of schooling in the United States, established in the Progressive Era and based on "standardized school districts, strict hierarchies of authority, age-graded classrooms, and regular testing for performance-evaluation." Additionally, he concedes that a consortium of select academics, along with a handful of politicians and corporate leaders, were responsible for the introduction of a regime high-stakes testing in the 1980s, which remains to this day.[75] With respect to higher education, The Carnegie Commission for Higher Education led efforts in the late 1960s and early 1970s for comprehensive reform of postsecondary schooling in accordance with the "needs" of a changing economy and, let us recall, at a time of unprecedented protest tied to university campuses. Economic imperatives dictated that universities be transformed from the exclusive breeding grounds of the elite, into training institutions for a white-collar bureaucracy. The Carnegie Commission issued twenty-one monographs, eighty additional publications, and an extremely influential *Final Report*, over the course of its six years in existence. Its conclusions include the following highlights: increased support for alternatives to four-year college study, such as "on-the-job training, proprietary schools, apprenticeship programs, education in the military . . . off-campus work extension, and national service opportunities"; in general, the "two-year planning module," as the study called it, should be the basis of higher education. The commission recommended the creation of 200 new public community colleges by 1980, in a time of general educational retrenchment. With respect to four-year colleges, however, it cautioned against allowing elite institutions to be "homogenized in the name of egalitarianism" and, to this end, advocated a retreat from public university education in favor of a "market model."[76] The first step in this direction, it claimed, should be a sharp rise in tuition fees that the influential Committee on Economic Development, which endorsed the Carnegie Report, specified as entailing a doubling of tuition at public universities, a two and half times increase at four-year colleges, and a tripling of fees at two-year colleges—in order to "narrow the . . . tuition gap with private institutions."[77] In the event that its readers were still unclear as to the practical significance of the extensive tracking and stratification program being proposed, the report concludes: "We recognize that some of these options reduce the chances of a common culture among college graduates within which people communicate, but this has been happening anyway, and we believe the gains will outweigh the losses."[78] That probably depends on who is counting.

Through their careful documentation of the historical progress of school development and reform and, in particular, through demonstrating the influence of corporate capital on the institutionalization of testing regimes, tracking, teacher training and certification, education funding, and so on, Bowles and Gintis go a considerable distance toward refuting accusations of teleological explanation. Yet the school remains a site of controversy and business involvement, although still prevalent and often decisive in the case of government policy, is not the only voice clamoring for influence. In fact, as Bourdieu and Passeron argue, the school must maintain relative autonomy despite this sort of influence, if it is to be able to fulfill its legitimizing function. This autonomy provides the space for parents, cultural communities, and teachers to sometimes effectively voice their own concerns, and so Bowles and Gintis need also to relate the influence of teachers and parents to that of administrators, politicians, and the corporate capitalists who support them. How is correspondence maintained in the face of this semi-autonomy, and are there cases in which correspondence fails?

The key premise behind Bowles and Gintis' explanation of the maintenance of correspondence is the Durkheimean one that they share with functionalists: that the impetus for educational change originates outside the school, in broader social or economic developments. And, in fact, they argue that this premise is shared with parents and teachers, too: Because one of the primary functions of the school as seen by both groups is to prepare young people for economic success, it is considered imperative that the school adapt itself to changes in the economy. This adaptation lags behind the changes that inspire it not only because it is inherently reactive; as a semi-autonomous institution, the school possesses a kind of institutional inertia reflected in settled teaching patterns, available materials and tools, and so on. This lag often results in strident predictions of crisis, imminently to result from the failure of the schools to prepare students for the so-called "jobs of tomorrow." The point, in other words, is that parents and teachers alike actively demand that the school maintain a form of correspondence. It is nearly universally agreed among sociologists of the school that this attitude is refracted through the prism of class-based work experience, such that working-class parents support comparatively authoritarian forms of discipline in the school, because their work experience has taught them that the ability to follow orders and to discipline oneself is key to occupational success; middle- and upper-class parents, on the other hand, expect more flexibility and avenues for independence and creativity, which similarly reflects an assessment of the skills required in their own work experience.[79] There is a broader insight to be gained here, however, which is offered by Bowles and Gintis without being widely observed by others: An ostensibly democratic organization of school boards, mechanisms of community consultation that are reasonably responsive to parents' concerns, lend to the school the appearance of a decentered institution that defies control by a single force, and that would seem relatively well guarded by this pluralism against the imperatives of economic and class reproduction. And yet the economic transformations with which the school struggles to keep pace, which are among the deepest concerns of parents, teachers, and school boards, are indeed driven by the interests of a single social class.[80] Semi-autonomy is ideology; the institution is like a well-trained dog, which needs no leash.

Despite its demonstrable truth, this nevertheless overstates the case. If by and large the school has succeeded generation after generation in rendering service to economic stability and growth—and, at present, no one could deny that this is the case, despite the fact that educational history is riddled with cries of crisis—it has at the same time occasionally produced misfits and radicals. More importantly, if it has effectively produced and maintained a reserve army of skilled labor, it has also sometimes raised expectations that capitalism has proved unable to satisfy. In other words, there are historical and empirical suggestions of the possibility of a contradiction in the school that could precipitate a motivation crisis, just as Habermas described, and that would in turn undermine the basic meritocratic legitimation of capitalist society. This is how Bowles and Gintis understand the "crisis" of the 1960s:

It was the result of a conflict between the imperatives issued by the economy, demanding expansion of university-level education to meet the needs of the proletarianization of white-collar, bureaucratic labor, and the residual, inertial features of these educational institutions connected to their higher-status past—for example, liberal arts requirements—that foster motives and attitudes incompatible with alienated labor. We have seen that the solution proposed by the Carnegie Commission was a more thorough stratification of education; but this demand, although successful in many ways, encountered the opposition of underprivileged groups demanding meaningful access to university education, as well as curricular reform, as a right.[81]

The sorts of disjunctions between the economy and the school, of which this is an example, are the result of distinct but intertwined historical processes and, according to Bowles and Gintis, represent rare opportunities for educational transformation. At the same time, they caution their reader not to be naïve about the significance of individual disenchantment with occupational opportunities or economic values. The "job blues," as they call it, can just as easily degenerate into dissolute hedonism as build constructively into political action[82] (which was more or less McCarthy's point about the significance of youth protest for Habermas). As a matter of fact, this is what largely occurred in the United States over the course of the 1970s. Nevertheless, the job blues *can* be the basis for practically effective social critique if coupled with the sort of pedagogy necessary for individuals to perceive the nature of the obstacles they face. It is Bowles and Gintis' hypothesis that, where educational reform precedes economic reform, the job blues are the likely result: that is, a failure of motivation to perform. But insofar as they identify the absence of apparently credible alternatives as the primary obstacle to a legitimation crisis, the link between motivation and legitimation deficits is, for them, a mediated one: Unlike Habermas, they are willing to call a society "legitimated" if individuals continue to carry out necessary functions, even while they explicitly consider it unjust. For Habermas, this signals the very end of the idea of legitimation on the basis of norms. My sense, shared by Held and McCarthy, is that—terminological differences aside—Bowles and Gintis are in the right here. The dominant problem today is the asymptotic approach toward something like a socialization without norms, the domination of the lifeworld by contexts of strategic action as the only "realistic" alternative. To oppose this trend, they argue,

> [w]e must press for an educational environment in which youth can develop the capacity and commitment collectively to control their lives and regulate their social interactions with a sense of equality, reciprocity, and communality. Not that such an environment will itself alter the quality of social life. Rather, that it will

> nurture a new generation of workers—white and blue collar, male and female, black, white, brown, and red—unwilling to submit to the fragmented relationships of dominance and subordinacy prevailing in economic life.[83]

In broad strokes, this argument is also my own: A certain transformation of the school could ground an anticipation of a renewed practical addressee for critical theory. Yet there are a number of differences that are worth observing here before proceeding. First, Habermas, like Bowles and Gintis, saw that the marginalization of the underprivileged is instrumentalized by capitalism: For Habermas, this was evident in the unequal distribution of the social burdens accumulated by the state in its service to capital, which prevents deficits of legitimation from arising among the politically powerful or among those on whose labor the system depends; for Bowles and Gintis, this is seen in the way the imposition of hierarchy is partially parasitic on patterns of social prejudice and disparities of status, which it thus also serves to reinforce. This insight is the basis for another shared argument: The key to meaningful transformation is the establishment of solidarity between the excluded and at least significant portions of the privileged. But Bowles and Gintis project this solidarity on to a long-term commonality of interest. Like Habermas, then, they subscribe to an improbable reductionistic account of human motivation: Habermas, recall, argued precisely from the perspective of considerations of interest that the prospects for the requisite solidarity seemed dim. The greater confidence of Bowles and Gintis comes from their sense, in the 1970s, that increasingly more people were beginning to realize the real force of Dewey's Progressivist insights, better indeed than had Dewey himself:

> Education can foster personal development and economic equality while, at the same time, integrating youth into adult society only under one condition: a thorough extension of democracy to all parts of the social order. For personal development consists in the acquisition of the full range of powers—physical, emotional, cognitive, spiritual, and aesthetic—to control one's life. Economic justice is built on a society of individuals capable of interpersonal relationships on the basis of equality and reciprocity.[84]

Dewey's failing was that, at least at the time of *Democracy and Education*, he considered the institutions of American society to be genuinely democratic; Bowles and Gintis, to the contrary, argue that because of the authoritarian character of the capitalist social formation into which students are to be integrated, the school's roles in material reproduction and socialization are mutually incompatible. Where social movements succeed in demanding a form of socialization suited to the human being, the citizen, and not merely the worker, the outcome for the economy is pathological and resistance becomes a possibility.

My argument differs most basically from this in that it no longer seems possible to me to sustain this level of confidence regarding the expectations young people have of their careers, and so on, even while alienation proceeds apace in the professions and while the old compensations of job security, pensions, and health benefits wither and disappear. In short, privatism is alive and well among the workers of tomorrow. There is, however, another change afoot in the broader society, rich with implications for education: Multiculturalism—broadly inclusive of issues of gender, race, ethnicity, although much less frequently of class—has profoundly challenged the role of the school in cultural reproduction and, more importantly, the use of shared cultural patterns of socialization for the manufacturing of social integration. My argument in the Concluding Reflections is that maintaining social integration in this situation, characteristic of those states that have explicitly relinquished policies of assimilation/normalization, requires that the school foster forms of socialization, sets of competencies, that are also dysfunctional from the perspective of the economy. So the immanent contradiction is not directly between socialization and material reproduction, but between the forms of socialization that serve material reproduction and those that serve social integration. More than this, however, the prospect for solidarity across lines of difference is not in this case an *ad hoc* practical condition on the social significance of change; it is instead built into the argument for the transformation of personal identity that, I claim, multiculturalism itself entails. The substance of this argument is presented in the Concluding Reflections; my goal in the rest of this chapter is to further illuminate the first half of the contradiction, the forms of socialization requisite to capitalist reproduction. The reason we must go beyond Bowles and Gintis on this score is, as I already noted, that they are in the end unable to avoid trivializing the agency of those so socialized. The following two sections, discussing the work of Jean Anyon and Paul Willis, respectively, provide the necessary supplementation.

Jean Anyon and the Differentiation of the "Hidden Curriculum"

Bowles and Gintis argued that the socialization of young people for participation in a stratified workforce is necessarily differentiated according to the station for which they are "destined"; but the authors do not provide much evidence for this thesis. That is where Anyon comes in. Anyon describes her research as an attempt to empirically test this assumption, which is found in nearly all reproduction theories. Her study is based on observation and assessment of classroom activity of both students and teachers (where all of the latter were described as "good" or "excellent" by their principals), as well as on interviews with teachers, students, and administrators. This method was employed in fifth-grade classrooms in five elementary schools in New Jersey, chosen on the basis of their social-class composition. Two were working-class schools, one was predominantly middle class, one "affluent-professional," and the last, "executive elite." All the schools employed the same fifth-grade math text, had "at least one boxed set of an individualized reading program available in the room," and in all the schools the "language arts curricula included aspects of grammar, punctuation, and capitalization."[85]

It is worth noting at the outset that, although Anyon herself concedes the point most commonly made against her study, that the size of the sample limits warranted generalizability very severely,[86] there is also a sense in which this objection begs the question behind a basic methodological difference. Macro-social analysis of statistical trends can tell us interesting things about the outcomes of education, and indeed relies on large samples to reduce margins of error and the probability of anomalies unduly influencing results, while the sort of ethnomethodological approach adopted by Anyon (and Willis) is unavoidably limited to small samples studied in detail, a kind of micro-analysis of reproduction. But these studies are intended to show something different and equally important: How it is that the statistical patterns illuminated by researches like Bowles and Gintis actually emerge from the behavior, choices, and action contexts of the individuals concerned.

To be brief, Anyon's research confirms differences in pedagogical style and classroom social relations between working-class, middle-class, professional-class, and executive-class schools; these differences in patterns of socialization reflect divergent expectations with regard to occupational trajectories. Anyon observed, correlated to ascending levels of social-class composition:

> increased variety and abundance of teaching materials in the classroom; increased time reported spent by the teachers on preparation; higher social class background and more prestigious educational institutions attended by teachers and administrators; more stringent board of education requirements regarding teaching methods; more frequent and demanding administrative evaluations of teachers; increased teacher support services such as in-service workshops; increased parent expenditure for school equipment over and above district and government funding; higher expectations and demands regarding student achievement on the part of teachers, parents, and administrators; more positive attitudes on the part of teachers as to the probable occupational futures of the children; an increase in the children's acceptance

> of classroom assignments; increased intersubjectivity between students and teachers; and increased cultural congruence between school and community.[87]

In particular, working-class schools were characterized by the stultifying relationship to knowledge and repressive relations of authority that Bowles and Gintis lead us to expect. Work, for the students in these schools, consists in following mechanical, step-by-step procedures, which leave little or no room for decision making; it often is evaluated according to whether the student has followed the procedure, rather than whether the final answer is correct. In many cases, the point of the procedure is not explained in advance, so that the children have no idea why they are doing what they are doing. Nor does the teacher in general explain the rationale behind assignments or its connection with other assignments. In class, the teacher poses questions to students in rapid succession, like a drill major, regarding the stages of the procedure: "What next, what goes here, etc." Teachers control both classroom time and space, without student input and without explaining their decisions. As a result, this control appears quite capricious:

> Teachers, for instance, very often ignored the bells to switch classes—deciding amongst themselves to keep the children after the period was officially over, to continue with the work, or for disciplinary reasons or so they (the teachers) could stand in the hall and talk. There were no clocks in the rooms in either school, and the children often asked "What period is this?" "When do we go to gym?" The children had no access to materials. These were handed out by teachers and closely guarded. Things in the room "belonged" to the teacher.[88]

The students required permission to be out of their seats and, in order to leave the room, a pass from the teacher on which the date and time were recorded. In short, the experience of such children, the "hidden curriculum" implied by the nature of their educational experience, indeed appears to shape their expectations and attitudes regarding work in ways that correspond to their likely occupational futures. That is, they are prepared for meaningless, externally directed, wage labor that is degrading, devoid of the human qualities of creativity, and carried out in an overall context of authoritarian social relations. Because it is the working-class level on which I largely want to focus, I do not go into the contrasting details of the other schools studied by Anyon. Suffice it to say that they move progressively in the direction of greater freedom, intrinsic motivation, personal responsibility, flexible thinking and problem solving, and holistic understanding; patterns of interaction tend toward greater reciprocity, maturity, and respect. However, at the middle-class level, which also is relevant for my argument, these changes are still quite minimal: Work still strikes students as an imposition, as something lacking in intrinsic interest or significance; but there is an appearance here of the instrumental value of education. As one student reported to Anyon, what you do in school is "store facts in your head like cold storage—until you need it later for a test, or your job."[89] Such students accept that performance in school is important for college entrance and occupational success. In short, they display the socialization patterns Habermas earlier described as typical of the middle class: They are well prepared by their educational experience for a bureaucratic relationship toward capital; they are the future appliers of technical rules, valued for possessing the right information. They expect and indeed achieve little fulfillment through work, but they are better able to put their (better) wages to use in satisfying their human needs for expression and creativity—although these needs are subject to consumerist redefinition.

Overall, Anyon's research provides strong confirmation for Bowles and Gintis' thesis of a correspondence between practices of socialization—which shape the attitudes of young people toward authority, work, order, and their own skills and abilities—and expected occupational trajectories. Yet a difference appears when she turns to consider the degree of success achieved at the various levels: There is a pronounced break at the lowest rung, the level of working-class schools on which the thesis of reproduction rests most heavily. Anyon reports that, despite the already authoritarian character of such classrooms, teachers nevertheless complain of having less control than they would like. The reason is that they are in a constant struggle with the students who, it turns out, are not the docile bodies reproduction theories lead us to expect. "The children continually resist the teachers' orders and the work itself. They do not directly challenge the teachers' authority or legitimacy, but they make indirect attempts at sabotage and resist the flow of assignments."[90] The children often are successful, so that there are long periods in which they are permitted to do nothing at all, as long as they are quiet. In other cases, teachers permit a constant hum of chatter during the rote copying of board work. In this sense, too, their socialization in the school is good preparation for their future on shop floors, where this conflict relationship with authority continues to play itself out in the attempt of workers to control the pace of work, to maintain forms of solidarity and cultural resistance. This socialization cannot be directly interpreted as serving the needs of capital since it is, to the contrary, quite antagonistic toward it. But, at the same time, it would be easy to overstate the point: While workers engage in forms of resistance, which their own children also develop over the course of schooling, these forms are "highly constrained and limited in their ultimate effectiveness." That is, just as the tactics employed by workers to maintain some space for personal freedom, and some control over the pace of production, do not ultimately challenge (or even attempt to challenge) the basic authoritarian structure of their workplaces, "the methods of resistance that the working-class children are developing in school are only temporarily, and *potentially*, liberating."[91]

Anyon's argument in this respect is really just a suggestion. To be sure, it is an intuitively well-supported suggestion since, as a matter of fact, capitalist-class society motors on without serious challenge, indicating that whatever resistance exists does not effectively contest the basic parameters of our collective occupational futures. Nevertheless, this insight serves to introduce the basic problem of vindicating reproduction theory within a more adequate account of society, one that is sensitive to the role of agency and culture: How is it that the oppositional culture of the working class serves, paradoxically, to stably reproduce the very structure responsible for its oppression? Paul Willis has provided what is, it is widely agreed, the most compelling and persuasive answer.

Paul Willis and "the Lads"

As Stanley Aronowitz wrote in the preface to the U.S. edition of Willis' *Learning to Labor*, it was Willis' idea that, employing the methods of ethnography at the cultural level of the school, he could both supplement and go beyond Bowles and Gintis by detailing "the processes by which [as Willis' subtitle declared] 'working class kids get working class jobs.' Willis," Aronowitz continued, "addresses the issue of *how* the reproduction of labor power—for him, the indisputable function of the schools—becomes subjectively apprehended."[92] As a practical matter, the articulation of this mediated process is an obvious necessity: In an ostensibly liberal democratic society, in which people are rarely forced against their will into given occupational or educational choices, we need to give some explanation of why individuals make the choices they do, especially where these choices evidently lead to the majority of individuals being poorly paid for work they find unrewarding. At both the practical-empirical and the theoretical levels, structuralist conflict theories are naïve in suggesting that working-class students simply accept at face value the "evidence" of their own stupidity, and so resign themselves to a life of "screwing nuts onto wheels in a car factory" when they fail to excel academically. We must be able to explain how economic and structural imperatives pass through a "semi-autonomous" culture and a culturally formed agency, and so fill in the "black box" of reproduction theory.[93] Like Anyon, Willis believes that what we find in such microanalyses is considerably less stable and monolithic than reproduction theory alone would suggest. The key to the process of reproduction, he believes, is the development among certain working-class youths—young men, in Willis' study—of a counter-school culture, a set of meanings, relationships, and interpretations that structure their decisions and even their perceptions of available choices, at a key point in their lives. Paradoxically, the culture developed by such youths identifies manual labor with masculinity, independence, and resistance and, in so doing, grounds what is to a significant degree a process of "self-damnation." As Willis argues, the irony is that there is a strong component of truth to the insights on which this culture is based, which are definitively superior to the interpretations of the reality of working-class students proffered by the school, with its meritocratic, middle-class orientation. Yet these very real insights remain partial, deformed by prejudices, and practically contradictory: They promise freedom while delivering waves of young people over to a life of oppression.[94] The principal advance Willis makes over Anyon is that his account in no way relies on the assumption, demonstrably false in a not insignificant number of cases, that the majority of schools are so stratified with respect to the socioeconomic background of their students that a hidden curriculum differentiated by institution can explain the reproduction of the requisite attitudes toward work.

Willis' main study is of twelve working-class "lads," as they call themselves, all part of a network of friends and a shared counter-school culture. "The lads" attend a school in a town Willis dubs "Hammertown." It is an all-boys institution, although it is paired with an equivalent all-girls school. Both schools draw heavily on working-class families, but "the lads" school nevertheless has a reputation for being a "good" school, although it is a comprehensive (i.e., not exclusively geared to preparation for postsecondary schooling). Although it had previously been streamed, as part of ongoing reforms it was destreamed into mixed-ability classes at the time Willis' study was conducted. The Hammertown school contains substantial West Indian and Asian minorities. The study followed "the lads" through their last eighteen months of high school and into their first six months of working life.[95] The oppositional culture of "the lads," on which the study focuses, is a kind of lived "style" that permeates their relationships and interactions in the school, both with teachers and with their classmates. The largely conformist students who comprise the latter are referred to by "the lads" as the "ear'oles" (i.e., the "earholes") an expression aptly conveying the kind of passivity with which they are associated in the minds of "the lads." "The lads" do not merely reject the values of the "ear'oles"; they feel superior to them, which superiority expresses itself through the pursuit of precisely those things the "ear'oles" are persuaded to deny themselves: independence, excitement, having a "laff": "It is not so much that they [the ear'oles] support the teachers, rather they support the idea of teachers . . . [they have] invested something of their own identities in the formal aims of education and support of the school institution."[96] The distinction between the activity of "the lads" and the passivity of the "ear'oles" maps onto the division between manual activity and mental labor and is more or less consciously taken by "the lads" as a projection of the future division of occupations—although, as Willis stresses, "the lads," even in accepting this differentiation, reject the conventional relative assessment of the categories. The superiority "the lads" feel is also more specifically manifested in what they perceive—accurately, it appears—to be their sexual superiority, their greater sexual experience, over the childish "ear'oles." The theme of association with adulthood is key as well to the material goods around which their opposition to the school and teacher authority crystallizes: smoking, drinking, and clothes. Drinking and smoking, both of which are persistently and openly flaunted, are intended as conspicuous signals to teachers that "the lads" possess "an alternative, superior and more mature social being."[97]

The social group—indicated collectively in the self-designation "the lads"—is the basis for their culture, which is to say that there is a strongly collectivist dimension to their individual identities. This is expressed clearly in the strong taboo against, and apparently irreversible consequences for, "grassing" (i.e., ratting-out a fellow "lad" to school authorities). The group provides the contacts as well as the meanings and interpretations that allow a "lad" to construct "an alternative map of social reality," which contrasts with the meritocratic, achievement-oriented individualism of the school. The groups formed in the school eventually link up with neighborhood groups, creating a network through which are reproduced forms of knowledge and meaning ("cultural capital") that ultimately make the school appear peripheral to the overall reality of a working-class teenager.[98] The struggle "the lads" wage against the school and its values is basically reducible to a question of control: They resist the domination of space and time by teachers and by the rigid school routine, and the overriding aim of the school to make you "work." They find myriad ways of carving out time, avoiding work, "moving about the school at their own will . . . being out of class, being in class and doing no work, being in the wrong class, roaming the corridors looking for excitement, being asleep in private," sneaking out to smoke, and simply being truant. They are, Willis observes, remarkably successful in this, often reducing their participation in the school to the bare minimum act of registering for classes. Social activities outside the school, especially drinking but also smoking and the need for fashionable clothes, place the lads under enormous financial pressure. The need for cash leads most to part-time work during school and, as a side effect, introduces them to the nature of low-paid labor and authority in the workplace.

The Educational Exchange and the Counter-School Insight

Willis describes the position of the teacher within the classroom today as a precarious one in that their powers of coercion are extremely limited: The catalogue of approved sanctions is a short one and, in the event of any confrontation, can be exhausted with astonishing speed, while doing so threatens to unmask once and for all the fact that the pedagogical control exercised by the teacher ultimately relies on nothing more than the acceptance of the controlled. The authority of the teacher, according to Willis, therefore rests on "moral not coercive grounds."[99] Yet any attempt on the part of each individual teacher to establish personal moral superiority over each student and class would be Sisyphean; the only viable strategy is to attach the legitimacy of the teacher to the *idea* of the teacher. The principle on which this relies, which grounds "the basic teaching paradigm which . . . locates all others . . . and which . . . remains massively dominant in our schools," is the idea of "teaching as fair exchange."[100] The terms proposed for exchange are respect and obedience on the part of the student and, on the part of the teacher, useful knowledge leading to market-worthy qualifications. Because knowledge is the rarer commodity, according to Willis, the teacher's participation in the exchange grounds their "moral superiority." Willis' choice of adjective, however, strikes me as an unhappy one: The orientation toward exchange marks out the teacher–student relationship as strategic, not moral. Willis' own argument confirms this, as we will see.

It is the crucial need to maintain this paradigm—on which the more or less progressive pedagogical styles of individual teachers are, according to Willis, parasitic—and to "exclude or suppress the contradictory, murky cross-currents of normal life which can give the school a cloying, claustrophobic feel of arrested development," against which "the lads" react.[101] The oppositional culture of "the lads" is based on a penetration of the real terms of the educational exchange, and its real lack of fairness for them.

> In particular, this involves a deep-seated scepticism about the value of qualifications in relation to what might be sacrificed to get them: a sacrifice ultimately, not of simply dead time, but of quality of action, involvement, and independence. . . . The sacrifice might, then, be exorbitant, but so too might the object of the sacrifice be meaningless. Cultural values and orientations suggest that the outcome which qualifications bring is not always an unmixed blessing. Qualifications are likely to be low anyway and not likely to affect job choice . . . and are not seen to be such an important criteria for selection anyway in the jobs "the

> lads" are likely to obtain. . . . But what would be the meaning, in any case, of academic "success" and its likely result of moderate upwards movement in the hierarchy of jobs? The possibility of real upward mobility seems so remote as to be meaningless. For "the lads" "success" means going into an apprenticeship or clerical work. Such jobs seem to offer little but to take a lot. And this assessment is clearly made in the cultural mode. Free cultural involvement, social collectivity, the risk of the street and factory floor, and independence of mind would all be lost for a mainly *formal*—not *real*—prize.[102]

This insight—reflected more in cultural patterns, values, and behaviors than in the conscious, expressed awareness of its members—is tantamount to an unmasking of the absurdity of the liberal-meritocratic premise that education actually creates opportunities, that qualification can exert an upward push through the job market. In fact, job opportunities are in no way created by education, but by processes internal to a market which can in no meaningful way be described as meritocratically governed.[103] If Dewey's basic conceptual error was to mistake the possibility of a harmony of developmental and integrative functions under capitalism, the conceptual error of the liberal technocrat is to argue that the occupational market could be directly responsive to a meritocratic educational system. The insight "the lads" gain in this respect is achieved through their collectivist orientation: Capitalism may well be compatible with a great deal of individual mobility; but it is patent that this does nothing to alter the relative position of the working class as a group. So understood, such mobility is *not for them*.[104] To the contrary, like Bowles and Gintis, Willis regards the proliferation of subtly differentiated credentials as achieving no more than the legitimation of existing occupational hierarchies. Moreover, the deskilling of industrial jobs is so nearly complete that any jobs that "the lads" are likely to encounter are equally meaningless.

"The lads," then, see through the ideological individualism of the capitalist myth of meritocracy, which is crucially anchored in a schooling system, a proposed educational exchange, in which "those attitudes needed for individual success are presented as necessary in general. The contradiction is never admitted that not all can succeed, and that there is no point for the [likely] unsuccessful in following the prescriptions for success—hard work, diligence, conformism, accepting knowledge as an equivalent of real value."[105] From the perspective of teachers, however, the breakdown of the paradigm is registered as an outrage; that is, as plain rudeness and disrespect on the part of "the lads."[106] From the perspective of "the lads," on the other hand, once the proposed exchange is seen through and rejected, the school appears more and more openly repressive, since the general authority of the teacher (i.e., aside from their legitimized control within the classroom) continues to be backed up by all elements of the school and, in the final instance, by the law. This authority is now regarded as arbitrary, deprived of its "moral" justification; but it remains ubiquitous, something from which "the lads" struggle to escape. The architecture of the school, the lack of privacy enjoyed by students, the control of access to materials, classrooms, buildings (typical of all but the most elite schools, according to Anyon), control of discussion by teachers—all reinforce the inferior position of the student. Willis sums up his basic thesis as follows:

> It is the school which has built up a certain resistance to mental work and an inclination towards manual work. At least manual labour is outside the domain of school and carries with it—though not intrinsically—the aura of the real adult world. Mental work demands too much, and encroaches—just as the school does—too far upon those areas which are increasingly adopted as their own, as private and independent. "The lads" have learned only too well the specific social form of mental labour as an unfair "equivalent" in an exchange about control of those parts of themselves which they want to be free. In a strange unspecified way mental labour henceforth always carries with it the threat of a demand for obedience and conformism. Resistance to mental work becomes resistance to authority as learnt in the school. The specific conjunction in contemporary capitalism of class antagonism and the educational paradigm turns education into control, (social) class resistance into educational refusal and human difference into class division.[107]

"The Lads'" Culture and the Role of Race and Gender

In addition to the "ear'oles," the two groups against whom "the lads" define themselves are ethnic minorities and, more importantly still, women. I have already mentioned that one of the main axes employed by "the lads" in differentiating themselves from the "ear'oles" is sexual experience, but beyond the patent sexism this reinforces, the attitude of "the lads" toward women is bifurcated by a traditional contradiction. On the one hand are the young women who provide the opportunity for their important sexual experience: These women are entirely objectified; they are denied active sexuality because the woman, as a commodity, "is actually diminished by sex; she is literally worthless; she has been romantically and materially partly consumed. To show relish for this diminution is seen as self-destructive."[108] On the other hand is the image of women as domestic comforters, strongly modeled on the mother, and into which category "girlfriends" are subsumed. Despite strong feelings of affection, the role is categorically one of inferiority. Girlfriends cannot be considered sexually experienced and any rumors to that effect are a serious challenge to a lad's masculinity. This complex of expectations leads, on the part of the young women with whom "the lads" are associated—who must be sexually desirable but not sexually experienced—to patterns of behavior which, in the estimation of "the lads," provides confirmation for their inferiority, their silliness, shyness, and so on, and that contrasts with "the lads" own frankness about their desires. In question here is the culture of the "crush":

> sublimation of sexual feelings into talk, rumours and message-sending within the protective circle of the informal female group. . . . The contortions and strange rituals of the girls are seen as part of their girlishness, of their inherent weakness and confusion. Their romanticism is tolerated with a knowing masculinity, which privately feels it knows much more about the world. . . . The girls are clearly dominated, but they collude in their own domination.[109]

It is the sexist attitudes of "the lads" that provide the crucial nexus explaining the process of reproduction, according to Willis. In short, the perception of a passivity shared by women and the "ear'oles" allows "the lads" to devalorize mental work through its association with femininity (independently ascertained to be of low social status), while charging meaningless manual labor with the affirming cultural significance of masculinity:

> Gender and mental/manual difference provide the atavistic divisions to be worked up into contemporary concrete cultural forms and relationships, but it is only the learning that division is not always and automatically to its own disadvantage which prevents sectors of the working class from seeing division as oppression. For "the lads," a division in which they take themselves to be favoured (the sexual) overlies, becomes part of, and finally partially changes the valency of a division in which they are disadvantaged (mental/manual labour power).[110]

The school thus provides the crucial, contradictory context in which, at the very moment that the operation of a dominant aspect of capitalist ideology—individualism—is destroyed among an important sector of the population, the larger structure of the system is accepted and deeply naturalized. This nexus explains the great mystery of liberal-democratic capitalism, according to Willis: the voluntary adoption of low-status, low-paid occupations by large sections of the population. It is quite clear from a structuralist or functionalist perspective that capitalism cannot do without this stratification; but needing something does not explain achieving it. The liberal-meritocratic picture of how this need is satisfied assumes that all students strive, as individuals, to attain the prerequisites of success understood in a uniform manner; those who fail or succeed only moderately simply accept their lot in life as the fruits of their own incompetence. Willis shows this to be false and explains to the contrary why so many students remove themselves voluntarily from the competition. It is indeed hard to believe that, were it the case that all those at the bottom rungs of the social ladder had genuinely striven for the purportedly coveted occupational stations, they would come so easily accept this outcome. And that acceptance, of course, is the basis of the stability of the system. Were it not going so thoroughly against the accepted wisdom of both school and economy, it might seem rather obvious that those who find themselves in positions despised according traditional value patterns will seek to positively revalue their reality in order to maintain their self-esteem. As Willis notes, "[n]o amount of conditioning in state agencies could provide a fully human identity for those at the bottom of the class structure: coercion or permanent struggle, not free consent in submission, would be the basis of this social order."[111] The inversion of the status scheme overlaying the mental/manual division is decisive for capitalism: The exclusion of the working class simultaneously serves as the basis of the competitive, positive identification of middle-class individuals with the values of the system, despite the fact that their actual work very often is equally meaningless and intrinsically unrewarding. They accept the "educational exchange" in a strategic mode, and see in the lot of the working-class confirmation of their own prudence and success.

Racial divisions, according to Willis, also help legitimize the stratification of the labor market, although in a different and less central way than sexism. Low-status racial groups primarily serve as an underclass that is "more heavily exploited than the white working class, and is therefore indirectly and partially exploited by the working class itself."[112] The oppression of such groups can bolster prejudicial bases for self-confidence among others and so serve an ideological function as well. The combination of these functions, however, is a little tricky because, to the extent that immigrant minority groups often fill the "worst and roughest jobs," they would seem to challenge the superior masculinity of white working class males. The solution, which Willis shows to be prefigured by the response of "the lads" to sexual competition with West Indian males in the school, is to reclassify such jobs (and those that occupy them) as falling off the bottom end of the "cultural scale of masculinity" and into the category of the "dirty," "messy" and "unsocial."[113] Thus, although light or mental labor is considered "sissy," the roughest jobs are not necessarily masculine, but are deemed "unacceptable through association with immigrant labour." It is patent today that public political discourses throughout "the West" seek to explicitly reinforce this association, attempting to ease fears among the working class that immigrants are taking "their" jobs by arguing that the latter "do the jobs Americans (for example) won't do."

Thus, we can say that, from a structuralist or functionalist perspective, the operations of the capitalist occupation system, and indeed the processes of capitalist reproduction in general, instrumentalize existing status distinctions for the sake of stability, legitimacy, and profit. But these three functions do not operate in the precisely the same fashion: The exclusion and super-exploitation of those of low status, both women and racial or ethnic minorities, directly serves the maximization of profit. Yet it also provides some measure of stability by buttressing feelings of superiority among the dominant within the working class. At the same time, instrumentalizing social prejudice serves two purposes of legitimation: Negatively, the asymmetrical burdening of marginalized populations with the consequences of crises of public finances, incurred as a result of servicing capital growth, shields the system from the legitimation deficit that would result should such deprivation be demanded of socially or politically powerful groups; and positively, authoritarian hierarchies within employment, the main significance of which is the maintenance of control through division, are legitimated not only through appeal to the purportedly meritocratic significance of credentials, but also through feeding parasitically on a reified, "naturalized" status order. In light of the significance of racism and sexism, however, Willis rightly cautions that it would be a mistake to equate patriarchy under capitalism with "male-dominance"—or "hegemonic masculinity," as Morrow and Torres put it—or to view racism as natural ethnic hostility. To do so is to risk serious practical and theoretical shortcomings. In the case of gender, Willis makes two points. First, there is a

> potential danger of the women's movement being vitiated by a too-short-run notion of a patriarchical sexism which oppresses them directly in some way outside capitalism. The need is for a dialectical and connected notion of a determinate capitalist patriarchy which transforms and fixes the whole social totality. This clearly has implications for men as well as women—though it is undoubtedly women who suffer the sharpest, most obvious and visible oppression.[114]

And, connected to this, Willis argues that because the operations of capitalism entail the persistence of divisions in society that manifestly result in the subordination of "the lads," the patriarchal terms that allow them to revalue and affirm their subordination "must be continuously reproduced and legitimated. If the currency of femininity were revalued then that of mental work would have to be too"[115]; but under the prevailing conditions of capitalism, that would present a serious threat to the identity of individuals like "the lads." The practical point here is that it is the determining circumstances that are principally responsible for the cultural distortions that, at the level of the working class, tyrannize both men and women, if neither equally nor in the same manner. If there is such a thing as "hegemonic masculinity," it results in oppression that cannot be confined within the barriers of gender divisions. Thus, a principal obstacle—if not *the* principal obstacle—faced by struggles for economic, sexual, and racial equality and justice, is one and the same.

Fatalism, Positivism, and Working-Class Culture

Not only does the school, in a paradoxical way and mediated by their cultural opposition, cultivate in "the lads" a positive acceptance of meaningless manual labor that they identify with freedom from the school, disposable income, and adult status; in addition, "the lads," by drawing heavily on the cultural resources of their community and often their home, have developed a culture that is very much in keeping with that of the shop floor—a consonance that helps them make an easy transition into the world of work.[116] Willis documents on the factory floor the same patterns of opposition: attempts to gain control over time, collectivism, having a "laff," masculine chauvinism, and a deep suspicion of "theory" in favor of practical know-how. This coheres with the cultural criteria by which "the lads" "choose" their jobs: Particular jobs do not much matter because "the lads" correctly perceive the absence of material differences between unskilled positions; what matters is the sort of people with whom they will work and the sort of social environment in which they will work. The criteria, in short, is that there be as few "ear'oles" as possible; that they be able to speak plainly about sexual feelings and drinking; that there be opportunities for having a "laff"; that their co-workers not be the type to squeal if they steal small things at work, or leave early. These values are independent of the nature of any specific task to be performed. The insight into the essentially meaningless and undifferentiated character of modern labor is one of the clearest produced by the culture of "the lads"; it is permitted to arise because their culture provides an alternative to finding meaning through work. This is particularly interesting because, as the professions are not only deskilled and increasingly alienated, but are also increasingly unstable and unrewarding in terms of status and income, middle-class students who have invested their identities in the meritocratic promises of education are increasingly unprepared for the realities they face.

A kind of *Bait and Switch*, as Barbara Ehrenreich has titled her book on this topic, appears to be perpetrated on those who accept at face value the offer proposed by the school.

In other respects, however, Willis stresses that the insights manifested in the culture of "the lads" are deeply compromised. The most important instances of such limits have already been discussed: sexism and racism. But these conspire with other elements to produce their "self-damnation." In particular, the "us" versus "them" mentality that is the basis for the attitudes developed by "the lads" toward authority in the school perversely entails a kind of *a priori* acceptance of the very relations of authority in question, "of a framework in which there is a 'them' and an 'us.'" Acceptance of this framework is the first step in carving out a place for cultural expression; but at the same time it signals a renunciation of all hope of direct challenge or deep transformation, a resignation to the inevitability of such division. For this reason, although "ear'oles" are typically preferred for positions in skilled labor, employers evidence a strong preference for a "lad" when it comes to unskilled work. Conformists in the school enter the workplace with expectations in which a "lad" does not indulge, regarding the quality of labor, opportunities for promotion on the basis of merit, and so on. Although, in the first instance, and "ear'ole" may appear less insolent or difficult, they lack the deeper acceptance of a "timeless" authority structure, and the absence for them of a cultural diversion of the search for meaning ultimately threatens profound dissatisfaction with the conditions of their labor.

To a "lad," such expectations demonstrate a lack of "common sense," a practical accommodation of demands for independence to a structure that is, overall, oppressive and exploitative but which, from this perspective, appears natural and inevitable in its divisions and finely grained hierarchies. That is not to say that oppression and exploitation pass unseen; to the contrary, their daily experience sustains the basically oppositional posture of working-class culture. The problem, according to Willis, is that there is no awareness that these experiences all point in the same direction, toward the same set of obstacles. From the fractured perspective of "the lads,"

> [i]nstead of a centred world of oppression from a specific and determinate social organization of thought, production and interests we have the naturalistic world of a thousand timeless causes. Multi-determination brings misery and is the human condition. A single enemy might be fought, but never a million little ones pricking out the contours of the human condition. . . . If some exploit and some are exploited, if some are equal and others unequal this does not happen with the systematization of classes. All have the chance to exploit others as well as be exploited.

> Nor can any system even hope to change this. Chance, fate and luck basically deal the same cards in any game. A quite marked degree of disenchantment with the prevailing system and a degree of knowledge of exploitation, coupled with culturally mediated (though distorted) and partially lived out penetrations of the capitalist system, can co-exist with a calm acceptance of the system and belief that there is no systematic suppression of personal chances in life. Suppression is recognized, but as no more than a random part of the human condition. Human nature, not capitalism, is the trap.[117]

Willis maintains—as Habermas argued in *Legitimation Crisis* and in *The Theory of Communicative Action* of those excluded (voluntarily or involuntarily) from the wage economy—that the working class is the only class under capitalism not burdened by a structural interest in mystification regarding the nature of production. Nevertheless, its insights into the true nature of society fall short of the ability to see the possibility of alternatives; to the contrary, it suffers from a strong tendency to naturalize social structures, to substitute fate for the consequences of human choices. In short, the partiality of the insights of "the lads"—which compensates for the shortfall of legitimation at this level of the occupational hierarchy—stems from the basically positivistic, strategic, fatalist character of their perspective on the social order.

Finally, the insights of "the lads" suffer from an additional perspectival limitation deriving from their origins in the school. The circumstance of the school produces, for a moment—and, as Willis writes, "it only needs to be this for the gates to shut on the future—when the manual giving of labour power represents both a freedom, election and transcendence, and a precise insertion into a system of exploitation and oppression for working class people."[118] As time passes and "the lads," too, become disillusioned with their "liberty," they find that their leap into the dungeons of the occupational order is all but irreversible; ironically, education is often identified retrospectively, and hopelessly, as the only means of escape. "The lads" are husbands and fathers, and have undertaken financial and personal commitments that practically preclude an unpaid return to schooling.

Conclusion

The primary benefit to Habermas' social theory of being brought into dialogue with the sociology of schooling is that his theory thereby receives both confirmation as well as critical modification; the primary benefit to the sociology of schooling of using Habermas' social theory in this integrating way is not just that it helps to overcome the descriptive partiality of research strategies that reduce the reproductive function of the school to one dimension, but that it provides a means of justifying the very much implied critical sense that this one-dimensionality is unjust. Of course, there are ways around this problem: One can identify the social system served by educational reproduction as unjust, as violating independently justified norms of equality, and argue on that basis that any institution that supports, reproduces, or legitimizes that system must also be unjust. I think that argument is basically right, but I also think that there are additional, specifically educational concerns and norms that make it possible not only to critique what goes on in the school under capitalism, but to justify alternatives. Most of the theorists I have discussed seem to be attracted to some version of this strategy, as is evidenced by the proliferation of demonstrations that the school in fact violates its own purported normative system, meritocracy. On the other hand, leaving the matter there suggests that these theorists would be content were the school simply to live up to this competitive, individualist credo; the reader can probably surmise for themselves that none of these authors would likely accept that suggestion. So there is a pressing need to find some grounds for arguing that the use of the school for the reproduction of the capitalist social order, both in terms of its legitimating or reifying of status hierarchies and its inculcating of the required sorts of possessive individualist motivations, is an illegitimate encroachment on the *true* or legitimate functions of education and educational socialization. In short, we need some means of showing that the role of the school in material reproduction is, under present conditions, a *colonization* of education. It is for this task that recourse is required to the sort of broader normative social theory, for which Habermas' seems to me eminently suited.

Indeed, employing the norms of communicative action to pedagogic discourse can go some way toward providing a normative foothold for theory within education itself. At the same time, it would be a mistake tantamount to the abandonment of a social-theoretical perspective to reduce the problem simply to one of the philosophy of education, an argument that current pedagogical practices on the part of teachers violate the norms summarized in the ideal speech situation and are thus normatively criticizable. Evidence suggests, especially in lower-class schools, that there is no small amount of truth in this accusation. R. E. Young, for instance, summarizes the "traditional" conception of teaching as based on a curriculum that is preformulated without concern for its relation to the lifeworld of the learner; that is comprised of apparently certain and unchanging knowledge; that is to be "transferred" to students in accordance with what Paulo Freire called the "banking" concept of learning; that views evaluation as the assessment of levels of success in receiving and storing transmitted information; and that precludes any possibility of critique.[119] Young then offers a sophisticated analysis of a large body of classroom talk that conforms to this model, and demonstrates that the pursuit of a preformulated curriculum on the part of the teacher has the effect of subordinating "the individual illocutionary claims inherent in the teacher's question and the student's answer . . . to the constraints of a perlocutionary structure which is created through tacit rules for speaking which specify that student answers should be 'what the teacher wants' and that teacher questions should be read as in some sense closed questions no matter how open in form."[120] That is, the cycle of question and answer, which comprises the largest single component of "official classroom talk" (typically around 60 percent) is a kind of pseudo-dialogue that is tacitly directed by the undeclared intent of the teacher to produce a predetermined outcome. Young details a number of mechanisms through which this is achieved, such as recontextualization and reformulation of student responses. His point, however, is that

> the structure of the cycle [of question and answer] may well be more deeply involved in both the colonization of the lifeworld and in the reproduction of ideology than first meets the eye. The typical structure of teacher reactions is not merely evidence of a perlocutionary instructional intent which prevents the lesson proceeding by way of rational assent by pupils [as a result of the form of pedagogy, irrespective of the rationality of its content], but it is an active form of colonization, since it seeks to replace the frameworks of learners with other frameworks, while mimicking the surface forms of genuine dialogue.[121]

It is undoubtedly the case that this "traditional" form of pedagogy strongly reinforces the passivity of students, their positivistic and fractured relationship to knowledge, that this indoctrinating form is antithetical to the development of student autonomy. And, indeed, Young demonstrates convincingly that this perlocutionary structure is normatively criticizable on Habermasian grounds. To the extent that this reflects a displacement of communicative action by strategic action, I can see why Young wants to describe it directly as colonization of the lifeworld by system. However, according to the analysis of Chapter 2, his presentation cannot effectively support that claim. Perhaps misled by Habermas' own inconsistent use of language, Young has conflated system generally and media-steered subsystems, and then portrayed both as coterminous with strategic action orientations. That interactions in the school can be analyzed from the perspective of a systemic connection of action consequences does not at all prove the illegitimate interference of money and power in communicative contexts, nor does the mere existence of elements of strategic action. We cannot claim that the "perlocutionary" teaching method is colonizing per se unless we can demonstrate its (non-teleological) connection with the reproductive imperatives of the capitalist economy and the state administration; in short, we must explain the role of the latter in the institutionalization of this paradigm—which Young does not do—after the fashion of Bowles and Gintis, Brint, and Habermas himself. This account includes the corporate manipulation of the political process as it relates to educational reform, its enormous role in funding and creating the system of agencies involved in the standardization of education, the deskilling of teachers, and the streaming of education, teacher training, and so on. But beyond this, when we turn our attention—as I attempted to do in this chapter—at once to the macro-sociological functions of the school as well as to their subjective mediation as described by ethnomethodological research, we see that the presence or absence of such perlocutionary aims on the part of individual teachers is no longer decisive for the reproduction of capitalist society. When students approach the school in a strategic attitude, as a system of social selection alone, it no longer matters whether individual teachers adopt a communicative orientation, make their motives and justifications explicit and open to criticism. Habermas has rightly argued that within a communicative orientation, we cannot understand a reason as such without taking a position on it as either persuasive or not; but where reasons are simply perceived as another undifferentiated element of teacher "talk," subject to the same "banking" imperatives and with an eye to expected evaluation, their ability to engage the convictions and identities of students dissolves. From such a strategic perspective, both the limits of their own lifeworld—background presuppositions, including those regarding gender and race, for example—as well as the systemic structuring of choices available to individuals, remain off limits to thematization and critique. The terrible pervasiveness of this attitude on the part of students, just as the ubiquity of strategic teaching methods on the part of teachers, is today an effect of colonization; as such, it requires explanation in terms of broader social processes.

What Habermas enables us to see is that the school, as an institution rooted in the lifeworld and charged with tasks of (cultural or developmental) socialization, social integration, and (hopefully, inclusive and reflexive) cultural reproduction, is intrinsically reliant on communicative action, on the basis of which alone these functions are possible. This reliance appeals at minimum to a counterfactual presupposition of communicative orientations, although it must be conceded that were such orientations *never* actually present, this would entail serious breakdowns in the reproduction of the lifeworld and widespread social pathologies (the existence and extent of which is an empirical, not a theoretical question). The school, therefore, can be described as "colonized" by the imperatives of the material reproduction of the economic and political subsystems, both of which rely on the cultivation (socialization) of strategic orientations—toward individual reward, monetary compensation, success as defined within established hierarchies—and, in general, on a fractured and positivistic attitude toward existing social structures and relationships, to the extent that a context of openly strategic action comes to predominate in education.

The evidence discussed in this chapter offers substantiation of the claim that this colonization is occurring today on a massive scale and in a variety of ways, and that this situation has been brought about through the influence of both power and money in the service of nongeneralizable interests. The influence of money, the interests of capital, was exhaustively documented by Bowles and Gintis and confirmed by Brint. Recall, however, that contrary to the technocratic argument endorsed by Habermas in *Legitimation Crisis*, it had comparatively little to do with the enhancement of worker productivity, the public funding of processes aimed at maximizing the quantity of surplus value available for private appropriation. This argument ran up against a great deal of evidence that credentialism fails to reflect cognitive ability, that credentials unequally benefit those who are selected as suitable for employment for other reasons entirely, and that the skills provided by education are of little cognitive significance for the vast majority of actual employment situations. The school serves the interests of capital, was worth the enormous investments of the Carnegies and Rockefellers of the world, because when organized according to their wishes, it serves indispensable functions of legitimation and stabilization. The hijacking of Progressivism by the corporate-funded school of "scientific management" issued in a system that is highly streamed (whether formally or informally) and hardwired into the occupational system, based on frequent high-stakes and standardized testing, and that fosters the idea that social inequality is natural and just while failure reflects no more than personal incompetence or bad luck. This ideological ruse has been so successful that, ironically, parents and the public generally perceive the significance of educational outcomes to be so great that they are often equally encouraging of the interference of power in the school, of legislating what goes on in the classroom. That is not at all to say that they would endorse the form that interference ultimately takes; the response of political administrations to public demands (a case of planning meeting opportunity) has most often been to artificially fuse them with the demands of business, as well as to their own concerns to maintain legitimation and motivation among a depoliticized citizenry. They accept the need for action, and implement the plan of reform that is ready to hand: namely, the corporate-supported plans produced by sponsored academics and so-called "think-tanks." At the same time, many of the legislative attempts to protect students from potential biases or incompetence among administrators and teachers—for example, through the development of "litigation-proof" grading procedures mentioned by Habermas—are responsive to the worries among parents who see the stakes with respect to their children's performance as being terribly high. Interestingly, this suggests a kind of resolution of a disparity between *Legitimation Crisis* and *The Theory of Communicative Action* noted in Chapter 2: that in the former, the interventions of the state into the lifeworld had been in the service of capital whereas, in the latter, they had been ostensibly well intentioned. In the case of education, we have seen that the need for the state to evidence responsiveness to the demands of parents as voters and taxpayers does indeed explain some of the motivation behind colonization. But that does not in fact prove beneficence: To the contrary, the demand for the state to act is often seized upon as an opportunity to better service capital.

The result has been the same since the Progressive era: What began as a movement toward "a more student oriented ethos," ends with what Brint describes as the "bureau-corporate/mass consumption" pattern of schooling that, although it "may be an American original . . . has gained strength in all advanced societies, because it corresponds to the impersonal bureaucratic regulation, pressure for cultural pluralism, and mass consumption priorities of early twenty-first century life."[122] Not only did corporate support for the expansion and reform of education serve to undermine the control of workers over training, and so also to hinder their ability to resist further deskilling; the bureau-corporate/mass consumption pattern is an exercise in socializing possessive individualism and civil privatism, accustoming students to control through hierarchies of power, to life in environments controlled in nearly every detail by the "owners" of the institutions in which they find themselves. Students are socialized in "bureaucratic ways of seeing themselves and others," including not just the individual achievement orientations implied by the constant repetition of assignment, performance, and evaluation, but also the tendency to see ourselves and others as belonging to certain categories in light of specific aspects of the person,[123] and so increasingly ignoring "whole" persons whom—paradoxically—one is today permitted to be only in one's private life. The features constitutive of "whole" persons, their values and commitments are, as we saw in Chapter 2, to be "checked at the door" of bureaucratically regulated institutions: to the extent that the colonization of education plays a crucial socializing role in this respect, it is "in the front line of the loss of motivation and meaning."[124]

But what the research presented throughout this chapter also has shown is that the agency of students is a key component in the explanation of educational interactions. This socialization, in other words, is not the passive shaping of "docile bodies." Despite the fact that so much of the energy of the school is dedicated to maintaining social control, there is very little evidence that its messages are "internalized" to produce genuine legitimation in Habermas' sense. Instead, "compliance mostly indicates a pragmatic stance"; that is, a strategic acceptance of the educational exchange as described by Willis, of minimal respect for market worthy credentials. As Brint notes, for example, swearing at teachers when they are out of hearing distance is quite common, and those who oppose their teachers in an open manner are often admired by their peers (who nevertheless consider such behavior to be foolish from the perspective of self-interest). More strikingly still, as many as four in five students confess to having cheated at some point in their academic career.[125] As the normalized occurrence of plagiarism and cheating testify, education is, for the vast majority of students, of purely instrumental value: The aim—as they have long been told—is credentials. Except in pursuit of exclusive professions and at relatively high educational levels, knowledge itself takes a distant second place or fails to register as a value at all. But as Willis and Brint both argue, although students may not be very interested in the knowledge proffered by the school, they are not stupid; they are well aware that credentials correspond to a stratification of the occupational sphere, which is precisely why the stakes are so high. Whether or not they personally believe this to reflect actual cognitive attainment, they are equally well aware that the substance of credentials is almost never tested outside the school. The diploma from a prestigious institution is all that matters. In many cases, students seem to feel—not wholly without justification—that the exorbitant tuition fees demanded by such institutions entitle them to that much, more or less irrespective of performance, as the paying customer.

I cannot fully articulate the significance of this conclusion here because the cognitive and developmental consequences of a process of socialization that dead ends in a dominantly strategic attitude must be cashed out in the context of a comprehensive theory of socialization, to be presented in the following chapters. Let me just note some additional conclusions that are supportable on the basis of the arguments presented so far. The hardwiring of the school and the occupational system at all levels creates a social context that makes adaptive a general predominance of the strategic attitude, including pathological resistance strategies in the lower classes (which see through the official technocratic ideology in a way that Habermas did not) as well as forms of possessive individualist orientations in the middle and upper-middle classes, at least. The acknowledged role of the school in assigning life prospects—that is, the general acceptance of the meritocratic ideology—motivates parents, teachers, students, and administrators to shape education and their own expectations in accordance with external imperatives. This represents a colonization of the lifeworld insofar as it undermines the communicative basis for its reproduction, in which the school must play an important part. The rejection of the technocratic argument by many students—unaccounted for by Bowles and Gintis, who refute the technocrats at the theoretical level alone—appears to give credence to Held's position with respect to the account of social legitimation presented in *Legitimation Crisis*. However, this is not so much a critique of Habermas' theory as a differing assessment of the relative integrative weight of social and systemic integration, which Habermas himself explicitly considered to be an empirical question. But as Willis and Anyon stressed—and which Held seems not fully to appreciate—in a perverse way, resistance to the ideology of the school actually contributes to the reproduction of the social order that the school services. The basic stance of strategic action accepts that the parameters for resistance, for choice generally, are fixed as though by nature. On the other hand, this resistance is an eminently modern response to the situation in which "the lads," for example, find themselves; it appears to owe nothing to the persistence of religious fatalism, as Habermas suggested in his response to Held.

The inverse implication of this argument for the colonization of the school is, of course, that successfully fulfilling—indeed, even seriously pursuing—the communicative functions of the school would render education dysfunctional from an economic standpoint: It would undermine the cultivation of privatistic motivations and so also the legitimation of the capitalist social order. Of course, even in an emancipated society, the school would play some role with respect to the material reproduction of the lifeworld and, specifically, of the occupational system. But as Bowles and Gintis argued with respect to Dewey, this role could be brought into harmony with the communicative tasks of the school only through the democratization of social and economic life. I am arguing in this work as a whole that there are reasons immanent to advanced capitalist societies to think that the impetus for this change could emerge in the school, in that its communicative functions cannot be dispensed with indefinitely. These reasons relate to the challenges of multiculturalism. Moreover, I intend to show that meeting these challenges would not only be economically dysfunctional under the present order, but could point the way toward forms of solidarity that transcend interest positions and so present the possibility not just of "job blues," but of successful mobilization against capitalist exploitation. Much of this argument, to be made in the Concluding Reflections, rests on the confirmation provided here for the way in which capitalism instrumentalizes status distinctions, relies on the exploitation of such inequalities for its reproduction. Morrow and Torres argue that the most important aspect of the move beyond simple Marxian reproduction theory has been precisely the attempt to formulate a nonreductivist account of the interactions of status and class. But their description of this advance is misguided: Noting that racism and sexism predate capitalism, they argue that, therefore, racism and sexism "are not inevitably required for (and may in fact contradict) capitalist development."[126] In so arguing, they implicitly reinstate the technocratic premise which, in other places, they claim to reject:

The capitalist economy should be viewed as a technical system focused on efficiency. They fail to heed Bowles and Gintis' critique of the hypocrisy of the hand-wringing of technocrats over the potential "lost" to the "premodern" vices of racial and sexual prejudice. To the contrary, the exclusion and subordination of these groups *is* productive: It is a central means not only of producing a reserve army of un- and underemployed, but of ensuring the legitimation that an inherently unequal social system sorely requires. We can argue, at a level of considerable abstraction, that capitalism need not require racism or sexism per se; but at the concrete level we must concede that it will always depend upon some form of functional equivalent. To that extent, capitalism is inextricably wedded to systems of prejudice.[127] As Robert Miles observed, in the historical situation of contemporary societies this means that racism and sexism—the dominant forms of prejudice—could be described as the permanent temptation of capitalism. Miles himself notes this temptation wherever there is a surfeit of potential workers relative to available positions.[128] But the age of full employment even as an administrative goal has long since past. Today this describes capitalism everywhere.

Chapter 3

Moral Consciousness and Postconventionality

In Chapter 1, we saw something of the socially transformative potential that Habermas had, in his earlier writings, linked with changing patterns of socialization; in the Intermediate Reflections, we saw the contrasting pattern of socialization in a "colonized" system of education. However, we have not yet seen in any detail just what he means by a "postconventional identity," or a "postconventional outcome to the adolescent crisis," how this outcome is brought about, what it involves, and what happens if it is thwarted. In short, we haven't yet seen Habermas' *theory of socialization*, on which the idea of a politically significant transformed subjectivity is based. But that way of putting it is a little misleading: Habermas' comments on socialization are scattered throughout his writings, early, middle, and late; they are offered from various perspectives and are introduced in the service of various problems. In that sense, he has never formulated *a* theory of socialization. But from his early interest in the protest potential of the student movement to his later interests in the genesis of moral consciousness and ego identity, a developmental conception of socialization has remained a crucial element of his critical theory. Even where it becomes less thematic, as in his writings on the philosophy of law, the conception of autonomy or "postconventionality" that is the culmination of these developmental processes, forms the normative core of, as well as a practical prerequisite to, his social theory and his endorsement of deliberative democracy. Much earlier in his career, Habermas himself had in fact noted that the concept of the autonomous ego has always in this way been normative for critical theory, even in its darkest hours when, as in the work of Adorno and Horkheimer, "it makes the gloomy prognosis that this ego is losing its basis."[1] That is, the norm of the autonomous ego is present in these works by its absence, as precisely that personality formation which the totalizing society will not allow.

But although Habermas concedes his reliance on the concept of autonomy as a critical reference point, the comparative gloom or optimism of his own "prognosis" regarding its reality, its possibility, and its practical significance, is difficult to discern and seems to vary without explanation over the course of his career. We already glimpsed a kind of snapshot of this variation in the transition from the comparatively hopeful, anticipatory argument of *Legitimation Crisis*, to the overly modest assessments of *The Theory of Communicative Action* and, finally, to the surprising complacency of *Between Facts and Norms*. In the following two chapters, I propose to track this variation in much greater detail as it relates to the question of ontogenesis and to examine its significance for the overall project of Habermas' critical theory. First, however, I attempt to draw together a comprehensive account of his developmental theory of the subject and of socialization, which culminates (theoretically, at least) in what he calls the postconventional stage. This development is comprised of two strands whose interrelation will be one of my principle interests in what follows: The first (dealt with in this chapter) is the development of moral consciousness; the second (dealt with in Chapter 4) is the development of ego identity.[2]

On Lawrence Kohlberg

Habermas' principal source for mapping the development of moral consciousness is the six-stage, three-level schema devised by Lawrence Kohlberg. Although Habermas departs from Kohlberg in a number of ways, most importantly as regards the culmination of the process of development, it is helpful to briefly rehearse the stages as Kohlberg saw them:

Level 1: The Preconventional Level

STAGE 1

The child is oriented to punishment and obedience; that is, the child's conception of what is right, which is in a sense *pre*-moral, is directly linked to obedience as the means of avoiding punishment, usually inflicted as a result of damage to property or harm to persons. Avoiding punishment is the principal motivation for "moral" action.

STAGE 2

The child's actions are guided by his or her own private purposes, advanced through instrumental (i.e., self-interested, means–ends) exchanges. What is right is the satisfaction of interests, which includes one's own but also non-interference in the satisfaction of the interests of others. This is the basis for a conception of fair, instrumental exchange. The child is motivated by his or her own needs and interests but has begun to recognize that others have needs and interests, too.

Level 2: The Conventional Level

STAGE 3

The child's social interactions are guided by "mutual interpersonal expectations, relationships, and conformity."[3] Children judge themselves and others in terms of roles described by Kohlberg as "nice girl/good boy"; "good" behavior refers to conformity with roles (e.g., demonstrating trust, loyalty, or respect where appropriate) and includes concern for the feelings of others. The desire to be seen as good by others (especially key reference persons, such as parents), and to see oneself as good, is the primary motive for moral action. This is linked to an increasing ability to put oneself in the shoes of others and the resolve to care for others as one would want to be cared for oneself (i.e., the Golden Rule).

STAGE 4

The young person at this stage is oriented by the existing social system and by the maintenance of his or her own conscience. What counted as good behavior according to one's role at Stage 3 is now generalized into the imperative to do one's duty, to uphold social expectations and roles, and to serve the welfare of the social group or society to which one belongs. In short, the system of roles is expanded to the broader community and motivation is generalized into a *concept* of role conformity. Maintaining one's own conscience is the primary motive for moral action, but the individual is also subject to an imperative to maintain the social order with which his or her identity is, at this stage, inextricably intertwined. The generalization of roles that has taken place leads from the personalized version of the Golden Rule (Stage 3), to the first acts of universalization: The young person asks him or herself, "What if everyone did that?" although "everyone," in this case, takes in only the known community.

Level 3: The Postconventional Level

STAGE 5

The young person is guided in his or her moral judgments by the idea of preexistent, natural rights, the norms arising from a social contract, or by principles of utility (the greatest possible happiness). As other societies and communities come into view, the young person recognizes the relativity of values to groups and determines that these values should generally be upheld; not, that is, because they are objectively correct but out of a sense of impartiality, and because they are part of existing social contracts. There is, however, a limited set of values, including the right to life or liberty, which is seen as truly universal, natural (i.e., as preceding any contract) and that must therefore be upheld in every society. One's own participation in social contracts, including friendship, family, employment, and so on, is the primary motive for moral conduct.

STAGE 6

The young person is guided by universal ethical principles to which all human beings are subject and that form the basis for judgments regarding the validity or invalidity of the laws and contracts of any society. The commitment of the individual to these principles takes precedence, in cases of conflict, over the laws of their community. At Stage 5, those values that transcended any given community were essentially brute claims: It must simply be recognized, for example, that all persons are equal. Although that "fact" may be understood as a statement of principle, it is not a principle that can be directly used to make decisions. At Stage 6, however, the principles to which one is committed and that form the basis of a new, fully autonomous motivation, are decision procedures like Kant's categorical imperative. They allow us to reflect on what makes a principle right.

Kohlberg's argument, which Habermas is at pains to vindicate once the schema just presented has been modified appropriately, is that these stages represent a process of *development*, an ordered hierarchy characterized by increasing adequacy:

> Kohlberg conceives the transition from one stage to the next as *learning*. Moral development means that a child or adolescent rebuilds and differentiates the cognitive structures he already has so as to be better able to solve the same sort of problems he faced before, namely, how to solve relevant moral dilemmas in a consensual manner. The young person himself sees this moral development as a learning process in that at the higher stage he must be able to explain [with maeutic help] whether and in what way the moral judgments he had considered right at the previous stage were wrong.[4]

As a matter of fact, Habermas' own criteria for justifying the developmental claim (i.e., that traversing the stages represents progress) are more involved than this. But the main point here is that the development in question is not the result of a simple maturational process of unfolding, nor is it (strictly) the result of environmental influences; rather, it is a series of insights or cognitive achievements on the part of the developing subject that need not occur or succeed. Kohlberg's account of this learning process appeals to a series of "sociomoral perspectives" to which each of the above stages is correlated, from the egocentrism of the preconventional level, through a limited degree of perspective-taking between concrete individuals (children and reference persons), to the moral point of view per se. According to Habermas, however, in so arguing Kohlberg conflates two things that must be differentiated. First, there are what he calls the "sociomoral conditions" for judgment, which refer to the degree and kind of access the subject has to the social world—for example, whether he or she is able to differentiate between the intentional action of a person and a physical event perceived in the world (i.e., between the objective world and the social world). These cognitive conditions of perception and interpretation are distinct from (the second thing) the structure of the judgments themselves that are actually made at each level, for instance, whether they are rooted in a universal principle or are justified by the interests of concrete individuals. There are two problems with Kohlberg's confusion on this point, in Habermas' estimation. The first is that part of what needs to be explained is *how* individuals derive a conception of justice or right (e.g., the greatest possible happiness, or avoidance of punishment) from the available "sociocognitive inventory" of any given stage, the repertoire of concepts the individual has at their disposal for the interpretation of social interactions. Because it is the perspective structures that are going to be linked hierarchically, explaining this connection helps prove that their ordering really explains what it is supposed to explain: the development of the capacity for moral judgment.

The second problem Habermas has with Kohlberg's argument is that "the sociocentric conditions [as Kohlberg presents them] lack sufficient analytical rigor to make it immediately evident why this sequence represents a hierarchy in the sense of a logic of development."[5] Habermas proposes to clarify the structure of the perspectives themselves by drawing on the work of Robert Selman. However, just as he departs from Kohlberg regarding the culminating stage of the development of moral consciousness, he breaks with Selman too regarding the highest levels of development in perspective structures. In both cases, Habermas extends the direction of moral development into the competence for discourse as defined by his own theory of discourse ethics. He makes his case by offering an argument that is one remove further still from what he sees as Kohlberg's superficiality: Perspective structures themselves, he claims, are rooted in and related to one another through structures of social interaction, and so his theory of communicative action can be used to ground a sequence of levels of interactive competence, which embody hierarchically ordered perspective structures, from which can be derived the conceptions of justice with which moral judgment operates.

It will perhaps be clearest to first detail Habermas' use of Selman's work in place of Kohlberg's system of sociomoral perspectives and then afterward to explain how he substitutes his own theory of discourse for the culmination of both moral judgment and perspective-taking. But let me first reiterate just what Habermas is hoping to explain by drawing on Selman: The claim that perspective structures are embodied in interaction structures means that the story Habermas is looking to tell should trace the emergence of the competence for communicative action at the ontogenetic level, which follows a trajectory toward the "decentered understanding of the world" that is, according to Habermas, the basis of communicative action. In Chapter 2, I offered a sketch of the *telos* of this process and we saw there its phylogenetic complement; now we turn to its onto-*genesis*.

Interactive Competence and the System of Speaker and World Perspectives

Let's begin with a summary of the perspective structures as Selman understood them:

Selman's Three Levels[6]

LEVEL 1

Comprising approximately ages five to nine, this level involves a differentiated concept of the person. That is, people begin to be differentiated in terms of their physical versus psychological properties, which distinction forms the basis for an awareness of the private inner lives of each individual. Psychological states themselves, however (e.g., feelings, beliefs, etc.), remain undifferentiated. Although there is an awareness of the psychological independence of others, social relations nevertheless are conceived of in a rigidly one-sided, nonreciprocal manner. This level of "perspective taking" lies at the basis of Kohlberg's Stage 1.

LEVEL 2

Comprising approximately ages seven to twelve, this level involves an increasing ability to adopt a reflective or second-person stance on one's own actions and thoughts, as well as an increasing awareness that others, too, can do the same. Psychological states are differentiated and ordered, although they are still seen as relatively atomic. "Persons are understood to have a dual, layered social orientation: visible appearance, possibly put on for show, and the *truer*, hidden reality."[7] The child recognizes the uniqueness of the perspectives of others, based on their own values and purposes, and interprets these differences relativistically. The ability to put oneself in the place of the other, and the awareness that others can do the same, introduces reciprocity in relations between individual actions, thoughts, and feelings.

> In strictly mechanical-logical terms, the child now sees the infinite regress possibility of perspective-taking (I know that she knows that I know that she knows . . . etc.). The child also recognizes that the outer appearance-inner reality distinction means selves can deceive others as to their inner states, which places accuracy limits on taking another's inner perspective. In essence, the two-way reciprocity of this level has the practical result of détente, wherein both parties are satisfied, but in relative isolation: two single individuals seeing self and other, but not the relationship system between them.[8]

This level makes possible the instrument moral reasoning reflected in Kohlberg's Stage 2.

LEVEL 3

Comprising approximately ages ten to fifteen, at this level the young person develops the concept of the person as a system of attitudes and values that more or less retain consistency over time (in contrast to the atomism of states at the prior level). Additionally, he or she develops the ability to adopt an observer's perspective, removed from the positions of both ego and alter, on the system of social interactions. From the vantage point of what Habermas (following Mead) calls the "generalized other," all participants are seen from the third-person perspective simultaneously, including the actor themselves, which means that the young person is able to see how his or her actions or role fit into the interaction as a whole. This abstraction overcomes the futility of the infinite regress model for understanding interactions, allowing the actor to coordinate perspectives rather than merely alternating between them. This innovation simultaneously makes possible both what is called conventional moral reasoning in Kohlberg's scheme (Stages 3 and 4), as well as genuine strategic action, the capacity for which depends on insight into the relationship between the perspectives of alter and ego.[9] But, Habermas claims,

> [o]nce the perception of social interaction is differentiated in this way, the growing child cannot avoid the necessity of also reorganizing types of nonstrategic action that had been left behind in

> his development, so to speak, to bring them into line with the new conventional level. What this means is that a social world of norm-guided [as opposed to interest-guided] interactions open to thematization comes to be set off against the background of the lifeworld.[10]

To explain how this happens and just what it is that is being transformed, we have look to Habermas' interpretation of Selman's three levels.

The first thing to note, for Habermas, is that even Selman's Level 1 relies on "a firm foundation of linguistically mediated intersubjectivity." That is, between the ages of five and nine, the process of language acquisition essentially has been completed.[11] Following Mead, Habermas argues that children acquire knowledge of shared meanings through the assumption of the perspective of a concrete other in interaction: This is how ego establishes the confidence that the meaning *is* shared. This entails that perspective taking in speech, the I–thou relation of speakers and hearers (not yet the third-person observer perspective) has already been established prior to Selman's Level 1: "Thus our point of departure is a situation where reciprocal speaker–hearer relations have been established at the level of *communication* but not yet at the level of *action*,"[12] where the coordination of action perspectives is still wanting. The reason for that is that the child at Selman's Level 1 is not yet able to consider his or her own actions from the perspective of the other, which is required if the two action perspectives are to be brought together. A further obstacle to this achievement is that, although the outer and inner realms have been distinguished, the outer realm has not yet been differentiated into the objective world and the social world, where the latter is the basis of the specifically normative concepts needed for moral judgment. As a result, the child does not differentiate between a speaker's assertion of power and his or her claim to normative, "nonpersonal" validity.[13] These limitations are overcome through the extension of the reciprocity of speaker and hearer relations, with which the child is already familiar, to the perspectives of two actors who each interpret a common situation with reference to their own desires, intentions, and so on. This accomplishment signals the transition to Selman's Level 2, in which not only are the speaker perspectives of ego and alter seen to be reversible—they each take turns in the roles of speaker and hearer—but the action perspectives as well—they each consider their actions from the perspective of the other. As we have already seen, however, there are also limits to the usefulness of the I–thou, first- to second-person relation as the basis for the coordination of action: It is stuck with the possibility of infinite regress.

It is the integration into the social world of the observer perspective, developed earlier in the course of perceptual-manipulative interactions with the (at that point, undifferentiated) objective world, that overcomes this limitation and signals the transition to Selman's Level 3. Although the observer perspective is correlated to the third-person grammatical role, this is not to suggest that children have until this point been unable to employ third-person pronouns in coming to an understanding *about* others; as I have just mentioned, they are also already able to adopt an objectivating attitude toward external nature. The point, rather, is that when the young person acquires the ability to turn that neutral, objectivating view on the action orientations of ego and alter that have already become accessible to him or her (in the concrete, first- and second-person forms), he or she becomes aware for the first time of the systematic character of their relations. This completes the system of action perspectives and makes manifest in action the full system of speaker perspectives (first-, second-, and third-person) that is implicit in the already mastered grammatical system of personal pronouns. It is on this basis that the social world as such is constituted for the subject and strategic, and ultimately norm-guided action as well, are made possible. So far, however, only the former has been explained: Interest-governed conflict is transformed into strategic action when the observer perspective is integrated into the system of action perspectives. But there remain from the preconventional level three other types of action situations: forms of interest-governed cooperation, as well as authority-governed conflict and cooperation. These, too, must now be reorganized; thus, the developing subject, emerging into Kohlberg's conventional level, faces the following problems.

Coordination of action at the preconventional level had relied on appeal and deference to the authority of reference persons, or was guided by an immediate connection to individual needs. This is no longer adequate. Habermas himself does not explain precisely why, but there are at least a couple of possibilities: (a) it seems to follow that the introduction of reciprocity into action perspectives has a corrosive effect on the strength of authority and this means, in turn, that situations of interest conflict have to be mediated by the subject's own efforts; and/or (b) as the scope of interaction widens beyond the family, appeals to the authority of reference persons become moot for attempts to coordinate actions, since reference persons are not shared; in this case, a new sort of authority is required.

The attitude appropriate to strategic action has been separated from that required for the pursuit of understanding and, as a result, the child is faced with the problem of whether or not he or she will, in engaging in any given social interaction, choose it as a means for coordinating action. If not, a new means of pursuing understanding is required that is similarly loosed from the connection to immediate interests and authority relations with specific reference persons. In other words, the basic concepts used to interpret interactions at the preconventional level—authority and interest—must be overhauled, translated into genuinely normative concepts.

The latter occurs, in the first instance, as follows: The social bonds and behavior patterns originally formed in relations of obedience and friendship with specific reference persons, with whom the child is emotionally connected, are detached from those contexts and generalized into a conception of the "normative validity of authoritative commands," that is, imperatives which are seen to be normative when they flow from a recognized authority (the supra-personal will) and not merely from the arbitrary will of a specific person.[14] Both Freud and Mead hold that the sanctions associated with particular behavioral expectations are internalized through socialization and in this way are detached from concrete reference persons who originally wielded the power of sanction. Freud investigated the psychodynamics of this process of internalization; Mead investigated its sociocognitive conditions. These conditions serve to explain why certain behavioral patterns can only be generalized once "A [the child] has learned to take an objectivating attitude toward his own actions" and is able to separate the system of actions perspectives that becomes visible thereby from the accidental nature of the fact that A and B (reference person as alter) in particular happen to embody them at this moment. Specifically, in the first instance, it is only by adopting the perspective of a neutral member of their own social group, the perspective of the "generalized other," that the positions occupied by A and B are seen to be interchangeable:

> A realizes that what he thought was a special behavior pattern applicable only to this particular child and these particular parents has always been for B the result of an intuitive understanding of the norms that govern relations between children and parents in general. As he learns to internalize concrete expectations, A forms the concept of a social behavior pattern that applies to all group members, a pattern in which the places are not reserved for alter and ego but can in principle be taken by any member of their social group.[15]

The social group, in other words, is the supra-personal will referred to previously. Once authority has been transferred from the concrete reference person to it, imperatives or expectations issued by any specific individual in interaction will be recognized through derivation from the expectations and imperatives in force within the group. These, in turn, underwrite the system of social roles within which individuals are oriented by a form of reciprocity: Although specific social roles may be hierarchically ordered in terms of their content (e.g., the roles of parent and child), individuals filling any social role have both obligations to and legitimate expectations of others who fill social roles within the same system.

At this entry level to the conventional stage, the authority of the group still retains the character of a higher-order imperative, qualitatively similar to the commands of reference persons. Not until the power of institutions, which had previously stood over against the child as facts to be accepted, is itself internalized in the form of a system of behavioral controls does it begin to lose this external character. Only when the young person conceives of the sanctions of the group as his own, "which he himself has set up against himself, does he have to presuppose his consent to a norm whose violation he punishes in this way. Unlike socially generalized imperatives, institutions possess a validity that is derived from intersubjective recognition, the approval of all concerned."[16] The recognition accorded to such institutions is, at this conventional stage, not yet the "yes" offered in response to a criticizable validity claim since, as Habermas concedes, most social norms are introduced through repressive forms of social control and their acceptance is merely *de facto*. At the same time, it is important to stress that the exercise of social norms cannot be carried through by coercion or power alone—in which case we would be dealing still with external imperatives rather than with norms—and so the "yes" of acceptance at this stage also is not the mere compliance of a subordinate.

> This equivocal traditionalist understanding is already based on a conception of the legitimacy of norms of action [albeit an inadequate one]. Within the horizon of this conception, social roles can cease to be properties of primary groups and can become generalized components of a system of norms. What emerges is a world of legitimately ordered interpersonal relations. Similarly, the concept of role behavior is transformed into that of norm-guided interaction. Through reference to the legitimate validity of norms, duties become distinct from inclinations, and responsible action from contingent or unintended violations.[17]

This is the culmination of the conventional level and the point at which nonstrategic action has been completely reorganized into norm-governed interaction. In other words, the solidified and differentiated forms of communicative and strategic action have emerged on the basis of Selman's Level 3 of perspective taking. All that remains to be added before addressing Habermas' attempt to vindicate Kohlberg's developmental logic is its culmination: The postconventional level of interaction manifested in the competence for discourse.

Postconventionality and Discourse

Kohlberg's Stages 5 and 6 are two levels of moral reasoning on the basis of principles, distinguished from one another by the sort of principle to which one appeals. Social contractarian and natural law principles, for instance, fall within Stage 5 for the reason that their claim to legitimacy is essentially brute: They are principles to be accepted as just no matter what the circumstance (social, cultural, etc.). As such, they advance a claim that cannot be ignored in decision making, but they do not themselves serve to make decisions. The principles of Stage 6, on the other hand, are in fact decision procedures, such as Kant's categorical imperative or Rawls' veil of ignorance. However, these two examples have something problematic in common: They are both, in Habermas' terms, "monological," forms of reasoning in which you can engage by yourself. According to Kant, for example (at least on Habermas' reading), you do not need to ask the other whether your action will respect their humanity as an end in itself; you do not need to engage in public deliberations within the kingdom of human beings as ends-in-themselves; rather, as a person possessed of univocal reason, you can anticipate the outcome of those deliberations by putting yourself in the perspective of all others affected, and determining whether you can still consistently will your action. It is not necessary to treat Habermas' critique of Kant's at length:[18] What is important here is his claim that the procedure of discourse ethics better captures the operations that Kohlberg himself has identified as definitive for the postconventional level. These operations include "complete reversibility of the perspectives from which participants produce their arguments; universality, understood as the inclusion of all concerned; and the reciprocity of equal recognition of the claims of each participant by all others."[19] To see why Habermas believes this, we need to say more about the procedure of discourse.

In a sense, we can do so quite succinctly: The procedure of discourse is rational argumentation. But what is argumentation, according to Habermas? As we saw in Chapter 2, it is the discursive redemption of problematized validity claims. In our context here, the key question then becomes the developmental one: How does the competence for discourse or argumentation arise ontogenetically? This competence requires completion of the concept of a criticizable validity claim, which was still somewhat ambiguous at the conventional stage. Habermas explains this as follows:

> In anticipating from alter a negative answer to his own speech act, and raising against himself an objection that alter might raise, ego understands what it means to make a criticizable validity claim. As soon, then, as ego masters the orientation to validity claims,

> he can repeat the internalization of discursive relations once more. Now alter already encounters him with the expectation that ego is not assuming the communicative role of the first person only in a naïve manner, but will expand it, if necessary, to the role of proponent in argumentation. If ego makes this attitude of alter his own, that is to say, if he views himself through the eyes of an arguing opponent and considers how he will answer to his critique, he gains a reflective relation to himself. By internalizing the role of a participant in argumentation, ego becomes capable of self-criticism.[20]

This achievement makes possible not critical self-transparency, but participation in processes of argumentation the most important feature of which is the adoption of a hypothetical attitude toward communicative claims the validity of which has been problematized, including one's own claims. Habermas argued that at the culminating stage of the conventional level, internalized expectations of the recognized institutions of one's society took on the function of proto-norms, so to speak. But this is to say that action is guided by the norms governing the institutions that *as a matter of fact* happen to be recognized in the societies into which we *as a matter of fact* happen to be born; this says nothing about the worthiness of such norms to be recognized. The introduction of the hypothetical attitude deprives the social world "to which one was naively habituated and which was unproblematically accepted . . . of its quasi-natural validity."[21] As a result, the only alternative to sinking, in a kind of bad faith, back into the unquestioned traditionalism of the conventional stage is yet again to reconstruct the normative concepts that had undergirded the conventional view and to put in their place a structure that is stable enough to withstand critical evaluation.[22] In the first instance (Kohlberg's Stage 5), judgments of the worthiness of norms for recognition are guided by universalistic moral-legal principles. But once it is recognized that those principles themselves stand in need of justification, Habermas argues that the shift must be made to a *procedure* for the justification of norms, namely, argumentation: "justificatory power resides only in the discursive procedure that redeems normative claims to validity. And this justificatory power stems in the last analysis from the fact that argumentation is rooted in communicative action."[23]

It is the introduction of the hypothetical attitude that makes this shift to argumentation possible. This new attitude represents a break with the "ingenious straightforwardness with which people have raised the claims to validity on whose intersubjective recognition the communicative practice of everyday life depends" [24]; it also at least partially brackets the pressure to act while the validity claims that are naively raised in ordinary communicative action are tested in the giving of reasons for and against, with an eye to the establishment of truth or rightness. At the same time, the divergence between discourse and communicative action must not be overstated: Within the practice of everyday communication there is implicit reference to the possibility of discourse. That is, in ordinary communicative action, it is not the validity of what is said that directly, rationally motivates a hearer to accept the proposed claim, but the implicit promise that the speaker will, if challenged, redeem it through reasons. It is that promise of the possibility of discourse that grounds the communicative coordination of action or, put more broadly, the socially integrative power of language.[25]

The connection between discourse or argumentation and the specifically moral theory of discourse ethics is established through Habermas' claim that a normative principle of universalization (U) is deducible from the structure of argumentation as such. Habermas does not regard this principle as transcendental in the strong sense employed by Kant; rather, his claim is that it is an unavoidable presupposition for engaging in the only form of argumentation that appears to us as possible.[26] The principle, in one of Habermas' formulations, states that every valid norm must meet the following condition:

> (U) *All* affected can accept the consequences and side effects its *general* observance can be anticipated to have for the satisfaction of *everyone's* interests (and these consequences are preferred to those of known alternative possibilities for regulation).[27]

Habermas intends to capture with this the basic intuition that is shared by all of the various historical attempts to ground universalist moral demands; namely, that only those norms are valid that could be rationally accepted by all affected.[28] The principle as stated here goes beyond the monological decision procedures of Kant and Rawls to demand what Mead called "ideal role-taking" or "universal discourse," in which generalizability is tested through everyone affected taking the perspective of everyone else. In fact, given that argumentation or discourse grows out of the interruption of ordinary communicative action and is undertaken in the service of restoring communicative consensus, it is obvious that a monological principle for moral reasoning would be both inappropriate and useless. One could employ such a principle in the service of formulating one's own contribution to argumentation, but it could not stand in the place of actual argumentation: How would those with whom one had suffered disagreement become thereby convinced, such that action might be resumed?

Habermas' primary justification for the claim that principle (U) is an unavoidable presupposition of argumentation draws on Karl Otto Apel's notion of "performative contradiction." The idea is that a speaker involves him or herself in a performative contradiction when he or she advances a claim the content of which contradicts (the content of) some unavoidable presupposition of his or her claim-making. Apel employs Descartes' famous *cogito ergo sum* ("I think, therefore I am") for the purpose of illustration: Although Descartes claimed that the truth of this statement was brutally self-evident, on closer examination it is convincing because the attempt by any skeptic to refute it ends in performative contradiction. That is, the skeptic objects, "I do not exist (here and now)"; yet, in so claiming, he simultaneously and unavoidably makes an additional, contradictory existential assumption, the content of which can be made explicit as: "I exist (here and now)."[29] The argument, then, is that the skeptic who would deny the possibility of achieving consensus in the absence of antecedently shared value orientations, or who would generically deny the possibility of grounding moral principles, commits the same error. The presuppositions in question here are those that Habermas had, earlier in his career, gathered under the rubric of the "ideal speech situation," a situation of discourse purified of all forms of force save for the force of the better argument. These same presuppositions have also been articulated by Robert Alexy as a set of "rules" for discourse:

> (1) "Every subject with the competence to speak and act is allowed to take part in a discourse."
>
> (2) Every participant may introduce or question any assertion, and may express his or her needs, desires, and attitudes.
>
> (3) "No speaker may be prevented, by internal or external coercion, from exercising his rights" as described above.[30]

These rules do not merely reflect a set of preferences or conventions regarding argumentation; they are inescapable presuppositions, a point that is to be proved by demonstrating that anyone who would deny it involves him or herself in a performative contradiction. These presuppositions are manifested in the intuitive preunderstandings that competent language users bring to argumentation. They can be highlighted, according to Habermas, through our sense of the difference between the following claims:

1. "Using good reasons, I finally convinced *H* that *p*."[31]

This statement, Habermas argues, can be considered a description of the outcome of a discourse in which the speaker rationally motivated the hearer, *H*, to accept the validity of the claim "that *p*." This is to be contrasted with a report such as the following:

2. "Using lies, I finally convinced *H* that *p*."[32]

Habermas contends that competent language users consider such a claim to be malformed or inapt because what is intended is clearly:

3. "Using lies, I finally talked *H* into believing that *p*."[33]

The second statement is a "semantic paradox," not simply in light of a prescriptive definition of the verb "to convince," but because of our intuitive understanding of the difference between convincing or reasoned agreement, and mere persuasion or manipulation, where the latter terms imply the presence of force other than that of the better argument (which is quite clear in the colloquial equivalent, "I *made H* believe that *p*"). We intuitively recognize that what has been achieved is not legitimate consensus because the conditions for such a consensus are clearly undermined by the situation described in the second statement. The crucial point is that anyone who sought to refute this argument, to defend the aptness of statement 2, could only do so by attempting to convince us on the basis of good reasons: in other words, the (performative) attempt to refute the distinction between rationally motivated consensus and agreement on the basis of coercion of any kind ends in contradiction, since the would-be defender cannot but rely on that distinction in attempting to launch a meaningful defense.

Habermas offers, as an additional example, a report which claimed that "[h]aving excluded persons *A*, *B*, *C*, . . . from the discussion by silencing them or by foisting our interpretation on them, we were able to convince ourselves that *N* is justified."[34] The agreement that is concluded to is clearly not rationally acceptable, so long as *A, B, C* are among those affected by *N*; anyone who sought to argue otherwise could only do so convincingly by allowing everyone affected to raise and question assertions, and so on. But,

> [i]f every person entering a process of argumentation must, among other things, make presuppositions whose content can be expressed in rules [1–3] and if we understand what it means to discuss hypothetically whether norms of action ought to be adopted, then everyone who seriously tries to discursively redeem normative claims to validity intuitively accepts procedural conditions that amount to implicitly acknowledging (U). It follows from the aforementioned rules of discourse that a contested norm cannot meet with the consent of the participants in a practical discourse unless (U) holds.[35]

Once principle (U) has in this way been demonstrated to be an unavoidable presupposition of the procedure of argumentation, and thus the pursuit of consensus at this level defended as meaningful, discourse ethics—whose procedure is argumentation—can be described as a theory that maintains that "[o]nly those norms can claim to be valid that meet (or could meet) with the approval of all affected in their capacity as participants in a practical discourse."[36]

One final argument needs to be observed here by way of forestalling a misunderstanding of remarkable persistence. The objection seeks to refute Habermas' description of the ideal speech situation (or its later equivalent formulations) by appeal to the fact that actual discourses are never free from constraint and force. The persistence of this misunderstanding is indeed remarkable since Habermas has always been clear that it is *presuppositions* that are in question: No one would bother pursuing argumentation, the adoption of the hypothetical attitude and the offering of justifying reasons, if they were convinced from the outset that this process was merely one of manipulative persuasion. If they did decide to proceed in such a case, their attitude would be strategic: To influence alter's perception or interpretation of the relevant situation by whatever means are deemed most effective, in the hope of provoking a predetermined, desired outcome (in which case, the considerations adduced would likely be very different). Of course, this happens; it might even happen most of the time. Insofar as the ideal speech situation is precisely ideal, we are faced with presuppositions that are counterfactual to various degrees. Yet the distinction between the pursuit of rationally motivated agreement and the pursuit of influence in the service of private interests remains irrevocably in force: Anyone who sought to demonstrate that every case of argumentation was reducible to such manipulation could never do so through argumentation itself, on pain of performative self-contradiction. The ideal speech situation, which models the presuppositions identified by Alexy, thus summarizes the presuppositions that participants must regard as sufficiently approximated for argumentation to be possible, at the same time as it serves as the critical point of reference by which the legitimacy of actual discourses may be judged.

Vindicating the Developmental-Logical Argument

With the sketch of Habermas' theory of discourse ethics complete, we can return to its position and significance within the hypothesized developmental hierarchy. Structurally, the transition to discourse represents the linking of the system of world perspectives with that of speaker perspectives: Both systems had been completed at the conventional level, but were not yet put into relation with one another. In discourse, however, the world perspectives are thematized in the hypothetical attitude as the domains referenced by problematic validity claims (depending on the situation in question, truth in the objective world, rightness in the social world, and sincerity in the subjective world). The system of speaker perspectives (first-, second-, and third-person), now fully reversible, provides the framework for argumentation, in the sense that the process of constructing and critically evaluating reasons requires interchangeably addressing the issue from all three perspectives.[37] However, although the reversibility of relations is a prerequisite for argumentation, participants nevertheless attribute to their own position (for or against a validity claim) the force of the better argument (otherwise, why would they hold and defend it?).

From within the hypothetical attitude that characterizes argumentation the connection is interrupted between the lifeworld and the world, which connection underwrites the ease of ordinary communicative action, resting as it does on a wealth of unthematized and potentially problematic assumptions. The pseudo-normativity of factually recognized norms evaporates; truth becomes a matter of theory and rightness a question of morality. According to Habermas, in the case of the latter, the separation of questions of justice from forms of life and their limitations comes at a cost: He claims that the "vigorous historical coloration of a particular form of life" is lost, and that by contrast, "[i]nteractions become strangely abstract when they come under the aegis of principled autonomous action."[38] Norms that have lost their basis in the taken for granted lifeworld must be stabilized by some other means, which entails that the sociocognitive concepts that had earlier been reorganized into the conventional form be reorganized yet again. Duty, for example, had been interpreted at the conventional level as responsiveness to recognized laws and expectations. But the mere factual recognition of a law is now insufficient ground for its legitimacy: Moral motivation must give up this heteronomy in favor of autonomy, the rational recognition of the validity of the norm as determined by its redemption through the process of argumentation. Moral responsibility is redefined at the postconventional level as action on the basis of such insight, a form of rational accountability.

It was true at the conventional level as well, of course, that a form of consensual resolution was available for conflict situations, albeit a comparatively superficial one that relied on the antecedent agreement of the presuppositions and values of socialized subjects. Once the social world is cut loose from its moorings in the lifeworld, however,

> autonomous justification of morality [becomes] an unavoidable problem. The very perspectives that make consensus possible are now at issue. Independently of contingent commonalities of social background, political affiliation, cultural heritage, traditional forms of life, and so on, competent actors can now take a moral point of view, *a point of view distanced from the controversy*, only

> if they cannot avoid accepting that point of view even when their value orientations diverge. Consequently, this moral reference point must be derived from the structure in which all participants in interaction *always already* find themselves insofar as they act communicatively. As discourse ethics shows, a point of reference of this kind is contained in the general pragmatic presuppositions of argumentation as such. . . . The sought after moral point of view that precedes all controversies originates in a fundamental reciprocity that is built into action oriented to reaching understanding.[39]

At the conventional level, the point of view "distanced from the controversy" between individuals and employed for the resolution of their disagreement is that of the "generalized other," the impartial member of the social group to which they both belong. But this resolution, as I said earlier, is really manufactured by their socialization according to a shared form of life: That is to say, in a very real sense, their agreement is not the result of their own communicative or rational efforts; rather, it is the result of a common accident of their personal histories. Postconventionality, the competence for discourse, entails an alternative "distanced" point of view, the truly "decentered perspective" on the world that is rooted in the structure of argumentation itself.

Having outlined and ordered the sociocognitive perspective structures, the next step in the argument is to explain how a conception of justice or of the good is derived at each level. As I mentioned earlier, this serves to show that the hierarchy of perspective and interaction structures really proves what it is intended to, namely, the developmental logic underlying moral judgment. These justice conceptions function as reference points in the subject's attempts to transitively order conflicting interests in pursuit of consensus (e.g., "whose claim will better serve the greatest happiness of the greatest number?"), and it is Habermas' contention that they are derived from the form of reciprocity available at each stage of interaction. He begins by noting that, although morality proper does not emerge until the postconventional stage, insofar as norms and their violation are at issue at each level there is a moral dimension to the normative concepts employed throughout the developmental sequence. At the preconventional level, this moral dimension is admittedly very thin, since a conception of the social world as such is lacking. However, the complementarity of order and obedience at Stage 1, and the idea of fair exchange at Stage 2, function in the place of justice conceptions. The reciprocity found at this level is described by Habermas as "the natural embryonic form of justice conceptions inherent in the structure of action as such."[40] At the conventional stage, when the social world is delimited through the integration of the observer perspective, ethical (*Sittlichkeit*) imperatives—that is, demands that flow unquestioned from the system of roles, expectations, and values rooted in the lifeworld—and properly moral (*Moralität*) imperatives remain undifferentiated.

> At this stage, issues of justice are posed within the framework of questions of the good life, question which have *always already been answered*. . . . As we have seen, this syndrome disintegrates when a hypothetical attitude is introduced. Before the reflective gaze of a participant in discourse, the social world dissolves into so many conventions in need of justification. The empirical store of traditional norms is split into social facts and norms. The latter have lost their backing in the certainties of the lifeworld and must now be justified in light of principles. Thus the orientation to principles of justice and ultimately to the procedures of norm-justifying discourse is the outcome of the inevitable moralization of a social world become problematic. Such are the ideas of justice that, at the postconventional stage, take the place of conformity to roles and norms.[41]

Perhaps the most interesting question here is whether the problematization of the social world—which inevitably, he says, leads to its moralization, the orientation to justice and to discourse—is itself inevitable. However, discussion of this issue must be postponed for the time being as it bears on Habermas' prognosis regarding the empirical basis of postconventionality in the contemporary world. With respect to the derivation of conceptions of justice, the conventional level interprets justice or goodness as the performance of one's duty, which is in turn interpreted as conformity to role expectations. Social roles at this stage serve as the basis for a more recognizable form of reciprocity of expectations, notwithstanding the asymmetries that may still be present in the content of the roles themselves.

The postconventional stage finally sees through to the truth of justice contained "embryonically" even at the preconventional level: "that the idea of justice can be gleaned only from the idealized form of reciprocity that underlies discourse."[42] Because social roles and expectations themselves are no longer seen to be normatively valid without further ado, the principles on which they rest must be discursively examined. If there is a form of reciprocity beyond the accidents of shared lifeworlds it must be available to individuals as participants in such a process of argumentation, who are able on this basis to adopt a decentered perspective on the world. Once we see that a decentered understanding of the world is the culminating perspective structure, Habermas claims, we can see that the sequence of earlier stages is "directed and cumulative."[43] Each stage is distinguished by coordination or integration achievements: at the preconventional level, the perspectives of I and thou are coordinated; at the conventional level, the observer perspective is integrated; at the postconventional level, the systems of world perspectives and speaker perspectives, which had developed separately, are coordinated in argumentation. Moreover, each new level involves an *Aufhebung* of the previous one: It transcends the previous level and its conflicts while preserving elements of its cognitive content in a reorganized form. The conventional level represents the overcoming, in action guided by norms, of the "opposition between authority-governed complementarity and interest-governed symmetry," which were characteristic of different types of action at the preconventional level; and the postconventional level represents the overcoming of the opposition between strategic and communicative action in argumentation because, in the latter, the orientation to success is translated into the attitude of competitors attempting to convince one another of the validity of their respective arguments and so reach a consensus (provided that these arguments are not advanced simply as attempts to influence).[44] These sublations also involve a repeated process of decontextualization and reassessment of earlier norms from the perspective of the changed context: as the transition is made from (a) loyalty to reference persons and (b) the pleasure/pain orientation, to the conventional level, these earlier conceptions are recast (a) as "*mere arbitrary* will" (of reference persons), as contrasted with "legitimate expressions of will" (of the supra-personal will, or social group), and (b) as "*mere* inclination" in contrast to duties. In turn, with the transition to the postconventional level, conventional normative concepts are recast as based on "*mere* social acceptance, which is contrasted with ideal validity, while action based on concrete duties is now contrasted with autonomy as something *merely* heteronomous."[45] These devaluations of previous normative concepts are the basis for the growing child's own ability to conceive of their development as a learning process, in the sense required by Kohlberg: namely, that they be able at higher stages to explain what was wrong with their judgments at lower stages. Habermas takes this to have established, at least as a starting point for argument, that Kohlberg's scheme when appropriately modified and reconstructed indeed represents a developmental logic. He turns, then, to attempt to show how these modifications and reconstructions also solve a number of problems with which Kohlberg's position has been confronted.

Problems in Kohlberg

It is his formulation of the culmination and critical reference point of development that has inspired the majority (but not all) of the criticisms of Kohlberg's position, and so Habermas' divergence from Kohlberg at just that point is fortuitous (although, of course, Habermas' position here is perhaps equally controversial). The objections are several, but they include

1. It has been difficult to "prove experimentally the existence of a hypothetical Stage 6 of moral judgment"—this raises the worry that postconventional morality, rather than being a "natural" development, may instead be a mere philosophical construct. In fact, Kohlberg revised his scheme for testing levels of judgment repeatedly and, in the most recent version, eliminated Stage 6 claiming "studies in the United States, Israel, and Turkey no longer provide evidence for its existence"[46] (a "gloomy prognosis" indeed!).

2. The existence of a phenomenon of regression in the third decade of life raises the worry that postconventionality might not be the appropriate normative reference point for the developmental logic, that perhaps adult moral reasoning—as Carol Gilligan maintained—is not, after all, amenable to "cognitive and formalist theories."

There are two other issues that are less closely related, but that are in fact more significant for my argument: the question of where to locate relativists and value skeptics along the developmental path; and the fact that "the question of whether structuralist theory can be combined with the findings of ego psychology in a way that would do justice to the *psychodynamic aspects of the formation of judgment* remains an open one."[47] Habermas focuses, in *Moral Consciousness and Communicative Action*, on finding an answer to the question of relativism, and on defending cognitive and formalist theories against Gilligan. He also offers considerations to suggest that the fact that full postconventionality may only be open to philosophical and not psychological corroboration is not, after all, an objection. On the question of ego psychology, however, he points the reader to an essay from seven years earlier, "Moral Development and Ego Identity."

Chapter 4

Socialization and Ego Autonomy

The basic problems surrounding the development of ego identity, the second strand of Habermas' developmental theory of autonomy, have been taken up in diverse ways in analytic ego psychology (H. S. Sullivan, Erikson), in cognitive developmental psychology (Piaget, Kohlberg), and in symbolic interactionist theories of action (Mead, Blumer, Goffman, and others). Although there are a number of common features that have emerged from these diverse research programs, Habermas argues that none of these theoretical perspectives has yet satisfactorily fixed the concept of ego identity in a way that is amenable to adequate empirical corroboration. In order to construct his own synthetic conception of the development of ego identity, he appeals again to the cognitive side of moral development and to Kohlberg, arguing that "moral development represents a part of the development of personality that is decisive for ego identity."[1] Although his discussion of Kohlberg here diverges in a number of details from the later and more extensive one already presented in the previous chapter,[2] it follows the same essential strategy of reformulating Kohlberg's stages within the context of the theory of communicative action, culminating in the competence for discourse. In short, the theory of communicative action sets out the stages of interactive competence—for example, role behavior, or participation in discourse—from which are derived the stages of moral consciousness. Here, however, Habermas includes a fuller discussion of the demand that ego be able to achieve recognition for his or her needs and identity within the demanding communication-interaction structures of discourse; if these needs remain excluded, or continue to be interpreted in accordance with concepts derived from lower, conventional levels of development, then, classically put, *akrasia* will result and postconventional moral consciousness will founder on the lack of grounding in a stable, autonomous identity.[3]

Habermas' account of ego development begins with the level of preoperational thought, which empirically refers to *pre*school-age children and which he claims falls below the threshold of Kohlberg's developmental typology. Preoperational thought is, in a sense, presymbolic, in that the "symbolic" world is seen as totally concrete: in the "incomplete interactions" of this level, the child is focused on concrete actions and consequences (sanctions and gratifications), is motivated by pleasure and pain ("action intentions," or wishes), and views agents including the self in terms of the "natural identity" of a bounded organism. The "role" qualifications for such interactions involve the ability to understand and follow concrete behavioral expectations.[4]

The cognitive level of concrete operational thought, which follows in sequence, encompasses Kohlberg's Stages 1 through 4 and, in it, individuals engage in competent role behavior. Social roles, in turn, eventually come to be understood as reflecting socially legitimate behavioral expectations. At the highest stage within this level of development, corresponding to Kohlberg's Stage 4, the know-how for role performance that has underwritten competent action throughout is transformed into an explicit know-that: The individual, through the incorporation into the interactive domain of the observer's perspective, gains insight into the systemic character of role relations (an insight that also makes strategic action possible). Individuals see themselves and others in terms of role identity. In order to engage in such behavior, they must possess the following cognitive requirements: They are able to "understand and follow reflexive behavioural expectations (norms); they are able to distinguish between duty and inclination in motives, and between actions and norms, i.e., individual subjects as such and as the bearer of roles."[5] The motivation for such behaviour comes from what are in fact (although not yet in consciousness) culturally interpreted needs.

At the culminating level of formal operational thought (discourse-competence), action is guided by principles and motivated by competing need interpretations, rather than cultural interpretations masquerading as "natural." Individuals at this level are able to adopt a critical distance toward norms and social roles. It is here alone, according to Habermas, that ego identity in the true sense is achieved: The agent must be able to "understand and apply reflexive norms (principles)," to distinguish autonomous and heteronymous sources of motivation, as well as actors in accordance with "particular and general norms, individuality and ego in general."[6] This strong claim that true ego identity occurs only at the postconventional level (ultimately correlated with the competence for discourse) is not adequately defended by Habermas until much later, in a paper on Mead's theory of individuation that I discuss later.

The transformation of the role of needs in motivation is a key element of ego identity and needs to be explained carefully. At the first level, need gratification is the sole reference point for action orientations; at the second level, needs are initially referred to primary reference persons (e.g., parents), and then to larger social groups that provide (or withhold) recognition for individual needs to the extent that they, and the individual's behavior, fall in line with role-based social behavioral expectations: It is through this that "motives for action acquire the form of culturally interpreted needs."[7] Finally, at the third level, the apparently natural character of the cultural tradition, including its social behavioral expectations, is dissolved; the culture and its institutional system, as well as the need interpretations rooted in both, can now be subjected to processes of discursive will formation. "In this way, beyond already culturally interpreted needs, the critique and justification of need interpretations acquire the power to orient action."[8]

But there is an important question left unanswered here. In order to see it, it is helpful to recall the teleological structure of action as Aristotle described it: Our ends, that to which we are "oriented," are the beginnings of action (i.e., the motive). The early child, then, aims at (is oriented by) gratification, the pursuit of which motivates his or her action; the older child aims first at the approval/love of reference persons, and later at the recognition of the community for good role performance (e.g., that he or she is indeed a "good boy" or a "nice girl"). At the highest level, the level of discourse, however, the connection is less straightforward, since discourse represents, to a certain extent, a *break* with action: It suspends immediate action pressures through the adoption of the hypothetical attitude, although it is at the same time a means of continuing communicative action in the face of disagreement or misunderstanding. The question is: for what reason or on what basis could the critique and justification of need interpretations through discourse become an aim—the orienting aim or motive—of individuals? It is clear that this can occur only when cultural need interpretations have been seen through as *merely* conventional, such that genuine recognition for one's needs is sought in accordance with a standard of legitimacy rather than conformity (i.e., true recognition is now recognition of the worthiness-to-be-recognized). Habermas has already described this devaluation of the conventional as a product of the transition to postconventionality, the reorganization prompted by the disintegration of a conventional social world that has become problematic. But this leaves the force of the transition unaccounted for: What is it that causes the social world to become problematic, in response to which it must be "moralized," made normatively thematic? This further question goes unanswered in this early paper, but I return to it later.[9]

By the time the child is able to make moral judgments of any kind, initially in terms of punishment and obedience, he or she has already distinguished him or herself as a bounded organism set off against the environment: The child has a "natural identity." But that environment is itself not yet distinguished into social and physical objects, because the incorporation of the objectivating attitude into interaction is what delimits the social world as such. As a result, there are no social expectations per se attributable to responsible agents, but only natural agents with action intentions (wishes). The differentiation of bodily appearance and personal identity replaces this natural identity with role identity, in the family and then in the wider community (although Habermas notes that some bodily features, such as sex, are not simply replaced but are sublated in social roles). At this level the identification of individuals with their roles is complete, first in the case of reference persons (e.g., that the identity of one's teacher or parent is exhausted in their role as teacher or parent), and later in the case of "anonymous role bearers"[10] (e.g., "police officer"). As I noted earlier, Parsons held that the change of teacher each year over the course of one's schooling helps to bring about the ability to differentiate persons from their roles; for Habermas, however, the general recognition that behind roles are persons who may "assert their identities independent of concrete roles and particular systems of norms," comes only fully at the third level of formal operational thought.[11] This distinction itself relies on the distance provided by the differentiation of *de facto* accepted norms, and principles according to which norms may be judged and potentially found wanting, merely conventional, or irrational. But that insight necessitates a reorganization of identity, which had been derived from its place in the now critically challenged cultural system.

> Thus [the youth at this level] has to retract his ego behind the line of all particular roles and norms and stabilize it only through the abstract ability to present himself credibly in any situation as someone who can satisfy the requirements of consistency even in the face of incompatible role expectations and in the passage through a sequence of contradictory periods of life. Role identity is replaced by ego identity; actors meet as individuals across, so to speak, the objective contexts of their lives.[12]

Individual identity of every kind, however—whether conventional or postconventional—is stabilized only through reciprocal recognition, for reasons to be discussed further later. But the passage just presented leaves the source of that required recognition unspecified: *To whom* does one credibly present oneself as an autonomous ego? Adequate recognition, it would seem, cannot be had within the context of a conventionally structured society because the role recognition available therein will not meet the needs of an individual who does not identify completely with any single role or sequence of roles. And, as we have seen already, if individual needs and identities cannot gain recognition at the postconventional level, then the motivations for acting on the available level of moral judgment (which is postconventional, since the individual has adopted a hypothetical attitude toward recognized norms) will be lacking and *akrasia* will result[13]:The individual will refrain from acting on the basis of socially critical, autonomous insights into normative legitimacy, because to do so would threaten the security of his or her identity, his or her opportunities to have his or her needs recognized.[14] Habermas, correctly I think, sees this as undermining the individual's claim to postconventional moral development. What this means—and Habermas is not anywhere near as unambiguous about this in his later work—is that there is a necessary reciprocity between social formations and individual ego formations: "basic psychological and sociological concepts can be interwoven [in critical theory] because the perspectives projected in them of an autonomous ego and an emancipated society reciprocally require one another."[15] In other words, postconventional (or "true"—for reasons that, as I said earlier, are not adequately explained here) ego identity can only be stabilized in a postconventional society that, by the same token, could only come about insofar as (the majority of) its members possessed the requisite competencies.[16] The "vicious circle" (as Dewey called it) formed by this reciprocity is precisely the problem of the critical theory of socialization.

Habermas attempts to vindicate the developmental ordering of these stages in light of the following considerations: The three levels of development discussed portray a gradually expanding access to symbolic reality; the competencies required of individuals in order to function in this reality indicate "the general qualifications for role behavior that together form interactive competence."[17] These qualifications involve the perceptions of norms, motives, and actors, described previously, which correspond to the "general structures of communicative action," and are ordered toward the increasing autonomy of the ego, achieved through a series of abstractive steps. I discussed this argument in the previous chapter: Interactive competencies are hierarchically ordered in terms of increasing reflexivity and generalization, and embody increasingly adequate forms of reciprocity from which are derived corresponding levels of moral consciousness understood as "the ability to make use of interactive competence for consciously processing morally relevant [i.e., amenable to consensual resolution and not merely compromise] conflicts of action."[18] Let me just add here some additional observations specific to identity and motivation.

According to Habermas, the changing view of moral actors (from natural to role to ego identity) presupposes the changes in the perception of norms and motivations discussed earlier and so has both cognitive and motivational conditions. At Level 1, there are only concrete actors; at Level 2, individual normative behavior is judged as an instance of a norm (i.e., role behavior is seen in the light of role bearing). Only at the third level, however, does it become possible to view these norms and roles themselves from the perspective of generalizability: "Actors can no longer be understood as a combination of role attributes; rather they count as individuated subjects who, through employing principles, can each organize an unmistakable biography."[19] The nature of motivation undergoes a similar process of abstraction (and devaluation) from concrete wishes, to duties associated with social roles (contrasted with *mere* inclination), to "the validity of norms justified by principle (autonomy)" as opposed to "norms imposed by tradition (heteronomy)."[20] This last postconventional level is internally differentiated in accordance with whether action motivations (needs) have become accessible as components of the symbolic world. If not, we get a form of utilitarianism and equivalent legal norms (Kohlberg's Stage 5) in which maximum scope is given for the "strategic pursuit of private interests, under the condition that that egoistic freedom of each is compatible with that of all."[21] On the other hand, if needs are recognized to be culturally interpreted, although they are still ascribed to given individuals as natural properties, we get Kohlberg's Stage 6 in which individuals monologically test possible maxims of action and norms against universalistic principles. For Habermas, of course, that isn't the end of the story: At the highest level of development "need interpretations themselves—that is, what each individual thinks he should understand and represent as his 'true' interests—also become the object of practical discourse."[22] This process is risky for the individual, as Habermas concedes, but it is the only means by which recognition can be attained for the *legitimacy* of needs mentioned previously (or for the *validity* of a claim to uniqueness of identity, as we will see later). This culminating transition opens the realm of inner nature to discourse and, in so doing, reveals the possibility of full ego autonomy, the self-formation of an individual for whom cultural tradition serves as a resource (but only as a resource) for self-interpretation.

So, despite having claimed that the relationship between ego development and moral consciousness remains "an open question," Habermas appears to have formulated a sophisticated hypothesis regarding their relation, mediated by the theory of communicative action. In so doing, he has answered part of the question of the dynamics of individual development, although the connection to social formations established through the need for recognition also shows that there must be a phylogenetic component to the explanation as well. At the ontogenetic level,

> [t]he correlation between levels of interactive competence and stages of moral consciousness . . . means that someone who possesses interactive competence at a particular stage will develop a moral consciousness at that stage, insofar as his motivation structure does not hinder him from maintaining, even under stress, the structures of everyday action in the consensual regulation of action conflicts. In many cases, however, the general qualifications for role behavior that are sufficient for dealing with normal situations cannot be stabilized under the stress of open conflicts.

> The party in question will then fall back in his moral actions, or even in both his moral actions and moral judgment, below the threshold of his interactive competence.[23]

Along the way to reaching this answer, however, we uncovered two crucial questions:

1. What is Habermas' justification for claiming that true ego identity is only attained at the postconventional level, such that throughout this paper he simply refers to this stage as the attainment of ego identity *simpliciter*?
2. What causes the undermining of cultural need interpretations, or alternately, what causes the problematization of the conventional social world, such that individuals are left having to seek need-recognition and identity-stabilization through the psychologically dangerous medium of discourse?

Both of these questions are answered in a late paper by Habermas on Mead's theory of subjectivity.

The True Individual

According to Habermas, classical sociology from Durkheim to Parsons suffers from a fatal ambiguity with respect to its conception of individuality. Both Durkheim and Parsons recognize increasing individuation as a characteristic feature of modernity, but both implausibly tie this trend directly to a distinct (albeit related) phenomenon: increasing social differentiation. According to Durkheim, social differentiation drives role differentiation, which he simply equates with individuation. The problem with that should already be clear since, at the highest level of individual development, of true individuality or autonomy, the equation of persons with roles has been undermined. According to Parsons, social differentiation multiplies the life options that are subject to purposive rational (i.e., to strategic, interest-based) choice on the part of the individual, which he sees as demanding increasing individuality or autonomy from the chooser. On this account, the deterministically conceived process of social evolution establishes a voluntaristic, selective relationship between the individual and the particular subsystems into which they choose to be integrated; but, Habermas objects, the role of the modern individual who must select integration into *some* subsystems on the basis of considerations of interest is no less a determined role for them than the old roles had been, chosen from among their limited options *within given systems*[24] (e.g., the limited range of occupational and marriage options open to a member of a particular feudal class). In light of the irony of this development, thinkers like Foucault and Arnold Gehlen indict the very idea of progressive individuation in modernity as an illusion. According to Habermas, however, the basic problem is one of conceptual poverty: The language of singularity that sociology inherited from Hegel, and that Hegel inherited from a philosophical tradition reaching back to Duns Scotus, is a language of deficiency and deviation. As a result, sociologists struggle to express a legitimate intuition about modern life in a vocabulary according to which the individual is an accident of substance, of the universal or species or essence. This problem is particularly evident in Durkheim, who is reduced to characterizing individuality as the spontaneous, as that which allows the individual to deviate from the universal—defined, for him, by the social environment—and so to be him or herself. This process is absorbed into the description of social differentiation, however, such that even these deviations eventually crystalize into standard forms of life within a now internally differentiated social group, at which point the individual is subordinated to these pluralized behavioral patterns no less than he or she was to the comparatively homogenous patterns that had previously characterized the life of the group. As a result, individuality, which Durkheim had aimed to capture, slips through his conceptual net.[25] It is in the work of George Herbert Mead that Habermas finds the only plausible path to a solution, specifically, in Mead's theory of individuation through socialization. On this basis, one can illuminate the connection between social differentiation—in particular, role differentiation—and increasing individuality or autonomy, without conflating the two.

Mead's interest in ego development began as an epistemic concern and, in his early work, he took up the problem from within the perspective of Dewey's functionalist psychology. He began with an investigation of the very problem that confronted Fichte and Kant: that the spontaneous "I"—which is how Mead describes the agent of reflection—always comes across the self as already objectified, factual or empirical—in Mead's terms, as the "me." The paradox is that what is supposed to be subjective, the self, appear to be accessible only as an *object* of introspection. The solution to which Mead eventually turned was the abandonment of the perspective of the philosophy of consciousness, moving instead to the intersubjective perspective of the communicative situation of a speaker and hearer in dialogue. It is only here that the apparent objectification of the "me" is undone: the self in dialogue can see and understand him or herself as "the alter ego of another ego," the hearer of his or her hearer. Hearing oneself speak, raise claims and make replies, is the nonreifying point of access to subjectivity in which, unlike in introspection, the self is not confronted in the objectivating attitude of the third person but in the performative attitude of the second. The second person encountered here, then, is still the "me" and not the "I"; but it is not an objectified "me." The "me" as seen from the performative attitude is the direct shadow of the spontaneous "I," the "I" that I just was. Habermas writes, "[t]he self that is given for me through the mediation of the gaze of the other upon me is the 'memory image' of my ego, such as it has just acted in the sight of an alter ego and face-to-face with it."[26]

But there is still a problem with this approach: Speech acts, even communicative gestures, *presuppose* self-consciousness, an intentional relation to the self. So taking the perspective of the other cannot function as an account of origin of self-consciousness unless this structure is actually rooted in a level deeper than or prior to linguistic competence. Mead turns to gestural communication and argues that, even prior to actual linguistic communication, it is possible for one actor to regard the reaction to his or her gesture on the part of another actor as though it were an interpretation of that gesture. Thus, although this "gesture-mediated interaction" is in fact guided by instinct, it is possible to explicate the origins of self-relation in the process of recognizing oneself in the (apparent) "interpretive accomplishment" of an other.[27] Of course, it is the observing ethologist who assigns objective meanings to what is in fact instinctually guided behavior (e.g., flight, defense). These objective patterns do not take on the character of actual interpretations on the part of participants until the gesture is a vocal one. It is, in the first instance, the vocal gesture that I hear simultaneously with my alter that enables me to interpret my own behavior through the orientation of my other; for it is here, for the first time, that the gesture affects both parties simultaneously and in the same way which, "in light of the other's interpreting behavioural reaction," allows me to perceive myself from the perspective of the other as a social object.[28] For example, an instinctively produced sound, a growl, which would be objectively interpreted as signaling "aggression," is revealed to me as my own aggressiveness turned toward the other who reacts. My vocal gesture takes on a meaning, becomes a sign. The "me" emerges here as the shadow of the performative "I," since the "I" as "the author of a spontaneous gesture am given to 'me' only in memory."[29] The "me" is, as it is for the other, the second person; it is not the third-person object as it is for the observing ethologist. In this way, self-consciousness is intersubjectively and communicatively produced.

Thus far self-consciousness has been considered as an epistemic problem: self-consciousness as a nonobjectifying relation to self, dependent on language or communication. The question of practical identity, however, must be distinguished. In the practical domain, the domain of ego development and motive-formation, although the structural division of the self into an "I" and a "me" is retained, their significance and relation is transformed. Mead continues to explain the emergence of the practical relation-to-self along the same lines as the epistemic, in that it results from "a reorganization" of behavior guided by instinct; but in this case the transition is to another form of behavioral control rather than to another form of communication.[30] Moreover, in question is not simply the self-referential control made possible by a conscious self-relation since, Mead argues, this could not adequately replace the "coordinative accomplishments" (based on the ability to anticipate the reaction of the other) that had been attained through common instinctual responses to species-specific stimuli. Rather, it is the emergence of normative behavioral expectations that ultimately assume the role of integrating actions that had been filled by shared instinctual patterns; however, unlike instinct, such expectations become effective only through being internalized by acting subjects.[31] Mead uses the mechanism of taking the perspective of the other yet again to explain how the connection between social institutions and such internalized behavioral controls is formed. This story is in part already familiar to us: Perspective taking assumes the form of role taking at the conventional level: "Ego takes over alter's normative, not his cognitive expectations. Through the fact that I perceive myself as the social object of an other, a new reflective agency is formed through which ego makes the behavioral expectations of others into his own."[32] This new agency, the practical "me," is the seat not of self-consciousness but of internalized self-control, described by Mead as the "generalized other." This is the conventional moral self, the embodiment of an existing form of life and institutions into which the individual is socialized. The "me," in this practical domain, is no longer charged with the task of recording the spontaneous "I," but with controlling and limiting it. This is necessary because not only does the practical "I" retain the character of spontaneity that escapes direct consciousness itself (as in the case of the epistemic "I"), it here forms an unconscious that is made patent in two ways: "as the onrush of impulses that are subjected to control and as the source of innovations that break up and renew conventionally rigidified controls."[33] The practical "I" is, in this sense, both presocial—composed of natural drives, and the like—and a source of "creative fantasy" and social transcendence. In both cases, the "I" is a force to be countered by the conservative "me," which stands as representative of the recognized norms of a given society.[34]

This fact impacts the nature of the distinction between the "I" and "me": In the epistemic domain, although the "I" still cannot be strictly identified with the self, it is very closely attached to it, because the aim of epistemic self-consciousness is maximally complete knowledge of the self. Practical self-consciousness, on the other hand, seeks the stabilization of its identity as a responsible agent in control of its actions. This occurs, in the first instance, through the internalization of the norms already in force in our community, which allows us to freely—and therefore responsibly—follow (or violate) socially legitimized expectations.[35] So the conservative, conventional "me" stabilizes its identity through the recognition provided by the society in which it finds itself, which recognition is earned on the basis of voluntary conformity to existing norms. The "I," by contrast, (the dual, unconscious force of spontaneity) cannot plausibly claim for itself the status of accountable actor in this way. It is by becoming a "me" that we take responsibility for ourselves, that we choose ourselves or appropriate our own facticity. As a result, however, the responsibility of the practical "me," the conventional self,

> represents the power of a *particular* collective will over an individual will that has not yet come into its own. The latter is *not completely* able to recognize itself in its own identity, generated through socialization, as long as this identity requires us to "attack ourselves in blind fury." The "me" characterizes an identity formation that makes responsible action possible only at the price of blind subjection to external social controls, which remain external in spite of the internalizing effect of role-taking. *The conventional ego-identity is at best a steward for the true one.* And in virtue of this difference, the difference between the "I" and the "me" may not be retracted, even for the practical relation-to-self.[36]

And so we discover the answer to our first question: On what basis did Habermas claim that true ego identity is only attained at the postconventional level? At the conventional level, individual identity remains subsumed in the universal (in this case, in *Sittlichkeit*), a mere instance of (ethical) substance or species or essence. The next question, of course, is how true individuality or ego identity comes about; although framed differently, this brings us to the second question we had in mind in turning to Mead: What causes the undermining of cultural need interpretations, or alternately, what causes the problematization of the conventional social world, such that individuals are left having to seek need-recognition and identity stabilization through the psychologically dangerous medium of discourse?

The Causes of Postconventionality

The formation of the practical "me" comes about as the growing child internalizes the expectations of concrete reference persons and then of the broader community or "generalized other." The child must integrate "diverse and even contradictory expectations by means of abstraction" and, in so doing, forms a "conscience," an internalized center for behavioral control. This development necessitates

> a degree of individuation, which in turn requires a detachment from roles, a distance from the expectations others exact when we play these roles. Such detachment and individuation come about when there are conflicting expectations exacted, along the sequence of our careers and currently among our circles of significant others. Individuation of the self results from the variety and scope of voluntary action [imputed to us] which we undertake. It involves the reality of individual decisions and being held responsible for personal choices.[37]

Habermas elaborates on this quote, taken from Hans Gerth and C. Wright Mills, linking the ontogenetic and phylogenetic levels: The process of societal differentiation is what explains the proliferation of diverse and often contradictory normative expectations, out of which the "autonomization of the self" occurs. That is to say that social differentiation multiplies the roles that any individual must fill in various domains of life and so is the driving force behind conflict of expectations. Individuals resolve the conflict by positing themselves as autonomously acting subjects distinct from any and all of their roles and, thus, their individuality becomes something that is no longer imputed to them to the extent that they fulfill expectations, nor is it merely the singularity of a unit of the group, but is instead an achievement of the individual. Accordingly, the process of individuation becomes a process of self-realization and not simply a specialization of roles or a product of the expanding scope for personal choice.[38] Even still, as Mead insisted, the experience of breaking free from rigid, traditional forms of life and social roles does not issue in nihilism; it is accompanied by integration into social groupings and contexts of interaction that, also as a result of social differentiation, are "both more comprehensive and functionally differentiated."[39] In other words, the self is socially constituted even at the level of ego autonomy; there is no striking out beyond intersubjectivity. Moreover, we see once again that there is a parallel or reciprocity in the developmental directions of society and individual.

This brings us back to an issue we already encountered: Postconventional ego autonomy, and thus also moral consciousness, only can be achieved if recognition for one's needs and identity can be secured; and because identity is intersubjective to the core, in constructing such an identity, "one appeals to others on the assumption that there is a group of organized others that answer to one's appeal—even if the appeal be made to posterity. In that case, there is the attitude of the 'I' as over against the 'me.' "[40] This occurs most clearly in cases where individuals find themselves iconoclastically at odds with their society, a situation that is unendurable as a solitary individual. In those few cases where it is endured, according to Habermas, it is so only by stabilizing one's identity through appeal to a universal or unlimited communication community, often including a posterity that will recognize the legitimacy of one's claims and the valuable uniqueness or irreplaceability of the claim-maker. So, the "I" in its role as socially transcendent source of "creative fantasy" breaks the constrictions of the conventional "me" by projecting a universal community of discourse, the approval of which is the presupposition of normative legitimacy at the postconventional level, and that can ground an *anticipation* of recognition on the part of a nonconventional ego identity. Thus, the projection of such a community not only delimits a Kantian regulative ideal, but also points to a condition on autonomous action (i.e., on grounding the motivation needed to carry postconventional moral judgments through to action/transformation of identity). The critical self-appropriation of one's life history, "as if it were the product of decisions for which I am responsible," is only possible through the mediation of a projected, universal communication community before whom I am responsible.[41] In my own community, by contrast, responsibility continues to be linked to the "me," to the performance of social roles, and so on. As we know, the self is constituted at this level through the adoption of the perspective of the "generalized other," the anonymous member of my ethical community. By contrast, the fully individuated person, characterized by autonomy both in moral judgment and ego identity, "comes upon itself as the alter ego of all others in every community. . . . Thus, the relationship between the 'I' and the 'me' remains the key even for an analysis of the socially imputed postconventional identity. But at this stage the relationship of the two is reversed,"[42] in that it is the "I" that is responsible for the anticipatory projection through which the self is assured of its autonomy and individuality. The "me" continues to follow behind the "I" here, but the "me"

> is now no longer made possible through an antecedent interactive relationship. The "I" itself projects the context of interaction that first makes the reconstruction of a shattered conventional identity possible on a higher level. This reconstruction is made necessary by processes of societal differentiation. That is, the latter have set in motion a generalization of values and, especially in the system of rights, a universalization of norms, and these processes demand a specific kind of independent accomplishment from the socialized individual. The onus of these decisions requires a nonconventional ego-identity. Although the latter can only be thought of as socially constituted, still a social formation

> corresponding to it in any way does not yet exist. This paradox is resolved in the temporal dimension.[43]

If a contemporary postconventional community cannot be appealed to, the autonomous individual projects such a community, appeals to posterity (and so *anticipates* such a community), to resolve the tension and to stabilize their identity beyond the conventional level. That this is the situation faced by postconventional individuality today, according to Habermas, appears to be at least indirectly confirmed by what he regards as the "acceleration of the historical process and a constant expansion of the future horizon,"[44] which are characteristic of modernity.

We can begin to see here Habermas' assessment of the reality of postconventional moral judgment and ego structures, and the evidence suggests a belief in their widespread existence. In fact, he explicitly claims that "[i]n modern societies *it is ever more common* for moral decisions to overtax a merely conventional moral consciousness; these decisions must now be made under the conditions of a universal discourse. The transition to a postconventional morality becomes *unavoidable*."[45] Because action on the basis of such judgment—on the basis of the moral and legal norms by which, he claims, modern society is characterized—requires autonomous ego structures to provide the needed motives, individuals find themselves more and more appealing to a future community in whose eyes such action, such an identity, would receive recognition. Viewing our present actions under future premises in this way, results in an expansion of the future horizon, an acceleration of the historical process. Although it is grounded in the requirement for unforced reciprocal recognition that underlies autonomous moral action and ego identity, Habermas claims that this projection is also responsible for the increasing "consciousness of crisis that is becoming more and more prevalent in modern societies."[46] But there is something rather surprising and more than a little discomforting about Habermas' "prognosis" regarding the state of postconventional identity today, and it is well worth pausing to be as clear as possible about his position. Let us note, then, that we have answered our second question: Conventional role structures and the recognition they provide are undermined by social differentiation, which requires that the individual reorganize their identity on a higher level; this identity, in turn, can only be stabilized by a form of recognition that extends beyond the parochialism of the conventional perspective. The new form of postconventional social interaction in which recognition is to be sought (or anticipated) is ultimately discourse (i.e., autonomous interaction with an unlimited communication community). Although the specific causal imputation is to his general theory of social evolution, Habermas unambiguously claims that the structures of modern law and morality, which also have been brought about by societal differentiation, *require* nonconventional moral judgment ("postconventional morality becomes *unavoidable*") and ego identity ("generalization of values and . . . a universalization of norms . . . *demand* a specific kind of independent accomplishment from the socialized individual"). But if so much postconventional action is, as it were, *going on* in contemporary society, why is it that the community that would stabilize this identity remains a mere idealizing projection? Whence the disjunction between social and psychological forms that had been maintained at all the prior levels? I don't mean to ask why there isn't an international, directly democratic order through which a universal communication community could pursue collective will formation. That is a different sort of difficult, practical question. What I mean to ask is at once more general and more basic: What happened to the link between critical ego autonomy and the emancipation of society?

Habermas' most recent major writing, *Between Facts and Norms*, strongly reinforces this surprising change in his work: Not only does he there seem to presume widespread realization of postconventional identity as a social requirement, which I discussed in the Postscript to Chapter 2; but he goes out of his way to trivialize the significance of this accomplishment, which had earlier been the great hope of social transformation. In contrasting postconventional morality (contingent, as we now see, on a realized ego identity) with its legal equivalent, Habermas emphasizes the "complementarity" of the two that results from the compensation the latter is able to provide for the weaknesses of the former. These weaknesses paradoxically include the dependence of postconventional morality on peculiar processes of socialization that must nevertheless, *at one and the same time*—and according to Habermas' own argument—be presumed widespread in order for such complex societies to function. Habermas writes,

> [a] morality that depends on the accommodating substrate of propitious personality structures would have a limited effectiveness if it could not engage the actor's motives in *another* way besides internalization, that is, precisely by way of an institutionalized legal system that *supplements* postconventional morality in a manner effective for action. Law is two things at the same time: a system of knowledge and a system of action. . . . Because law is simultaneously established in this way at the levels of culture and society, it can *offset* the weaknesses of a morality that exists primarily as knowledge. . . . The person who judges and acts morally must independently appropriate this moral knowledge, assimilate it, and put it into practice. She is subject to unprecedented (a) cognitive, (b) motivational, and (c) organizational demands, from which the person as legal subject is *unburdened*.[47]

This "overtaxing" of the cognitive, motivational, and organizational capacities of the individual, which I discussed earlier, appears to completely trivialize the social significance of the attainment of postconventional morality, which is reduced to its legitimating functionality for the legal and economic systems. That is, its value is to be found in its permitting individuals to participate in legal discourses limited to the determination of the appropriate boundaries within which strategic action may be pursued, as well as in informal discourses in the political public sphere to which elected officials should be responsive. This represents an enormous concession to the technocratic and elite democratic theorists Habermas himself had earlier criticized: Postconventional identity is so beleaguered by the demands of increasingly complex societies that, rather than representing the saving grace sought by earlier critical theorists (including Habermas himself), it must itself be saved from utter annihilation by legal permissions to relinquish its *constitutive responsibility*, its "communicative freedom," as Habermas says (i.e., the freedom to participate in discourse, to challenge and respond to validity claims, etc.).[48] Habermas cites the following as an example of the organizational overburdening of postconventional morality:

> the unmistakable duty to preserve even anonymous neighbours from starvation conspicuously contrasts with the fact that millions of inhabitants of the First World allow hundreds of thousands in poverty-stricken areas of the Third World to perish. Even charitable aid can be transmitted only along organized paths; the convoluted route taken by food, medicine, clothing, and infrastructures far exceeds the initiative and range of individual action. As many studies have shown, a structural improvement would require no less than a new economic world order. Similar problems that can only be managed by institutions arise in one's own region, and even in one's very neighborhood. The more that moral consciousness attunes itself to universalistic value orientations, the greater are the discrepancies between uncontested moral demands, on the one hand, and organizational constraints and resistances to change, on the other.[49]

Following McCarthy, I noted in Chapter 2 that Habermas makes no attempt to explain how the empirical limits of communicative resources are to be ascertained. I want to sharpen this criticism here into what is one of my essential conclusions in this work: Not only does Habermas not address this question as an empirical one, but given what we have subsequently discovered with respect to the link between *akrasia* and identity-stabilizing social recognition, it now appears that there would be no way, on Habermas' own terms, to determine whether the empirical evidence for communicative failure (of which there is plenty) is the result of the overburdening of a *fully developed* interactive capacity, or an instance of socially induced moral failure. Given that, in the previous example, Habermas entertains no doubts regarding our recognition of the basic injustice of world hunger, we seem to be presented with a case in which we fail to act on the level of moral judgment available to us—that is, it appears at least as plausible to interpret this as a case of *akrasia* as to see it as one of insurmountable complexity overwhelming our moral resources. There is no way to decide between these interpretations *unless we assume that postconventionality and ego autonomy have been realized*; only then could we safely interpret reversions to strategic action, artificial limitations to the communication community, moral renunciation generally, as capitulation in the face of complexity that calls for supplementation by the legal and systemic mechanisms that morally "unburden" the individual.

So everything rests on whether postconventional individuality is in fact realized on a broad scale. We have already seen reasons to doubt that claim since if it isn't clear, on the one hand, how an idealizing projection could stabilize such an identity in the first place, it is equally unclear, on the other, why we can do no better than idealizing projections at the societal level if postconventional individuals are no longer rare. But consider this as well: What other reasons does Habermas give for his belief that postconventionality is widespread? By the time of *Between Facts and Norms*—although this is also the dominant argument in his discussion of Mead—only the fact that postconventional legal institutions and, indeed, the structure of society as a whole, appear to require it. Yet this inference from the existing level of development of social structures, including especially moral and legal institutions, to the state and capacities of individuals, is precisely what the theory of the colonization and cultural impoverishment of the lifeworld served to undermine: The rationalization that made these postconventional legal innovations possible in response to steering problems (the emergence of market economies, etc.) eventually threatens the reproduction of the lifeworld itself by setting loose the imperatives of autonomous subsystems that overrun their borders. The forms of fragmented consciousness and alienated personality structures that result from cultural impoverishment and colonization destroy the lifeworld foundations of communicative action and, *a fortiori*, *necessarily the possibility of postconventionality as well.*[50]

In the example cited earlier, Habermas appears to suggest that the fact that the alleviation of world hunger could only come about as a result of a new economic world order is, if not morally, at least practically exculpatory given the complexity of the task. He seems to have forgotten that the point of critical theory has always been critique in favor of a new economic world order; as he had once realized, the link to autonomous, postconventional identity was forged in the insistence that this new order could not be brought about by a revolutionary vanguard hoping for retrospective justification. Instead, it waited on the widespread emergence of individuals unsatisfied by the palliatives of merely formal democratic participation, symbolic politics, and the "trickling down" of economic growth; individuals committed to the realization of the ideals of the Enlightenment, the overcoming of the discrepancies between the demands of universal morality and the reality of the present social order, and to breaking the resistance of existing institutions to this change by transforming or destroying them. In a different context, it might well be worth inquiring into whether possible motives for this change in Habermas' thinking are derivable from his intellectual biography. For my purposes, however, it is both more suggestive and more helpful to ask: If the later Habermas is confident that postconventional identity is a reality, then what stands in the way of the realization of a postconventional, that is, an emancipated *society*? "Societal complexity" certainly would be his first reply. But we also have seen that this contention is basically unsupported: As I observed in Chapter 2, Habermas posits the "complementarity" of a communicatively burdensome lifeworld and communication-replacing subsystems entirely at the level of theory; we can now add that this direct inference from complexity is in fact insupportable except on the basis of empirical evidence that admits of more than one relevant interpretation (communicative overburdening or socially induced *akrasia*). Ironically, however, if you ask this same question of the earlier Habermas, the answer is rather different: His answer then appeared to be that it is the lack of emancipated, postconventional individuals that is the chief obstacle to social emancipation. In 1974, he maintained not just that "an autonomous ego and an emancipated society reciprocally require one another" but that, unfortunately, the realization of ego autonomy "is *by no means a regular occurrence* . . . in fact, *it is usually not attained*."[51] We are back, then, in the vicious circle: From where will such individuals come, when the vast majority continue to be shaped by more or less conventional societies concerned with their own reproduction? What is to be done if the issue is in fact *akrasia* as Habermas describes it, if the problem is that social structures are lacking for the stabilization of postconventional identities—indeed, that advanced capitalist economic and political systems conspire against the cultivation of individual autonomy—while such structures cannot come about except through processes of individual and then cultural learning? If we continue to insist, as Habermas has ceased to do, that the emancipation of individuals is meaningless if it is not the first movement of a dialectical process that includes the emancipation of society—if we continue to insist, for instance, that the administrative and economic subsystems as they operate today are inherently unjust in their internal operations (in the alienation and exploitation of labor, the trivializing and undermining of the democratic regulation of social life), and that *stalemate* with their inherently expanding dynamics brought about through social struggle is insufficiently radical a response to such injustice—then our questions regarding obstacles to emancipation become the following:

1. On what basis could postconventional forms of socialization be instituted in a society that is not yet postconventional (although, as a matter of fact, neither is it stably conventional)?
2. Can we identify points of leverage (i.e., potentials for protest or transformation) within the status quo that could save this argument from the charge of utopian thinking, of sociopolitical elitism or paternalism?
3. Are there functional connections between stalled developmental forms and the status quo social structures that would indicate systemic obstacles to such changes?

The first two questions are linked and will be answered by the argument of the concluding chapter. Only question (c) really falls within in the purview of Habermas' theory of socialization and so needs to be answered before this chapter is through.

Before I turn to this question, however, I consider in more detail a puzzling feature regarding the solution Habermas gleans from Mead, as well as some issues regarding his interpretation of Mead's theory. The puzzling feature is the question of how it is that at the postconventional level alone the mere anticipation of recognition from a projected community is able to stabilize one's identity, breaking the reciprocity between social and psychological forms that had been maintained to this point. How is it that the lack of reality of such a community of recognition does not result in *akrasia*, in the manner just discussed, since the needs and identity of the postconventional moral reasoner do not receive recognition within the contexts of their actual social interactions? As Peter Dews argues in a similar vein, "the anticipation of such a community cannot answer the question of 'who I am'; it cannot furnish me with the *concrete meaning* of my individual existence. This is because the specific meaning of my life can only be unfolded in *actual* interactions with others."[52] Is there, as *Between Facts and Norms* seems to presuppose, some domain of society in which such interactions could take place? Habermas has maintained quite explicitly that the abstractness of postconventional morality (ultimately, of discourse ethics) can be overcome only by reinserting it into the context of everyday life, which is only possible where

> a form of life meets it halfway. There has to be a modicum of congruence between morality and the practices of socialization and education. The latter must promote the requisite internalization of superego controls and the abstractness of ego identities. In addition, there must be a modicum of fit between morality and sociopolitical institutions. Not just any institutions will do. Morality thrives only in an environment in which postconventional ideas about law and morality have already been institutionalized to a certain extent.[53]

Although the claim that postconventional morality has, in light of the differentiation of modern society, become "unavoidable" certainly implies that such congruence indeed attains, in the very paper in question Habermas concedes that the crucial processes of socialization, and the crucial institutions that would ground the possibility of discourse, are often lacking in practice.[54] Appeal to a rationalized form of life, then, is not an option for satisfying the kinds of objections made by Dews and by me; but even if it were, we would have to be extremely careful about how we tried to justify that response since the caveat, "halfway," is important.

Dews also accuses Habermas of having misrepresented Mead in suggesting that the discrepancy between the "me" and the "I" is an historical rather than a metaphysical problem. The idea, in Dews' reading of Habermas, is that in the right kind of society, where a form of life met postconventional morality (at least?) halfway, the socialized personality—the "me"—would itself be postconventional. Dews maintains, however, that the coincidence of the "I" and the "me" can never be brought about "because of a moment of coagulation which is built into (linguistic) self-presentation as such. Thus the duality of the self cannot be considered as a merely historical feature, which would be overcome in a hypothetical society founded on fully mutual recognition."[55] Although Mead did entertain the idealized notion of a universal discourse that would reflect such recognition, claims Dews, "he never suggests that in such a society the distinction between 'I' and 'me' would disappear."[56] It seems to me that this objection rests on a misunderstanding of Habermas, one that is also evidenced, yet in a surprisingly inverted way, in the work of Mitchell Aboulafia.

Aboulafia's concern is to defend Mead against Habermas' (mis)reading of him and to suggest in addition that Mead's actual position is more adequate than the conclusions Habermas draws on the basis of his misunderstanding. Insofar as Habermas hopes to get out of Mead no more than a set of conceptual tools for the construction of a hypothesis that is amenable to empirical verification, I think we can mostly put to the side the question of Mead's true position. In addition to agreeing with Dews that Habermas' version of a projected, abstract universal communication community is too thin and procedural (for Mead, the universal remains rooted within the concrete), Aboulafia contends that Habermas misconstrues the "I" and the "me" by presenting them as a rigid binary, as forms of transcendence and conservatism, respectively. In fact, Mead saw the relationship between the two as "dialectical," a position that is, in addition and according to Aboulafia, more adequate since as a matter of fact the "me" can contain the perspectives of communities that Habermas would think of as postconventional, as is the case with an institution such as the United Nations.[57] This is the connection with and inversion of Dews: is it therefore the case that the "me" and the "I" would coincide in such an example, which Dews believes Habermas illegitimately allows but which Aboulafia considers him to have too categorically ruled out?

The answer, I think, is that both readings miss their mark. Habermas issues a warning regarding the limits of the homologies between individual moral consciousness and social development that is crucial in this respect: The parallels refer to structure, *not content*; "individual consciousness and cultural tradition can agree in their content without expressing the same structures of consciousness."[58] As a result, as R. E. Young writes, "[t]he potential paradox of a fully enlightened society is that it could not simply impose its enlightenment on the coming generation."[59] In other words, in Aboulafia's counterexample, it doesn't matter that the content of the norms internalized through the process of taking the perspective of the other—by which means the conventional "me" is formed—embody the postconventional insights *of others*: One can be a dogmatic and uncritical defender of a universalist conception of human rights, of democracy or the rule of law. The transcendence of socialized roles by the "I," its break with the "me," signals the process of autonomous insight, the "yes" or "no" to the validity of the norms proposed by one's community, whether it be postconventional or not. In another context, Habermas expresses the same difference of form in the language of William James, in which the "twice-born" differ from the "once-born" in light of the reflective, critical form in which they have appropriated the same belief content.[60] Whether that position is authentically Mead-ean may well be another matter. But, on this basis, we can also see that it cannot be the case, as Dews charges, that Habermas intends the differentiation between the "me" and the "I" to be relinquished in the case of an ideal, future, emancipated society. Just the opposite, the distinction is a necessary condition for autonomous self-realization, the critical appropriation of one's life history and socialization (including the possibility of both "yes-es" and "no-s" to the validity of cultural norms). In fact, with respect to structure, it isn't entirely clear that a postconventional practical "me" is possible after all (which doesn't entail anything about the possibility of an emancipated society). Habermas writes, apparently with guarded approval, the following:

> In discussion, Klaus Eder advanced the thesis that there could be collective identities corresponding to personal identities only at the stage of conventional (role) identity. Postconventional ego identity would have to do without support from a collective identity. The fictions of a cosmopolitan state of affairs, a socialist order of society, an association of free producers, and so on, would then merely signify stages in the dissolution of collective identity as such. . . . Nevertheless, such identity projections illustrate the conditions of a universalistically regulated domain of communicative action, against which the provisionally constructed, collective identities of particular reference groups can be relativized and rendered fluid. From this perspective the question of whether complex societies can construct a rational identity would have to be answered as follows: a collective identity becomes superfluous as soon as the mass of the members of a society are sociostructurally forced to lay aside their role identities, however generalized, and develop ego identities. The idea of an identity become reflective, to be collectively established in the future, would now be the last illusory husk before collective identities as such would be given up and replaced by the permanent variation of all reference systems.[61]

The "me," as we know, is the internalized representative of a collective identity and so this passage, although tentative in tone, is consonant with the possibility that in practical terms the "me" is dissolved in postconventional insight (which is to say nothing about the continued existence of an epistemic "me," and a "me" that is the "object" of introspection and sincere self-presentation, etc.). At the same time, it is with good reason that Habermas is not unequivocal in his endorsement of this suggestion from Eder: He has already made the development of postconventionality conditional on a form of life, practices of socialization and institutions that "meet it halfway." So there must be some sense in which there remains a collective *component* to postconventional identity—that is, a form or forms of rationalized collective life that are prerequisite to and supportive of the development of postconventional ego identity—even if, in the last instance, they must be relativized, made into a resource for self-interpretation and formation. We should note, however, that such a collective identity meets postconventional ego structures and morality *no more than halfway*. Habermas, in response to a criticism by

Albrecht Wellmer, retracts an early formulation in which he suggested that it would be possible to derive a substantive, fully rational (collective) form of life from the standards of discourse ethics—and, in fact, by the time of *Between Facts and Norms*, Habermas appears never to tire of criticizing such views himself. To the contrary, forms of life, unlike questions of justice or truth, cannot be judged according to the universalistic criteria of procedural rationality: Every form of life contains ethical content that is not susceptible to this sort of judgment, but can at best be characterized (from a different perspective) as healthy or unhealthy, more or less alienated.[62] Habermas quotes Wellmer himself in this connection:

> For this reason we can specify only certain formal conditions of a rational life—such as a universalistic moral consciousness, a universalistic law, a collective identity that has become reflective [*pace* Eder], and so forth. But insofar as we are dealing with the possibility of a rational life in the substantial sense, with the possibility of a rational identity, there is no ideal limit value describable in terms of formal structures. There exists rather only the success or failure of the efforts to achieve a form of life in which the unconstrained identity of individuals, along with unconstrained reciprocity among individuals, becomes an experienceable reality.[63]

Habermas himself concludes on this basis that, at the level of theory, this leaves only the critique of distortions inflicted upon substantial life forms in advanced capitalist societies. This takes us full circle: His account of these distortions *is* his account of the obstacles that prevent the formation of postconventional identities, namely, the colonization of the lifeworld and cultural impoverishment. I would add, however, that although this conclusion is certainly not wrong, it does seem to me unnecessarily chaste: It is also possible to reflect positively on the tentative, precarious empirical achievements of recognition that structural changes in developed societies have made possible. It seem to me that multiculturalism, very broadly speaking—recognition theory, feminist and queer theory, and the development of civil rights movements, counter-publics, and some multicultural social policies—as well as cosmopolitanism—the development of global civil society and international law—are the most interesting and important phenomena in this regard. It is my aim in the Concluding Reflections to offer an appraisal of the potential significance of these changes as the positive, hopeful counterpart to the discussion of the distortions of postconventionality that have occupied us thus far.

Arrested Development and the Systems-Theoretical Individual

Even in later writings, in which he regards postconventionality as a requirement exacted of members of modern rationalized societies, Habermas concedes that the empirical situation is to some extent confused by contradictory or apparently contradictory trends. In particular, although he is critical of the systems-theoretical *concept* of increasing individuation as the expansion of the scope for strategic decision making, Habermas does not deny that these theorists can point to very real evidence in support of their view. At the stage at which rationalization takes the form of the differentiation of media-steered subsystems, there is indeed an expansion of situations in which strategic action is demanded of individuals. Habermas' description of the strategically oriented self is significant:

> Under conditions of strategic action, the self of self-determination and of self-realization slips out of intersubjective relations. The strategic actor no longer draws from an intersubjectively shared lifeworld; having himself become worldless, as it were, he stands over against the objective world and makes decisions solely according to standards of subjective preference. He does not rely therein upon recognition by others. Autonomy is then transformed into freedom of choice, and the individuation of the socialized subject is transformed into the isolation of a liberated subject who possesses himself.[64]

Like Habermas himself, the systems theorist Ulrich Beck concedes that the "liberation" effected by the disintegration and detraditionalization of the lifeworld, as a result of which such strategic action contexts proliferate, is at least in the first instance experienced "fatalistically" by those who undergo it.[65] Whereas traditional social roles and ascriptive status positions had "normatively bundled" marriage, family, career, and other life options—particularly those most important to the individual—in modern societies the number of possibilities between which the individual must decide explodes.[66] In Beck's characterization, the isolated individual confronts such social options, opportunities, possible roles, *externally*, although at the same time the decision must be made under system conditions that do not lie in the sphere of control of the chooser. Individuals who select their inclusion into specific subsystems are thereby subjected to new forms of dependence: They must orient themselves to pregiven steering media such as money or power. "These media exercise a behavioral control that, on the one hand, individualizes because it is tailored to choices of the individual that are steered by preferences; but on the other hand it also standardizes because it only allows options in prestructured dimensions (having or not having, commanding or obeying)."[67] Each decision further entangles the individual in a net of pregiven dependencies in the market, the education system, the health system, and so on[68]; through this limited self-selection individuals are made to fill the grid of social reproduction, as it were. But if this is so, Habermas argues, the release and isolation of individuals, through which they adopt the external, strategic relation to subsystems, cannot be equated with "successful emancipation."

Far from describing increasing individuation, the system theorist captures at most a process of singularization and, far from an increase in autonomy, this represents "at most a transformation in the mode of social control."[69] Habermas does not intend to deny that it occurs; as we have seen, he considers it an empirical question the extent to which system integration or social integration prevails in any given society. My own interest at this point is not in arguing generally that system integration has empirically gained the upper hand; instead, I want to suggest that this conceptualization of modern "individuality" better captures stalled forms of development than Habermas' own account of value relativism, positivism, and so on. That is, as Habermas himself admits, the differentiation of media-steered subsystems calls for decision-making structures rooted in a view of the self—a form of self-understanding or identity—as an isolated, strategically acting individual choosing among pregiven options on the basis of subjective preferences. Such an identity, it seems to me, is significant relative to the stabilization of the social order in that it reflects what Horkheimer called the "idolatry of the actual": Such individuals do not critically thematize the validity of the options with which they are presented, but see them as quasi-natural features of the social world, just as "the lads" saw the occupational sphere. As this strategic orientation, suited to the needs of steering media, colonizes domains of the lifeworld for which it is unsuited, it undermines (together with phenomena of cultural impoverishment) the development of the sorts of postconventional personality structures—through undermining the basis of their development in communicative action—on which alternative, nonconventional forms of social integration rely.

In order to vindicate my hypothesis, however, it is necessary first to investigate the form of interrupted development, the situation in which the individual is left whose process of development has been undermined by these obstacles prior to attaining postconventionality. We already know, of course, what a conventional identity looks like, so if development does not at all proceed beyond that point, we have our answer. But given the effect of social differentiation and colonization on the stability of the conventional social world, this form of underdevelopment is increasingly uncommon according to Habermas' own argument. His social-theoretical writings offer some hints regarding what the consequence of this might be: According to *The Theory of Communicative Action*, the outcome of colonization and cultural impoverishment is either rigid traditionalism (which is not the same as immersion in a living, albeit conservative cultural tradition), or the fragmentation of consciousness that is unable to construct for itself a holistic interpretation of the world against which social critique could be posed; in *Legitimation Crisis*, Habermas described the phenomenon of cultural impoverishment—connected there to the discrediting of traditional worldviews by science—as resulting in an increasing positivism in everyday consciousness, the inability to construct a holistic interpretation of the world, and a consequent, pervasive value irrationalism. Most importantly, he had suggested in that earlier work, albeit obliquely, that this value irrationalism in particular plays a role in the maintenance of bourgeois privatism and the depoliticization of the public sphere. In his later moral writings, however, Habermas appears to give a different sort of answer.

Arrested Development and Moral Consciousness

This discussion returns us to a question left unanswered some time ago: Among the list of problems with which Kohlberg's developmental account was faced were the empirical reality of Stage 6, as well as the challenge of value skeptics and relativists. On the subject of the former, I have already noted that in his later formulations, Kohlberg himself omitted Stage 6, claiming that the most recent empirical data available to him had ceased to provide evidence of its existence. It is interesting that Habermas does not even suggest (as the theory of colonization clearly implies, or as Adorno or Horkheimer certainly might have argued) the possibility of a sociological explanation for this change; that is, that the declining empirical basis for Stage 6 might actually reflect social trends rather than an error in earlier interpretations. Habermas, however, defends the reality of Stage 6 as he construes it (as the level of discourse ethics and not Kantian or Rawlsian "monological" proceduralism) through an entirely different sort of argument. In short, he claims that Stage 6 is unique in that it represents a reflective turn, as opposed to the sort of linear development that characterizes Stages 1 through 5, and that it would be inappropriate to conceive of such a reflective stage along the lines of natural psychological development. The claim he makes for Stage 6, then, is unabashedly normative: "One must be able to show that a person relying not on the self-evident nature of universal principles [as do reasoners at Stage 5] but on the legitimating power of procedures for justification is in fact better equipped to oppose skeptical objections and thus also better able to judge consistently."[70] As long as there are individuals who deny that there is any difference between ultimate principles and proceduralism, Stages 5 and 6, discourse ethics requires defense in the philosophical arena, not as a claim about the natural culmination of psychological development but about theoretical adequacy. Kohlberg's account, in this light, can be seen to supply only indirect confirmation for the theory of discourse ethics through the "consonance" between the two theories; direct validation is to be sought through competition with other moral theories.[71] In fact, Habermas suggests that this isn't merely the temporary historical situation of discourse ethics, a peripheral issue to be resolved prior to resuming the psychological perspective. Nor does he seem to believe it is a cop-out of the real issue at hand, which is whether the highest stage of moral development should be located in the competence for discourse (I say this is the "real issue" because, according to his own argument, it is the ordering of interactive competencies that are the product of socialization that justifies the developmental logic, not the conceptions of justice that flow from them). His explanation is that what we are talking about at this level is the existence and nature of a form of moral reasoning in which we engage in reflection on the validity of moral principles themselves: That is to say, we are talking about the capacity to engage in moral-theoretical, or moral-philosophical debate. Citing McCarthy, Habermas notes that in cases in which a hypothetical attitude is taken toward moral questions, the asymmetry is overcome that had existed between the intuitive competence of an experimental subject (their "know-how")—for example, a child unreflectively manifesting pretheoretical knowledge in an experimental setting—and the psychologist with his or her explication of that pretheoretical knowledge into theoretical claims ("know-that") which are themselves inaccessible to the subject. The reflective turn at Stage 6 puts the subject on a par with the moral psychologist. This explains why the asymmetry of the psychological perspective must be relinquished not only temporarily; but it doesn't actually answer the question about the competence for discourse, whether a Stage 6 of this form really exists. We have already seen one possible answer: Although he does not do so, Habermas in this situation might appeal to the "performative contradiction" argument discussed earlier, by claiming that anyone who denied that discourse competence could be empirically grounded could only do so through participating in discourse. Note, however, that this argument (which is not Habermas') and the previous one (which is) both simply presume that the competencies necessary for participation in discourse are in fact accessible to the interlocutors: This potentially counterfactual presumption is an unavoidable part of communicative action. But the real issue with the empirical data is that it suggests that competent participation in such a discourse is not possible for at least a majority of individuals and, if so, the performative argument would fail pragmatically. In that case, explanation would be required for how communication can nevertheless be maintained (e.g., via the theory of ideology or distorted communication).

There are some commentators who consider such an empirical assessment to be so patently absurd on its own as to undermine the plausibility of Kohlberg's (or Kohlberg-like) approaches. Gilligan and Murphy, for instance, incredulously declare that "Kohlberg's criteria would put half the population of the United States at some level below the postconventional in terms of their moral consciousness."[72] From the perspective of social psychology, one can see how such a claim would suggest that the researcher was importing normative assumptions into the interpretive schema, which is problematic for a science that conceives of itself along descriptive lines. But from the perspective of a critical theory of society, there is nothing at all surprising about the fact that the majority of people in a stable yet unjust society should be fundamentally uncritical, and apparently unable to be really otherwise. Habermas' assertion in his earlier work that postconventionality is rare, or Adorno or Horkheimer's claim that it is practically nonexistent, would suggest that a figure of half the population of the United States would almost certainly be overly optimistic (imagine the postconventionally inspired election victories!).

Although the question of the reality of Stage 6 has not been answered to any satisfactory degree, we have seen how Habermas conceives of and defends the transition to discourse ethics, namely, how he evades the problem at the descriptive level, which is the only part that is really crucial for my own discussion. Assessing the reality of postconventional development is, after all, the point of this entire chapter and I am, in that sense, attempting to take a significantly wider view of the problem than Habermas does in the single paper under discussion here. The remaining problem, then, is how to interpret value skeptics and relativists. The reason that it is important to come back to this issue is that it is my hypothesis that some form of relativism not wholly unlike what Kohlberg described is in fact the most common outcome of moral development as arrested by the sorts of obstacles described here and in earlier chapters.

Kohlberg formulated Stage 4½ to accommodate relativistic judgments that were predominantly made from a strategic and not a moral point of view. Although such a perspective resembles the hedonism of Stage 2, it was combined with a level of argumentation too sophisticated to be of the preconventional kind. Kohlberg's description—which I hope will strongly remind the reader of both the concept of the modern individual described by systems theorists, as well as Habermas' own description of the individual acting under the premises of strategic action—is as follows:

> This level is postconventional but not yet principled. . . . At Stage 4½, choice is personal and subjective. It is based on emotions,

> conscience is seen as arbitrary and relative as are ideas such as "duty" and "morally right." . . . At this stage the [social] perspective is that of an individual standing outside of his own society and considering himself an individual making decisions without generalized commitment or contract with society. One can pick and choose obligations, which are defined by particular societies, but one has no principles for such a choice.[73]

Although this description comes from an essay written several years before Habermas' paper on Mead, in which he discusses Beck, it is remarkable that Habermas himself does not draw the connection in either place. Instead, he adds of such individuals that,

> [t]he hypothetical attitude with which they judged the social world without moralizing it also spoke for an affinity of their statements with judgments on the postconventional level. For those reasons, Kohlberg has placed these relativistic judgments between the conventional and the postconventional levels, assigning them to a transitional stage of their own, a stage that calls less for structural description than for psychodynamic explanation and is the expression of an unresolved crisis of adolescence. This interpretation leaves something to be desired, since it cannot explain the possibility of this level of judgment being stabilized. That such stabilization is indeed possible is indicated, among other things, by the fact that a philosophical version of the value skepticism of stage 4½ has been developed and defended as a position to be taken seriously by thinkers in a line that starts with Weber and extends to Popper.[74]

The position in question—which takes in core aspects of postmodern relativism in addition to the positivist lineage mentioned—maintains essentially that moral conflicts cannot be decided "on the basis of valid (i.e., intersubjectively binding) reasons."[75] There is something very curious about the means by which Habermas defends the seriousness of this position: Why does the existence of a philosophical version suggest stability, especially when Habermas himself has spared no effort in attempting to prove these philosophical theories to be contradictory? Why can't such a development find stabilization, after the pattern of ego identity, through consonance with society and social norms, or as an adaptive mechanism of the sort described by Held under the title of "pragmatic acquiescence"? Why might it not be that positivist and postmodernist forms of moral consciousness are stabilized through the harmony they enjoy with a positivist, postmodern society, one characterized by the transformation of processes of social integration to coordination via steering media—that is, by the spread of colonization—the description of which is linked to an account of the individual that is basically identical? It is true that *theories* of all kinds could be said to pursue stability through internal coherence or consistency, but it is far from obvious that the same can be said of individuals. Habermas is pragmatist enough to recognize in other contexts that inconsistencies need only be dealt with (contra Descartes, they *can* only be dealt with) if they are somehow problematized by our experience and made thematic; but that is just what is unlikely to occur the more this form of consciousness effectively mirrors social trends.

It is my hypothesis that the continued persistence of obstacles such as the colonization of the lifeworld and the absence of a source for identity-stabilizing recognition at the postconventional level, explains the prevalence of this form of relativistically stalled development. At this later point in his career, however, Habermas offers a different sort of account:

> My own explanation for this troubling phenomenon of a transitional stage is that the group of respondents in question have only partially completed the transition to the postconventional level. If the integration of speaker perspectives with world perspectives has not been fully achieved and does not take in the social world and the norm-conformative attitude corresponding to it, there will fail to occur the coordination of the success-oriented attitude of the subject who acts strategically with the attitude oriented toward reaching understanding of the person who continues to communicate through argument—a coordination that discourse ethics presupposes. Moreover, it will fail to occur precisely in those cases in which problematic *normative claims to validity* are thematized. In such cases the sociocognitive inventory of the conventional stage of interaction can be said to have been only partly reorganized in the sense that while the adolescent has learned to reason theoretically, he stops short of moral argumentation.[76]

As explanations go, this seems to me pretty opaque and, more importantly, ultimately question-begging. Recall that the system of world perspectives and speaker perspectives were completed at the conventional level; Habermas maintains, however, that they are not put fully into relation with one another until the level of discourse is attained, in which the opposition between strategic and communicative action is also overcome. His explanation of the way this occurs is as follows: In discourse, the world perspectives are thematized in the hypothetical attitude as the domains referenced by problematic validity claims (i.e., truth in the objective world or rightness in the social world). The system of speaker perspectives (first-, second-, and third-person) form the "constitutive framework within which participants in argumentation can reach rationally motivated agreement,"[77] that is, adopting the perspective of the other as well as the systematic observer's perspective are necessary stages in producing and evaluating rational arguments with respect to the thematized "worlds." To say that this process fails to take in the social world is simply to say that, for some entirely unspecified reason, although all the cognitive prerequisites appear to be in place, the young person simply does not realize that one can argue about norms, at least not in the attitude of norm conformity. In short, it is to restate the problem rather than explain it. It isn't hard to see, in this light, why Kohlberg turns to psychodynamic explanation: Habermas himself already suggested to us that an individual with the cognitive and interactive capacities of a certain level will acquire the corresponding level of moral consciousness unless threats to ego identity, failures of recognition, and so on, undermine this process. And it would appear that, at this stage, these young people have all the tools they need for discourse, in which Habermas claims they are indeed able to engage where matters of truth are concerned, while being unable to do so when morality is at issue. As a result, these individuals address themselves to norms in the objectivating attitude, considering them as quasi-natural features of the social world to be taken into account in the process of making strategic decisions. That is, the result is the adoption of a self-understanding complementary to media-steered subsystems and described by systems theory as the essence of the modern form of individuality.

So what exactly is missing here? It appears that what is doing all the work for practical discourse is the adoption of the hypothetical attitude *within* the norm-conformative perspective on the social world. It is my hypothesis that the subjects in question fail to achieve this precisely because they cannot seriously adopt a hypothetical attitude toward norms as such, cannot seriously conceive as a rationally grounded possibility that the social world could be otherwise than it is, and that this incapacity, in turn, is to be explained sociologically. The key difference between the participant in discourse and the strategic reasoner just described is that the latter does not question norms or view them as one possibility among others, but takes them, in Habermas' language, as prestructured options. This should hardly be surprising since, in other contexts, Habermas is perfectly unambiguous about the fact that the transition to discourse, the undermining of the conventional social world, is brought about by the introduction of the hypothetical attitude that, he claims, deprives the social world "to which one was naively habituated and which was unproblematically accepted . . . of its quasi-natural validity."[78] Again, referring to the uncritical acceptance of norms, roles, and definitions of justice at the conventional level, Habermas repeats, "[a]s we have seen, this syndrome disintegrates when a hypothetical attitude is introduced. Before the reflective gaze of a participant in discourse, the social world dissolves into so many conventions in need of justification. The empirical store of traditional norms is split into social facts and norms."[79] But this is precisely what doesn't happen for the popular positivist or postmodern relativist consciousness: Although traditional norms are undermined, especially in light of the insight into cultural pluralism, they retain the character of social facts over which no criteria for justification presides. And, paradoxically (this is part of the inconsistency of such a position), the social facts that continue to be recognized are fatalistically linked with purportedly "realist" views of human nature and so attain a kind of pseudo-normative force simply because they are "the facts." This view is consonant with both Kohlberg's description of Stage 4½ as well as with the model of the individual derived from systems theory. It also is precisely what Horkheimer described as the "idolatry of the actual": Alternatives to the status quo can be entertained in the abstract alone; they are all to be met with the pseudo-realist rejoinder that, although indeed it sounds "nice," "people just aren't . . ." or "the world just isn't like that." It seems to me that this complex manifests itself also at the communicative-logical level as a persistent confusion of descriptive and normative claims: normative suggestions based on a hypothetical approach to the social world from within the norm-conformative attitude are discounted as "unrealistic."[80] On this basis, the line demarcating communicative from strategic actions in the social world is deeply blurred, a symptom that Habermas had—earlier in his career—described as characteristic of systematically distorted communication.[81] He has since more or less ceased to talk about distorted communication, but it is clear from his account of the nature of discourse described here that this rejection of the distinction between rationally motivated consensus and agreement on the basis of coercion is not only self-contradictory, but precludes participation in discourse.

Habermas himself concludes his explanation by claiming that the undermining of the certainties of the conventional world leaves the young person two options. The first is that the individual can engage in the reflective reconstructions of his or her cognitive inventory ("duty," "validity," "responsibility," etc.) necessary for the transition to postconventionality, a process that was described in the previous chapter. On the other hand, however, the adolescent can make the break with the conventional mode without transitioning to the postconventional:

> In this case, he views the collapse of the world of conventions as a debunking of false cognitive claims with which conventional

> norms and prescriptive statements have hitherto been linked. The basic moral concepts in their cognitively devalued conventional form then appear retrospectively as requiring explanation. The adolescent's task is to come to terms with the dissonance between his moral intuitions which continue to determine his unreflective everyday knowledge and actions, and his (presumed) insight into the illusory nature of this conventional form of consciousness which reflection has discredited but which has not ceased to function in everyday life. For the second developmental path, metaethical explanation of moral illusions takes the place of postconventional renewal of ethical consciousness. The more successfully theoretical skepticism has been reconciled with the intuitions that go unchallenged in practice, the more easily such explanation can handle the dissonances.[82]

Habermas cites Weber as an example of such "successful" ethical skepticism. In other words, here too Habermas appeals to philosophically articulated theories in a teleological explanation of what is supposed to be a common, unreflective (or, at least not fully reflective) form of consciousness. But the problem of reconciling the debunked pretences of conventional morality with what Habermas and I both regard as the continued quasi-natural acceptance of these norms in practice, only becomes an issue for the individual if somehow problematized or made thematic.[83] Otherwise, ordinary young people are not aspiring Max Webers. To the extent that they are increasingly socialized in circumstances in which strategic attitudes prevail, as a result of colonization—or, for Habermas, sometimes acceptable mediatization—there is little reason to expect that problematization will occur or, for that matter, to expect that it will be dealt with consciously if it does so only very rarely. We saw in the Intermediate Reflections that research in the sociology of schooling confirms phenomena that, for Habermas, would count as colonization and that serve to explain the predominance of strategically oriented, stalled forms of development and self-identity, including the dominance of possessive individualism, status orientations, and so on. More importantly still, we saw the reciprocally stabilizing effect these ontogenetic developments have on the status quo social order, the reproduction of class structure; what we have added to this diagnosis in this chapter is that such colonization has the practical effect on the individual of undermining the development of normative discourse competence and, at the same time, the possibility of a normative critique of society. In doing so, it frustrates not a philosophical ideal but an immanent potential of autonomous human beings.

Concluding Reflections

Multicultural Identity as Postconventionality

In these concluding reflections, my principal aim is to defend a deliberative democratic account of multiculturalism or, better, of multicultural integration. I mean by this an account according to which citizens must determine for themselves, collectively, how they will govern themselves as a political society characterized by irreducible cultural and ethnic diversity, how they want to understand themselves as a society relative to that diversity. In so arguing, I am rejecting the idea that protecting cultural pluralism requires recognizing a new kind of group right, such as a right to indefinite cultural survival, as well as the old kind of national right, such as the right to self-determination of "peoples." These interpretations entail unavoidable forms of injustice (in particular, with respect to internal minorities) and appeal to spurious normative bases. But defending the superior justice of a deliberative democratic account might, in a sense, seem to overshoot the mark. Recall that the overall argument to be advanced in this book is that there is an incompatibility between advanced capitalism and multicultural social integration, so it is the ability of specific policies to foster integration that we must keep in our sights. At the same time, it is my position that the deliberative democratic proposal is both most in keeping with moral insight, and represents the most stable policy alternative. There is an obvious reason to suspect this convergence of legitimacy and stability, namely, the fact that the stability of an unjust social formation is always threatened by the possibility of that injustice being unmasked. Nevertheless, the fact that the argument centers on the question of integration is relevant for considering its status, to which I turn in conclusion.

The confluence of the requirements of justice and stability is fortuitous, however, in that it should forestall any impression of paternalism, as though I were recommending to political elites a means of advancing their own interests in social stability at the expense of the true interests of subaltern groups. The historically typical version of such an argument has been the opposite of the one offered here: namely, that total assimilation would offer the greatest degree of stability. However, not only have such policies never actually worked in the past but, as Will Kymlicka has argued, in the past twenty years multiculturalism as a political framework for negotiating minority-state relations has spread across the globe, led by relative successes in developed nations and by attempts to formulate international standards for minority rights protection at the United Nations and in other regional bodies.[1] The result is to have made programs aimed at assimilation definitively unfeasible and to have provided a standard in light of which minorities themselves perceive their oppression as a violation of their basic rights. Thus, the adoption of some kind of multicultural policy is required for the integration of diverse societies and it is my argument that policies normatively rooted in the ideals of deliberative democracy would be the most effective, precisely because they best realize the constitutional and human rights of all those affected. Once I have defended this conception of multiculturalism, I argue that it represents a form of life that meets postconventionality—as described in the previous chapter—halfway. That is, effective participation in cross-cultural practical discourses offers the potential for widespread identity-stabilizing postconventional recognition in diverse societies, while the societal need to socialize individuals with the competence for participation in integrating, multicultural discourses presents an immanent pressure toward the cultivation of postconventionality. Defending this position will require the refutation of persistent criticisms—such as those advanced by Charles Taylor and Axel Honneth—of the "abstraction" of Habermas' proceduralist account of democracy and of discourse ethics.

So my argument concludes here with the following claims: As we have seen, postconventionality and advanced capitalism (in light of phenomena of colonization and cultural impoverishment, in particular) are incompatible; but genuine (stable and just) multicultural integration requires postconventionality (through requiring the competence for participation in integrative discourses); therefore, multiculturalism and advanced capitalism are incompatible. However, the argument goes beyond this to outline an immanent possibility for the widespread realization of this incompatibility, and for the cultivation of a politically significant kind of solidarity not confined to potential congruencies of self-interest, in the form of an identity transformed through multicultural discourses such that diversity itself has become constitutive for it, in a decentering, nonassimilative manner. Of course, noting an incompatibility does not in any way amount to a prediction that things will turn out one way rather than another; but the argument intends to prove that, where the contradiction is resolved in favor of the capitalist instrumentalization of socialization processes, it will necessarily do so at the expense of social integration in diverse societies. Habermas himself seemed to have thought as much in *Legitimation Crisis*, but assumed that the burden of integration might be assumed by systemic forms instead, thus preventing any resultant destabilization. The irreducibility of cultural diversity, however, entails that this is no longer a viable alternative: Persistent and irreconcilable cultural conflict is the cost of capitalism's victory over autonomous socialization.

New York Multiculturalism and the "Contact" Hypothesis

When I taught multiculturalism to undergraduates at Fordham University, in New York City, I often used the example of New York itself to clarify what I had in mind. For those who self-identify as "New Yorkers"—and for many residents of the city this is a central aspect of their identity, easily rivaling national identifications—the diversity of the city is an indispensable element of its meaning: New York would not be New York if it did not contain the sorts of diversity it does. As a result, self-identifying "New Yorkers" are in a position to perceive threats to the existence of cultural groups and forms of life—let's say, to Chinatown, or Little Italy—as threats to their own identity, even while they do not themselves (let's say) have any genealogical connection to the affected groups. As Hegel would have said, such individuals have become "at home in otherness," where *particular* forms of otherness have become a constitutive part of the meaning of their identity. This possibility can be described as illustrating the form of a kind of *interest-transcending solidarity*, at least on the usual interpretations of "interest" as a function of socioeconomic (status/class) position. Of course, in a much broader sense, we all have an interest in not having our identity threatened; but the "interest" in this case is moral rather than utilitarian.

Clarissa Rile Hayward discusses a number of writers who appeal to the potential of urban life for effecting something like this transformation of identity: Although they all concede that, in practice, the city is a highly anti-democratic, bureaucratic political institution, they nevertheless see in it a more or less unrealized potential for fostering inclusive and democratic forms of citizenship. According to this account, it isn't just that the city is small enough to make genuinely democratic participation possible, while being sufficiently significant politically such that participation can realize meaningful forms of self-determination (although this, too, is important). The allure of the city scale is "its capacity to foster, at the level of the psyche of individual citizens, a sense of the self as an actor in public."[2] In short, the argument is that mere habitual contact among strangers in public places fosters a sense of "association," "a conscious awareness of the stranger and a regard for her as a partner in a joint political venture, which cultivates . . . an openness and a receptivity to her claims."[3] Living in a diverse city structured in such a way as to encourage these interactions (which obviously is not a given) is regarded as fostering a kind of mutual concern among individuals who nevertheless do not experience one another as "sharing an identity based on a supposed social sameness and/or common interest."[4]

The problem with this proposal is that, as Hayward notes, it ignores the foundational contribution of a commitment to certain kinds of moral-political principles on the part of citizens, for example, to democratic equality, popular sovereignty, and human rights. Can contact alone bring about such commitments or, in their absence, will it merely result in an increased awareness of conflicting interests, resentment-inspiring inequalities, and the like? Fortunately, there have been extensive attempts to empirically test what has been termed *the contact hypothesis* (i.e., this idea that contact and interaction between members of various groups can reduce prejudice).[5] The upshot of this research is that, under the appropriate conditions, the contact hypothesis appears to hold some water; the problem is that the "appropriate conditions" are both extensive and largely lacking in practice. In Gordon Allport's early assessment, they include the following:

> contact must take place (1) under conditions of cooperative independence in which participants work to achieve a shared goal, (2) [participants must] enjoy equal status, and (3) work in a context in which group stereotypes are disconfirmed, [and in which] (4) egalitarian social norms prevail, and [where] (5) the potential for becoming acquaintances (that is, for getting to know members of other socially defined groupings as individuals, and not merely as group members) is high.[6]

Research in the past fifty years confirms that in the absence of these conditions, the contact hypothesis fails. That the nontrivial and largely principled prerequisites that qualify the contact hypothesis are indeed lacking in actual social practice can be seen quite clearly in the example of New York: It would not be uniformly easy to include all groups in the inclusive sense of "New Yorker," nor is such an inclusive identity equally accessible to all groups residing in the city. In this respect, the examples of Chinatown and Little Italy were not randomly selected, but represent two groups that enjoy relatively high levels of education and mobility in American society as a whole. The obvious counterexample is the African American community and, increasingly, the Hispanic community; this appears clearly in the uneven and overall pathetic degree of solidarity with the African American community in the face of recurring instances of police harassment and brutality, catastrophic unemployment among young black males, and so on, and with the Hispanic community in the face of discrimination, increased government harassment and racial profiling by immigration enforcement agencies in cooperation with local authorities, and the like. What is crucially important, however, is that multicultural policies often are and certainly can be designed precisely to secure those conditions Allport describes: As I argue, following Habermas' account of "constitutional patriotism," multicultural policies should be aimed at facilitating political (but not cultural) integration through the reform of public institutions, thus encouraging all citizens to see themselves as inheritors of a common constitutional project (satisfying Allport's first condition); these policies aim to establish concrete, practical equality among citizens, understood as individuals integrated around various, rational conceptions of the good, cultural values (satisfying Allport's second and fourth conditions); they aim to do so precisely by undermining the operation of stereotypes in public culture and in institutions, by moving beyond anti-discrimination measures to positive forms of recognition (satisfying Allport's third condition); and, finally, they *ought* (were they to be organized along deliberative democratic lines) to aim to create institutional spaces for dialogue among individuals and so, as far as the political form of such institutions permits, encourage individuals to come to know one another *as individuals* rather than merely as (more or less representative) members of an ascriptive group (satisfying Allport's fifth condition).

So, in the example of New York, we get a very partial view, but still, a glimpse at what it would mean to be "at home in otherness," to have a diversity-valuing identity; yet we can see that the contact hypothesis, so far from explaining this sort of successful multiculturalism, actually presupposes it.

Multiculturalism as a Fact and Multicultural Integration as an Aim of Policy

Before I go any further, it is important to be clearer than I have been so far about my use of terms, specifically, what I mean by *multiculturalism*, and what I mean by *integration*. Multiculturalism might mean one of two things: On the one hand, one might intend to point to the fact that an increasing number of countries are characterized by internal cultural, ethnic, racial, and religious diversity. To some extent, this has always been true: In particular, many states contain what Will Kymlicka terms *national minorities*, that is, formerly self-governing "societal cultures" that were incorporated into the state through conquest, colonization, or treaty. In his earlier work, Kymlicka had included in this category both national minorities such as the Québécois in Canada, the Catalans in Spain, the Flemish in Belgium, and Puerto Rico in the United States, as well as indigenous peoples in Canada, the United

States, Russia, Australia, New Zealand, South America, and elsewhere. Given the implausibility of this categorization, he later distinguishes national minorities from indigenous groups, although he still wants to retain the claim that both belong together in their difference from "polyethnicity," or immigrant group diversity, where the key differentia are, first, the lack of a viable "societal culture" for immigrant groups that are territorially dispersed and that migrate one family at a time and, second, what is in Kymlicka's estimation the morally relevant fact that immigrants emigrate "voluntarily."[7] These distinctions are seriously overdrawn insofar as they are intended to justify differential normative claims; in fact, they seem to rest inescapably on a morally spurious appeal to rights of "national self-determination," rights attributable to "having been there first," or to "territorial attachment."[8] Not surprisingly, this leads to a subordination of the question of immigrant rights to those of national minorities that is common to both Kymlicka and Charles Taylor, and that leads in practice to the endorsement of policy proposals intended to "protect minority cultures" that are inherently illiberal. On deliberative democratic premises, there are no grounds for making such distinctions as a matter of normative principle, although there is ample room for sensitively addressing differing conditions on the realization of "effective participation," which reflect practical, empirical, and historical differences between immigrants, national minorities, and indigenous groups. On the other hand, I follow Kymlicka in maintaining that "accommodating ethnic and national differences is only part of a larger struggle to make a more tolerant and inclusive democracy. . . . An adequate theory of the rights of cultural minorities must therefore be compatible with the just demands of [all] disadvantaged social groups [inclusive of struggles for gay rights, rights for the disabled, etc.]."[9] In what follows, then, I propose to use the expression *diversity* to capture the factual pluralism that encompasses all of the groups described by Kymlicka; my focus, however, largely is on the diversity that results from immigration, because it (a) applies in some form to pretty much all states (legal or illegal, in the form of refugees, "guest workers," etc.), as well as to the partially self-governing territories of national minorities; (b) has been poorly treated by influential theorists like Kymlicka and Taylor; (c) is against this group that a "backlash" against recognition is now underway.

Using *diversity* to capture these factual conditions frees up the term *multiculturalism* for a more specific employment: When one uses this expression, one might intend to refer to factual diversity, as I have said, or one might intend to refer instead to the spectrum of policies that respond to the challenges presented by the aforementioned fact, policies directed at any of the abovementioned groups and that seek to "go beyond the protection of the basic civil and political rights guaranteed to all individuals in a liberal-democratic state, to also extend some level of public recognition and support for ethnocultural minorities to maintain and express their distinct identities and practices."[10] It is in this sense that I talk about multiculturalism. My argument is that these policies should aim at creating the conditions under which deliberative democratic resolutions of cross-cultural conflicts can succeed at once in providing a postconventional form of individual recognition, and in securing a just and stable form of nonassimilative social integration. And this brings us to our second and somewhat more complicated term: What exactly is meant by the expression, *multicultural social integration*?

Habermas provides a helpful starting point here: He distinguishes between two levels of assimilation that a society might demand of minorities and newcomers. The first entails acceptance of the constitutional principles that govern the state. For the sake of clarity, let's call this integration rather than assimilation: In other words, integration would mean accepting and conforming to "the ways in which the autonomy of citizens is institutionalized in the recipient society and the way the 'public use of reason' is practiced there."[11] Assimilation, on the other hand, would go beyond this political integration to demand that minorities "become accultured, that is, not only to conform externally but to become habituated to a way of life, the practices, and customs of the local culture."[12] Multicultural integration, then, refers to political integration, to inclusion in the political culture of the society in a manner that does not demand that those so included relinquish or conceal their own cultural form of life or identity; it intends thereby to prevent social disintegration, anomie, or the collapse of society into a series of unrelated subcultures.

This will serve as a preliminary specification: Our question now becomes, how are we to gauge whether my hypothesis is correct, that multicultural policies as described here can actually foster such integration? There are at least two ways in which we can attempt to answer this question: First, we can consider evidence concerning whether countries with active multicultural policies do a better job of integrating immigrants as measured by levels of civic engagement and political participation. Second, we can ask a less direct question, but one with regard to which there has been considerable recent research: Do multicultural policies erode the forms of solidarity necessary for the redistributive measures of the welfare state, as some critics have alleged? Such measures require a relatively strong sense of social trust, confidence in the reciprocity of relations (that others would help you if you were in need), as well as the kind of mutual recognition manifested in the sense that others are "like me" in the relevant, not intrinsically reductive manner (that I could find myself in their position, I can put myself in their shoes). Given that the widespread retrenchment of the welfare state has coincided temporally with the expansion of multicultural policies (roughly, 1980 to the present—of course, as has been widely observed, this also is the period of extensive economic globalization), the possibility of a causal relation is very much a live question.

Multiculturalism as Political Integration

There certainly exists some evidence that, at first glance, might appear deeply troubling for my thesis: A not-insubstantial body of literature suggests that increasing ethnic and cultural diversity may be correlated negatively with the degree of social solidarity and, as a result, with the strength of the welfare state. Thus, one might think that if diversity itself were problematic, highlighting it in the sorts of ways required by multiculturalism is likely only to exacerbate the problem. The idea that ethnic diversity might be an obstacle to effective class mobilization is, of course, very old in the Marxist tradition. But it has been bolstered by a large body of empirical work, such as John Stephens' cross-national study, which found that "ethnic and linguistic diversity was strongly and negatively correlated with the level of labour organization"; the latter, in turn, is one of the crucial factors in explaining statistical variations in social spending in the Organization for Economic Cooperation and Development countries. However, it was economists at the World Bank who initiated research directly into the effects of diversity on social spending, suggesting that it accounted for poor economic performance and social instability in sub-Saharan Africa. At issue in their researches was almost exclusively the question of economic growth; however, investigations undertaken subsequently have revealed that, although ethnic diversity is not necessarily correlated to small government in general, a correlation can be demonstrated (in developing countries) between the degree of religious and linguistic diversity and degree of private instead of public funding for such social goods as health care and education.[13] Similarly, studies of the United States have long cited racial diversity as a main obstacle to the development of a stronger welfare state system, and specific studies have shown that the size of racial minorities in individual U.S. states correlates with increasing restrictions on welfare programs like Medicare.[14]

There are a variety of explanations for the fact that interethnic redistribution encounters obstacles not evidently faced by homogenous communities, the most convincing of which links two arguments:

1. As already mentioned, citizens are only willing to participate in redistributive measures as long as they trust that the would-be recipient will reciprocate, and this sort of trust is more difficult to generate across ethnic and cultural difference.

2. This trust itself is "a component of social capital," while "the sort of associational life that generates social capital is lower in ethnically heterogeneous neighbourhoods."[15]

This thesis is supported by R. D. Putnam, who demonstrated that social capital, understood as levels of "trust and engagement in social networks," is prerequisite to collective engagement in the public sphere. Levels of social capital, however, correlate negatively with increasing ethnic diversity; for example, individuals living in ethnically diverse regions of the United States have been shown to be significantly less engaged in their community and in broader social networks than those living in ethnically homogenous regions.[16] This provides additional confirmation that things cannot be as simple as the contact hypothesis would suggest. Finally, although in their cross-national empirical study they did not discover any connection between the size of immigrant populations and the scope of social spending, Banting, Johnston, Kymlicka, and Soroka demonstrated that *changes* in the size of the immigrant population (no matter its initial absolute size), especially rapid changes, correlate with decreases in the strength of support for the welfare state.[17]

So there is some evidence to suggest that, in some cases, and particularly with respect to the category of immigrants, ethnic and cultural diversity can threaten social integration as measured relative to the index of wealth redistribution. What, then, is the effect of the adoption of multicultural policies on these trends? It is this question that is at the heart of the research commissioned by Banting and Kymlicka, the overwhelming upshot of which is that, at minimum, there is no evidence suggesting that states with robust multicultural policies have any more difficult a time sustaining the welfare state than those states that have weak or no such policies. Not only is this the conclusion of Banting et al.'s cross-national study of social spending; it is also the conclusion of Markus Crepaz's cross-national study of public opinion with respect to diversity and redistribution; and, by and large, it is the outcome of a series of more detailed national studies of the United States, Canada, Germany, Britain, and the Netherlands.[18] To the contrary, there are a number of intriguing evidential suggestions that adopting multicultural policies may actually mitigate the negative effects of increasing factual diversity:

> If the critics were correct, we would expect countries with strong MCPs [multicultural policies] to have fared worse than average. Focusing on the case of immigrant minorities, however, the result is exactly the opposite for four of our five measures. Countries with strong MCPs have done better than average on changes in social spending, reduction in poverty, reduction in inequality, and overall child poverty.[19]

In light of the fact that the countries with the strongest multicultural policies—Canada and Australia—are also the two countries with the highest proportional levels of ethnic and racial diversity, their superior performance with respect to social spending suggests "the intriguing possibility that MCPs may in fact have a positive impact on social spending, in the sense that they help to mitigate the negative impact that ethnic and racial diversity as such is predicted to have."[20] Thus, while there is a certain logic to the inference from the negative effects of diversity to the claim that publicly acknowledging diversity could only worsen social fragmentation, it turns out that multicultural policies may thematize diversity in ways which render it less threatening to dominant groups or that "reduces the 'otherness' of ethnic and racial minorities, enabling members of the dominant group to view minorities as 'one of us.' "[21] In his studies of public opinion as an expression of social trust, Crepaz arrives at the same conclusion: Increases in the percentage of foreign-born population correlate with decreases in the level of social trust, but the adoption of multicultural policies counters this trend. Indeed, more so than the statistical suggestions in the Banting et al study, Crepaz found the effect of multicultural policies to be "significantly positive, indicating that those countries with stronger MCPs generate more trust as compared to countries with weaker MCPs."[22] And as with Banting et al, these findings are most pronounced relative to immigrant diversity.

Considering public support for redistribution, as well as actual levels of social spending, as indexes on the degree of social solidarity yields the significant conclusion that, while increasing diversity may indeed present a considerable challenge, the adoption of multicultural policies in fact serves the goal—and meets with some success—of fostering integration. So far, however, the relevance of the arguments presented for multicultural integration per se have been indirect; that is, precisely in the form of an index and not a direct observation. But what about political integration itself? Do multicultural policies encourage the balkanization of political society, or do they succeed as they intend in facilitating the participation of immigrants in mainstream political culture? This question is a rather tricky one to answer because it is important to keep in mind (as very little sociological research does) that the "political culture" of advanced capitalist, multicultural states bears all the marks of refeudalization, superficiality, and privatism. Nevertheless, it is still possible to speak of relative levels of engagement, to contrast comparatively hospitable and inhospitable public spheres, and so on.

We have seen some evidence already that ethnic diversity itself not only adversely effects redistributive measures, but also impoverishes the social capital and trust that are necessary for political engagement; what affect, if any, do multicultural policies have on this phenomenon? Perhaps the most relevant study in this connection is one (of several) conducted by Jean Tillie and Boris Slijper on immigrant political integration in Amsterdam, a city that is relatively unique in its ambitious approach to fostering political participation specifically among immigrant groups. Focusing on those groups who are the primary addressees of these multicultural policies—Moroccans, Turks, and Surinamese—Tillie and Slijper's research points to the conclusion that, on the whole, all four groups show higher levels of participation than Dutch citizens, but that Moroccans and Turks evidence higher levels than Surinamese.[23] Investigating the potential determinants on political participation with an eye to explaining these results yields some interesting suggestions: With respect to individual circumstances, neither gender nor employment, but level of education alone "has a significant influence on political participation. That is, a lower [level of] education results in a lower participation score."[24] At the collective level, ethnic organizational membership and "social activities in the network of the respondent," and no other kinds of organizational memberships (e.g., union membership, residents' associations, sports or cultural organizations, churches, school associations, political parties, etc.), have a significant effect on levels of political participation. The inclusion of the collective component represents an explicit attempt to capture the level of "social capital" available to individuals: The authors operate on the assumption that organizational membership gives one access to the social capital of the organization and to that of organizations with which it is associated; a similar assumption is made with respect to having friends/associates who are members of such organizations. Their results in this regard demonstrate that, among immigrants, ethnic communities uniquely "serve as a mobilizing device and promote the political integration of the members." The explanation offered by the authors is that "voluntary organizations generate social capital. This social capital in turn leads to social trust, and finally this social trust is an important precondition for political participation."[25] This finding is particularly interesting in that it contradicts the common perception that access to nonethnic social capital (so-called "bridging capital," which crosses group lines) must be crucial for social integration, whereas social capital tied to ethnic organizations has been thought to foster cultural isolationism. In fact, the opposite appears to be true, at least insofar as we want to connect social integration with political participation (perhaps a noteworthy caveat).

What is also interesting, however, is that it appears not to hold equally true of all immigrant groups. Tillie and Slijper appeal to R. D. Putnam's concept of "civic community" in their attempt to explain both the success of ethnic organizations in fostering political participation, as well as the group differences in the extent of this success. "Civic community" refers to a particular constellation of civil society characterized by a "balance of horizontal and vertical ties," that is, horizontal ties directly between various organizations, as well as vertical ties to the state and its institutions. But it is the former that are key to their explanation: Analysis of the extent of interorganizational connectedness among the main ethnic groups in Amsterdam reveals a sharp disparity between Surinamese, who registered lower levels of political participation and evidence a similarly lower frequency of such horizontal ties, and Turks and Moroccans, who evidence higher levels of participation and more extensive horizontal ties. All three groups evidenced roughly similar levels of integration with organizations outside their own cultural community ("bringing capital"), although this does not license the inference that such connections are not a precondition on participation; to the contrary, the authors interpret this evidence to mean that, although such "bridging capital" is indeed important, it is not sufficient, as many have argued.

> It seems to be the proper mix between ethnic community and social integration (the combination of bonding and bridging social capital) that provides the breeding ground for political participation. . . . Contrary to the current tendency to consider a strong ethnic community and/or identity as frustrating the process of integration, the results here indicate the exact opposite: A strong ethnic community seems to be a necessary precondition for successful integration, at least as far as political participation is concerned.[26]

The aim of multicultural policies is to provide support for and recognition of ethnic and cultural identities, in symbolic as well as material forms. The outcome, if these policies are effective, should be a strong ethnic or cultural identity and, as Tillie and Slijper have shown, the ability to maintain such an identity appears to have a salutary effect on political integration. At the same time, although Tillie and Slijper focus on the groups targeted by Amsterdam's multicultural policies, and intend their research to inform policymaking, they do not attribute their results directly to the effect of existing policies (nor do they discount this possibility, but it is plausible, e.g., that the activism of immigrant communities independently of the state is the primary causal factor). So, it is worthwhile to ask how, other things being equal (including the origin of immigrants, level of occupational and educational skill, etc.), immigrant political integration fares in countries with multicultural policies as compared to those without. Irene Bloemraad has conducted just such a controlled study of Vietnamese and Portuguese immigrants to Toronto, Canada, and Boston. Even taking into account variations in local labor markets and political structures, her study concluded that the immigrants to Toronto—a diverse city in a country with an official multiculturalism policies—were better integrated and more active in public life than those who had immigrated to Boston—a diverse city in a country lacking an official multicultural policy. For example, although the rate of immigration is significantly higher in Canada than in the United States, immigrants to the former naturalize at twice the rate of immigrants to the latter. Additionally, further studies by Bloemraad confirmed that cultural elites within these groups were more representative of their communities—in particular, that they were better balanced along gender lines—in Toronto as compared with Boston, suggesting an internal liberalizing effect resulting either from the nature of multicultural policies themselves or, what seems more likely, from the experience of participating in a liberal, political culture.[27]

In summary, there is convincing empirical evidence to suggest that some actual multicultural policies are aimed at and to a measurable extent succeed in cultivating social integration, not cultural and ethnic balkanization. This evidence is especially convincing in the case of immigrant multiculturalism, where immigrant diversity both presents the greatest challenge to social cohesion and, as a matter of fact, is suffering under the burden of a racist immigrant backlash, a "chauvinism of affluence," manifesting itself in the full spectrum of developed nations to varying degrees. But this last observation introduces one further worry: Granted multiculturalism may be salutary from the perspective of support for the welfare state and with respect to immigrant political participation; but perhaps even taken together, these findings do not discount the possibility that it is the very success in encouraging political participation that has driven the apparent increase of conflict in diverse societies—particularly when we consider that this participation often emerges from social capital generated at the level of ethnic communities. In other words, given the largely depoliticized character of all developed nations today, the evidence presented thus far remains compatible with the hypothesis that the dual effects of multicultural policy actually work at cross-purposes: Paternalistic, depoliticized policies successfully foster passive solidarity (e.g., along affective lines) and so an acceptance of redistribution, while active political participation among immigrants, especially where it takes the form of identity politics, may yet threaten social fragmentation precisely in the political sense. This tension would represent a kind of multicultural refraction of the basic conflict of a depoliticized society that must nevertheless legitimize itself "democratically." Participating in politics is, after all, no guarantee that a resolution to conflicts will be found. Unfortunately, I know of no empirical attempts to study this possibility; but with this problem in mind, I want to look more closely at the deliberative democratic model of multicultural integration and the correlated hypothesis of a diversity-valuing identity.

Constitutional Patriotism as Multicultural Identity

What sorts of commitments are necessary in order for social integration to be maintained even when political actors recurrently encounter one another across the lines of conflicting versions of the good? One common answer, described by Habermas under the title "constitutional patriotism," suggests that it is through maintaining a consensus with respect to political principles—namely, those reflected in legitimating legal-political procedures—that disagreements can become tolerable among legal consociates in a diverse society.

> Citizens who are politically integrated in this way share the rationally based conviction that unrestrained freedom of communication in the political public sphere, a democratic process for settling conflicts, and the constitutional channeling of political power together provide a basis for checking illegitimate power and ensuring that administrative power is used in the equal interests of all. The universalism of legal principles is reflected in a procedural consensus, which must be embedded in the context of a historically specific political culture through a kind of constitutional patriotism.[28]

To the extent that such constitutional patriotism is a *precondition* for successful political discourse, it appears to have the same sort of counterfactual force as the norms that, according to Habermas, shape all forms of discourse. In other words, if there is not a consensus regarding the legitimacy of the procedures by which collective decisions are made, and so a presumption of legitimacy that extends to decisions made according to those procedures (whether the ultimate decision reflects your own position in the debate or not), then there is nothing to prevent groups who lose out in the course of democratic debate from saying, "to hell with this: If I am not going to get what I want, I'm not going to bother to participate." In this case, the threat to social integration against which constitutional patriotism is posed is obvious. But although Habermas often seems to want to confine constitutional patriotism to this procedural element, it seems to me that it implies something further: If I do not also presuppose that those with whom I debate are oriented by rational conceptions of the good, from which I could conceivably learn something, then although I may engage in political participation of some form, it cannot be considered participation in a form of discourse. Implicit in this openness is the ability to adopt a hypothetical attitude toward my own existing commitments. To put the same point the other way around, if I assume from the start that you are irrational, that your values are dogmatic, or that I already possess incorrigible insights in the matter at hand, then I cannot engage in interaction with you except strategically—I can try to disillusion you, manipulate or threaten you, but I cannot engage in meaningful dialogue with you.[29] It is also clear that, lacking *this* element of constitutional patriotism, multicultural integration as a form of political integration is not possible.

But this second element is telling for what it means for the constitutional project of a society to be rooted in its lifeworld: A consequence of realizing constitutional patriotism, of succeeding in the cultivation of multicultural integration through political discourse, seems to be that part of what it must come to mean to be "Canadian," for instance, will include reference to the attempt to pursue political self-determination in partnership with a sometimes-separatist Québécois national minority, with reference to a shameful past and present of subjugation and exploitation of indigenous peoples, and in cooperation and negotiation with a myriad of ethnic and cultural immigrant groups, all of whom must also be able, if the legal structure and political culture of the society is to be legitimate and stable, to see themselves as the authors of the laws to which they are subject.[30] Canada, of course, is just an example: The nodal points around which such "social imaginaries" revolve are, as Habermas observes, an historically contingent matter and immigration is one of the main sources of their transformation, putting new issues on the agenda and requiring the constant renegotiation of the meaning of the whole.[31] If constitutional democracy reflects the form of political association of its members, through which they attempt to regulate their interactions and shared life together nonviolently, this commitment must ultimately be reflected in and supported by the sort of decentered identity I have described.

It hardly need be said, however, that this claim is normative: Not only is it the case that in most of the world, the meaning of national identity remains tied up with monocultural, exclusionary assumptions. Even where it has been decentered to some extent, that in no way entails that is authentically inclusive: My earlier discussion of the meaning of being a "New Yorker" already suggested as much. Where groups are excised from the meaning of the polity in which they live, however, social integration is in peril and, in most cases, struggles for recognition and inclusion ensue in some form (although, of course, not necessarily in a directly political form—crime, gang memberships, etc., are relevant here, too).[32] The dual significance of constitutional patriotism, on my reading, suggests that the existence of common value commitments is not sufficient to ground the sort of "shared identity" that is a necessary part of social unity.[33] Some postmodern critics like Hayward argue against any form of advocacy for such a "shared identity" on the grounds that it threatens to reproduce a "Rousseauean" totalization of "the people." To a significant degree, these criticisms rest on the presumption that the issue must be formulated hierarchically, rather than as a matter of decentering existing identities, as I maintain. The reason for so arguing is that it has seemed to many that if a shared "civic identity" is to support integration, the features or values on which it is based will have to take precedence over any competing claims or values arising from "subpolitical identities": For example, one's civic commitment to democratic equality will have to trump culturally rooted attitudes of sexism. But this way of putting the problem is deeply misleading. First, it is not a question of having two distinct and potentially competing identities, where those elements of one's "subpolitical identity" that do not overlap with the shared "civic identity" would have to be screened out of one's public self-presentation. But perhaps the more basic error is to assume that shared "civic identity"—although, in fact, it must be far more substantive than that term implies—is a condition for political integration, rather than its result.[34] As studies by Tillie and Slijper, as well as Bloemraad, obliquely suggest, it is by adopting multicultural policies that allow minorities to participate in public life *as themselves* that the conditions are ultimately created for the socialization of the required sort of diversity-valuing identity—and this, it seems to me, is only comprehensible on a deliberative democratic account.

In a general way, the history of multicultural policy in Canada appears to bear this out. To summarize rather briefly: In 1963, in an attempt to mitigate spreading ethno-cultural nationalism in Québec, the federal government instituted the Royal Commission on Bilingualism and Biculturalism; the idea was to include the Québécois within the fold of federalism by fostering a narrative of Canada as a pact between "two founding peoples." That this narrative was radically out of touch with the realities of Canadian society as a whole became immediately clear as non-British and non-French citizens and immigrant groups, who quite understandably saw themselves as excluded by and subordinated within such an account, confronted the government through organized lobbies. The policy that eventually resulted from the Commission, under the force of this pressure, was the Official Multiculturalism Policy of 1971 which, in an attempt to accommodate both groups, described Canada instead as a multicultural society in a bilingual framework. Although initially quite vague, with the passage of the Fourth Supplement to the 1985 Multiculturalism Act (in 1988), the role of multiculturalism in shaping Canadian identity, itself to be understood as an evolving project, is explicit; the Act declares its aim as the protection and recognition of cultural and ethnic identities such that they may continue to evolve as vital heritages, as well as to "promote the understanding and creativity that arise from the interaction between individuals and communities of different origins"; to that end, it aims to "encourage and assist the social, cultural, economic and political institutions of Canada to be respectful and inclusive of Canada's multicultural character" and to "promote the full and equitable participation of individuals and communities of all origins in the continuing evolution and shaping of all aspects of Canadian society and assist them in the elimination of any barrier to such participation."[35] However, the Canadian case is interesting not because of the policy itself, but because of one of its primary effects: Data gathered in the past ten years concerning the identities of the first generation of young people to grow up under the policy (and the Charter of Rights and Freedoms, which offers its underlying justification) reveals not only historically surprising levels of national identification (in a nation long thought too large and diverse to foster identifications more robust than affective attachments to hockey, beer commercials, and anti-Americanism), but a marked transformation of the meaning of "being Canadian." In short, young people cite the diversity of the country, the multicultural policy, and the Charter itself as key features of their identity.[36] Despite being the most diverse generation of young people in Canadian history, they also are more likely than any other age group to list "Canadian" as part of their ethnic origin.[37] The point, then, is that multicultural policies aimed at fostering the political integration of diverse ethnic, cultural, and linguistic groups, in the sense of creating opportunities for their participation in public life *as the groups and individuals that they are* has had the result, at least to some measurable extent, of producing a broader context of socialization within which individuals increasingly see the diversity of their society as a part of their identity.

It would be a serious error, however, to think that, despite the suggestive language of the Multiculturalism Act itself, political integration in Canada has in fact proceeded along such deliberative democratic lines. This would require a politicized public sphere that Canada, like other advanced capitalist democracies, ultimately lacks. Instead, the described changes in Canadian identity appear to have resulted largely from two things: moderate success of targeted multicultural policies in realizing the conditions under which contact among strangers can itself have this effect; and, likely more important, the use of what Richard Rorty calls "sentimental manipulation," that is, essentially affective appeals to the unity of diversity in Canada.[38] In this manner, a sense that others are, after all, "like us" in the relevant way can indeed be cultivated; but—and this speaks to my hypothesis regarding the possibility that multicultural policies may in fact work at cross-purposes—the political uselessness of such a program reveals itself anew in each case of conflict. Groups who advance demands that contain challenges to the identity of the majority, their understanding of multiculturalism, or their self-interest, rupture this affective bond instantaneously; individuals for whom multiculturalism is not tied to deliberative commitments are left without any way of seeing their way past the conflict. Some arguable examples are the response of many Canadians to the plight of Lebanese-Canadians in the 2006 Israeli invasion of Lebanon, or to the attempt in Ontario to gain protection for the use of sharia law in family arbitration. It isn't that there aren't real issues in both cases (in the latter much more than the former), but that the public reaction—which included immediate denunciations of multiculturalism, particularly in conservative circles—was basically affectively motivated, and uncritically taken up in mainstream media coverage.[39] Such affectively rooted integration is intrinsically unstable, requiring constant "management" of the public sphere, and is unable to provide the basis for actually solving the sorts of problems that are inevitable in diverse societies.

Benhabib provides some additional justification for this position. Arguing, as I have, that although a presupposition of equal respect and reciprocity must be made in order for discourse to get off the ground, she notes that it is only through participating in multicultural discourses that we can begin to see "what such respect requires or entails in the face of deep cultural conflicts; while some of us may consider certain practices and judgments an affront to human dignity [for example,], others may consider our evaluations a species of ethnocentric imperialism."[40] Often, multicultural discourse will require that we first come to an agreement about the kind of practice that is in question—whether it is political, cultural, religious, moral, and so on—since, in the absence of such an agreement it is meaningless to talk about normative appraisal: What sort of norm would apply? *L'affair foulard* is a good example of this. Although the same issues have played out in several countries (e.g., Canada, Britain, Belgium), in France the controversy surrounded the expulsion from school of several Muslim-French citizens, all teenage girls, for refusing to remove headscarves that had been deemed a violation of France's prohibition on conspicuous religious symbols in public schools. The possibility of rational debate surrounding Muslim veiling in Western immigrant communities was thoroughly undermined by the failure to first sincerely consider the significance of the practice today—was it a symbol of gender subordination, the manifestation of social and political separation, or a contestation of older generations' interpretation of religious imperatives? As it happens, no one bothered to ask the young women how they sought to understand themselves through this practice.[41] Of course, the meaning of one's action is not a matter of univocal self-determination, and there is ample room to consider the possibility of self-misunderstanding, deception, or indoctrination. But without engaging in these debates first, we cannot even hope to fairly answer the question of whether the practice is compatible with equal human rights. And in this connection, as James Bohman argues, part of the problem facing immigrant communities to which multicultural policies are supposed to respond is the need to develop the capacities for effectively employing "established practices of adjudication," in the service of articulating their differing interests and needs.[42]

"Mosaic multiculturalists," like Taylor, avoid this necessity mostly by privileging cultural contributions to the constitution of personal identity and, moreover, largely conventional interpretations of culture (as can be seen in his endorsement of a restriction of the autonomy of members of threatened cultural groups[43]). There is, in this way, a parallel between their view of the self and their view of culture, where the internal complexity of both is reduced in the same dimension. As a matter of fact, however, all forms of identity are the result of a fragile synthesis of differing and even conflicting narratives "into a unique life history"[44] within which there is no way to nondogmatically privilege, on behalf of others, cultural affiliation over gender, race, political commitments, personal interests, biographical events, and so on. This applies in spades to postconventional identities that, as discussed in Chapter 4, emerge from a successful attempt to reconstruct an autonomous identity in the face of conflicting role commitments. According to the developmental schema outlined in Chapters 3 and 4, then, the sort of privileging of cultural identity in which Kymlicka and Taylor engage is inherently conservative, in the sense that it attempts to enforce a conventional-level interpretation of the meaning of selfhood.

Of course, as communitarians like Taylor will here loudly insist, given the depth and scope of the disagreements sometimes reflected in cultural differences, it is actually the consensus-oriented deliberative-democrats who, in their appeal to discursive negotiation of cultural conflicts, are naïve about real levels of cultural harmony. But, to the contrary, in the account that Benhabib and I more or less share,

> [t]here is no presumption that moral and political dialogues will produce normative consensus, yet it is assumed that even when they fail to do so and we must resort to law to redraw the boundaries of coexistence, societies in which such multicultural dialogues take place in the public sphere will articulate a civic point of view and a civic perspective of "enlarged mentality." The process of "giving good reasons in public" [and, I would add, sincerely entertaining such good reasons in public] will not only determine the legitimacy of the norms followed; it will also enhance the civic virtues of democratic citizenship by cultivating the habits of mind of public reasoning and exchange . . . [Moreover,] [p]recisely because multiculturalism, in so many of its manifestations, challenges key assumptions of liberal democracies, it needs to release its conflictual and explosive potential in the public civil sphere through the dialogue, confrontation, and give-and-take of ordinary citizens. . . . How else can moral and political learning take place, except through such encounters in civil society?[45]

Without disputing the consequence she wants to draw from participation in discourse with respect to democratic habits (certainly part of the procedural commitment of constitutional patriotism), I have argued that "enlarged mentality" takes the form of a diversity-valuing identity (the substantive element of constitutional patriotism), an identity that is itself decentered and multicultural. This identity provides a possible ground for the crucial ongoing commitment to take up the shared constitutional project despite the recurrent conflicts and challenges that irreducible diversity entails, to debate sympathetically another day. This commitment is prerequisite to the stability of democratic forms of multicultural integration and, I have argued, would result from multicultural policies that succeeded in securing the conditions for effective democratic participation. Indeed, to some extent, it has resulted in restricted forms from policies that realize this aim only to a very limited degree.[46] As Benhabib too concedes, such a model suffers from no illusions about the fact that we will often fail to discover a solution acceptable to all affected; but in deciding what path to pursue at that point, "we" (as an inclusive society) will have to do much better than Taylor's nativist retort (to be discussed in more detail in the next section), "this is just how *we* [privileged majority group] do things here."[47]

The remaining question, however, is whether participation in discourse could actually stabilize the sort of identity I have described by providing it with a source of recognition at the postconventional level. And, indeed, for some that will seem too easy a formulation: One of the primary problems to be treated by multicultural theory is that marginalized and stigmatized groups suffer misrecognition, the internalization of demeaning images that forms an additional barrier to effective political participation. So, a discourse-oriented approach also will have to consider whether it is up to the task of dealing honestly with this issue.

The Actualization of Democratic Rights as a Source of Postconventional Recognition

Nancy Fraser, who also argues for a deliberative democratic model of multicultural justice based on the critical standard of participatory parity, attempts to avoid the problem of misrecognition by rejecting the "internalization model" on which Taylor's endorsement of the "politics of recognition" is based. In fact, she regards the recognition-oriented politics of both Taylor and Honneth as one-sided, and theoretically as well as practically problematic.[48] These thinkers both identify recognition as a basic human need and interpret misrecognition "in terms of impaired subjectivity and damaged self-identity."[49] From the perspective of the model of participatory parity, on the other hand, "misrecognition" is seen as a form of status subordination in which "some individuals and groups are denied the status of full partners in social interaction simply as a consequence of institutionalized patterns of cultural value," patterns that are discriminatory or demeaning.[50]

Such subordination is therefore objectively ascertainable through analysis of social relations. Fraser gives an extensive list of the advantages she sees as accruing to this justice-based, sociological approach, as contrasted with the internalization model employed by Honneth and Taylor, according to which misrecognition causes "psychic harm" that must be assessed on the basis of a theory of individual or interpersonal psychology. Two of these reasons are germane to my argument: (a) the injustices identified by the recognition-theoretical approach ("psychic harms") stand and fall with the psychological theory on which the internalization model is based, unlike an account grounded in an independent theory of justice; and (b) it suggests that repairing "psychical damage" is the appropriate aim for social justice.[51] With respect to the former, Fraser's case seems considerably weakened by the fact that she advances no considerations whatsoever to suggest that the internalization model might in fact be wrong. To the contrary, she actually goes on to claim that her account "accepts that misrecognition can have the sorts of ethical-psychological effects described by Taylor and Honneth. But it maintains that the wrongness of misrecognition does not depend on the presence of such effects."[52] Her normative insistence seems correct to me: Misrecognition is unjust because it prevents the realization of democratic equality and so equal autonomy. But there are two problems with this: Fraser's account of the way status subordination undermines full participation in society is crucially underdetermined, insofar as she never explains *how* misrecognition, on her model, has this effect. Beginning with Frantz Fanon, on the other hand, internalization theories have investigated the ways in which misrecognition can cripple effective agency, social integration, and the like.[53] Thus, more than merely "accepting" that misrecognition can have such psychological consequences, Fraser may need such a theory to bolster her own argument.

But, and this is the second problem, it isn't clear how Fraser can accommodate this and still maintain the second argument against the internalization model mentioned earlier. We might not want to make the repair of "psychic damage"—that is, the overcoming of misrecognition through recognition—the central aim of a theory of social justice; but once we recognize that social exclusion, misrecognition, and status subordination can have such effects, we should at least want to be sure that alternative proposals for social transformation are adequately responsive to this problem. Otherwise, we risk advocating formal, objective improvements that nevertheless fail to change the reality of the experience of the marginalized. This is where Honneth's argument holds real weight: We must at least ask whether participatory parity, effective participation, or the realization of democratic rights, holds out the prospect of the sort of recognition required. Fraser, it must be conceded, does not make this case; Honneth, Taylor, and Steven Lukes, among many other critics of discourse ethics, deny that it can be made. As it seems possible to introduce their objections together without serious equivocation, I will do so prior to offering my defense.

Taylor's endorsement of the "politics of recognition" is based on an account of historical transformations of the meaning of liberalism, itself understood as based on the principle of equality or equal recognition.[54] The collapse of the social hierarchies that were the foundation of the feudal social order gave rise, in the course of the bourgeois revolutions and the slow evolution of law in Britain, to a politics of universalism: that is, to a form of liberalism that interpreted the principle of equality to mean treating all persons the same and, in so doing, equally recognizing what everyone shares in common—their humanity. But as our conception of human identity changed under conditions of modernity and, in particular, as we became aware not just of the deep nature and significance of our differences, but also of the crucial harm that misrecognition can inflict on individuals and groups through internalization, we came to see that this older model was naïve about what it means to be a person. That is, recognizing someone for what they have in common with everyone else is not really recognizing them at all, or not adequately, as the person that they are. This realization gives rise to the politics of difference, according to which "[e]veryone should be recognized for his or her unique identity."[55] The political ideal here is still equality, but we have realized that if individuals only become and are who they are through socialization, as Habermas has also argued, then inequalities in the socializing circumstances of individuals threaten to produce a form of second-class citizenship. For example, those who lack access to education in their native language, or who are exposed only to interpretations of history in which their ancestors are marginalized, are put at a disadvantage relative to others when it comes to the formation of a healthy, stable identity; the latter, in turn, is a prerequisite for the realization of autonomy and so a matter of equal rights. Taylor identifies Kantian proceduralism with the politics of universalism (Liberalism 1, for short), and something like the model he sees operative in Québec with the politics of difference (Liberalism 2, for short). He considers proceduralism to be hostile to difference because it can't permit what groups like the Québécois really want, namely, indefinite cultural survival. For this reason, Taylor does not believe that proceduralism possesses the kind of cultural neutrality its proponents claim for it. The fact of the matter, as he sees it, is that the procedural model requires that we make a certain kind of distinction between what is public and what is private, and relegate contentions cultural differences—whatever they may be—to the sphere of the private. It is this argument against proceduralism that is common to objections to discourse ethics and deliberative democracy generally, and in a way that also overlaps with the view that the politics of universalism is homogenizing. As Habermas himself summarizes him, Steven Lukes, for example, argues that "[t]he conditions set forth for participating in practical discourse are . . . idealized to such a degree that we cannot imagine how actors who are tied to their social contexts even into the innermost regions of their persons could possibly be equal to the role of participants in discourse. And if one tries to imagine it, the actors lose their flesh and blood, take on unearthly forms."[56] So, procedural universalism in ethics as in politics cannot permit individuals *as such* to participate.

Taylor's problem with this isn't the idea that some cultural matters are private; his point is that any way we might choose to draw this line is itself going to be culturally contentions. "Gag rules" that aim to keep controversial religious demands off the table, for example—which would conflict, say, with free speech, as was the case with the controversy surrounding Salmon Rushdie's *Satanic Verses* and in the Danish cartoon affair—reflect cultural values, not neutral procedures. That doesn't mean we should surrender "our" values, but we should accept that "[l]iberalism is also a fighting creed," and continue to insist upon the way "we do things here," when it is a question of free speech or other fundamental values that might become the subject of a culturally inspired challenge.[57] In summary, Taylor's argument is that universalist, proceduralist politics is homogenizing and, in practice, culturally particularistic, a fact which it conceals from itself through the use of "gag rules."

Honneth argues that the evolution of modern societies should be understood, not as the shift from the politics of universalism to the politics of difference, but as "the result of the differentiation of three social spheres of recognition": namely, love, law, and achievement/esteem.[58] Love refers to caring for the needs of another, in the absence of which children cannot develop a healthy sense of self, and on which adults too depend for basic self-confidence. Like Taylor, Honneth sees the recognition sphere of law, governed by the principle of equality, to have emerged from the crumbling feudal "honor" system, a system that unilaterally defined both one's social and economic standing at once.

> The new normative structural transformation that went along with this institutionalization of the idea of legal equality should not be underestimated, since it led to the establishment of two completely different spheres of recognition, revolutionizing the moral order of society: the individual could now—certainly not in actual practice, but at least according to the normative idea—know that he or she was respected as a legal person with the same rights as all other members of society, while still owing his or her social esteem to a hierarchical scale of values—which had been set on a new foundation.[59]

Equality in the sphere of law entailed that legal recognition was "democratized," while in the economy (market) and connected status order of society, achievement, or esteem was "meritocratized." Following Hegel's critique of "legal status" and of Kantianism, Honneth sees the development of a sphere of recognition "over and above" legal recognition as crucial because the rights and capacities that the latter values are necessarily shared with all other citizens. As a result, "one cannot yet, as a legal person, relate positively to those of one's characteristics that precisely distinguish one from one's partners in interaction. For that, a form of mutual recognition is needed in which each individual is affirmed not only as a member of his or her community but just as much as a biographically individual subject."[60] It would be possible to multiply the citations *ad nauseam* to show that Honneth, too, although appearing loathe to admit it, sees legal recognition as an kind of abstraction from what makes a person the person they are and so is, in that sense, homogenizing.[61] As a result, where misrecognition has taken the specific form of legal exclusion, legal recognition may be able to repair the damage; but in all other cases where the injury exceeds this, where it is of an individual order—even if the same injury is shared by many—then legal rights or participatory parity will be inadequate to the task.

Habermas' answer to Taylor is that his contrast of "a politics of consideration of cultural differences on the one hand, and a politics of the universalization of individual rights on the other," is a false construal.[62] The problem stems from Taylor's misleadingly "paternalistic" account of the politics of universalism. That is, in Taylor's presentation, when individuals pursuing the realization of constitutionally protected liberties come into conflict with one another, the courts sort out whose rights deserve precedence. What this misses is the intrinsic connection between democracy and the constitutional state or, to put the same point another way, the connection between public and private autonomy: We are only really free in our use of private autonomy to the extent that we have had a hand in shaping the laws to which we are subject when we do so. Once we realize that private autonomy can only be protected through realizing the conditions necessary for activating the public autonomy of citizens, the homogenizing character of universalist law disappears. The legitimacy of the state relies on providing the sorts of social and cultural rights needed to facilitate political participation. This cannot be achieved through equally paternalistic welfare state legislation, which reifies groups and stereotypes their needs; rather those affected must, through participating in discourses in which they seek to clarify their needs, establish for themselves the conditions necessary for achieving equality. Both sorts of error, welfare state paternalism as well as Taylor's "paternalistic" account of liberalism, result from a failure to adequately apprehend the internal connection between public and private autonomy.[63]

Habermas' rejection of Taylor's account of proceduralist "gag rules" is connected to this. It is true that rights have precedence over "goods" such that the goals of ethnic and cultural communities cannot be permitted to dissolve the structure of the law; but "it is inherent in the concrete nature of the matters to be regulated that in the medium of law—as opposed to morality—the process of setting normative rules for modes of behavior is open to influence by the society's political goals."[64] All legal systems and accompanying political cultures are, in this sense, reflections of the goals and identities of their citizens, mediated by the structure of universal basic rights and principles of democratic self-determination. As a consequence of immigration and social change, these reflections are dynamic: The goals and nodal points around which political culture revolves are a contingent matter that cannot legitimately be fixed. In the course of attempting to justly regulate conflicts in an impartial way, these societies at the same time come to an understanding about how they see themselves "as citizens of a specific republic, as inhabitants of a specific region, as heirs to a specific culture."[65] There are a couple of implications that follow from this: As Habermas says, "the theory of rights in no way forbids the citizens of a democratic constitutional state to assert a conception of the good in their general legal order, a conception they either share or have come to agree on through political discussion."[66] It is the concerns and values of individuals and groups, in addition to the experience of conflict, that motivates them to participate in politics in the first place; thus, a procedural politics that forbade citizens to pursue the legal protection for or expression of all values or concerns connected with a conception of the good would leave them with little or nothing to talk about. As Habermas writes in reply to Lukes, "if the actors did not bring with them, and into their discourse, *their* individual life-histories, *their* identities, *their* needs and wants, *their* traditions, memberships, and so forth, practical discourse would at once be robbed of all content."[67] That said, the mediating structure of basic rights does prohibit that one conception of the good should be privileged at the expense of others in the society; but this prohibition does not work by way of antecedent restrictions on debate. To the contrary, in maintaining that valid conceptions of the good, ethical-political self-understandings, can be the product of discourse—indeed, in maintaining a proceduralist conception of political legitimacy generally—Habermas cannot stipulate in advance what kinds of reasons individuals may offer in support of their position and which may be found convincing by rational citizens.

In point of fact, I think we can explain the basic error of Taylor and Honneth even more simply. In their more or less common account of legal recognition—in which they do occasionally make passing reference to democracy—they conflate the level of abstractness at which legal rights are described and defended with a claim about the level of abstractness by which the experience of the actualization of these rights is supposedly characterized. Although the capacity to engage in democratic will formation is indeed abstract and shared, there is no reason whatsoever to think that in the act of doing so, individuals who are able to raise for the sincere consideration of their peers questions and claims that emerge from the concerns and values of their unique biography, would experience the recognition involved as "abstract." As Habermas himself argues, the recognition of individuals who are individuated only through socialization in particular cultural contexts entails simultaneously that they be recognized as irreplaceable individuals and as members of a group and, in so doing, forges a link between justice and solidarity.[68] No doubt, this can hardly be said of participation in periodic plebiscites on administrative personnel; but the problem there is the nature of merely formal democracy, not the inherent character of legally ensured recognition—that is, more robustly democratic institutions are called for. Nor does this argument rely on an implausible requirement for wholly direct democracy since, in the sort of vibrant political culture that would accompany not-merely formally democratic institutions, there would be ample opportunities for participation in the shaping of opinion in the public sphere, directly and through engagement in the counter-publics created by various social movements, voluntary associations, and so on. As discussed in Chapter 2, in connection with McCarthy's critique of Habermas' "seducement" by systems theory, we cannot specify in advance the limits of democratic self-determination: unmanageable forms of complexity can only be identified relative to existing institutional innovations and, as I concluded in Chapter 4, relative to the level of deliberative competence enjoyed by citizens. In other words, participation in discourse—political, moral, ethical—extends a form of genuinely individual recognition or respect (understood along post-conventional rather than conventional lines), and so stands at least as good a chance as any other form of recognition of being adequate to the task of repairing the "psychic damage" inflicted through misrecognition. Indeed, it stands a better chance, insofar as it ensures the victims an opportunity to clarify their own needs, an intuition that seems at least partially reflected in the organization of "truth and reconciliation" commissions in response to various historical injustices. What is more, it suggests that if multicultural integration requires participation in discourse—in the absence of which, cultural diversity threatens to undermine social integration, or threatens the politicization of the desiccated public sphere either by ethnic and cultural struggle or by increasingly totalitarian repression—then a stably integrated, genuinely multicultural society would present a context of socialization that would meet postconventionality halfway.[69]

Multicultural Education and Capitalist Colonization: A Social Contradiction

To the extent that multiculturalism means, among other things, that diverse individuals and groups will be encouraged to maintain their own cultural traditions and attachments, it is clear that the family must become a primary site of subnational cultural socialization. This is not to say that it will be the only such site, which would not reflect a multicultural policy at all but merely traditional liberalism; to the contrary, public support for community centers, cultural events, language courses, and various "accommodations," are all ways of protecting this cultural reproduction as well as its public expression. Nor is this to suggest that the family must be a site of the reproduction of traditionalist versions of minority culture, any more than it must be for families belonging to the majority culture. What it is to say, however, is that in a multicultural society, the conditions for social integration cannot be reliably met through socialization in the family; a society concerned about its level of integration will have to express that concern through the organization of public institutions with a role to play in socialization. In capitalist societies, that disqualifies the media (as overwhelmingly private); but it points rather obviously toward the school. However, it also requires a rejection of the view that multiculturalism entails, not reform of traditional curriculum and pedagogy aimed at inclusiveness, but at least at the primary and secondary levels, parallel and independent schooling systems with curriculum differentiated according to cultural background.[70] Such an interpretation of multiculturalism is incompatible with social integration, and does nothing to prepare individuals for the challenge of self-governance in cooperation with their diverse legal consociates. Schools have become virtually unique among public institutions in contemporary societies in that, unlike other forms of civic association, they are not voluntary: Everyone must be admitted, everyone has a right to be one's classmate, one's peer. The school and the democratic polity itself are, in this sense, uniquely homologous.

At the primary level, then, multiculturalism would mostly entail ensuring the inclusiveness of curriculum with an eye to realizing the conditions for democratic equality; in other words, ensuring that conceptions of history, language, and social interaction do not reflect stereotypical or demeaning images of minority groups, do not exclude them as marginal or unimportant, and do not, as Susan Wolf warns, assimilate them as implicitly "honorary" members of majority culture.[71] Success in this provides the sorts of conditions under which the "contact" hypothesis becomes at least partially operative (depending still on conditions of socialization in the home). This is not to suggest, however, a purely monological pedagogy at this level; to the contrary, an active engagement in the world as well as discursive reasoning of a limited type is both possible and appropriate.[72] But by the secondary level, as individuals approach the crisis of adolescence, and as their social lives, centered around the school, take on (at least for many) a greater importance for their identity than home life, multicultural integration demands that schools go beyond this to find a way to cultivate opportunities and competencies for the discursive negotiation of conflict situations by students themselves. That is, multicultural schooling must facilitate—but not manufacture—the thematization of students' background presuppositions in light of challenges and problems that arise within the experience of students themselves, in their society and in their classroom. In contrast to "nonreflexive" learning, or the "banking" model of education, in which "implicitly raised theoretical (technical) and practical validity claims are naively taken for granted and accepted or rejected without discursive consideration," this entails a process of reflexive learning that "takes place through discourses in which we thematize practical validity claims that have become problematic or have been rendered problematic."[73] College- and university-level education must continue this cultivation of informed, deliberative competence.

It is patent that, to the extent that education (and, indeed students' attitude toward knowledge generally) is reduced to the strategic exchange relation described by Willis—of deference for qualification—student identities, core values, and commitments remain closed off from the educational process that raises, not challenges to the validity of one's presuppositions, but strategic problems whose successful resolution is signaled by quantitative evaluation—grades. It is only by engaging students themselves in genuine dialogue that these presuppositions can be problematized by the arguments of others, whether of the teacher, the curriculum, or fellow students. On the other hand, in the absence of the competencies for such discursive resolution, and as cultural pluralism in society and in the school undermine the level of intuitive confidence students have in unreflectively held convictions, they slip into something akin to Kohlberg's Stage 4½: a relativistic view of values and culture and a strategic attitude toward the social world and social conflict, both of which lend themselves to fatalism with respect to fundamental social structures. The end result is that, as Todd Gitlin observed of his students at UCLA and, indeed, "of American citizens generally," they lose "faith in their capacity to influence the structure of economic inequality." Along with the economic, social and political structures too take on the mantle of a "second nature," a collection of facts and not a series of meanings, decisions, and priorities. As social actors, individuals become utterly passive, just as Habermas describes them under the conditions of merely formal democracy; or, as Willis claimed, the limited character of their rejection of the current system perversely reinforces its most basic lineaments.

I don't want to spend much time detailing the sort of educational praxis that would foster multicultural integration and, at the same time, necessarily counter these tendencies. There are a number of plausible candidates and it strikes me as an empirical matter which would be most effective or practicable. But I do want to note a few important features common to all such programs and to point in the direction of research that aims to formulate them. First in this connection is that, although the introduction of discursively run civics classes eschewing the usual attempts at patriotic obfuscation and glorification, and focusing on current conflicts in the social world and communities of students, would surely be a good idea, critical educationalists are quite clear that it is not a matter of teaching substantively in one class a day or a week what is performatively denied in the other seven or eight.[74] Autonomy is a function of one's relationship toward knowledge, understanding, and insight; you cannot teach a student that thinking for oneself is crucial to democratic citizenship while stultifying their autonomy in rout learning of math, science, history, and so on. The sign of all knowledge is the measure in which it illuminates our world and experience, natural and social, rendering meaningful what was confused, opaque, and especially, what was taken for natural in such a way that no explanation seemed to be required. To my mind, the best single educational theory that aims at precisely this form of insight, at the discursive cultivation of autonomy as the confident capacity to intervene in social reality, is that of Paulo Freire; but one could easily multiply the list of educationalists emerging from a critical theoretical, discursively oriented perspective whose proposals are at least broadly compatible. Australian educationalist R. E. Young has provided a comprehensive account of the possibilities for developing a specifically Habermasian pedagogy; but Michael Apple, Henry Giroux, and Stanley Aronowitz all have contributed to tracing out the educational implications of critical theory.[75]

So far as my basically sociological argument goes, nothing in particular hinges on accepting one version of such an educational theory over others; the main reason I mention Freire is that he provides the clearest solution to the problem that has vexed educationalist proposals for radical social change since Plato's allegory of the Cave: Who educates the educators? Is there not a deeper authoritarianism or paternalism in a proposal that would make the autonomy of students the charge of their teachers?[76] Freire's proceduralist model of curricular development and pedagogy suggests that it is not necessary, after all, to presuppose in the teacher the level of insight we wish to inspire in students: In fact, to do so would be severely problematic on deliberative democratic grounds because it would suggest that we have preformulated the proper outcome of discourses that are supposed to be carried through by others. Young has also been particularly cautious in this regard and has repeatedly rebuked superficial attempts to invoke Habermas in the service of emancipatory education by portraying the ideal speech situation as a kind of model of freedom to be imposed on students by enlightened education—that is, rather than seeing it as an outgrowth of the students own efforts to achieve understanding, which the teacher can do no more than shield from external coercion as much as possible.[77] As I already stressed, in the case of multicultural education, this means that the problematization prerequisite to discourse has to arise endogenously from the communicative interactions of students. Any attempt by teachers to impose problematization on students could only be based on an ascription of identities and values, and would not only demonstrate a lack of the pedagogical restraint or "tact"—which Brumlik argued could alleviate the asymmetry of power between teacher and student—and so threaten student autonomy; it would also violate the right of students to a kind of privacy with respect to their identities.[78] To express the merit of such insistence in another way: This provides us a means of breaking into the mutual reinforcement of phylogeny and ontogeny, of social and individual formations. Education can be no more than a point of entry into this circle, which attempts to dissolve the obstacles to the open-ended process of human development; the ultimate stability of the changes it might bring about on a wider scale than is evidenced today rests on the subsequent achievements of social struggles. But it is nevertheless the only point of entry compatible with democratic legitimacy and, as far as I can see, the most promising place of traction for the critical ideals of justice in an increasingly totalized world. Of course, this is as much as to say that social struggles themselves will ultimately determine the justification for any optimism or pessimism. But, at present, it does not seem to me that there are empirical grounds for optimism regarding existing movements. Although feminist, environmental, antiglobalization, immigrant rights groups, and the like, all serve to create mini counter-publics and undoubtedly help to stabilize autonomous identities in some small number of people, they cannot exert formative influence unless they succeed in impacting the basic institutions of socialization. On this point, the prospects seem to me much better regarding the school than either the family or the media.

The Practical Significance of the Contradiction

Successful, stable forms of multicultural integration that meet the demands of justice, particularly with respect to internal minorities, requires discourse and so the socialization of discourse-competent individuals; but the colonization of the school by capitalist imperatives, the reduction of education to the strategic pursuit of qualification, disrupts the development of discourse-competence or the attainment of postconventionality. Societies that are both multicultural and advanced capitalist are therefore internally contradictory: They advance two distinct reproductive demands with respect to the socializing functions of the school that cannot both be satisfied and that cannot be hierarchically ordered, one beneath the other. There is nothing predictive about this: There is a mutual incompatibility that might be resolved in either direction. At present, things look favorable for capitalism: Even in the face of the most serious economic crisis since the Great Depression, at least in North America there remains neither space for nor willingness to engage in the rational consideration of alternatives to the status quo. Nevertheless, my argument serves to put a serious qualification on Habermas' thesis of the possibility of "socialization without norms," of a more or less total shift to systemic forms of integration: Given the irreducibility of cultural difference in contemporary societies and the role of recognition in individual development, the victory of capitalism in the school and over processes of socialization generally will necessarily come at the expense of social integration. Habermas suggested that system integration could, at least in principle, fully compensate for this loss; but although system integration can succeed in meeting many of the individual's needs, to the extent that they can be translated into money or access to social services, and so on, it cannot meet a need for recognition that, under conditions of cultural pluralism and conflict, also cannot be met by conventional role satisfaction within homogenous groups. There are a variety of more or less Orwellian ways in which these conflicts could be "managed" without pursuing resolution: Anti-immigrant legislation, racial profiling, government harassment, legal and social exclusion, all are examples evidenced in many places today. But it is at least debatable whether such a strategy is in the long-run sustainable for nations dependent on immigration for economic growth and population stability.

But this argument does not yet meet the bar of critical theoretical argumentation, since the objective incompatibility I have observed is not reflected in the experience of subjects who could become the agents of social change. To be sure, where things work themselves out in favor of the capitalist instrumentalization of education, individuals do experience the high level of recurrent and apparently rationally insoluble cultural conflict as anxiety provoking. In the absence of solutions to the so-called "clash of cultures," such feelings provide ample fodder for the sorts of far-right, Orwellian policies just mentioned. On the other hand, if things were to work out in favor of postconventionality, what might happen? To be sure, such individuals would and do experience contemporary mainstream political society as irredeemably shallow, electoral politics as approaching meaninglessness, the occupational sphere as thoroughly alienated even throughout most of the professions; most importantly for my argument, however, such individuals also have and would have a kind of diversity-valuing solidarity that transcends their individual and group interest position. In what way might this translate into social struggle?

In Chapters 1 and 2, we considered Habermas' claim that conflicts in advanced capitalist societies no longer take the direct form of class conflict. In *The Theory of Communicative Action*, this was supported by the altered account of protest potential relative to the threat to the lifeworld posed by colonization. In *Legitimation Crisis*, and in *Towards a Rational Society*, he reminded us that the displacement of class struggle does not entail the end of conflicts related to disparities in the distribution of social wealth:

> But unless they are connected with protest potential from other sectors of society no conflicts arising from such underprivilege can really overturn the system—they can only provoke it to sharp reactions incompatible with formal democracy. For underprivileged groups are not social classes, nor do they potentially represent the mass of the population. Their disenfranchisement and pauperization no longer coincide with exploitation, because the system does not live off their labor . . . as long as no coalitions are made with privileged groups, such a civil war lacks the chance of revolutionary success that class struggle possesses.[79]

What is interesting is that a diversity-valuing identity suggests, not a coalition between the privileged and the underprivileged in which each would consider their alliance strategically, but a form of solidarity that transcends interest positions. It seems to me that something like this is behind protests in developed nations against globalization: Although there is ample evidence that economic globalization, as it has been practiced, is of benefit to very few even within developed nations, much of this protest has been in principled solidarity with the oppressed elsewhere. The possibility of this kind of solidarity has been very poorly accounted for in philosophical theories of social struggle. Indeed, critical theory as whole has painted itself into a corner through an insistence on an unrealistic and overly narrow account of motivation tied too exclusively to the idea of interest. This much Honneth has indeed shown: Real social actors more often than not find effective motivation in their sense of identity and fundamental values; considerations of personal (or even group) interest are by no means paramount. More than just the "job blues," a specifically multicultural postconventionality simultaneously threatens a crisis of motivation and of legitimation.

Yet if it were true, as Habermas claimed, that capitalism does not rely on the labor of the underprivileged groups in question, it would indeed not be clear that solidarity relations of this sort would present a genuinely radical challenge. But we have already seen this claim refuted in several places: first, in Chapter 2, following Fraser, we saw that the capitalist economy instrumentalizes status distinction in its pursuit of profit; in the discussion of the school, we saw that status hierarchies, along with (or, better, overlaid by) educational credentials, are employed to legitimate the occupational hierarchy that is crucial to capitalist control and to its ability to appropriate socially created wealth; we saw, with Bowles and Gintis, that racially, ethnically, and sexually marginalized groups form a reserve pool to be drawn into the economy in times of growth and expelled back into poverty without consequence in times of economic contraction; and we saw, in the case of "the lads," how the stable reproduction of the capitalist occupational order at the lowest levels relies on the maintenance of sexist and racist value patterns. Closest to popular consciousness today are the exploitation and underprivilege of immigrant labor (legal and illegal) in the developed world, and the exploitative relationship between the developing world (from which most immigrants today come) and the developed. These facts allow us to give a more convincing answer to the question of the practical significance of the objective social contradiction for which I have argued: Again, if things turn out in favor of capitalism, then individuals and societies are left to cope in some fashion with the anxiety produced by recurrent cultural and ethnic conflicts (and, as Habermas noted, strategies for repressing these conflicts often risk the repoliticization of society); but if things turn out in favor of deliberative democratic contexts of socialization and the cultivation of a diversity-valuing identity on wide scale, then individuals are in a position to see not just the shallowness of their political culture and society, and not just the moral unacceptability of an asymmetrical distribution of social burdens over stigmatized or marginalized populations, but also the exploitation of racialized and ethnic immigrant populations and of the developing world, the persistence of the cultural subordination of women that justifies their unequal economic position, as threats or challenges to their own identity. That is, they are in a position to see multiculturalism and capitalism as incompatible, and to see the latter not as an inevitable, quasi-natural expression of human nature, but as an unjust and alterable system of social and material relations. As Marx and history have both demonstrated, *capitalism means poverty*, always and in some quarter; as we saw in the Intermediate Reflections, *capitalism means dominance, subordination, and hierarchy*, legitimized according to some pattern of privilege and prejudice. As Habermas argues in *Legitimation Crisis*, a welfare state reliant on capitalist growth, on the one hand, and perceptions of legitimacy, on the other, will always be faced with the problem of distributing the effects of that pathological correlation. Of course, it is not that individuals who attain postconventionality or discourse competence, and who experience the injustice of the current social order, would somehow intuitively see its systemic sources. As always, it is the job of theory to illuminate the sorts of obstacles faced by social struggles; but at this point, there would again be an addressee for such theory, a socially and politically significant number of individuals able and willing to listen.

Conclusion: The Status of the Argument

Rather than offering one more summary of my argument and critique of Habermas, I conclude by reflecting on an outstanding question: To whom is such an anticipatory argument addressed, in the sense of practical agent? Answering this question will hopefully vindicate a claim I made in Chapter 1 in connection with McCarthy's criticisms of *Legitimation Crisis*; namely, that I proposed to offer here an argument that, although resembling that of *Legitimation Crisis*, would not be predictive, and yet would do a better job of making the return trip from universal normative standards of critique, to pointing out practical addressees of critique under current social conditions. McCarthy had accepted that Habermas, through the theory of communicative action, identifies a suppressed interest that is universal or generalizable at the level of humanity as a whole: namely, the emancipatory interest in communication free of domination, which is embedded in language itself but that has practical consequences for the realization of autonomy, the openness of the political public sphere, and so on. He noted that, as a result, the addressee of critical theory appears also to be universalized. But it is hard to see, according to McCarthy, how such an abstract interest could serve as the motive and guide for effective political practice. Who will engage in political struggle for the sake of communication free from domination? The bourgeois appeal to the universal values of liberty, equality, and justice was politically effective precisely because they were ideologically interpreted to be of service to the particular interests of an emerging class. Marx's critique of these same values, which rested on a moral critique of capitalism, retained a similar connection to the interests of a particular social class, the proletariat.

McCarthy is more or less right that, in *Legitimation Crisis*, Habermas does not identify any particular social group, or particular group interests, as the lever of social transformation: In pointing to the transformative potential of altered socialization processes, he at most suggests the possibility of future struggles that would satisfy this requirement. And McCarthy is also right to point to Habermas' contention regarding the end of direct class conflict as the underlying cause of this assessment, which robs critical theory of a concrete practical addressee much as Adorno and Horkheimer believed. In the meantime, Habermas maintains that the struggle of underprivileged groups who bear the burden of displaced class conflict lacks revolutionary potential so long as common cause is not made with members of privileged groups. But he never pursues that question. Instead, in *The Theory of Communicative*

Action, Habermas answers McCarthy by moving from the identification of a universal interest in undistorted communication, via the theory of colonization, to the articulation of the interests of potential protest groups confronted with the encroachment of system imperatives. As we have seen, the argument there manifests a dramatic scaling down of the transformative significance of protest compared to the crisis argument of *Legitimation Crisis*: Only stalemate with media-steered subsystems is possible, even while Habermas has argued that capitalism will continue to generate a more or less irresistible tendency toward encroachment upon the lifeworld. Finally, *Between Facts and Norms* offered further details regarding Habermas' increasingly modest vision of how citizens could reign in the capitalist Leviathan, through participation in discourses in the public sphere on the appropriate limits of strategic action, to which discourses legislators *ought* to be responsive. Absent is any reference to the practical potentials for bringing about the realization of even these conciliatory ideals, and any consideration of the availability of the necessary competencies for effective participation in these demanding discourses on the part of individuals who, for the most part, appear quite content with merely formal democracy or, at most, with its merely periodic invigoration.

There is no way around the fact that contemporary society offers little grist for optimist mills. It seems to me inevitable that anyone committed to the theoretical and practical ideals of critical theory, that is, anyone committed to the creation of a truly just, egalitarian, and democratic society, yet who is also sensitive to the need to ground this "ought" through the identification of immanent, nontotalitarian potentials for achieving this end, will have to adopt an approach something like that of Habermas in *Legitimation Crisis* and my own here. While rightly eschewing "predictions" regarding the outcome of history, one can today do no more than search for causes to *anticipate* the conditions under which democratic social transformation could become a possibility. This, it seems to me, rather highly recommends processes of socialization, including perhaps especially schooling, as an area of great interest to critical theory. Such an anticipation is what I have attempted to offer, in a way that is significantly more concrete than anything found in *Legitimation Crisis*, but that does not commit the error of *The Theory of Communicative Action* and *Between Facts and Norms*, and pursue concreteness at the expense of the very ideals that send the critical theorist looking for practical potentials in the first place.

My admittedly normative account of deliberatively democratic multicultural integration, and the hypothesis of a consequent, interest-transcending solidarity, is the primary buttress for this alternative to Habermas' argument. It seems to me that the first thing that must be noted about this argument, relative to the model of critical theory, is that it could be accused of suffering from a kind of undemocratic institutionalism. As Fraser notes:

> [c]alls for deconstructing binary oppositions are far removed from the immediate concerns of most subjects of misrecognition, who are more disposed to seek self-respect by affirming a depreciated identity than by espousing the blurring of status distinctions. Similarly, calls for economic transformation are experientially remote from most subjects of maldistribution, who stand to gain more immediate benefit from income transfers than from democratic socialist planning.[80]

With respect to recognition and culture, I have not argued for the "deconstruction" of identities as an aim; I have suggested that a similarly decentered identity could result from success in democratic inclusion justified as a question of individual right. But it is nevertheless the case that what many mobilized cultural and ethnic groups want has little to do with the overall character of multicultural integration. It is often the case that integrative accommodations are sought that aim to make public institutions more inclusive; it is even sometimes the case that accommodations are sought that would give this inclusiveness a democratic form. But on the whole, groups engaged in struggles for recognition are concerned with their rights, with their own interpretations of their needs that—just as with the majority—are not typically the result of processes of discursive contestation: Parents seek the right to raise their children as members of their own culture without their suffering discrimination as a result; they most often do not intend that the identities of their children or indeed, that their own identities, should be pluralized and decentered through social inclusion. Like Fraser, I believe that such claims to recognition are justified insofar, but only insofar as they contribute to realizing substantively equal participation; thus, the articulation of a critical standard is relevant both for struggling groups seeking to justify their demands, and for their addressees, who require some such standard for judgment. But my argument connects up with these normative questions only because I have defended a congruence of justice and stability in this regard. To be sure, to the extent that social integration proceeds through mutual recognition and communicative action, there is indeed a universal interest at stake here. Yet under current undemocratic conditions, where systemic forms of integration are widespread, where attempts are still made to manufacture mutual recognition between (certain) citizens in advance through unreflective processes of cultural reproduction, the practical significance of my argument answers a question of policy: Its immediate addressee can only be those for whom social integration is their determining concern. This is what I intended to capture with the term *institutionalism*: namely, that my argument recommends itself as a guiding norm for policy with respect to fostering integration in diverse societies, especially in the school.[81] Indeed, my point has been that this macro-social imperative suggests an immanent pressure toward a potentially transformative reform of socialization in the schools, from an unjust subordination of communicative contexts to the strategic imperatives of system maintenance, to an emancipatory release of the inherently communicative potential of education. Thus, through using Habermas to integrate alternative conceptions of the role of the school in society, I have connected a universalizing normative critique of what occurs in the school today with a particular, concrete set of motives for ending this injustice, albeit among a specialized group of actors. Still, it is at least possible that this impetus could overcome the resistance to democratic educational reform noted by Habermas in *The Theory of Communicative Action*.

Things stand somewhat differently with respect to the economic: As I have insisted already, I do not intend to suggest that individuals socialized in the manner I have recommended would somehow see the systemic injustice of the capitalist order written plainly across the face of society, as though scales had fallen from their eyes. What is at issue, rather, is the transformation of attitudes toward the social and economic order, from one of passivity—a strategic, instrumental orientation at the level of the individual, and a fatalistic acceptance of the social—to one of activity. Only once individuals are able to perceive the status quo as but one possibility among others, as the product of human agency, as a series of meanings and not a series of natural and unalterable facts, is there any meaningful role for practically oriented theory, whose task it is to clarify alternatives and, most importantly, to illuminate the nature of the obstacles faced by struggles for justice. In this respect, most important to my argument is the claim that the economic structures of capitalism represent a permanent obstacle to the achievement of recognition: that, after all, is the meaning of the claim that multiculturalism and capitalism are incompatible. This argument is continuous with Marx's practical aim that, in works like *Capital* and the *Communist Manifesto*, was very largely intended to demonstrate to his addressees, to workers, that capitalism could never include everyone under the umbrella of its munificence, that the system itself was their obstacle and not this or that employer, or even this or that industry.

The question of attitude toward the social world is worth considering in closer detail: In Habermas' terms, my argument regarding the irreducibility of cultural struggle today intends to say that struggles for recognition represent the most potent possibility for a repoliticization of the public sphere. As Habermas himself more or less noted in his pessimistic assessment of the political significance of "underprivilege," the suppression of such struggles—the war on "illegals" in the United States, for example, or the status of the "*sans papiers*," in France—equally risks increasing levels of politicization that are incompatible with merely formal democracy. On the other hand, where mobilization is effective in transforming social institutions, it is at least plausible that the quasi-natural façade of the economic order is dented. Banting and Kymlicka make a similar claim in the course of rejecting the worry that identity politics displaces economic politics; to the contrary, they argue, this could only hold true were there a body of individuals who, were it not for their engagement in cultural struggles, would certainly invest their time in questions of economic justice.[82] Yet there is so little sense that economic structures are open to modification, they agree, that the possibility of economic struggle seems to wait upon a renewed sense of the competence of individuals for effective social action. In this light, the politics of identity may well be propedeutic to the politics of class. And, as a matter of fact, they cite at least a couple of cases where this seems to have been true, the most suggestive of which are, first, the role struggles for indigenous rights in Latin America seem to have played in building a social base on which challenges to neoliberalism have been built[83] and, second, the possibility that the politics of recognition "helped to inspire some of the protest around globalization."[84]

As Habermas has come to stress rather often, the list of problems confronted by the citizens of the world today, when they open a newspaper, turn on a television or a computer, is unprecedented both in terms of length and seriousness: Increasing poverty and unemployment coupled with exploding corporate profits and share prices; the dramatic rise or return of racism in developed nations; continually growing disparities of wealth and life chances between the prosperous North and West and the impoverished South and East; the prospect of "civilizational" conflict between the East and the West; spreading fundamentalism in Islamic, Christian, Judaic, Hindu, and other cultural and religious forms; ongoing and imminent environmental catastrophe; uncontrollable migrations of refugees. This frightening list of dangers, threats, and difficulties can only become "a political agenda for a public which maintains a degree of trust in the possibility of a conscious transformation of society—and which can in turn be entrusted with it."[85] But that, in turn, rests on the possibility of a reinvigoration of the political public sphere in diverse, complex societies, such that a democratically integrated citizenry could gain confidence in its capacity for effective intervention and self-direction. Habermas concludes,

> Margaret Thatcher—the first genuinely "postmodern" politician—must have had some intuitive understanding of this situation when she hit upon the slogan that "there is no such thing as society." In the political public sphere, conflicts on a national, European, or global scale develop their power to disturb us only when they are seen, against the background of a normative understanding of social inequalities and political oppression, not as natural phenomena but as social products—hence as changeable.[86]

Yet, in the end, despite the enormous rigor and fruitfulness of his theoretical approach, Habermas is never able to answer how that normative understanding is to be encouraged, spread, and made effective, where the footholds can be found that would allow us to dig in our heels and so resist the terrible weight of the forces of capital and the power that speaks in its name. More and more his ideals and his practical proposals find themselves on awkward terms with one another. With the argument I have presented here, I hope to have adequately defended the possibility of an alternative framework, on the basis of which we can assess our current situation with reasonably clear eyes, while not being forced to compromise our ideals in order to maintain that they are more than idle fancies. Finally, I hope the argument may offer some grounds for educators, struggling cultural and ethnic groups, and leftists generally, to see themselves as engaged in a struggle against a shared set of obstacles, in a common cause that can be named, without equivocation, the cause of social justice.

Notes

Introduction

1. Horkheimer, "Authority and the Family," 95.
2. See Benhabib, *Critique, Norm, and Utopia.*
3. Young, "Habermas and Education," 532.
4. Habermas, "Moral Development and Ego Identity," 72.
5. See Honneth "The Social Dynamics of Disrespect," *The Struggle for Recognition*, and "Redistribution as Recognition." Honneth, however, nowhere seems to suspect that any important consequences might follow for the very structure of identity as a result of the emergence of multiculturalism.
6. McBride, "Habermas and the Marxian Tradition," 431. A number of authors—including Habermas himself—maintain to the contrary that Habermas has, since the 1960s, held to essentially the same intellectual course and commitments (modifying them, as he says, no more "than was necessary to hold true to them in altered historical circumstances"). For some supporters of this view, and Habermas own statement just cited, see Habermas, *Autonomy and Solidarity*, 183–84; White, "Reason, Modernity, and Democracy," 5; and Morrow and Torres, *Social Theory and Education*, 12–13.
7. McBride, "Habermas and the Marxian Tradition," 432. That is not to suggest that McBride remains unconvinced: He takes it as quite incontrovertible when one addresses oneself instead to Habermas' practical political interventions, for example, in support of the NATO bombing of Serbia or the first invasion of Iraq.
8. Other notable attempts to make the same point have focused on a different issue, which does not have the simultaneous methodological implications of my critique here: namely, Habermas' work on the public sphere. In this connection, see Marsh, *Unjust Legality*, Scheuerman, "Between Resignation and Radicalism." Amy Allen's work on the Foucault–Habermas debate is probably closest, thematically, to the issue I deal with here; but although she spends some time dealing with issues of Foucault's development, her discussion of Habermas on this point is quite brief (see Allen, *The Politics of Ourselves*).
9. See Habermas, *Between Facts and Norms*, chapter 8, especially 358, 371.
10. Berger, "The Linguistification of the Sacred and the Delinguistification of the Economy," 169–70.

11. Simone de Beauvoir cites George Bernard Shaw's lampooning of this bad faith argument in her critique of its use relative to women. As Shaw wrote, "The American white relegates the black to the rank of shoeshine boy; and he concludes from this that the black is good for nothing but shining shoes" (cited in *The Second Sex*, xxx).

12. Young, *A Critical Theory of Education*, 14.

13. Ibid., 52.

14. Cited in Morrow and Torres, *Social Theory and Education*, 252. Moreover, the competencies in question do not pick out the fixed teleological goal of all development, but the conditions for an open-ended process of development or, better, the conditions for free self-development. Although no neoconservative, Richard Rorty is a good example of someone who would object to my argument here that it demonstrates a "phallogocentric" rejection of human beings as they really are, and fails to appreciate that the need for clarity and the ineffable felt by intellectuals is intrinsically esoteric (see Rorty, "Habermas and Lyotard on Postmodernity," 174). However, Rorty is so sanguine about the achievements of the so-called West, so certain in the absence of any argument that its outstanding problems are residual rather than systemic, that he dismisses out of hand the intellectual effort to achieve a deep understanding of social reality as a totality, considering it unnecessary to the project of justice.

Chapter 1: Capitalism and Contradiction in Legitimation Crisis

1. Habermas, *Legitimation Crisis*, 1.

2. Ibid., 3, 28; see also *Lifeworld and System*, 292.

3. Indeed, that is precisely Habermas' normative interpretation of the situation of post-war German society: Assuming responsibility for the perpetration of the Holocaust, he has argued, entails an irrevocable split with the nationalist traditions of the prewar period; postwar Germany can seek unity only through a "constitutional patriotism," a forward-looking, discursive democratic project. Unity on the basis of shared, once constitutive cultural and linguistic traditions is henceforth forbidden to it (see, e.g., Habermas, *The New Conservativism*; also, for a good summary, Pensky, "Universalism and the Situated Critic").

4. Habermas, *Legitimation Crisis*, 4.

5. Ibid., 4–5.

6. Honneth, "Redistribution as Recognition," 156.

7. Habermas, *Legitimation Crisis*, 6.

8. Ibid., 7.

9. Ibid., 8.

10. Ibid., 21.

11. See Marx, *Capital*, Parts Three and Four.

12. Habermas, *Legitimation Crisis*, 23.

13. Liberal capitalism was so successful because, for the most part, economic crises that erupt from structurally insoluble system contradictions "have the appearance of natural catastrophes that break forth from the centre of a system of purposive-rational action. . . . [I]n liberal capitalism, class antagonism is shifted from the

intersubjectivity of the lifeworld [i.e., from a question of the social relations between individuals and groups] into the substratum of this world. Commodity fetishism [the appearance that market relations are relations between things and not between laboring individuals] is both a secularized residual ideology and the actually functioning steering principle of the economic system. Economic crises thus lose the character of a fate accessible to self-reflection and acquire the objectivity of inexplicable, contingent, natural events" (ibid., 30).

14. Ibid., 27.

15. On the definitions of constant and variable capital, see Marx, *Capital*, chapter 8, especially 317; on the falling rate of profit, see ibid., chapter 25, especially 772ff. Surplus value is derived from variable capital because the cost of constant capital expense is passed along to the consumer, transferred to the product through the process of labor; there is no quantitative change in this. But by driving down wages relative to the value realized by selling the product, profit or a surplus quantity of value is produced beyond the original investment—violating the principle of exchange of equivalents and paying workers less than the value of their labor.

16. Habermas, *Legitimation Crisis*, 29.

17. Ibid., 33.

18. Ibid.

19. Ibid., 34.

20. Ibid., 35. The aim of full employment, which Habermas also mentions in this passage, has long since been surrendered as unattainable under the conditions of advanced capitalism in "Western" nations. Presently, in the aftermath of the financial crisis of 2008–09, an unemployment rate of around 8 to 9 percent seems poised to become the new "normal" in the United States and Canada.

21. Ibid.

22. Ibid., 56–57. Habermas tends to exaggerate the extent to which contemporary capitalism has left behind the liberal stage, which is almost certainly a function of Eurocentrism in his thinking: The exploitation of labor in the pursuit of absolute surplus value continues unabated in many developing nations with no serious or with unenforced labor regulations; it also continues domestically in North America and Europe, in the exploitation of "illegal" immigrant labor. The use of such labor in both cases has crucial effects on domestic economies: The cheaper consumer goods and services that result reduce the cost of the reproduction of labor power and so the market price of labor (wages). Habermas' main point, however, is that Marx's assessment of the inevitability of economic crisis relies on an underestimation of the significance of this directly unproductive labor (e.g., scientific research, education) which is aimed at increasing the productivity of labor and thus both contributing to surplus value and forestalling the fall in the rate of profit.

23. Ibid., 36.

24. Ibid.

25. Ibid., 37.

26. Ibid., 75. Habermas adds that vocational privatism "thus corresponds to the structures of educational and occupational systems that are regulated by competition through achievement" (ibid).

27. Ibid., 38.

28. Ibid., 39.
29. Ibid., 41.
30. Ibid., 9–10.
31. Ibid., 43.
32. Ibid., 67.
33. Ibid., 47, 70.
34. Ibid., 71.
35. Ibid., 70 (my emphasis).
36. Ibid., 47–48.
37. Ibid., 71. Other examples mentioned by Habermas include the role of the state in marriage laws and family planning, which has thematized normative conceptions of marriage and the family that had once been taken as natural, and also urban planning and health care planning, which inspire use-value demands in citizens.
38. Ibid., 71–72.
39. There are a number of additional problems confronted by the administration in its attempt to steer the economy that relate to the paradoxical situation in which the administration finds itself, faced by the imperatives of economic growth on the one side and by the use value-oriented demands of citizens on the other. Its need to conceal the interests behind its operations, for instance, appears in the question of taxation, which is used to generate resources to be deployed rationally for the avoidance of crises and the stimulation of growth; that is, it must do so while avoiding the withdrawal of legitimation that would result should the selectivity in the raising of money from taxation and the "discernible pattern of priorities in their use" (ibid., 62) come to public consciousness. Recent examples in which this "selectivity" is discernable abound in the "bailout measures" employed in 2008–09 by nearly all developed nations, especially regarding the financial industry.
40. Ibid., 48.
41. Ibid. Habermas adopts the term "post-auratic" from Benjamin, who intended to indicate thereby that whereas "traditional art was surrounded by a ritually induced aura that distanced it from everyday life, thus encouraging its cultic enjoyment as a beautiful illusion, modern art abandoned both its aura and the accompanying illusion of autonomy from society" (see Jay, "Habermas and Modernism," 127). Many of the papers collected in the volume with Jay's (Bernstein, ed., *Habermas and Modernity*)—including Habermas' response—explore the question of the significance of aesthetic rationality for his project.
42. Habermas, *Legitimation Crisis*, 74–45.
43. Ibid., 76.
44. Ibid., 77.
45. Ibid., 78.
46. Ibid., 79.
47. Ibid., 80.
48. Ibid., 81.
49. Ibid.
50. Ibid., 81–82.
51. Ibid., 83.

52. Naomi Klein's most recent work is worthy of note in this regard, in which she traces the connection between research on the psychological effects of shock, in particular, the inducement of regression, and strategies for the implementation of programs of neoliberal reconstruction that aim to circumvent the "problem" of legitimacy (see *The Shock Doctrine*).

53. See McCarthy, *The Critical Theory of Jürgen Habermas*, 375, for his agreement.

54. Habermas, *Legitimation Crisis*, 84.

55. For a much later attempt at suggesting a possible model for the dialectical reintegration of art and life, see Habermas, "Modernity versus Postmodernity."

56. Habermas, *Legitimation Crisis*, 92.

57. Ibid., 89.

58. Ibid., 92.

59. McCarthy, *The Critical Theory of Jürgen Habermas*, 385.

60. Habermas, *Legitimation Crisis*, 125.

61. Ibid., 128.

62. Ibid., 129.

63. Held, "Crisis Tendencies, Legitimation and the State," 188.

64. Habermas, "A Reply to my Critics," 280.

65. Ibid.

66. Held, "Crisis Tendencies, Legitimation and the State," 188.

67. Günther Dux argues a similar position with respect to *The Theory of Communicative Action*; he writes, "[i]ntellectuals have always overestimated the legitimacy of a social order and its individual norms. . . . Habermas believes that the viability of a lifeworld simply requires an awareness that one lives in legitimated relationships—this is decisively devalued by our own lifeworld: I simply cannot think of a single domain of life whose life-forms could be ascribed outright legitimacy—even though an awareness certainly does exist of that at least problematical legitimacy involved in conducting everyday life. At the same time, life is being conducted in them. If one agrees with Habermas in defining the social world as the world of legitimately regulated relationships, then this social world has collapsed in the present day." Dux, "Communicative Reason and Interest," 271, n. 11. Dux fails to note—as I argue of Held and McCarthy, as well—that Habermas, although disagreeing with this empirical assessment, has discussed this possibility under the heading of a socialization without norms.

68. Held, "Crisis Tendencies, Legitimation and the State," 188.

69. Ibid., 189.

70. Ibid.

71. Ibid., 190.

72. Ibid., 192.

73. Ibid., 191–92. In *Legitimation Crisis* itself Habermas notes that the socially integrative force of bourgeois ideologies applies predominantly to the bourgeois class. The proletariat, whom this ideology serves to oppress, offer loyalty to the system on the basis of a combination of tradition, precapitalist values, "fatalistic willingness to follow, lack of perspective, and naked repression," and admittedly not on the basis of "the convincing force of bourgeois ideologies" (Habermas, *Legitimation Crisis*, 22).

Habermas can concede this without adopting Held's position precisely because the crisis argument is not offered with reference to the class consciousness of the proletariat. Also, see ibid., 96, where Habermas adds that the factual recognition of a social order may be attained through "simple compliance engendered by the individual's perception of his own powerlessness and the lack of alternatives open to him (that is, by his own fettered imagination)." Habermas cites Weber in support of this contention but adds, as Weber did, that every social order nevertheless rests on a significant degree of recognition for its structure of rule. The latter, Held seems to deny.

74. McCarthy, *The Critical Theory of Jürgen Habermas*, 377.

75. Ibid., 378.

76. Ibid., 379.

77. Ibid., 380.

78. Ibid., 381.

79 Ibid., 383.

80. Cited in ibid., 384; originally, Habermas, "Technology and Science as 'Ideology,'" 109–10. More recently, Habermas has observed that in the face of the neoliberal dismantling of the welfare state a new "underclass" is being formed in the urban centers of the developed world that, as in the developing world, is left to fend itself, cut off from the rest of society and from political power (images of the aftermath of hurricane Katrina come to mind). Although he still foresees no transformative significance in such an underclass, he notes three consequences that follow from its creation:

1. It results in social tensions that occasionally explode in "self-destructive revolts" (e.g., the suburbs of Paris).
2. The increasing need for repression drives massive growth in the prison and security industries.
3. The effects of immiseration spread throughout cities, poisoning whole regions and, ultimately, leading to the "moral erosion of society, which inevitably undermines the universalistic core of any republican polity. Formally correct majority decisions that merely reflect the status anxieties and self-assertive reflexes of a middle class threatened by the prospect of social decline undermine the legitimacy of the procedures and institutions of the democratic constitutional state" (Habermas, "The European Nation State," 123).

As evidence of this last connection, I am inclined to cite the rhetorical incorporation of "illegal" immigration into the issue of "homeland security" and the so-called "war on terror," the cultivation and exploitation of xenophobia by "Western" politicians and pundits. Surprisingly, however, although he seemed to speak descriptively in the above, Habermas goes on to say that "[w]hile this scenario is by no means unrealistic, it illustrates just one among several possible future developments" (ibid). Sadly, it seems to me that this future has arrived.

Chapter 2: Rationalization and Social Pathology in The Theory of Communicative Action

1. Habermas, *Lifeworld and System*, 86.
2. Habermas, "Moral Consciousness and Communicative Action," 133–34.
3. Ibid., 134.
4. See also, Habermas, *Reason and the Rationalization of Society*. In his initial articulation of the theory of communicative action, Habermas postulated a fourth validity claim to intelligibility or comprehensibility (see Habermas, "Reflections on the Linguistic Foundation of Sociology," 90–93).
5. Habermas, "Moral Consciousness and Communicative Action," 134–35; *Lifeworld and System*, 122–23, 127.
6. Habermas, "Moral Consciousness and Communicative Action," 135.
7. Ibid., 130–31.
8. Ibid., 137–38.
9. Ibid., 87.
10. Ibid., 90.
11. Ibid., 107. Despite basically parallel developments in the differentiation of culture, morality is given by Habermas a special status (which he subsequently revokes, in *Between Facts and Norms*): Neither art nor science can assume something approximating the erstwhile function of religion as a total social institution; but morality, in the form of a communicative ethics, retains at least something of the social pervasiveness of religion in archaic societies: unlike science and art, it cannot be confined to the cultural sphere of the lifeworld; unlike law, it is not restricted to the sphere of society; and unlike formations of personality, it cannot be confined to the person. To be sure, morality is embodied diversely in these various spheres—in institutionalized social norms and in forms of moral consciousness—but it is nevertheless the same morality that is thus embodied.
12. Ibid., 140.
13. Ibid., 140–41.
14. Ibid., 141. The careful differentiation of the respective resources underlying these new disturbances seems especially intended to answer Held's critique of the underlying source of confusion in *Legitimation Crisis*.
15. Ibid.
16. Ibid., 143.
17. Ibid., 146.
18. Ibid., 147.
19. Ibid., 117.
20. Habermas concedes (to a criticism originally advanced by Axel Honneth) that the identification of action types and action systems that he had maintained in "Technology and Science as 'Ideology,'" was overly hasty (see Habermas, "A Reply," 251).
21. Habermas, "A Reply to my Critics," 253–54.
22. See Habermas, "A Reply," 257; for the whole discussion, 252ff. In general, the criticism that Habermas has reified both system and lifeworld is so common

that I could not give anything like a representative list of examples; to offer a few, without suggesting that they are more important than those I don't mention, see Fraser, "What's Critical About Critical Theory?"; Ingram, *Habermas and the Dialectic of Reason*, 115; Alexander, "Habermas and Critical Theory," 61–65; Berger, "The Linguistification of the Sacred and the Delinguistification of the Economy," 174.

23. Habermas, *Lifeworld and System*, 153.

24. See Habermas, "A Reply," 259, where he concedes that his language in *Lifeworld and System* had given the false impression that he believed the process of uncoupling to be complete. In a somewhat surprising note (ibid., 294, n.92) he also claims that he does not consider this uncoupling to be "irreversible" although he doubts, for unspecified empirical reasons, the prospects for success of a recoupling of the economy to the lifeworld through workplace democracy (ibid., 261).

25. Habermas, *Lifeworld and System*, 171.

26. Habermas, "A Reply," 256.

27. Habermas, *Lifeworld and System*, 173.

28. Ibid.

29. Ibid., 174.

30. Ibid., 176.

31. Ibid., 177.

32. Ibid., 176.

33. Ibid.

34. Ibid., 180.

35. Ibid., 183.

36. See Fraser, "What's Critical About Critical Theory," 118; McCarthy, "Complexity and Democracy," 123ff; and Ingram, *Habermas and the Dialectic of Reason*, 145.

37. Habermas, "A Reply," 257.

38. Habermas, *Lifeworld and System*, 308.

39. Ibid., 310. Habermas further concedes, however, that "the externalization of lifeworld contexts cannot be carried through without remainder, as the informal organization upon which all formal organization relies amply demonstrates. Informal organization covers those linguistically regulated, inner-organizational relations that, notwithstanding the juridification of the framework, may be moralized. The lifeworlds of members, never completely husked away, penetrate here into the reality of organizations" (ibid., 311). Unfortunately, he fails to offer any examples of the kind of relations he has in mind: Perhaps sexual harassment or other forms of workplace discrimination would count as an inner-organizational relation that can be moralized in light of normative, lifeworld orientations? Would the right to unionization so count, a right to the assertion of equality against power hierarchy?

40. McCarthy may be right to read this claim as saying that individuals (generically) act communicatively only "with reservation," since they know that at any point they can have recourse to formalized rules. This seems particularly true to me of superiors in relation to inferiors. Yet McCarthy has the opposite in mind: that authorities are only able to bypass communication "with reservation," since they know that sometimes they can only achieve their goals on the basis of mutual understanding and cooperation. He concludes, however, that the "ratio of power to agreement in the actual operation of administrations seems . . . to be a thoroughly empirical

question" ("Complexity and Democracy," 129). But I disagree that this precludes the basic truth of Habermas' general claim that bureaucratic systems are essentially hierarchies in which power functions as a medium; no one low down on this totem will harbor illusions regarding the number of cases in which they will find themselves in essentially reciprocal, communicative relations with their superiors. A deeper problem comes out when McCarthy argues that systems are supposed to be differentiated by systemic integration, that is, by the functional interweaving of action consequences yet, he claims, it is much harder to see what this would mean in bureaucracies as contrasted with markets (ibid., 129–30). It is true that a bureaucratic subsystem should be particularly amenable to analysis from a system perspective; but that isn't what differentiates a subsystem from the lifeworld. Subsystems are marked out by their legal organization, which institutionalizes a steering medium; so the primary question is not whether action consequences are functionally interwoven, but whether power actually operates as a medium. Steering media operate by manipulating the conditions under which self-interested decisions are made; thus, if power functions as a medium in bureaucratic organizations, we might interpret this to mean, for instance, that systems of promotion on the basis of performance evaluations conducted by superiors, emphasizing obedience, etc., or threats of dismissal on specific grounds, influence the boundary conditions for the strategic behavior of subordinates. Systems analysis can then also tell us how the consequences of the actions so motivated are functionally integrated in ways that reproduce the system of power.

41. Habermas, *Lifeworld and System*, 185.
42. Ibid., 312.
43. Ibid., 186.
44. Ibid., 341.
45. Ibid., 319.
46. Ibid.
47. Ibid., 321.
48. Ibid.
49. Ibid., 311.
50. Ibid., 321.
51. Ibid., 332.
52. Ibid., 322.
53. Ibid., 325.
54. Ibid.
55. Ibid., 356–57.
56. Ibid., 359–60.
57. Ibid., 361–62.
58. Ibid., 362.
59. Ibid.
60. Fraser, "What's Critical About Critical Theory?" 132. Fraser rightly rejects Habermas' contention that welfare reforms in the occupational sphere are less ambivalent because it is, as a domain, already formally organized. Accordingly, she notes that dependence on the state, which ultimately characterizes both kinds of welfare programs she describes, must, if it is pathological, be equally so in both cases even if in different ways (ibid., 133). With respect to the stereotyping domination involved in welfare

policies, see also Fraser, "Women, Welfare and the Politics of Need Interpretation." For Habermas' discussion of this example in light of the "feminization of poverty," see Habermas, "Struggles for Recognition in the Democratic Constitutional State."

61. Habermas, *Lifeworld and System*, 363.

62. Benhabib, *The Claims of Culture*, 74. Will Kymlicka also notes of multicultural policies that, "the bureaucratic categories used to identify beneficiaries . . . are often over-inclusive or under-inclusive, or reflect the logic of administrative convenience rather than the needs or aspirations of the intended beneficiaries. They may lump disparate groups into the same legal category, despite their different needs, or put similar groups into artificially distinct categories" (Kymlicka, *Multicultural Odysseys*, 158). As an example of over-inclusiveness in the case of Canadian welfare policy, Kymlicka cites the use of the category "visible minority," which is insensitive to the specific nature of anti-black and anti-Muslim racism; as an example of under-inclusion in the Canadian case, he points to the distinction between "status" and "non-status" First Nations persons that, although it initially had a practical purpose, has long been out of touch with the realities of indigenous people in Canada (ibid., 158–59, n.21). As with the case of the NAACP, these administrative distortions have forced indigenous groups to prioritize strategic considerations over a more open and genuinely communicative debate regarding the meaning of being "First Nations" and the associated conditions of membership. Benhabib and Kymlicka's examples both indicate why an administrative processing of cultural conflict is inadequate, something to which I return later.

63. In an attempt to respond to at least some of these types of problems, welfare states increasingly offer forms of therapeutic assistance as well; but this simply recapitulates the same basic ambiguity at a more specific level: "The form of administratively prescribed treatment by an expert is for the most part in contradiction with the aim of the therapy, namely, that of promoting the client's independence and self-reliance" (Habermas, *Lifeworld and System*, 363). Habermas refers to the complex of medical, educational, and carceral institutions that implement these additional measures as the "therapeutocracy." It includes the prison system, institutions for the treatment of the mentally ill, for the rehabilitation of addicts, public education systems, health care systems, and so on.

64. Ibid., 363–64.

65. Ibid., 359.

66. Ibid., 369. Both Amy Allen and Nancy Fraser dispute Habermas' conception of the family as a lifeworld domain characterized by communicative action (see Fraser, "What's Critical About Critical Theory?" and Allen, *The Politics of Ourselves*). Allen, however, seems to accept that Habermas' position is that the reproductive specialization of the family links it to a process that is essentially communicative—in other words, that the link between the lifeworld and communicative action orientations is more or less counterfactual. Fraser seems to miss this and to criticize Habermas for claiming that the family is, in practice, a purely communicative domain. Although I'm not certain she is entirely consistent on this point, Allen's critique seems most forcefully directed at the practical significance of the fact that, as far as she can tell, the connection is for the most part strongly counterfactual. If that is the case, she asks, what practical consequences result from the fact that individuals are socialized

very often under conditions of systematically distorted communication? She suspects that, even on Habermas' own terms, these consequences are such as to cast into doubt the feasibility of constructing a social theory based normatively on a strong idea of autonomy.

67. Habermas, "A Reply," 225.

68. Ingram claims that the colonization and cultural impoverishment (still to be discussed) theses are "an attempt to broaden the theory of social crisis developed in *Legitimation Crisis*," and not an attempt to displace it (*Habermas and the Dialectic of Reason*, 160); and, indeed, in his reply to Held, Habermas seems to make the same claim ("A Reply to my Critics," 278ff). It is less than clear to me that this can be true, however, since the correlated assessment of protest potential is similarly scaled down; Habermas now seems content with a sort of stalemate between subsystems and lifeworld. But if he continued to foresee the possibility of a motivation crisis, as he used to conceive of it, there would be no obvious reason to limit the potential for transformation to this exceedingly modest claim. This change is especially surprising because Habermas' basic diagnosis of the problem is, on the other hand, unchanged: It is the effect of the absorption of the contradictions at the heart of capitalist production that are at the root in both cases (see Habermas, "A Reply," 225). It is therefore hard to see how to reconcile the external correction advocated in *The Theory of Communicative Action*—in which the resistance of the lifeworld is to keep system "in bounds" but unaltered—and the hope for the transformation of advanced capitalism which a motivation-legitimation crisis had seemed to promise.

69. Habermas, *Lifeworld and System*, 343.

70. Ibid., p. 344. In the bailout measures employed in the United States in 2008–09, this restraint reached almost absurd proportions, with the Obama administration refusing itself voting privileges on the boards of corporations that had effectively been nationalized with public dollars.

71. Ibid., 347.

72. Ibid., 348.

73. Ibid., 350–51.

74. Ibid.

75. Ibid., 344.

76. Ibid., 345.

77. Ibid., 346.

78. Ibid.

79 Ibid., 346–47. Habermas has noted the way in which the manipulation of public opinion is aimed at the manifestation of apparently irreconcilable differences in values (for which positivistic common consciousness also is necessary), which then justifies the intervention of the state as arbitrator in the public sphere. See Dryzek, "Critical Theory as a Research Program," for examples of empirical research that employs and confirms something like a Habermasian framework in the analysis of the mass media and public sphere.

80. Habermas, *Lifeworld and System*, 351.

81. Ibid., 326.

82. Ibid., 327.

83. Ibid., 355.

84. Ibid.

85. Ibid., 313.

86. Ibid., 316. In fact, however, Habermas rejects the over-drawn contrast between Marx and Weber as purportedly and one-sidedly "materialist" and "idealist," respectively (see Ingram, *Habermas and the Dialectic of Reason*, 204, n.13).

87. Habermas, *Lifeworld and System*, 315.

88. Ibid.

89. Ibid., 328. As Joel Whitebook notes, a similar thesis regarding "unlearning"—although presented as intrinsic and inevitable—was advanced by earlier critical theory, according to which "the 'brief intermezzo of liberalism' constituted a short, self-liquidating phase of historical development in which autonomous individuality was articulated as a social norm, partially realized, and finally undermined. The same market that, in the first instance, had served to differentiate the individual from the precapitalist collectivity, in the long run destroys the conditions of individuality" ("Reason and Happiness," 146). Habermas also began his career with an account of something very much a part of this process of unlearning; namely, the rise of an enlightened political public sphere in the eighteenth century and its subsequent depoliticization and "refeudalization" under advanced capitalism (see Habermas, *The Structural Transformation of the Public Sphere*).

90. Habermas, *Lifeworld and System*, 386.

91. Ibid., 143; see figure 22.

92. Although Habermas' own analysis in *The Theory of Communicative Action*—and in *Legitimation Crisis*, as well—suggests that the importance of the school is, at minimum, equal to that of the family in this respect, it is worth noting that several years later he not only repeats the claim that the family is specialized in the area of socialization, but asserts that the school specializes in cultural reproduction (see Habermas, "Actions, Speech Acts, Linguistically Mediated Interactions, and the Lifeworld [1988]," 250). This restriction of the primary reproductive contribution of the school contradicts Habermas' own arguments regarding the migration of the achievement principle from the market to the school; nevertheless, as I argue in the Intermediate and Concluding Reflections, the school does, no doubt, also serve cultural reproduction.

93. This is reflected in a complementary sociopsychological change: The decreasing significance of the Oedipal phase during which Leo Lowenthal, for instance, had theorized that superego structures are shaped by functional imperatives. The resolution of the Oedipal problematic was supposed, according to Lowenthal, to signal "the internalization of societal repression which is simply masked by parental authority" (Habermas, *Lifeworld and System*, 388). This process is confronted with dangers that manifest themselves in symptoms of hysteria and compulsive neuroses. But "psychoanalytically trained physicians," according to Habermas, have long noted that these illness manifestations have been almost entirely displaced by "narcissistic disorders." This phenomenon remains impenetrable to accounts which take the Oedipal complex as key; instead, this new symptom presentation is attributable to the increasingly vulnerable and demanding conditions of socialization in a family in

which communicative structures have been set free. When this occurs, "[t]he potential for irritability grows, and with it the probability that instabilities in parental behaviour will have a comparatively strong effect—a subtle neglect" (ibid.). This neglect results in the aforementioned narcissism.

94. Ibid., 388.

95. Ibid., 391–92.

96. Ibid., 392.

97. Ibid., 393.

98. Ibid., 399.

99. Ibid., 395.

100. Habermas, "Technology as Science and 'Ideology,'" 109–10.

101. Fraser, "Social Justice in the Age of Identity Politics," 16–18.

102. Ibid., 19. As a matter of fact, Fraser thinks that all struggles are somewhere in the middle: Oppressed economic classes suffer from forms of cultural stigmatization that are not merely epiphenomenal, at least in the sense that they can undermine the ability of members to mobilize effectively; on the other hand, because homophobia is tied to pervasive workplace discrimination, for example, the economic threats that accompany attempts to openly struggle against heterosexist cultural values are not merely epiphenomenal either.

103. Ibid., 20.

104. Ibid., 21–22.

105. Ibid., 22–23.

106. Ibid., 51.

107. Ibid., 58.

108. Interestingly, Fraser's earlier work contained numerous good examples of the way the political system absorbs cultural prejudices, such as the division of welfare programs mentioned already. But, ironically, Fraser rejects Habermas' characterization of the political administration as a "system," and so cannot appeal to these phenomena in making her case.

109. See Fraser, "Distorted Beyond All Recognition," 216.

110. Such industries include the entire service industry in places like New York and Los Angeles, much of the construction industry, and the agricultural sector generally, but especially the fruit industries of South; the meatpacking industries of the Midwest, and so on.

111. McCarthy, "Complexity and Democracy," 131.

112. Ibid., 132.

113. Ibid.

114. Ibid., 132–33.

115. Having no desire to attempt to engage in my own *a priori* effort to talk about limits to democratization, allow me merely to point to one suggestive empirical counterexample. Michael Menser ("Disarticulate the State!") has explored a number of experiments in democratization in Central and South America, through which he reveals the errors of an insistence on all or nothing contrasts between reform and revolution. That is, the options facing social movements are not limited to participating in the current system with the aim of reform, or revolution aimed at the complete

overthrow of the current system. The successful resistance in Cochabamba, Bolivia, to the privatization of water resources provides an interesting instance of a middle ground. When mass mobilizations ultimately succeeded in forcing the government to repeal the privatizing legislation and "renationalize" the infrastructure and resources, the citizens were confronted with a new dilemma: In the face of the neoliberal transformation of their government into an administrative arm of capital realization, they were no longer willing to ensure management of the water department to government bureaucracy. As a result, they resolved not on the overthrow of the state, but on the democratization of this specific bureaucracy that, as is typical, already enjoyed a degree of institutional autonomy. One of the main difficulties citizens faced was the level of technical expertise required, the complexity of the matter to be regulated. Accordingly, they solicited (internationally) the advice of progressive engineers who indeed provided them with the expertise needed. The composition of the water board and the organization of its decisions procedures have been modified several times as the citizens have dealt with unanticipated problems; they have sought ways of avoiding the perils of direct democracy while ensuring community control over its own fate with respect to this vital resource. In short, it is true that they have required some forms of representation, some forms of hierarchical decision making; but the forms they have adopted are in stark contrast to the limited sovereignty and participation that Habermas has argued, on principle alone, to be inevitable.

116. Habermas, *Between Facts and Norms*, 22.

117. Ibid., 25–26 (my emphasis).

118. Ibid., 26–27.

119. Ibid., 55–56.

120. Rehg, "Translator's Introduction," xxx.

121. Scheuerman points to "a profound weakness in Habermas' contemporary democratic theory: namely, its failure to give adequate expression to legitimate unease and anxiety about the fate of representative democracy at the end of the twentieth century. Despite rapidly growing evidence of widespread dissatisfaction with the operation of contemporary capitalist democracy, Habermas' work at times offers a surprisingly moderate and even conciliatory picture of 'real-existing' democracy. . . . In his eagerness to integrate a mind-boggling array of alternative legal and political theories, *Between Facts and Norms* ultimately offers a deeply ambiguous account of modern democracy . . . at times [it] seems to point to the outlines of an ambitious radical democratic polity, based on far-reaching social equality, and equipped with wide-ranging capacities for overseeing bureaucratic and market mechanisms. Yet Habermas never adequately develops this line of inquiry. Despite his repeated attempts to overcome a false juxtaposition of normativity and facticity, this model remains at the level of an abstract 'ought. Second, Habermas simultaneously suggests a defensive model of deliberative democracy in which democratic institutions exercise at best an attenuated check on market and administrative processes, and where deliberative publics most of the time tend to remain, as Habermas himself describes it, 'in dormancy' " ("Between Resignation and Radicalism," 155–56).

122. Habermas, *Between Facts and Norms*, especially chapter 8, e.g., 358, 371.

Intermediate Reflections:
Habermas and the Sociology of the School

1. In addition to the material drawn from *Legitimation Crisis* and *The Theory of Communicative Action*, Habermas has also discussed university reform and the role of the university in society as a model of discourse (see "The University in a Democracy: Democratization of the University," "Student Protest in the Federal Republic," and "The Movement in Germany: A Critical Analysis," in Habermas, *Toward a Rational Society*; also, see *The New Conservativism*).

The relative silence of critical theory on the question of education, as compared to the question of the family or the media, is itself interesting, given the programmatic importance of socialization for the Frankfurt School as a whole. Granted, after their return from exile, Adorno and Horkheimer both participated to a limited extent in the debate surrounding the question of university reform. Most of their comments in this connection were derived from the thesis of the dialectic of enlightenment—that is, they saw the school as pulled between two equally unattractive options: The conservative forces of traditionalism and the technocratic forces of instrumental rationality (couched in language of "democratization"). Morrow and Torres write, "Adorno's notion of '*Halbbildung*' or 'half-education' conveys the sense of disillusionment with post-war educational systems, which had made certain ostensible gains in the direction of democratization but remained constrained within a new, more sophisticated system of domination known as 'total administration.' The most widely known variant of this argument was developed by Herbert Marcuse in the context of his theory of 'one-dimensional' society" (*Social Theory and Education*, 224–25).

The case of Marcuse, in fact, is an interesting one: lectures delivered by Marcuse on the topic of education were recently uncovered in the Marcuse Archive in Frankfurt, and have been published along with extensive secondary reflections—see Douglas Kellner et al. (eds.), *Marcuse's Challenge to Education*. Alongside *One-Dimensional Man*, these lectures reveal an approach to the current status and future potential of education that interestingly parallels my argument here, as I occasionally note, below. Allow me to add here only that Kellner et al offer a justification for their interest in the educational significance of Marcuse's work that is indeed quite similar to my reasons for focusing on the school: In light of arguments found in Marcuse (and, in fact, in Horkheimer as well) regarding the displacement of the socializing significance of the family in favor of direct imprinting by society, schools as "public social institutions" must "become increasingly responsible for fostering either (a) one-dimensional personalities or (b) critical, multidimensional human beings" ("Introduction," 10).

2. Habermas, *Legitimation Crisis*, 37, altered for purposes of agreement.

3. Ibid., 71–72.

4. Morrow and Torres, *Social Theory and Education*, 239.

5. Habermas, *Lifeworld and System*, 367.

6. Ibid., 368.

7. Ibid., 369.

8. Brint, *Schools and Societies*, 225, on scripted learning formats; see ibid., 262, on the long-term effects of No Child Left Behind with respect to deskilling,

regimentation, and so on. Brint notes that there appears to be some truth to the suspicion that the act may have, as its long-term intent, to bring about the complete privatization of the public educational system: The rate of improvement required to reach the Act's stated goal of 100 percent proficiency in reading, math, and science by 2014—or else risk privatization—"would be equivalent to the big automobile manufacturers being required to produce engines averaging 288 miles per gallon by 2014" (ibid., 265). Nigel Blake, Paul Smeyers et al. (see "Introduction") describe as deskilling a parallel transformation of teacher education, in which emphasis has shifted to training teachers "in skills and competencies that will equip [them] to deliver the curriculum effectively," while this training is increasingly severed from educational research that operates with a more inclusive sense of pedagogical purpose.

9. Habermas, *Lifeworld and System*, 371.

10. Morrow and Torres, *Social Theory and Education*, 239.

11. Habermas, *Between Facts and Norms*, 76.

12. Morrow and Torres, *Social Theory and Education*, 49.

13. Ibid., 50.

14. Feinberg and Soltis, *School and Society*, 25.

15. Ibid.

16. Morrow and Torres, *Social Theory and Education*, 56.

17. Ibid. As both Willis and Bourdieu and Passeron show, this claim is contradicted by the available evidence.

18. Ibid., 59.

19. See Ball, *Foucault and Education.*

20. Morrow and Torres, *Social Theory and Education*, 118.

21. See Bourdieu and Passeron, *Reproduction in Education, Society, and Culture.*

22. Feinberg and Soltis, *School and Society*, 81.

23. Aronowitz, "Preface to the Morningside Edition," xiii.

24. Feinberg and Soltis, *School and Society*, 104.

25. Ibid., 107–8.

26. Habermas, *Lifeworld and System*, 141.

27. Dewey, *Democracy and Education*, 93ff.

28. Bowles and Gintis, *Schooling in Capitalist America*, 11.

29. Ibid., 22; see Dewey, *Democracy and Education*, 76, 87–88.

30. Bowles and Gintis, *Schooling in Capitalist America*, 25; see Dewey, *Democracy and Education*, 85, 320, respectively.

31. Bowles and Gintis, *Schooling in Capitalist America*, 48.

32. Ibid., 26. Bowles and Gintis note that Dewey revised his assessment of the democratic character of American society and became increasingly critical of the use of education for the integration of young people into an alienated occupational sphere. In particular, he led an at least partially successful opposition to the introduction of a rigid system of vocational tracking in Chicago, which he saw as incompatible with the tasks of the school with respect to both self-development and equality (ibid., 309, n.85).

33. Ibid., 22; see also ibid., 110.

34. Ibid., 23.

35. Ibid., 30.

36. Brint reports that later studies from the 1980s confirmed that children from lower socioeconomic brackets are twice as likely as those from high-status backgrounds to end up in lower vocational tracks, to select or be streamed on the basis of tests scores and grades into vocational programs in high school; and such students remain far more likely to drop out of high school altogether (*Schools and Societies*, 212).

37. Bowles and Gintis, *Schooling in Capitalist America*, 32.

38. Brint, *Schools and Societies*, 163. Brint notes: "Among men and women born between 1955 and 1971, background was substantially more important as an influence on obtaining a college degree, while verbal ability, as measured by the GSS word recognition test, was hardly important at all. The gap separating sons and daughters of professionals from sons and daughters of blue-collar workers nearly doubled between the earlier and the later cohorts. . . . This is just one piece of evidence that the effects of family background may be increasing as an influence on adult attainments. Most studies suggest that growing income inequality lies behind this change" (ibid., 176–77).

39. Ibid., 164.

40. Ibid., 141. Updating and reconfirming their own analysis in 2002, Bowles and Gintis report that men born in the top decile of family income have a 40 percent chance of being in the top quintile themselves by mid-career, whereas those in the bottom decile have the same chance of being in the bottom quintile at that point (Bowles and Gintis, "Schooling in Capitalist America Revisited"). Brint sees such a figure as indicating that both reproduction theory and technocratic-meritocracy theory are equally overstated. But in addition to the fact that he notes that rising income inequality is increasingly reinforcing reproductive trends in the United States, the equation of the two arguments is misleading: Meritocratic theory, as a principle of legitimation, makes claim to universality at the level of the individual that reproduction theory, as a descriptive argument about classes, does not. For meritocratic theory to hold water, it has to be true that any individual who works hard enough and has sufficient ability can succeed irrespective of his or her background; for reproduction theory to hold water, it only needs to be the case that, by and large, those born into lower socioeconomic brackets tend to end up in lower socioeconomic brackets, irrespective of their talents. The figure reported by Bowles and Gintis offers substantial support for the latter, but rather little to the former.

41. Bowles and Gintis, *Schooling in Capitalist America*, 9. Although there is a correlation between parental socioeconomic status and childhood IQ, on the one hand, and childhood IQ and economic success on the other, IQ itself does not play the causal role in intergenerational transmission of socioeconomic status. This is demonstrated by once again holding IQ level constant across social class, which does not meaningfully change the rate of heritability of socioeconomic status (ibid., 119–20; see also, ibid., 112).

42. Ibid., 35. Thirty years later, this situation remains unchanged or, if anything, has worsened somewhat. In 2004, data from the U.S. Census Bureau predicted the achievement of parity in high school graduation rates by 2013; college graduation rates, however, despite considerable improvement, would not reach parity until at least 2075 and, in fact, some evidence suggests a movement back toward greater asymmetry, making even this prediction overhasty. Among those who do graduate

from high school, a black worker employed from age twenty-five to sixty-four can nevertheless expect to make $300,000 less than a white worker with the same level of education; among college graduates, the disparity rises to $500,000. See Muhammad et al., "State of the Dream 2004: Enduring Disparities in Black and White."

43. Brint, *Schools and Societies*, 185.

44. Bowles and Gintis, *Schooling in Capitalist America*, 35.

45. Brint, *Schools and Societies*, p. 190, see also 207–9.

46. Ibid., 181–82.

47. Bowles and Gintis, *Schooling in Capitalist America*, 33–34.

48. Brint, *Schools and Societies*, 185.

49. Ibid.

50. Bowles and Gintis, *Schooling in Capitalist America*, 114.

51. Blake, Smeyers, et al., "Introduction," 8.

52. Bowles and Gintis, *Schooling in Capitalist America*, 103 . . . 105 . . . 106.

53. Ibid., 97. The authors cite evidence showing that, among disadvantaged workers, the hiring and promotion decisions of managers are two to three times more likely to correlate with assessments of personal appearance than with job experience or education.

54. Brint, *Schools and Societies*, 98, 112. Bourdieu and Passeron also argue that in terms of comprehension and retention, "the information transmitted [by the school] tends towards zero" (*Reproduction in Education, Society, and Culture*, 21).

55. Bowles and Gintis, *Schooling in Capitalist America*, 9.

56. Ibid., 11, 55.

57. Ibid., 39.

58. Ibid., 41–42.

59. Ibid., 55.

60. Ibid., 55–56.

61. Ibid., 67. "These waves of integration of new groups into capitalist production have occurred at critical stages in the growth of the economy and, hence, their experiences have been qualitatively different, both in terms of occupation and mobility chances. Thus the experience of nineteenth-century native, white craft workers drawn into factory production with the ascendance of entrepreneurial capital cannot be equated with the experience of Northern European immigrants in the first wave of capitalist expansion, when the majority of jobs were essentially deskilled. Both are distinct from the later wave of Southern and Eastern European immigration associated with a second surge of corporate consolidation in the late nineteenth century when ethnic 'underclasses' became stable elements of the urban class structure. Similarly, the occupational shift of U.S. blacks from Southern agriculture to urban wage labor in the post-World War I period differs in a number of important ways from the experiences of their predecessors. . . . No less, the historical movement of women in and out of the wage-labor sector, while maintaining their position in household production, gives the analysis of female oppression a characteristic stamp. In the most recent period, this is marked by their appearance on the market as a vast number of highly qualified female workers in a period in which occupational growth is limited to low-level, white-collar jobs associated with bureaucratized production" (ibid., 65–66).

62. Ibid., 82.

63. Ibid., 98.
64. Ibid., 99.
65. Ibid.
66. Ibid., 98.
67. Ibid., 12.
68. Ibid., 132.
69. The authors themselves have subsequently conceded this point: see Bowles and Gintis, "Schooling in Capitalist America Revisited."
70. Bowles and Gintis, *Schooling in Capitalist America*, 29, see also ibid., 37.
71. Ibid., 30.
72. Ibid., 193.
73. Ibid., 196–97.
74. Ibid., 198.
75. Brint, *Schools and Societies*, 15.
76. Bowles and Gintis, *Schooling in Capitalist America*, 208, 213.
77. Ibid., 213.
78. Cited in ibid., 208.
79 Ibid., 133, Brint, *Schools and Societies*, 137.
80. Bowles and Gintis, *Schooling in Capitalist America*, 236.
81. Marcuse's reading of the situation in the late 1960s and early 1970s is remarkably similar. The school finds itself in a contradictory position, he claims: On the one hand, society is faced with an economic imperative to expand access to education as a result of the dependence of advanced capitalism on education and "unrestricted knowledge in the competitive economic process, and in the steering of the political process"; on the other hand, in light of the dangerous transformative power of knowledge, it must also " 'contain' knowledge and reason within the conceptual and value universe of the established society and its improvement and growth in order to protect this society against radical change." Marcuse was also quite aware of the proposed solution for resolving this tension, as was also hit upon by the Carnegie Commission: "The result: an emphasis on professional, vocational training, and a decline of the "humanities," of transcendent, critical thought" ("Lecture on Education, Brooklyn College, 1968," 34).
82. Bowles and Gintis, *Schooling in Capitalist America*, 254; see also ibid., 15, 49.
83. Ibid., 14. Here, too, Marcuse's hopeful response regarding the transformative potential of education is markedly similar: The aim is "to educate men and women who are incapable of tolerating what is going on, has always been going on, and why, and who are educated to resist and to fight for a new way of life" ("Lecture on Education, Brooklyn College, 1968," 35).
84. Bowles and Gintis, *Schooling in Capitalist America*, 101.
85. Anyon, "Social Class and the Hidden Curriculum of Work," 73.
86. Ibid., 72, 90. See Feinberg and Soltis, *School and Society*, 61. However, the authors add an additional point that is much more significant: Such socioeconomically homogenous schools are rather rare (although they are far more common than they should be). This introduces a problem not of generalizability but of analytical applicability: How, in a school of mixed social status, can one group of students be prevented from being socialized according the "hidden curriculum" intended for

others? This is what Willis will help explain. Feinberg and Soltis nevertheless note that Anyon's conclusions have been confirmed by a variety of researchers, some operating with very different theoretical perspectives (ibid., 61–62).

87. Anyon, "Social Class and the Hidden Curriculum of Work," 87.

88. Ibid., 76.

89. Ibid., 79.

90. Ibid., 76.

91. Ibid., 88.

92. Aronowitz, "Preface to the Morningside Edition," xi.

93. Willis, *Learning to Labor*, 175, 206.

94. Ibid., 3.

95. Ibid., 4. Willis also conducted five additional studies for the sake of comparative analysis, which included a group of conformist students attending the same school as "the lads," a group of working class conformists at a nearby school (considered to be "rougher"), a group of nonconformist lads in the Hammertown grammar school (a more academically oriented school structure), a conformist group in a comprehensive school in the nearby larger urban area, and a nonconformist group of young men from mixed-class backgrounds in a high-status grammar school in an affluent area near Hammertown.

96. Ibid., 13.

97. Ibid., 18–19.

98. Ibid., 26.

99. Ibid., 63–64.

100. Ibid.

101. Ibid., 66.

102. Ibid., 126. Elsewhere, Willis writes: " 'Qualifications' for [the 'lads'] constitute the practical arm of the power of knowledge as it is institutionally defined. Since knowledge [as defined by the school] is opposed so must qualifications be resisted and discredited. As in other things, the principal means of discrediting formal standards is to 'see behind' them, in the informal mode, to 'how things really work.' Experience, or at least projected experience, maneuvers around formal definition. At a certain level they really feel that they know better. It is possible to get on without qualifications and school work because what really matters is 'knowing a bit about the world,' 'having your head screwed on.' . . . Of course, the adult working class world, the air of practicality which prevails on the English shop floor, and the distrust of theory there, considerably strengthen this kind of perspective. . . . Qualifications, to them, seem to be a deflection or displacement of direct activity. They feel that they can always demonstrate any necessary ability 'on the job,' and that the doing of a thing is always easier than the account of it, or its representation in an exam, or its formal description seem to imply" (ibid., 94).

103. Brint confirms this point historically: Although an expansion of higher education in the United States correlated with a transformation of the occupational system that included an enormous expansion of white-collar jobs, this same occupational transformation occurred elsewhere without correlated educational reforms. But, of course, someone had to fill these jobs, so they were filled through processes of internal promotion and without credentials (*Schools and Societies*, 166). Inversely,

if the occupational structure continues to provide a large number of jobs that are menial and unrewarding, someone will have to fill these positions, too, whether or not they have a diploma to hang on the wall. In point of fact, however, in many places immigrants fill these jobs; the surplus of skilled labor simply feeds the reserve army of the unemployed.

104. As Willis argues, "[n]o conceivable number of certificates among the working class will make for a classless society, or convince industrialists and employers—even if they were able—that they should create more jobs" (*Learning to Labor*, 127). Bourdieu and Passeron agree: The self-selection of working-class youths is a key part of the explanation for the stability of the economic system. And, in fact, this self-selection is reciprocally related to the objective facts it produces: "The subjective expectation which leads an individual to drop out depends directly on the conditions determining the objective chances of success proper to his category, so that it must be counted among the mechanisms which contribute to the actualization of objective probabilities" (*Reproduction in Education, Society, and Culture*, 156). The purported democratization of education has resulted in a substantial gain in enrollment of working-class youths, in absolute terms, more or less representing a doubling. And yet, as Bourdieu and Passeron astutely observe, "[t]he fact that a manual worker's son has a 3.9 percent chance of going to university, instead of a 1.5 percent chance [the difference from 1961 to 1966], is not sufficient to modify the image of higher education as an unlikely, if not 'unreasonable' future, and one that is, so to speak, unlooked for" (ibid., 227). The authors do not note that a tendency to pose the question in terms of one's "category" is, as Willis shows, itself not uniform across social class. The middle-class individualism that the school fosters is, in this sense, requisite training for approaching the question of meritocracy from the, as it were, ideologically appropriate angle.

105. Willis, *Learning to Labor*, 128.

106. The teachers often retaliate by invoking the superiority of their element of the exchange in a new light, that is, by presenting knowledge as beyond "the lads" in any case, seeking to embarrass them in class, for example—a tactic to which "the lads" are quite sensitive. Alternatively, Willis documents, teachers may attempt to "mystify" the educational exchange—which is, for Willis, in fact an effort to reproduce the labor force—by moralizing the content to be received by the student. The inherently worthy values that are to be inculcated are the "right attitudes," which are then loosely linked to life success. The argument is that these attitudes are required for success in work, irrespective of academic achievement. However, this argument is utterly tautologous: The "right attitudes" turn out to be a catalogue of the very things the students were, on the traditional model, supposed to exchange for knowledge and qualifications—respect, obedience, and so on. Thus, in exchange for deference and obedience, the teacher now proposes to teach the students deference and obedience! (*Learning to Labor*, 69).

107. Ibid., 103.

108. Ibid., 44.

109. Ibid., 145–46.

110. Ibid., 148.

111. Ibid.

112. Ibid., 145.

113. Ibid., 152.

114. Ibid., 155, n.3.

115. Ibid., 149.

116. This is perhaps the main difference in circumstance between working-class and middle-class nonconformists studied by Willis: When the latter develop opposition to the school, they find within their available cultural resources much that pushes them back into its arms (*Learning to Labor*, 76). In many cases, the middle-class nonconformists begrudgingly completed their studies in order to give themselves options down the road, as they saw it. In fact, Willis had selected the group at the grammar school because they were the only students who had declared their intention of leaving the school at the same stage as "the lads"; in the end, however, only two actually did so, and one of these to become an assistant golf professional (ibid., 57). In general, the oppositional culture at this school is less collectivist, less permeated by a sense of inevitability; in fact, Willis discovered that a perceived comparative lack of authenticity was a sensitive concern among these young men.

117. Willis, *Learning to Labor*, 163–64, 165.

118. Ibid., 120.

119. Young, *A Critical Theory of Education*, 96–97.

120. Ibid., 94 and, for his analysis of classroom talk, ibid., 91ff.

121. Ibid., 95.

122. Brint, *Schools and Societies*, 143. Brint links the issue of consumption to the proliferation of electives at the secondary level, the attempt to integrate choice into primary curriculum, as well as, at both levels, variation of teaching methods, the nature of assignments, work with specialized teachers over the course of the day, and the categorizing emphasis of textbooks and reading anthologies on the basis of the variety of styles, theories, traditions, and so on. Brint along with colleagues has also documented the pervasive use of exchange "rewards" for obedience and performance, from pizza parties and candy to early dismissal (ibid., 147, 242).

123. Ibid., 146.

124. Young, *A Critical Theory of Education*, 23.

125. Brint, *Schools and Societies*, 152.

126. Morrow and Torres, *Social Theory and Education*, 379.

127. There are several clear instances of the economically functional way in which low-status groups can be absorbed into the economy in times of growth and expelled in times of contraction, without repercussions for legitimacy. For instance, by the time the United States officially entered a recession in 2008, economic indicators revealed that persons of color had been in a technical recession for five years and, by 2008, had entered a depression according to the standard definition. Moreover, if the current recession is as deep as is expected, median income among U.S. whites will fall by 4 percent; among people of color, however, the drop will be 6 percent; 33 percent of blacks, and 41 percent of Latino families would drop out of the middle class, compared with a national average of 25 percent. See Rivera et al., "State of the Dream 2009: The Silent Depression."

The subprime mortgage crisis provides additional evidence: Toward the end of the expansion of the real estate bubble—and not before—people of color were explicitly targeted for what, by this time, were increasingly predatory and sometimes plainly fraudulent mortgages. The first result is that in the United States, persons of color are more than three times as likely to have a subprime loan; the ultimate cost, however, is expected to be the single largest loss of wealth among people of color in modern U.S. history (between $164 and $213 billion). Inversely, if such mortgages had been distributed equitably across racial lines, losses among U.S. whites would have been 44.5 percent higher, and 24 percent lower for persons of color. See Rivera et al., "Foreclosed: State of the Dream 2008."

128. Cited in Morrow and Torres, *Social Theory and Education*, 384–85.

Chapter 3: Moral Consciousness and Postconventionality

1. Habermas, "Moral Development and Ego Identity," 72.

2. A note regarding this terminology: Although there are places where Habermas uses the term *ego identity* to encompass both self-determination (i.e., moral autonomy, the capacity for autonomous moral judgment) and self-realization (i.e., the construction of a unique, responsible identity inclusive of psychosexual and motivational aspects of development), I use the term *ego identity* as the earlier Habermas did, to refer only to the latter. See *Lifeworld and System*, 97, for an example of Habermas' inclusive use of ego identity. In his earlier work, the stages of moral consciousness are presented in distinction from, although correlated to, the stages of ego development, as in "Moral Development and Ego Identity."

3. Habermas, "Moral Consciousness and Communicative Action," 123.

4. Ibid., 125.

5. Ibid., 129.

6. Habermas omits discussion of Selman's Level 0, in which the extent of differentiation between the self, the world, and others, is insufficient for the establishing of specifically moral consciousness. Habermas also omits Selman's culminating Level 4, which he rejects as being insufficiently differentiated from Level 3 on the basis of perspective structure alone. It is the introduction of the link to communicative action that makes the required differentiation possible ("Moral Consciousness and Communicative Action," 90, n.24). James Swindal offers a useful summary of the relevant aspects of Selman and Habermas' use of them in *Reflection Revisited*, 202ff.

7. Habermas, "Moral Consciousness and Communicative Action," 142–43.

8. Ibid., 143.

9. See ibid., 149–50, where Habermas discusses a well-known experiment by J. H. Flavell that tests the capacity for strategic reasoning and so illuminates one aspect of the change that occurs between Selman's Levels 2 and 3.

10. Ibid., 140.

11. Ibid., 144.

12. Ibid.

13. Ibid., 145.

14. Ibid., 152.

15. Ibid., 154.

16. Ibid., 155.

17. Ibid., 155–56.

18. Mark Warren nicely explains one part of the problem: "Because individuals are unlikely to be able to challenge their own interpretations of needs and interests . . . they must be challenged by other individuals. [Furthermore,] [w]hen one must explain oneself to others, Habermas holds, individuals come to understand why they feel as they do in justifying their needs and interests to others. In doing so, they may alter their need interpretations, finding that their previous need interpretations, often absorbed uncritically from their culture, were inappropriate and perhaps even a source of unhappiness to themselves" ("The Self in Discursive Democracy," 179). See also *Lifeworld and System*, 95.

Amy Allen, it seems to me, loses sight of this aspect of his position in her critique of Habermas. Specifically, she objects that both Habermas and Benhabib overstate the self-transparency of the subject, the limits upon one's ability to thematize power relationships, especially where such relationships have become constitutive of the identity of subordinated subjects (see Allen, *The Politics of Ourselves*, e.g., 163–171). But Habermas always has been skeptical of the claim that we can do this for ourselves, whether or not our identities are healthy and relatively autonomous. On the other hand, if she means to question not the possibility of critical insight but only the efficacy of proposed insights—whether our own or those of others—then her critique of Habermas would, as the next chapter shows, largely converge with my own. In the end, Allen seems to make both critiques without clearly differentiating them.

19. Habermas, "Moral Consciousness and Communicative Action," 122.

20. Habermas, *Lifeworld and System*, 74–75.

21. Habermas, "Moral Consciousness and Communicative Action," 126.

22. Ibid.

23. Ibid., 126.

24. Ibid., 127. Habermas adds, "[t]his unnaturalness is like an echo of the developmental catastrophe that historically once devalued the world of traditions and thereby provoked efforts to rebuild it at a higher level" (ibid.).

25. Habermas, "Discourse Ethics: Notes on a Program of Philosophical Justification," 58–59.

26. Habermas, "Moral Consciousness and Communicative Action," p. 116. Habermas writes, "[w]e may no longer burden these arguments [for a principle of universalization] with the status of an a priori transcendental deduction along the lines of Kant's critique of reason. They ground only the fact that there is no identifiable alternative to our kind of argumentation" (ibid.) Despite considerable overlap in their work and interests, it is this claim regarding the strength of the justification for the norms governing discourse that continues to put Apel and Habermas at odds (see, e.g., Karl Otto Apel, "Openly Strategic Uses of Language"). The status of the "idealizations" invoked by discourse ethics remains quite controversial (see also Allen, *The Politics of Ourselves* and Benhabib, *Critique, Norm, and Utopia*).

27. Habermas, "Discourse Ethics," 65.

28. Ibid.

29. Ibid., 80.

30. Ibid., 89.

31. Ibid., 90.

32. Ibid.
33. Ibid.
34. Ibid., 91.
35. Ibid., 92–93.
36. Ibid., 93.
37. Habermas, "Moral Consciousness and Communicative Action," 159.
38. Ibid., 161.
39. Ibid., 162–63.
40. Ibid., 165.
41. Ibid., 164–65.
42. Ibid., 165.
43. Ibid., 168.
44. Ibid., 160. There is something *prima facie* odd about Habermas claiming both that discourse is defined by a cooperative search for truth as well as by competition on the basis of arguments. The tension, however, is merely apparent. Readers will perhaps be familiar with an argument Socrates makes against Thrasymachus in the first book of Plato's *Republic*: that the unjust person is like the ignorant person, who will seek to outdo both the knowledgeable and the similarly ignorant in any field, which is to say that they seek to win the argument irrespective of the actual merit of their position (their attitude is a strategic one, in Habermas' terms). The just person, on the other hand, is like the knowledgeable person, who will only seek to outdo the ignorant (349b–350c). That isn't to say that there is no competition among the knowledgeable—there is—yet the competition between doctors, for example, is aimed at attaining the perfect diagnosis, the right answer. Accordingly, their interactions are at once competitive and cooperative because they aim at the same independent thing: the truth. Elsewhere, Habermas offers a similar formulation: "The practice of argumentation sets in motion a cooperative competition for the better argument, where the orientation to the goal of communicatively reached agreement unites the participants from the outset" (Habermas, "A Genealogical Analysis of the Content of Morality," 44).
45. Habermas, "Moral Consciousness and Communicative Action," 169.
46. Ibid., 172.
47. Ibid., 171.

Chapter 4: Socialization and Ego Identity

1. Habermas, "Moral Development and Ego Identity," 78.
2. For example, the level of discourse is here construed as an additional Stage 7, rather than as a reinterpretation of Stage 6. In another writing still, Habermas appears to favor the view that there is only one postconventional stage, and that the dispute between competing moral theories regards how to characterize it (see Habermas, "A Reply to my Critics," 259–60).
3. Habermas, "Moral Development and Ego Identity," 78.
4. Ibid., 83.
5. Ibid.

6. Ibid.

7. Ibid., 84

8. Ibid.

9. The omission is not accidental: Habermas has been clear in arguing that the reconstruction of stages of development must be separated from the account of the (causal) dynamics of development (see "A Reply to my Critics," 252–54). Nevertheless, on practical grounds, the reconstruction is not much use without a connected discussion of its conditions.

10. Habermas, "Moral Development and Ego Identity," 85.

11. Ibid., 85.

12. Ibid., 85–86.

13. Habermas, "Moral Consciousness and Communicative Action," 182–83.

14. The question of the specific means by which socially critical insight is thus rendered ineffective is a tricky one, deserving of close attention by critical theorists: We should expect to see it manifest in various forms, from a more or less straightforward fatalism to a more sophisticated and paradoxical fragmentation of the personality. I suggest that this approach offers a highly plausible explanation of some of the phenomena at the heart of Amy Allen's critique of Habermas, which seems to vacillate between the claim that the inevitability of power relations makes Habermasian ego autonomy impossible in principle, and the more modest objection that the power relations current in society make the realization and plausible nature of autonomy problematic. Allen uses as an example the experience of Joan Jacobs Brumberg with her students in a women's studies course: These young women were able in their academic work to engage in critical analysis of gender norms and representations, while nevertheless having internalized the very norms and roles in question; in other words, their legitimate critical insights failed to break the spell of their cultural socialization (Allen, *The Politics of Ourselves*, 181ff). Does this mean that rational insight itself is insufficient? The answer I am suggesting here would be "yes and no": Rational insight is precisely what is required, but its maintenance, effectiveness and, ultimately, its reality requires that it be supported through adequate sources of recognition which, at present, are lacking. Clearly, the experience provided by this course alone was not sufficient to support a genuine reorganization of the identity of these students, who continued to see themselves through the lens of conventional and instrumentalized expectations and roles; indeed, in many cases, and for largely sociological reasons, the identities and basic commitments of students remain closed off to serious thematization within formal education (see Concluding Reflections).

15. Habermas, "Moral Development and Ego Identity," 71.

16. As Habermas notes, "[n]ot all individuals are equally representative of the developmental stage of their society. Thus in modern societies, law has a universalistic structure, although many members are not in a position to judge according to principles. Conversely, in archaic societies there were individuals who had mastered formal operations of thought, although the collectively shared mythological worldview corresponds to a lower stage of cognitive development" ("Historical Materialism and the Development of Normative Structures," 102).

17. Habermas, "Moral Development and Ego Identity," 86.

18. Ibid., 88.

19. Ibid., 87.
20. Ibid., 86.
21. Ibid., 89.
22. Ibid., 90.
23. Ibid., 91–92. In this light, Habermas argues that moral conflict resolution is a good indicator of the stability of interactive competence. Ego psychology has catalogued many of the mechanisms employed by the ego to avoid consciously processing conflict when the costs are too high in terms of threats to identity and need recognition. Thus, Habermas suggests that additional research might prove that such defense mechanisms themselves can be developmentally ordered as responses to the anxieties to which specific stages of development are susceptible, in which the capacity for moral judgment outstrips motivational development (*akrasia*) resulting in feelings of guilt, fear of punishment, and so on. In his own theory of systematically distorted communication, he offers a hypothesis regarding how distorted communication may be symptomatic of certain defense strategies, which in turn correlate with systematic problems in the fulfillment of the family's dual roles of need satisfaction and identity stabilization (see "Reflections on Communicative Pathology," 160ff).
24. Habermas, "Individuation Through Socialization," 149.
25. Ibid., 157–58.
26. Ibid., 172.
27. Ibid., 175–76.
28. Ibid., 176.
29. Ibid.
30. Ibid., 178. See also *Lifeworld and System*, 32ff.
31. Habermas, "Individual Through Socialization," 178–79.
32. Ibid., 179.
33. Ibid., 179–80. See also *Lifeworld and System*, 41ff.
34. In *The Theory of Communicative Action*, Habermas adds that "The 'me' represents not only the particularities of moral consciousness tied to tradition, but also the constraints of a character that impedes the development of subjectivity" (*Lifeworld and System*, 97). In other words, the "me" is a conservative force not only with respect to the development of moral autonomy or self-determination, but also with respect to the project of consciously developing a unique identity, of self-realization.
35. Habermas, "Individuation Through Socialization," 181.
36. Ibid., 182 (emphasis in the final case is mine).
37. Ibid., 152.
38. Ibid.
39. Ibid., 182.
40. Ibid., 183.
41. Ibid., 186.
42. Ibid., 187.
43. Ibid. See also *Lifeworld and System*, 106.
44. Habermas, "Individuation Through Socialization," 187.
45. Ibid., 184 (emphases are mine).
46. Ibid., 188.
47. Habermas, *Between Facts and Norms*, 114.

48. Ibid., 119.

49. Ibid., 116–17; for another example of "communicative overtaxing," see ibid., 115.

50. In an interview, Torben Hviid Nielsen posed a very similar question to Habermas: "[t]he preconditions of an ethics of discourse are fulfilled at the ontogenetic level only at Kohlberg's final, postconventional stages of moral-psychological development. But only a minority of the adult population ever reaches these stages (if we can rely on the relevant longitudinal studies). Then we are faced with the paradox of a society with postconventional social institutions while a majority of the population languishes at the preconventional or conventional stages of moral consciousness. How is this possible? How can it be reconciled with your claim that normative structures function as the pacemaker of social evolution?" (Habermas, "Morality, Society, and Ethics: An Interview with Torben Hviid Nielsen," 161). Interestingly, Habermas does not answer: He suggests that the fact that social innovations often are introduced through marginal groups may account for this discrepancy, but, as we know, that isn't quite how his own theory of social evolution works. Indeed, marginal groups initiate social change, but these innovations, he has claimed, migrate into the cultural background of a society through so-called "exemplary learning processes" and are drawn upon and institutionalized in the face of steering problems (this is the pattern for which Weber's analysis of the Protestant Ethic served as model). In the middle stage here, these insights have in principle become accessible to all or most members of society, which Habermas omits from his response to Nielsen and which undermines the response he does give. Habermas claims, to the contrary, "[t]his may explain why positive law in modern societies must be understood as the embodiment of postconventional structures of consciousness, although *many members* [my emphasis: note the change of scale] are found to have reached only a conventional stage of moral consciousness" (ibid). But Habermas then shifts gears and, still without having answered, deflects the question: "What's more," he continues, "findings concerning the moral consciousness of the general population are problematic; it is a matter of considerable controversy whether Kohlberg's methods of collecting data do not in fact lead to artificial results in the definition of stages. For instance, children master the moral judgments of a given stage long before they have the verbal resources to articulate this knowledge in response to familiar dilemmas" (ibid). Indeed, there are many controversies surrounding Kohlberg's method; but is Habermas really trying to suggest that the majority of adults are capable of postconventional moral judgments but are simply unable to articulate them? That would be problematic indeed for a discourse theory of postconventionality!

51. Habermas, "Moral Development and Ego Identity," 70 (my emphasis). Many prominent commentators on Habermas appear to have kept pace with him in his development, and have similarly accepted the apparently unremarkable existence of a critically neutered form of postconventionality: To offer just a couple of examples, see Rehg, "Translator's Introduction," xvii ff; Warren, "The Self in Discursive Democracy," 168ff; and Honneth, "The Other of Justice," 305.

52. Dews, "Communicative Paradigms and the Question of Subjectivity," 106.

53. Habermas, "Morality and Ethical Life: Does Hegel's Critique of Kant Apply to Discourse Ethics?" 207–8.

54. Ibid., 209.
55. Dews, "Communicative Paradigms and the Question of Subjectivity," 107–8.
56. Ibid., 108.
57. Ibid., 106.
58. Habermas, "Historical Materialism and the Development of Normative Structures," 102.
59. Young, "Habermas and Education," 549.
60. Habermas, *Legitimation Crisis*, 91.
61. Habermas, "Historical Materialism and the Development of Normative Structures," 224, n.30.
62. Habermas, "A Reply to my Critics," 261–62.
63. Cited in Habermas, ibid., 262–63.
64. Habermas, "Individuation Through Socialization," 192.
65. Ibid., 195.
66. Ibid.
67. Ibid., 196.
68. Ibid.
69. Ibid.
70. Habermas, "Moral Consciousness and Communicative Action," 172–73.
71. Ibid., 117. See also "A Reply to my Critics," 259.
72. Habermas, "Moral Consciousness and Communicative Action," 175.
73. Ibid., 185.
74. Ibid., 184.
75. Ibid.
76. Ibid., 185–86.
77. Ibid., 159.
78. Apparently to the contrary, Habermas in one place writes, "[t]here are different ways in which the adolescent can use this newly acquired detachment from a world of conventions that have lost the naïve force of social acceptance by being hypothetically relegated to a horizon of possibilities and have thereby become reflexively devalued" ("Moral Consciousness and Communicative Action," 186; this passage, as well as what follows it, appears nearly identically in "A Reply to my Critics," 260–61). But not only does it seem to me descriptively inaccurate in these cases to claim that the hypothetical attitude is taken up within the norm-conformative perspective on the social world; so arguing once again makes it incomprehensible why the young person cannot engage in moral argumentation.
79 Habermas, "Moral Consciousness and Communicative Action," 164–65.
80. It is worth noting, given Habermas' claims regarding the evidential value of philosophical articulations, that this view, too, has its more consistent and complex philosophical defenders whom Habermas himself discusses: for example, Niklas Luhmann and H. Lübbe. The later Habermas sympathetically suggests that such an argument may not be entirely unfounded as a reaction to the complexity of social systems today and the potentially catastrophic unanticipated side-effects of attempts at revolution or reform ("A Reply to my Critics," 222ff).
81. For example, I have very often encountered the following response among students when explaining Kant's attempt to formulate an unconditional, inescapable

argument for moral obligation: that the idea of unconditionality signals that he is "just trying to make you accept his opinion." In other words, an argument that intends to be binding is identified with a form of coercion.

82. Habermas, "Moral Consciousness and Communicative Action," 186–87.

83. Again, the persistence of discredited norms that this analysis leads us to expect sheds some light on the problem Allen discusses relative to the students in Brumberg's women's studies course: Because we cannot actually do without recognition—even if we conceive of most of our social relationships in strategic terms—the young women described by Allen are in the paradoxical position of being invested in the persistence of norms which, for them, have explicitly become arbitrary or worse, yet which remain without practical alternatives.

Concluding Reflections: Multicultural Identity as Postconventionality

1. Kymlicka, *Multicultural Odysseys*, see "Introduction."

2. Hayward, "Binding Problems, Boundary Problems," 189.

3. Ibid., 193.

4. Ibid., 192.

5. Ibid., 195. Initial investigations in the postwar period focused on racial and ethnic prejudices, but have since expanded to encompass age, sexual orientation, and disability (ibid., 195, n.50).

6. Cited in ibid., 196.

7. See *Multicultural Citizenship* (e.g., 78) for the older, two-tiered model; see *Multicultural Odysseys* for the new tripartite division. Kymlicka can't seem to decide whether or not the privileging of the rights of national minorities is simply a practical matter: that is, whether circumstances make a right to the protection of the societal culture of immigrant groups impractical, or whether such groups forfeit this right through having entered the political constellation "voluntarily." Benhabib is right to note that there are quite a number of minority groups who appear to fit neither category as Kymlicka draws them, the most obvious example being African Americans (see Benhabib, *The Claims of Culture*, 62–63). But the primary problem I have with this is the astonishing liberal naivety that Kymlicka manifests in discussing the voluntary character of immigration, the vast majority of which is the result of flight from poverty for which developed nations can claim a great deal of responsibility. For a critique of the hypostatization of "societal cultures" in Kymlicka's early work, see ibid., 60ff.

8. Although in his earlier work, Kymlicka claimed that multicultural rights were justified both by considerations of distributive justice and by the constitutive role of recognition in the cultivation of individual autonomy, in his most recent writings he supports the claims of national minorities and indigenous peoples over those of immigrants by claiming that generic rights "do not protect any claims based on historic settlement or territorial attachments" (*Multicultural Odysseys*, 285). In other words, "priority in time and attachment to a particular territory" (ibid., 276) are now supposed to shoulder a genuinely justificatory burden. But, in contrast to an appeal to distributive justice or autonomy, neither of these advances anything like a normative

claim. It is true, as a matter of fact, that appeals to priority in time and territorial attachment are often part of Indigenous rights claims that, in light of the outrageous injustices they have suffered, are certainly among the most morally persuasive. But we need to be clear that, whereas "having been there first" is not a moral claim, "having been illegitimately expropriated" is. So, restoring land and self-government powers to Indigenous groups is part of the just demand to rectify injustices. The legacy of these wrongs requires extensive remedial action to empower Indigenous persons to participate on equal footing both with other Canadians, for instance, and with others generally. But this has nothing to do with special attachments to particular pieces of land, but with violated legal treaties regarding specific pieces of land, and with the material prerequisites for protecting cultural contexts of socialization, which extends to preferential fishing and hunting rights, for example. The fact remains that should Indigenous communities in the future find themselves to have finally attained equal economic and political status through the success of projects of self-government, on moral grounds they would be subject to the same demands as every other wealthy community regarding (for example) liberal immigration policies, cultural accommodation, etc. The demonstrated willingness of indigenous groups in Canada to subject self-government regimes to the standards of international law suggests to me that this argument would be acceptable to them.

9. Kymlicka, *Multicultural Odysseys*, 19.

10. Ibid., 16.

11. Habermas, "Struggles for Recognition in the Democratic Constitutional State," 138.

12. Ibid.

13. Banting and Kymlicka, "Introduction," 24.

14. Ibid., 25. Rodney E. Hero and Robert R. Preuhs provide an overview of this research, noting that survey evidence in the United States confirms that the best predictor of support for welfare state measures "is not whether [individuals] self-identify as right or left, or liberal or conservative, or even whether they believe that the poor are lazy. Rather, the most powerful predictor is the belief that blacks are lazy" ("Multiculturalism and Welfare Policies in the USA," 25–26, n.19).

15. Banting and Kymlicka, "Introduction," 26.

16. Cited in ibid., 26.

17. Banting et al, "Do Multicultural Policies Erode the Welfare State?" 80, 83.

18. See Crepaz, " 'If You are my Brother, I may Give you a Dime!.' " There are nevertheless variations in each case: see chapters 4 through 8 in Banting and Kymlicka (eds.), *Multiculturalism and the Welfare State*, for studies by Hero and Preuhs (on the U.S.), Geoffrey Evans (on Britain), Hans Entzinger (on the Netherlands), Peter A. Kraus and Karen Schönwalder (on Germany), and Matt James (on "redress" movements in Canada).

19. Banting et al, "Do Multicultural Policies Erode the Welfare State?" 69

20. Ibid., 73, see also 80–81.

21. Ibid., 84.

22. Crepaz, "If you are my Brother, I may Give you a Dime!" 113.

23. Tillie and Slijper, "Immigrant Political Integration and Ethnic Civic Communities in Amsterdam," 216–17, see Table 9.4.

24. Ibid., 218.

25. Ibid., 218–19.

26. Ibid., 225.

27. Discussed in Kymlicka, *Multicultural Odysseys*, 156–57. John Myles and Sébastien St.-Arnaud's critique of Bloemraad's work seems to miss its significance when they assert that political and economic integration are the key factors in determining the effect of diversity on social solidarity and that, while multiculturalism policies are one element of broader immigration policies, they are not the only, "or even the major, determinant of successful economic and political incorporation" ("Population Diversity, Multiculturalism and the Welfare State," 341). Their argument is that low levels of incorporation on either or both these fronts increases the probability of the sorts of ethnic cleavages that undermine welfare state support and provide fertile conditions for the rise of ultra-right parties that combine laissez-faire economic appeals with nativist citizenship demands. But Bloemraad's study aims to show that, other things being equal—including the features discussed by Myles and St.-Arnaud such as worker skill and education level—countries with multicultural policies outperform those that lack them when it comes to immigrant social and political integration.

The question of economic integration, however, is an interesting and crucial one. I have argued elsewhere for the importance of recognition for one's labor as an element of an undistorted relationship to one's self and community, and for the claim that capitalism is systematically unable to make this recognition available to all (Borman, "Labour, Exchange, and Recognition: Marx contra Honneth"). This suggests yet another avenue for pursuing a contradiction between multicultural recognition and capitalism. The economic impulse toward the instrumentalization of status distinctions is strong enough that Canada, which is dependent on immigrants for economic growth and which, according to policy at least, selects over half of its immigrants based on a points system that favors skilled labor, nevertheless evidences widespread un- and underemployment among new immigrants and persistent problems regarding recognition of foreign credentials. According to Statistics Canada, 25 percent of well-educated male immigrants are absorbed into the unskilled, low-paid occupational sector, whereas among female immigrants, the figure is 38 percent ("How Canada Chooses its Newcomers"). Moreover, according to census data, "the employment prospects of immigrants are actually worsening relative to those of native-born Canadians, even as immigrants' educational qualifications have improved. By 1996, earnings of new immigrants had dropped to 60 percent of those of native-born Canadians. The employment rate of immigrants fell to 68.3 percent in 1996 from 85.4 percent in 1984. This trend has not been reversed with the economic recovery of the late 1990s" (Jimémez, "Is the Current Model of Immigration the Best One for Canada?"). And, in fact, in the recession that began in 2008, new immigrants have lost their jobs at more than three times the rate of native-born Canadians (Grant and Yang, "Immigrants Take Brunt of Recession, Recover Less Quickly," citing figures from Statistics Canada). This data indicates again the disjunction between technocratic economic planning, which views the economy as a technical system requiring increasingly large inputs of skilled workers, and the actual operations of hierarchical and alienated capitalism, which must secure legitimation for itself through socially acceptable asymmetries.

28. Habermas, "Struggles for Recognition in the Democratic Constitutional State," 135. This formulation is typical of the later Habermas' systematically ambiguous normative claims: though couched in ostensibly descriptive terms, the claim is patently normative, relying on a reinvigorated conception of the public sphere and an active citizenship that remains more or less without empirical referent.

29. In a slightly different context, Habermas himself makes this quite clear: "hermeneutical reflection on the starting points of a human rights discourse among participants of different cultures draws our attention to normative contents that are present in the tacit presuppositions of any discourse whose goal is mutual understanding. That is, independently of their cultural backgrounds all the participants intuitively know quite well that a consensus based on conviction cannot come about as long as symmetrical relations do not exist among them—relations of mutual recognition, mutual role-taking, a shared willingness to consider one's own tradition with the eyes of the stranger and to learn from one another, and so forth" ("Remarks on Legitimation through Human Rights," 129).

This element of a particularistic but inclusive loyalty to one's fellow citizens is absent from most discussions of "constitutional patriotism" in Habermas. When it is included, for example, in the work of Patchen Markell (see "Making Affect Safe for Democracy?"), reference often is lacking to this counterfactual aspect. Markell argues that a postnational form of citizenship may be able to dispense with the prior "vertical" identification of all citizens with a shared set of national images, in favor of a direct affective connection to fellow citizens that supports feelings of "love, sympathy, indebtedness" and also perhaps "fear, anger, and shame" (ibid., 55). And, in fact, he identifies such feelings as the motivational basis for solidarity with excluded groups, as evidenced in the public outrage and protest of masses of German citizens over the murder of three Turkish residents of Mölln (in 1992), and at a government perceived to have responded impotently, perhaps even with the intent "to drum up public support for a more restrictive asylum policy" (ibid., 56). This is precisely the sort of phenomena in which I, too, am interested. But Markell does not note the cognitive, quasi-transcendental nature of such loyalty in a democratic multicultural citizenry, which can only stably cultivate these affective ties to the extent that democratic rights are effectively realized. I will discuss below my worries about these ties remaining at the purely affective level.

30. As James Bohman notes, following Habermas, this is not to be interpreted overly rigidly: The final outcome of democratic deliberation can be subjectless, "in the sense that it does not accord with anyone's particular beliefs or desires. Each among a plurality of deliberating agents can accept such a goal or outcome to the extent that he can recognize his own intentions as part of the deliberative activity, even if it is not directly a part of its specific outcome. Like a good jazz trio, deliberation succeeds only when each individual maintains his or her distinctness and the group its plurality; cohesion is only a by-product of each person's distinctive contribution" (*Public Deliberation*, 56).

31. Habermas, "Struggles for Recognition in the Democratic Constitutional State," 137.

32. Axel Honneth is right to insist on this point: A critical theory that confines itself to forms of struggle articulated in more or less organized social movements

offers only a very partial picture of the injustices in a given social order (see Honneth, "Redistribution as Recognition").

33. Kymlicka argues this same point—see *Multicultural Citizenship*, 188.

34. Although Kymlicka at least argues that it is a mistake to think "civic" or "procedural" identities are sufficient for social integration, he similarly claims that the required substantive attachment is a prerequisite for integration: "The problem, of course, is that this sort of allegiance is the product of mutual solidarity, not a possible basis for it" (*Multicultural Citizenship*, 190–91). And so, for Kymlicka, we seem to be caught in a vicious circle.

35. *Canadian Multiculturalism Act, 1985*. Available at http://laws.justice.gc.ca/en/C-18.7/.

36. See "The New Canada," an Ipsos-Reid study jointly commissioned by *The Globe and Mail* and the Centre for Research and Information on Canada; in addition to the polling by Ipsos, the study also involved political scientist Matthew Mendelsohn working in the Public Opinion Archives at Queen's University, along with experts at Statistic Canada; it was published in *The Globe and Mail*, from June to July 2003, as well as through the Web site for the Centre for Research and Information on Canada.

Michael Adams confirms this research: "In 2003, 85 percent of Canadians said that multiculturalism was important to Canadian identity. More Canadians cite multiculturalism as central to the national identity than bilingualism or hockey. Also in 2003, four out of five Canadians (81 percent) agreed that multiculturalism has contributed positively to the national identity. . . . In 1985 we [Adams' Environics polling firm] asked Canadians to tell us in their own words what made them proud to be Canadian. Multiculturalism was in tenth place. People were more likely to cite the beauty of the land, Canada's natural resources, and even the physical size of the country. By 2006, though, multiculturalism had climbed to second place." Importantly Adams' notes, though this trend is very strongly reflected in immigrant communities, "at still only 19 percent of the population, immigrants are not the ones driving [it]" (Adams, *Unlikely Utopia*, 20–21).

The important exception to all of these trends is Québec, including young people in the province and, in particular, regarding the significance of diversity, multiculturalism, and the Charter. The exception is important not only empirically, but theoretically, given that Taylor's entire account of multiculturalism as "deep diversity" is written with an eye to defending the "Quebec model" of special "group rights," and so of shielding national minorities from precisely the sort of decentering of identity that I am defending here (see his "Shared and Divergent Values," especially). Although I cannot argue it here in detail, I have alleged that such a model is inherently illiberal, particularly with respect to internal minorities: the ongoing political controversies within Québec surrounding the chauvinistic "limits of reasonable accommodation" seems to me to be case and point; Taylor's participation in the so-called "Bouchard-Taylor Commission," set up to pander to this chauvinism in the aftermath of surprising electoral success by the right-wing nativist ADQ [*Action démocratique du Québec*], is thus also quite illuminating.

37. Forty percent of individuals in their twenties do so, as compared with 32 percent of those over age sixty-five (in other words, the most ethnically homogenous demographic). Some comparisons are illuminating: approximately one in three Ameri-

cans hold that blacks and whites should not intermarry; in Canada, fewer than one in ten agree and the percentage of those under age thirty who do so is statistically negligible. Studies conducted across a number of European countries, including France, Italy, and Britain, suggest that between 30 and 50 percent of the population views ethnic and racial difference to be a significant problem; in Canada, the equivalent question yields 12 percent (Mendelsohn, "Birth of a New Ethnicity"). Adams reports similar findings: in national studies, 75 percent of Canadians believed immigrants have a positive influence on the country; Australia, 54 percent; the United States 52 percent; Germany, 47; France 45; Italy, 44; United Kingdom, 43. The "net positive" results are more striking, that is, "the number of points by which positive attitudes towards immigrants exceed negative attitudes in each country. Australia, for example—with 54 percent saying that immigrants overall have a positive effect on the country and 39 percent saying they have a negative influence—registers a net positive attitude of 15 percent . . . Canada, with a net positive attitude of 55 percent, ranks a full forty points higher than the next most positive country" (*Unlikely Utopia*, 13–14).

38. See Rorty, "Human Rights, Rationality, and Sentimentality."

39. See Adams, *Unlikely Utopia*, e.g., 34, for some suggested confirmation.

40. Benhabib, *The Claims of Culture*, 11.

41. Ibid., 117–18. In the first ever survey of Canadian Muslims, Adams reports considerable differences in the symbolic significance of the hijab (*Unlikely Utopia*, 90–91).

42. Bohman, *Public Deliberation*, 143.

43. See Taylor, "The Politics of Recognition."

44. Benhabib, *The Claims of Culture*, 16.

45. Ibid., 115 . . . 129.

46. My argument in this connection involves a parsing of evidence to which I suspect anyone not persuaded by my account of multiculturalism might object: that is, I have based my account of diversity-valuing identity at least partially on empirical cases in which, I have argued, it has not resulted from participation in deliberative democratic self-determination. But the question must then be: Why do I think it would so result? The simplest answer (and a good one, I think) is that sociopsychological studies have demonstrated that shared projects can, under the right conditions, have these effects. But my argument has mostly taken a different form: The value and rationality of the views, concerns, and identities of one's interlocutors is a counterfactual presupposition of discourse; but if discourse is to be sustained such valuing must be more or less reciprocally redeemed through contributions to decisions reached and through the consequences of those decisions. This is a motivational necessity and, I have argued, one that ultimately entails that we incorporate into our own identities a sense of ourselves as cooperators in the shared project of self-determination. It seems to me that any attempt to ground normative arguments immanently in present trends is going to find such parsing inevitable: Critics avoid it by one of two means—either they endorse the status quo, or they ignore the critical need to ground their alternative norms in the possibilities of the present.

47. Taylor, "The Politics of Recognition," 63 (my emphasis).

48. Fraser states both that recognition theorists, like Honneth and Taylor, are "one-sided" in ignoring systemic aspects of contemporary society that present

recognition- (or culture-) independent obstacles to the norms they advocate, and that contemporary social movements display a similar partiality ("Social Justice in the Age of Identity Politics," 7–8). However, her argument is rightly focused on the former. As Kymlicka demonstrates with reference to the latter, the majority of actual "struggles for recognition" advance demands for access to resources, political power, and economic opportunities that are essentially redistributive, and do not merely demand cultural and symbolic institutional changes, such as curricular reform (*Multicultural Odysseys*, 80ff).

49. Fraser, "Social Justice in the Age of Identity Politics," 28.

50. Ibid., 29.

51. Ibid., 30ff.

52. Ibid., 32.

53. See Fanon, *The Wretched of the Earth*.

54. See Taylor, "The Politics of Recognition," 37ff. Honneth and others have misread Taylor as arguing that a politics of "cultural difference" displaces a "politics of legal equality," which "suggestive periodization," according to Honneth, is not only based on false opposition and on bad history, but on "a much too narrow notion of legal recognition" ("Redistribution as Recognition," 122). This last accusation is somewhat surprising since Honneth offers the same basic (Hegelian) criticism of legal recognition as Taylor: That it is a form of "homogenizing equal treatment" (ibid). But, in any case, as a reading of Taylor, Honneth is off the mark: not only is Taylor quite clear that the politics of difference and the politics of universalism (the contrast he actually offers) are both interpretations of the meaning of liberal equality or equal recognition, the example on which he spends the longest time, Québec and the Meech Lake Accord, is precisely an example of legal recognition.

55. Taylor, "The Politics of Recognition," 38. Of course, it is quite mysterious how group-based identity politics can hold out any hope of such recognition. The suppressed premise is that individuality is crucially defined by cultural and ethnic affiliation in a way that subordinates all other kinds of ties; instead of attempting to defend this implausible claim, Taylor simply slips into talking about recognizing the uniqueness of "this individual or group" ("The Politics of Recognition," 38).

56. Habermas, "A Reply to my Critics," 254; see Lukes, "Of Gods and Demons," 139.

57. Taylor, "The Politics of Recognition," 62–63.

58. Honneth, "Redistribution as Recognition," 137.

59. Ibid., 140.

60. Honneth, *The Struggle for Recognition*, 80.

61. For instance: legal recognition "brings to light the same quality of individual autonomy in all members of the community" (Honneth, *The Struggle for Recognition*, 110); legal recognition respects individuals in light of "the general feature that makes them persons at all" (ibid., 113); "modern law represents a medium of recognition that expresses the universal features of human subjects" (ibid., 122), and so on. In each case, law is contrasted with recognition for what makes an individual "distinct" from everyone else.

62. Habermas, "Struggles for Recognition in the Democratic Constitutional State," 111.

63. Ibid., 115–16.

64. Ibid., 124.
65. Ibid., 125.
66. Ibid., 128.
67. Habermas, "A Reply to my Critics," 255.
68. Habermas, "A Genealogical Analysis of the Content of Morality," 39.
69. Honneth appears to sense that such a position may be found in Habermas, and accuses him accordingly of "ambiguity" in his use of the "the concept of recognition" as including both the granting of social status and the acceptance of language-based validity claims by others ("Redistribution as Recognition," 247). But Honneth is never clear why, his own position to the contrary notwithstanding, we should consider such a usage equivocal. Moreover, he is off the mark in his description of the purported "ambiguity" itself. Habermas writes, "[t]he self of the practical relation-to-self reassures itself about itself through the recognition that its claims receive from an alter ego. But these identity claims aiming at intersubjective recognition must not be confused with the validity claims that the actor raised with his speech act. For the "no" with which the addressee rejects a speech-act offer concerns the validity of a particular utterance, not the identity of the speaker" ("Individuation Through Socialization," 189–90). As a matter of fact, the speaker must presume that the other recognizes his or her in her autonomy and, in anticipating a "yes" or "no" from the other, must already have recognized the autonomy of the other, as well. Of course, these presuppositions ground no more than expectations to be redeemed by the behavior of the participants. But the distinction Habermas describes above is crucial in this regard since if, as Honneth argued, the experience of recognition entailed the acceptance of the specific validity claim raised, rather than sympathetic consideration and response, the recognition available through discourse would necessarily be scarce indeed.
70. Benhabib, although denying the right of conservative cultural communities to limit the exposure of their children to forms of knowledge and pluralism that would challenge their own tradition, nevertheless surprisingly accepts the possibility of ethno-culturally streamed school systems, provided they teach publicly approved curriculum (*The Claims of Culture*, 123ff). I cannot see how this is to be reconciled with her conception of identity and endorsement of deliberative integration, and I rather suspect that it could only result from an underestimation of the significance of the school in both respects.
71. Wolf, "Comment," 79.
72. For a defense of the ability of children to engage in forms of discursive reasoning and problem-solving that are specific to developmental levels, see Young, *A Critical Theory of Education*, 110ff (Young relies on a co-worker of Habermas, M. Miller, in making this argument). The main idea is that, as Dewey long ago suggested, autonomous reasoning is not an all or nothing deal, as critics like John Stuart Mill and R. S. Peters argued in rejecting autonomy or critique as an appropriate goal for children. Miller has theorized a series of developmental stages over the course of which children develop the capacity to enter into argumentation or discourse. "In observation of group problem-solving argument among children, Miller identifies the stages of argumentation in terms of the kinds of problems which children can collectively solve in resolving a moral dilemma situation. At the first level, among children aged 5 years, the problem of justification is recognized and solved. At suc-

ceeding levels, problems of coherence, circularity, and language arise. All four levels are identifiable in the argumentation of older children, with, typically, a recapitulation of the developmental sequence in a series of contextual switches during the process of argument" (ibid., 115–16). This argument does not challenge the schema presented in Chapter 3 (nor does Young take it to); the idea is that argumentation is possible within certain limits. The broader point is that we can't expect autonomy to spontaneously become a real possibility for individuals who, although they have reached a material age of maturity, have had no opportunity to develop the skills and attitudes that are prerequisite.

73. Habermas, *Legitimation Crisis*, 15.

74. Young, "Habermas and Education," 539–40. On the other hand, as Paulo Freire recognized, this is not to say that lecture, memorization, etc., have no place whatsoever in education; the argument is that they have a secondary place, that only after a dialogical relation has been established can these techniques find their proper use (see Morrow and Torres, *Reading Freire and Habermas*, 121).

75. For some particularly interesting Habermasian proposals, see Young, "Habermas and Education" (who also endorses Freire as "one of the best sources for an account of the kind of restraint that critical pedagogy requires"—ibid., 548); Young, *A Critical Theory of Education*; and Morrow and Torres, *Reading Freire and Habermas*, which argues persuasively for a complementarity between Freire and Habermas. Recent research on Marcuse on education suggests another valuable avenue. And, interestingly, Kellner et al suggest that Marcuse and Freire are similarly complementary, though on different grounds: "Because Marcuse [in his critique of education] focused explicitly on academic subject matter, perhaps we could argue that in many ways he provides revolutionary content while Paulo Freire provides the particular educational form (dialogic and problem posing) for constructing a pedagogy that fights for freedom, transforms students into active participants in the production of knowledge, problematized notions of educational neutrality, and emphasizes critical consciousness-raising and social transformation and activism" ("Introduction," 23).

There is perhaps one major divergence between Habermas and Marcuse (and Freire) in this connection which is, in fact, a part of the ongoing family quarrel within critical theory regarding the proper conceptualization of critical reason: Marcuse's discussion of education gives much greater place to the aesthetic, the shaping of needs and desires, the psychological and existential elements of socialization and personhood; a Habermasian approach, centered on the question of discourse, (consciously) operates with a thinner, more formal account of the subject. This difference has been regarded as salient among some Habermasian educationalists: see, for instance, Morrow and Torres, who argue against Habermas in this respect, and for a care-oriented account of pedagogy (*Reading Freire and Habermas*); Tammy A. Shel's contribution to the aforementioned volume on Marcuse ("The Dialectic of Tolerance and Intolerance in the Ethics of Caring") suggests that Marcuse may, like Freire, offer a kind of supplementation or challenge to Habermas on this issue. Because I intend mostly to prescind from discussions of the philosophy of education in favor of the sociology of schooling—a task I regard as having theoretical priority for a critical theory—I do not enter into this debate here.

76. See Blake and Masschelein, "Critical Theory and Critical Pedagogy," 47. This is a problem with which Marcuse also wrestled.

77. Young, "Habermas and Education," 531, 537, especially 541–42; also, *A Critical Theory of Education*, 78ff.

78. See Young, *A Critical Theory of Education*, 78.

79 Habermas, "Technology and Science as 'Ideology,'" 109–10.

80. Fraser, "Social Justice in the Age of Identity Politics," 77–78.

81. In a sense, I have argued that the principal beneficiaries of multicultural policies with respect to the transformation of identities are the children of a society—immigrant and "native"—who are socialized under conditions of democratic plurality. This seems practically correct and coheres with empirical studies of immigrant integration, and so on, but it could easily be overstated: The argument, after all, is also that engaging in the shared project of peaceful, collective, self-determination, if it is successful and so able to redeem the more or less counterfactual presuppositions on which such discourse necessarily rests, will foster a decentered sense of oneself as a participant in this shared, challenging endeavor. This should apply to first generation immigrants as well. Nevertheless, many measures for assessing success in realizing effective political participation only become evident over time—for example, rates of social mobility—which is precisely why much of the research focuses on the second generation.

Let me also add (although this should be obvious) that, because the argument is for a decentered, pluralized identity, the means are not in contradiction with the ends: I do not rely on one set of individuals not having a hybridized identity so that their struggles can benefit others, who will share an identity. Although the reliance of developed nations on immigration means practically that challenges will be ongoing in any case, even conceptually the idea is that individuals with such a hybridized identity remain invested in their particular heritage, and so it is not the case that, by the second generation, everyone who identified as "Canadian" in the decentered sense would be in the same sort of manufactured agreement that nationalist models have always presupposed.

82. Banting and Kymlicka, "Introduction," 10–11, 15–16.

83. See Van Cott, "Multiculturalism versus Neoliberalism in Latin America," 283ff.

84. Banting and Kymlicka, "Introduction," 16; see also ibid., 16, n.13. Matt James argues that the politics of redress for historical wrongs in Canada—such as the internment of Japanese- and Ukrainian Canadians during World War II, the residential school policy for First Nations children, and the like—play a similar politicizing role, stimulating public discourse around the meaning of political society: "Thus, it appears that redress movements are transforming Canadian memory and historical identity in ways that help to promote a more accurate and inclusive public discourse—an absolutely vital basis for building solidarity and cohesion" (James, "Do Campaigns for Redress Erode the Canadian Welfare State," 244). A serious public debate concerning reparations for slavery in the United States would certainly serve in a much more extreme manner to politicize the relationship between race and economics in the country.

85. Habermas, "The Postnational Constellation and the Future of Democracy," 59–60.

86. Ibid., 59.

Bibliography

Aboulafia, Mitchell. "Habermas on Mead: On Universality and Individuality," *Constellations* 2:1 (1995): 94–113.

Adams, Michael. *Unlikely Utopia: The Triumph of Canadian Pluralism*. Toronto: Viking Canada, 2007.

Alexander, Jeffery. "Habermas and Critical Theory: Beyond the Marxian Dilemma?" in *Communicative Action: Essays on Jürgen Habermas'* Theory of Communicative Action, edited by Axel Honneth and Hans Joas.

Allen, Amy. *The Politics of Ourselves: Power, Autonomy, and Gender in Contemporary Critical Theory*. New York: Columbia University Press, 2008.

Anderssen, Erin and Micheal Valpy. "Face the Nation: Canada Remade," *The Globe and Mail*, 6 July 2003.

Anyon, Jean. "Social Class and the Hidden Curriculum of Work," *Journal of Education* 162 (Winter 1980): 67–92.

Apel, Karl Otto. "Openly Strategic Uses of Language: A Transcendental-Pragmatic Perspective (A Second Attempt to Think with Habermas Against Habermas)," in *Habermas: A Critical Reader*, edited by Peter Dews.

Aronowitz, Stanley. "Preface to the Morningside Edition," in Paul Willis, *Learning to Labour: How Working Class Kids Get Working Class Jobs*. New York: Columbia University Press, 1977.

Ball, Stephen J., ed. *Foucault and Education: Disciplines and Knowledge*. London and New York: Routledge, 1990.

Banting, Keith, and Will Kymlicka. "Introduction. Multiculturalism and the Welfare State: Setting the Context," in *Multiculturalism and the Welfare State: Recognition and Redistribution in Contemporary Democracies*, edited by Keith Banting and Will Kymlicka.

———, eds. *Multiculturalism and the Welfare State: Recognition and Redistribution in Contemporary Democracies*.

———, and Will Kymlicka, Richard Johnston, Stuart Soroka. "Do Multicultural Policies Erode the Welfare State? An Empirical Study" in *Multicultural and the Welfare State*, edited by Keith Banting and Will Kymlicka. Oxford: Oxford University Press, 2006.

Beauvoir, Simone de. *The Second Sex*, translated by H. M. Parshley. New York: Vintage Books, 1989.

Benhabib, Seyla. *Critique, Norm, and Utopia: A Study of the Foundations of Critical Theory*. New York: Columbia University Press, 1986.

———. "Afterword," in *The Communicative Ethics Controversy*, edited by Seyla Benhabib and Fred Dallmayr. Cambridge, MA: MIT Press, 1990.

———. *The Claims of Culture: Equality and Diversity in the Global Era*. Princeton, NJ: Princeton University Press, 2002.

———. "Another Universalism: On the Unity and Diversity of Human Rights," *Proceedings and Addresses of the American Philosophical Association* 81:2 (November 2007): 7–32.

———, and Ian Shapiro, Danilo Petranović, eds. *Identities, Affiliations, and Allegiances Identities.* New York: Cambridge University Press, 2007.

Berger, Johannes. "The Linguistification of the Sacred and the Delinguistification of the Economy," in *Communicative Action: Essays" on Jürgen Habermas'* Theory of Communicative Action, edited by Axel Honneth and Hans Joas.

Bernstein, Richard J. ed. *Habermas and Modernity*. Cambridge, MA: MIT Press, 1985.

Blake, Nigel, and Paul Smeyers, et al. "Introduction," in *The Blackwell Guide to the Philosophy of Education*, edited by Nigel Blake, Paul Smeyers, et al. Malden, MA: Blackwell, 2003.

———, and Jan Masschelein. "Critical Theory and Critical Pedagogy," in *The Blackwell Guide to the Philosophy of Education*, edited by Nigel Blake, Paul Smeyers, et al. Malden, MA: Blackwell, 2003.

Bohman, James. *Public Deliberation: Pluralism, Complexity, and Democracy*. Cambridge, MA: MIT Press, 1996.

Borman, David A. "Labour, Exchange, and Recognition: Marx contra Honneth," *Philosophy and Social Criticism* 35:8 (October 2009): 935–59.

Bowles, Samuel, and Herbert Gintis. *Schooling in Capitalist America: Educational Reform and the Contradictions of Economic Life*. New York: HarperCollins, 1976.

———. "Schooling in Capitalist America Revisited," *Sociology of Education* 75:1 (January 2002): 1–18.

Bourdieu, Pierre. "Preface to the 1990 Edition," translated by Loïc J. D. Wacquant, in Pierre Bourdieu and Jean-Claude Passeron, *Reproduction in Education, Society, and Culture*, Second Edition,.

———, and Jean-Claude Passeron. *Reproduction in Education, Society, and Culture*, Second Edition, translated by Richard Nice. London: Sage, 1990.

Brint, Steven. *Schools and Societies*, Second Edition. Stanford: Stanford University Press, 2006.

Canadian Multiculturalism Act. (1985). Available through the Department of Justice website, http://laws.justice.gr.ca/en/C-18.7/text.html.

Crepaz, Markus. ""If you are my Brother, I may Give you a Dime!" Public Opinion on Multiculturalism, Trust, and the Welfare State," in *Multiculturalism and the Welfare State*, edited by Keith Banting and Will Kymlicka.

Cronin, Ciaran. "Democracy and Collective Identity: In Defence of Constitutional Patriotism," *European Journal of Philosophy* 11:1 (2003): 1–28.

Dewey, John. *Democracy and Education: An Introduction to the Philosophy of Education*. New York: The Free Press, 1944.

———. *Human Nature and Conduct: An Introduction to Social Psychology*. Amherst, NY: Prometheus Books, 2002.

Dews, Peter. "Communicative Paradigms and the Question of Subjectivity: Habermas, Mead, and Lacan," in *Habermas: A Critical Reader*, edited by Peter Dews.

———, ed. *Habermas: A Critical Reader*. Oxford: Blackwell, 1999.

Dryzek, John S. "Critical Theory as a Research Program," in *The Cambridge Companion to Habermas*, edited by Stephen K. White.

Dux, Günther. "Communicative Reason and Interest: On the Reconstruction of the Normative Order in Societies Structured by Egalitarianism or Domination," in *Communicative Action: Essays on Jürgen Habermas'* Theory of Communicative Action, edited by Axel Honneth and Hans Joas.

Ehrenreich, Barbara. *Bait and Switch: The (Futile) Pursuit of the American Dream*. New York: Henry Holt and Company, 2005.

Fanon, Frantz. *The Wretched of the Earth*. New York: Grove Press, 1963.

Feinberg, Walter, and Jonas F. Soltis. *School and Society*, Fourth Edition. New York: Teachers College Press, 2003.

Fraser, Nancy. "What's Critical About Critical Theory? The Case of Habermas and Gender." Chapter 6 in *Unruly Practices*. University of Minnesota, 2003. Originally published in *New German Critique* 33 (Fall 1984): 127–54.

———. "Women, Welfare and the Politics of Need Interpretation." Chapter 7 in *Unruly Practices*. University of Minnesota Press, 2003. Originally published in *Hypatia* 2:1 (1987): 103–21.

———. "Social Justice in the Age of Identity Politics: Redistribution, Recognition, and Participation," in *Redistribution or Recognition? A Political-Philosophical Exchange*. New York: Verso, 2003.

———. "Distorted Beyond All Recognition: A Rejoinder to Axel Honneth," in *Recognition or Redistribution? A Political-Philosophical Exchange*. New York: Verso, 2003.

Giddens, Anthony. "Reason Without Revolution? Habermas' *Theorie des kommunikativen Handeln*," in *Habermas and Modernity*, edited by Richard J. Bernstein.

Grant, Tavia and Jennifer Yang. "Immigrants Take Brunt of Recession, Recover Less Quickly," *The Globe and Mail*, 25 July 2009.

Gregg, Allen. "Identity Crisis. Multiculturalism: A Twentieth-Century Dream Becomes a Twenty-First-Century Conundrum," *The Walrus* 3:2 (March 2006): 38–47.

Ha, Tu Thanh. "Québec Town Defends Conduct Code for Minorities," *The Globe and Mail*, 25 October 2007.

———. "Islam Sparks Fiery Debate in Québec," *The Globe and Mail*, 24 October 2007.

Habermas, Jürgen.———. *Knowledge and Human Interests*, translated by Jeremy J. Shapiro. Boston: Beacon Press, 1968.

———. "Technology and Science as 'Ideology,'" in *Toward a Rational Society: Student Protest, Science, and Politics*, trans. by Jeremy J. Shapiro. Boston: Beacon Press, 1970.

———. *Legitimation Crisis*, translated by Thomas McCarthy. Boston: Beacon Press, 1975.

———. "Historical Materialism and the Development of Normative Structures," in *Communication and the Evolution of Society*, translated by Thomas McCarthy. Boston: Beacon Press, 1979.

———. "Toward a Reconstruction of Historical Materialism," in *Communication and the Evolution of Society*, translated by Thomas McCarthy. Boston: Beacon Press, 1979.

———. "Moral Development and Ego Identity," in *Communication and the Evolution of Society*, translated by Thomas McCarthy. Boston: Beacon Press, 1979.

———. "Modernity versus Postmodernity," translated by Seyla Benhabib, *New German Critique* 22 (Winter 1981): 3–14.

———. "A Reply to my Critics," translated by Thomas McCarthy, in *Habermas: Critical Debates*, edited by John B. Thompson and David Held.

———. *Reason and the Rationalization of Society*. Vol. 1 of *The Theory of Communicative Action*, translated by Thomas McCarthy. Boston: Beacon Press, 1984.

———. "Questions and Counterquestions," translated by James Bohman, in *Habermas and Modernity*, edited by Richard J. Bernstein.

———. *Lifeworld and System: A Critique of Functionalist Reason*. Vol. 2 of *The Theory of Communicative Action*, translated by Thomas McCarthy. Boston: Beacon Press, 1987.

———. *The New Conservativism. Cultural Criticism and the Historian's Debate*, edited and translated by Shierry Weber Nicholsen. Cambridge, MA: MIT Press, 1989.

———. "Moral Consciousness and Communicative Action," in *Moral Consciousness and Communicative Action*, translated by Christian Lenhardt and Shierry Weber Nicholsen. Cambridge, MA: The MIT Press, 1990.

———. "Discourse Ethics: Notes on a Program of Philosophical Justification," in *Moral Consciousness and Communicative Action*, translated by Christian Lenhardt and Shierry Weber Nicholsen. Cambridge, MA: The MIT Press, 1990.

———. "Morality and Ethical Life: Does Hegel's Critique of Kant Apply to Discourse Ethics," in *Moral Consciousness and Communicative Action*, translated by Christian Lenhardt and Shierry Weber Nicholsen. Cambridge, MA: The MIT Press, 1990.

———. "A Reply," in *Communicative Action: Essays on Jürgen Habermas'* The Theory of Communicative Action, edited by Axel Honneth and Hans Joas.

———. *The Structural Transformation of the Public Sphere: An Inquiry into a Category of Bourgeois Society*, translated by Thomas Burger. Cambridge, MA: MIT Press, 1991.

———. "Individuation Through Socialization: On George Herbert Mead's Theory of Subjectivity," in *Postmetaphysical Thinking: Philosophical Essays*, translated by William Mark Hohengarten. Cambridge, MA: MIT Press, 1992.

———. "The Unity of Reason in the Diversity of its Voices," in *Postmetaphysical Thinking: Philosophical Essays*, translated by William Mark Hohengarten. Cambridge, MA: MIT Press, 1992.

———. *Autonomy and Solidarity: Interviews with Jürgen Habermas*, edited by Peter Dews. New York: Verso, 1992.

———. "Struggles for Recognition in the Democratic Constitutional State," translated by Shierry Weber Nicholsen, in *Multiculturalism*, Expanded edition, edited by Amy Gutmann. Princeton, NJ: Princeton University Press, 1994.

———. "Remarks on Discourse Ethics," in *Justification and Application: Remarks on Discourse Ethics*, translated by Ciaran Cronin. Cambridge, MA: MIT Press, 1994.

———. "Morality, Society, and Ethics: An Interview with Torben Hviid Nielsen," in *Justification and Application: Remarks on Discourse Ethics*, translated by Ciaran Cronin. Cambridge, MA: MIT Press, 1994.

———. *Between Facts and Norms: Contributions to a Discourse Theory of Law and Democracy*, translated by William Rehg. Cambridge, MA: MIT Press, 1996.

———. "The European Nation-State: On the Past and Future of Sovereignty and Citizenship," in *The Inclusion of the Other: Studies in Political Theory*, edited by Ciaran Cronin and Pablo de Greiff. Cambridge, MA: MIT Press, 1998.

———. "A Genealogical Analysis of the Content of Morality," in *The Inclusion of the Other: Studies in Political Theory*, edited by Ciaran Cronin and Pablo de Greiff. Cambridge, MA: MIT Press, 1998.

———. "Actions, Speech Acts, Linguistically Mediated Interactions, and the Lifeworld (1988)," in *On the Pragmatics of Communication*, edited by Maeve Cooke. Cambridge, MA: The MIT Press, 1998.

———. "Reflections on the Linguistic Foundation of Sociology: The Christian Gauss Lecture (Princeton February–March 1971)," in *On the Pragmatics of Social Interaction: Preliminary Studies in the Theory of Communicative Action*, translated by Barbara Fultner. Cambridge, MA: MIT Press, 2001.

———. "Reflections on Communicative Pathology (1974)," in *On the Pragmatics of Social Interaction: Preliminary Studies in the Theory of Communicative Action*, translated by Barbara Fultner. Cambridge, MA: MIT Press, 2001.

———. "The Postnational Constellation and the Future of Democracy," in *Post-national Constellations: Political Essays*, edited and translated by Max Pensky. Cambridge, MA: MIT Press, 2001.

———. "Remarks on Legitimation Through Human Rights," in *Postnational Constellations: Political Essays*, edited and translated by Max Pensky. Cambridge, MA: MIT Press, 2001.

———. "What is a People?" in *Postnational Constellations: Political Essays*, edited and translated by Max Pensky. Cambridge, MA: MIT Press, 2001.

———. "Is the Development of a European Identity Necessary, and is it Possible?" in *The Divided West*, edited and translated by Ciaran Cronin. Cambridge: Polity Press, 2006.

Hahn, Edwin Lewis, ed. *Perspectives on Habermas*. Chicago and LaSalle: Open Court, 2000.

Hayward, Clarissa Rile. "Binding Problems, Boundary Problems: The Trouble with "Democratic Citizenship," in *Identities, Affiliations, and Allegiances*, edited by Seyla Benhabib, Ian Shapiro, and Danilo Petranović.

Held, David. "Crisis Tendencies, Legitimation and the State," in *Habermas: Critical Debates*, edited by John B. Thompson and David Held.

Hero, Rodney E. and Robert R. Preuhs. "Multiculturalism and Welfare Policies in the USA: A State-Level Comparative Analysis," in *Multiculturalism and the Welfare State*, edited by Keith Banting and Will Kymlicka.

Honneth, Axel. "The Other of Justice: Habermas' and the Ethical Challenge of Postmodernism," translated by John Farrell, in *The Cambridge Companion to Habermas*, edited by Stephen K. White.

———. *The Struggle for Recognition: The Moral Grammar of Social Conflicts*, translated by Joel Anderson. Cambridge, MA: MIT Press, 1995.

———. "The Social Dynamics of Disrespect: Situating Critical Theory Today," in *Habermas: A Critical Reader*, edited by Peter Dews.

———. "Redistribution as Recognition: A Response to Nancy Fraser," translated by Joel Golb and James Ingram, in *Redistribution or Recognition: A Political-Philosophical Exchange*. New York: Verso, 2003.

———, and Hans Joas, eds. *Communicative Action: Essays on Jürgen Habermas'* Theory of Communicative Action, translated by Jeremy Gaines and Doris L. Jones. Cambridge, MA: MIT Press, 1991.

Horkheimer, Max. "Authority and the Family," in *Critical Theory: Selected Essays*, translated by Matthew J. O'Connell et al. New York: Continuum, 1999.

———. *Eclipse of Reason*. London and New York: Continuum, 2004.

———, and Theodor W. Adorno *Dialectic of Enlightenment: Philosophical Fragments*, translated by Edmund Jephcott. Stanford: Stanford University Press, 2002.

"How Canada Chooses its Newcomers," *The Windsor Star*, 5 November 2005.

Ingram, David. *Habermas and the Dialectic of Reason*. New Haven, CT and London: Yale University Press, 1987.

James, Matt. "Do Campaigns for Historical Redress Erode the Canadian Welfare State?" in *Multiculturalism and the Welfare State*, edited by Keith Banting and Will Kymlicka.

Jay, Martin. "Habermas and Modernism," in *Habermas and Modernity*, edited by Richard J. Bernstein.

Jimémez, Martina. "Is the Current Model of Immigration the Best One for Canada?" *The Globe and Mail*, 12 December 2005.

Kellner, Douglas, Tyson Lewis, Clayton Pierce, and Daniel K. Cho, eds. *Marcuse's Challenge to Education*. Lanham, MD: Rowman & Littlefield Publishers, Inc., 2009.

———, and Tyson Lewis, Clayton Pierce, Daniel K. Cho. "Introduction," in *Marcuse's Challenge to Education*, ed. Douglas Kellner et al.

Klein, Naomi. *The Shock Doctrine: The Rise of Disaster Capitalism*. Toronto: Alfred A. Knopf, 2007.

Kymlicka, Will. *Multicultural Citizenship*. Oxford: Clarendon Press, 1995.

———. *Multicultural Odysseys: Negotiating the New International Politics of Diversity*. Oxford: Oxford University Press, 2007.

LeBlanc, Daniel. "Duceppe Slams 'Multiculturalism,'" *The Globe and Mail*, 11 October 2007.

Love, Nancy S. "What's Left of Marx?" in *The Cambridge Companion to Habermas*, edited by Stephen K. White.

Lukes, Steven. "Of Gods and Demons: Habermas and Practical Reason," in *Habermas: Critical Debates*, edited by John B. Thompson and David Held.

Marcuse, Herbert. "Lecture on Education, Brooklyn College, 1968," in *Marcuse's Challenge to Education*, ed. Douglas Kellner et al.

Markell, Patchen. "Making Affect Safe for Democracy? On 'Constitutional Patriotism,'" *Political Theory* 28:1 (February 2000): 38–63.

Marsh, James L. *Unjust Legality: A Critique of Habermas' Philosophy of Law*. Lanham, MD: Rowman & Littlefield, 2001.

Marx, Karl. *Capital* Vol. 1, translated by Ben Fowkes. New York: Vintage, 1977.

McBride, William. "Habermas and the Marxian Tradition," in *Perspectives on Habermas*, edited by Edwin Lewis Hahn.

McCarthy, Thomas. *The Critical Theory of Jürgen Habermas*. Cambridge, MA: MIT Press, 1978.

———. "Reflections on Rationalization," in *The Theory of Communicative Action*" in *Habermas and Modernity*, edited by Richard J. Bernstein.

———. "Complexity and Democracy: or the Seducements of Systems Theory," in *Communicative Action: Essays on Jürgen Habermas'* Theory of Communicative Action, edited by Axel Honneth and Hans Joas.

Mendelsohn, Matthew. "Birth of a New Ethnicity," *The Globe and Mail*, 9 June 2003.

Menser, Michael. "Disarticulate the State! Bioregionalism, Transnational Anticapitalism, and the Maximalization of Democracy," forthcoming. Menser presented an abbreviated form of this paper at the *Eastern Division Meeting of the APA*, Baltimore, December 2007.

Michelman, Frank I. "Morality, Identity, and 'Constitutional Patriotism,'" *Ratio Juris* 14:3 (September 2001): 253–71.

Miller, David. "Multiculturalism and the Welfare State: Theoretical Reflections," in *Multiculturalism and the Welfare State*, ed. Keith Banting and Will Kymlicka.

Morrow, Raymond Allan and Carlos Alberto Torres. *Social Theory and Education: A Critique of Theories of Social and Cultural Reproduction*. Albany, NY: SUNY Press, 1995.

———. *Reading Freire and Habermas: Critical Pedagogy and Transformative Social Change*. New York: Teachers College Press, 2002.

Muhammad, Dedrick, et al. "State of the Dream 2004: Enduring Disparities in Black and White," *The Racial Wealth Divide Project* (United for a Fair Economy). Report available at www.faireconomy.org/files.pdf/StateoftheDream2004/pdf.

Myles, John, and Sébastien St.-Arnaud. "Population Diversity, Multiculturalism, and the Welfare State: Should Welfare State Theory be Revised?" in *Multiculturalism and the Welfare State*, ed. Keith Banting and Will Kymlicka.

"The New Canada," with Mendelsohn, Matthew. *The Globe and Mail*, with Ipsos-Reid and the Centre for Research and Information on Canada, June to July 2003.

Pensky, Max. "Universalism and the Situated Critic," in *The Cambridge Companion to Habermas*, edited by Stephen K. White.

Perreaux, Les. "Multiculturalism Threat to Quebec: Duceppe," *The Globe and Mail*, 11 December 2007.

Rehg, William. "Translator's Introduction," in *Between Facts and Norms: Contributions to a Discourse Theory of Law and Democracy*. Cambridge, MA: MIT Press, 1996.

Rivera, Amaad, et al. "Foreclosed: State of the Dream 2008," *The Racial Wealth Divide Project* (United for a Fair Economy). Report available at www.faireconomy.org/files/StateoftheDream_01_16_08_Web.pdf

———. "State of the Dream 2009: The Silent Depression," *The Racial Wealth Divide Project* (United for a Fair Economy). Report available at www.faireconomy.org/Dream.

Rorty, Richard. "Habermas and Lyotard on Postmodernity," in *Habermas and Modernity*, edited by Richard J. Bernstein.

———. "Human Rights, Rationality, and Sentimentality," in *Politics of Human Rights*, edited by Obrad Savić. New York: Verso, 1999.

Scheuerman, William. "Between Resignation and Radicalism: Democratic Theory in Habermas' *Between Facts and Norms*," in *Habermas: A Critical Reader*, edited by Peter Dews.

Shel, Tammy A. "The Dialectic of Tolerance and Intolerance in the Ethics of Caring," in *Marcuse's Challenge to Education*, edited by Douglas Kellner, et al.

Swindal, James. *Reflection Revisited: Jürgen Habermas' Discursive Theory of Truth*. New York: Fordham University Press, 1999.

Taylor, Charles. "Shared and Divergent Values," in *Options for a New Canada*, edited by Ronald L. Watts and Douglas M. Brown. Toronto: University of Toronto Press, 1991.

———. "The Politics of Recognition," in *Multiculturalism*. Expanded edition, edited by Amy Gutmann. Princeton, NJ: Princeton University Press, 1994.

"Ten Court Rulings that Cemented Canadian Freedoms," *The Globe and Mail*, 12 April 2007.

Tillie, Jean and Boris Slijper. "Immigrant Political Integration and Ethnic Civic Communities in Amsterdam" in *Identities, Affiliations, and Allegiances*, edited by Seyla Benhabib, Ian Shapiro, and Danilo Petranović.

Thompson, John B., and David Held, eds. *Habermas: Critical Debates*. Cambridge, MA: MIT Press, 1982.

Van Cott, Donna Lee. "Multiculturalism versus Neoliberalism in Latin America" in *Multiculturalism and the Welfare State*, edited by Keith Banting and Will Kymlicka.

Wacquant, Loïc J.D. "Translator's Note," in Pierre Bourdieu and Jean-Claude Passeron, *Reproduction in Education, Society, and Culture Second Edition*.

Warren, Mark E. "The Self in Discursive Democracy," in *The Cambridge Companion to Habermas*, edited by Stephen K. White.

White, Stephen K. "Reason, Modernity, and Democracy," in *The Cambridge Companion to Habermas*, edited by Stephen K. White.

———, ed. *The Cambridge Companion to Habermas*. Cambridge: Cambridge University Press, 1995.

Whitebook, Joel. "Reason and Happiness: Some Psychoanalytic Themes in Critical Theory," in *Habermas and Modernity*, edited by Richard J. Bernstein.

Willis, Paul. *Learning to Labor: How Working Class Kids Get Working Class Jobs*. New York: Columbia University Press, 1977.

Wolf, Susan. "Comment," in *Multiculturalism*. Expanded edition, edited by Amy Gutmann. Princeton, NJ: Princeton University, Press, 1994.

Young, Robert. *A Critical Theory of Education: Habermas and Our Children's Future*. New York: Teachers College Press, 1990.

———. "Habermas and Education," in *Perspective on Habermas*, edited by Lewis Edwin Hahn.

Index